Economics, Law, and Institutions in Asia Pacific

The Asia Pacific region is expected to steadily enhance its economic and political presence in the world during the twenty-first century. At the same time, many serious economic and political issues remain unresolved in the region. To further academic enquiry and enhance readers' understanding about this vibrant region, the present series, Economics, Law, and Institutions in Asia Pacific, aims to present cutting-edge research on the Asia Pacific region and its relationship with the rest of the world. For countries in this region to achieve robust economic growth, it is of foremost importance that they improve the quality of their markets, as history shows that healthy economic growth cannot be achieved without high-quality markets. High-quality markets can be established and maintained only under a well-designed set of rules and laws, without which competition will not flourish. Based on these principles, this series places a special focus on economic, business, legal, and institutional issues geared towards the healthy development of Asia Pacific markets. The series considers book proposals for scientific research, either theoretical or empirical, that is related to the theme of improving market quality and has policy implications for the Asia Pacific region. The types of books that will be considered for publication include research monographs as well as relevant proceedings. The series show-cases work by Asia-Pacific based researchers but also encourages the work of social scientists not limited to the Asia Pacific region. Each proposal and final manuscript is subject to evaluation by the editorial board and experts in the field.

All books and chapters in the Economics, Law and Institutions in Asia Pacific book series are indexed in Scopus.

Masayoshi Okabe

Economics of the Reversal in Gender Disparities in Education and Development

Poverty, Family Dynamics, and School Environment in the Philippines

Springer

Masayoshi Okabe
Faculty of Economics, Graduate School
of Humanities and Social Sciences
Saitama University
Saitama, Japan

School of Labor and Industrial Relations
University of the Philippines Diliman
Quezon City, Metro Manila, Philippines

ISSN 2199-8620 ISSN 2199-8639 (electronic)
Economics, Law, and Institutions in Asia Pacific
ISBN 978-981-96-9270-5 ISBN 978-981-96-9271-2 (eBook)
https://doi.org/10.1007/978-981-96-9271-2

This Springer imprint is published by the registered company Springer Nature Singapore Pte Ltd.
The registered company address is: 152 Beach Road, #21-01/04 Gateway East, Singapore 189721, Singapore

Foreword by Yasuyuki Sawada

Human capital accumulation, resulting from investment in education, is a critical driver of economic development, generating both intrinsic and instrumental values. Education is not only a fundamental element of individual welfare and empowerment but also a key determinant of labor productivity and technological progress. Over the past few decades, concerted efforts have led to significant improvements in educational access and gender parity, particularly in developing regions. Global initiatives such as the Millennium Development Goals (MDGs) and the Sustainable Development Goals (SDGs) have emphasized expanding educational opportunities for girls. However, a less-discussed yet equally pressing issue has emerged in recent years—reversed gender disparity, wherein boys are increasingly disengaging from education while girls continue to advance. Initially observed in high-income nations, this phenomenon is now becoming more pronounced in low- and middle-income countries, presenting new challenges for human capital development.

The Philippines serves as a compelling case study in understanding this trend. Despite persistent poverty and economic inequality, the country has consistently ranked high in gender equality indicators, particularly in education. Historically, the Philippines achieved near-universal primary school enrollment earlier than many of its regional peers, reflecting a strong national commitment to education. However, in recent years, the country's educational landscape has shifted, revealing a growing disparity where male students are lagging behind their female counterparts in both school retention rates and academic performance. This "boys' crisis" challenges conventional narratives of gender inequality and necessitates deeper examination.

In *Economics of the Reversal in Gender Disparities in Education and Development: Poverty, Family Dynamics, and School Environment in the Philippines*, Dr. Masayoshi Okabe investigates the economic and social dimensions of reversed gender disparity in education, with a particular focus on the Philippines. The book explores how cross-cutting structural factors such as poverty, along with family dynamics and school environments, contribute to boys' disengagement from education while girls' participation continues to rise. Drawing on unique field surveys and rigorous empirical research, the book provides an in-depth analysis of the structural and cultural factors driving this shift.

This book aims to contribute to a more nuanced understanding of gender and education in developing countries by shedding light on the economic and social mechanisms underlying the "boys' crisis." Its findings hold broader implications for creating a more inclusive, resilient, and sustainable society in the Philippines and globally. I am confident that this book will serve as an essential resource for scholars, students, and policymakers, offering valuable insights to address educational disparities and promote gender-inclusive development.

Yasuyuki Sawada, Ph.D.
Professor, Faculty of Economics
and Director, Center for Research
and Education in Program Evaluation
(CREPE)
University of Tokyo
Tokyo, Japan

Former Chief Economist
Asian Development Bank
Mandaluyong City, Philippines

Foreword by Melisa R. Serrano

The Philippines has consistently ranked high in closing the gender gap since 2006, based on the global gender gap index of the World Economic Forum. The country is also identified as the most gender equal country in East Asia and the Pacific. In 2024, the Philippines in particular achieved gender parity in educational attainment, which includes literacy rate, enrollment in primary education, enrollment in secondary education, and enrollment in tertiary education. This landed the country among the 33 economies that ranked first on the education subindex, among 146 countries.

But despite being portrayed as a top-tier country for gender equality, including women's educational advantages over men, women workers in the Philippines continue to experience inequalities in the labor market. Between 2018 and 2023, the country's gender parity index was declining suggesting a widening of the gender gap. This is mainly attributed to lower and declining scores in the economic participation and opportunity index, particularly the subindices on labor force participation rate and wage equality for similar work. In terms of the former, between October 2007 and October 2022, data from the Philippine Statistics Authority show that less than half (49.2 percent) of all women aged 15 years and older were in the labor force compared to over three-fourths (77.1 percent) among men.

The gender wage gap remains; women remain to be less compensated even within the same occupational groups, even if women workers bring in better human capital attributes. The combined effects of gender discrimination, women's low labor force participation rate, their overrepresentation in low-wage jobs and informal employment, and women's unpaid care work result in women's poorer labor market outcomes compared to men.

All these suggest that men (and boys) are better off than women (and girls) in terms of economic participation and opportunity and educational attainment.

The book *Economics of the Reversal in Gender Disparities in Education and Development: Poverty, Family Dynamics, and School Environment in the Philippines* by Dr. Masayoshi Okabe spotlights an important and often overlooked dimension of gender disparity particularly in education—boys' underperformance and disengagement from education or "boys' crisis"—that, as the book argues, may lead to a "girls' crisis". The observations and empirical findings of the book suggest that gender disparities in education of boys and girls mutually reinforce and transform each other at various stages—"against men at one stage and against women at another—and between schooling and post-schooling systems" (p. 262). In fact, one may argue that the boys' crisis may be an important albeit adverse factor that may have contributed to the country's purported success in closing the gender gap in education.

Using the Philippines as a case study, the book investigates how factors such as poverty, family dynamics, and school environments contribute to boys' disengagement from education while girls continue to improve their participation and performance. At the same time, the book critically assesses this perceived "reversed" gender disparity in education, arguing that it is not a true reversal when the broader link between education and the socioeconomic and cultural environment is considered. Thus, despite women's educational achievements, women still face disadvantages in the economic sphere or the labor market. However, centering discussions on gender disparity on women masks a broader crisis impacting individuals regardless of gender. As the book points out: "Boys' disengagement from education affects not only the boys themselves—some of whom will become fathers—but also the girls—some of whom will become mothers—resulting in long-term intergenerational effects when they assume these roles." (p. 262). Here, the book brings to light the "unintended" effect of poverty-induced mothers' labor force participation (MLFP) as an economic response to supplement the breadwinner roles typically filled by fathers. The effect of MLFP not only contributes to boys' underperformance, as the book highlights, but also reinforces the "dual burden"—childrearing and household duties and engaging in productive/paid work—that working women mothers face. In other words, MLFP bolsters up, through the role-model dynamic between mothers and daughters, women's dual burden.

This book contributes to a deeper understanding of the underlying factors that influence the dynamics between gender and education in poor, rural households in developing countries like the Philippines, and how, in turn, these dynamics later shape men and women's participation in the economy and the labor market. The book's interdisciplinary approach, which combines qualitative field surveys that used local languages and empirical econometric approaches, reflects a niche in educational development studies as well as in economics. The book's interdisciplinary approach and innovative research methodology are crucial in addressing the complex issues that the book convincingly tackled. It is no wonder that Dr. Okabe's earlier research on which this book is based received the Main Prize of the 19th Asia Pacific Research Prize (Iue Prize) by the Asia Pacific Forum, Awaji Conference Japan.

The findings of the book bear important implications for developing policies that address both educational and post-educational gender disparities, taking into consideration equally important factors such as poverty, family dynamics and school environments. Therefore, scholars, researchers and students across disciplines (economics, education, development studies, area studies) as well as policymakers will find this book an important resource.

Melisa R. Serrano, Ph.D.
Dean and Professor, School of Labor
and Industrial Relations (SOLAIR)
and Director, Center for Labor Justice
(CLJ)
University of the Philippines Diliman
Quezon City, Philippines

Preface

As I sit down to write this preface, my thoughts return to the experiences that first shaped the inquiries in this book. Their origins trace back to a series of defining moments—encounters that, in ways both immediate and enduring, set the course of my academic journey. One such moment occurred in the summer of 2009, right after I had completed the first semester of my master's program, when I first set foot in the Philippines—let alone in economically impoverished areas.

As part of a study tour group from the University of Tokyo, I ventured into the narrow alleys of Sitio Paz, a community nestled within a fishpond belt along a river and highway in northern Metro Manila. With every step, the tropical humidity became more palpable, carrying a faint yet distinct scent of daily life that grew stronger as we moved further in. Rather than feeling oppressive, the air brimmed with vitality, infused with the relentless energy of people's everyday existence. This very locality was the focal community of *Economics of Slums* (University of Tokyo Press, 1991), a work shaped by Professor Toru Nakanishi, renowned for his long-standing engagement with this community. I first encountered this book in 2007 as an undergraduate, when I visited Professor Takashi Kurosaki of Hitotsubashi University for academic guidance and he suggested I look it up in the university library.

As I delved into its pages, I was excited by its insights, never expecting that a few years later, I would find myself standing in the very community it depicted. The community's history was etched in its crammed yet resilient homes, in the smiles of children running barefoot through unpaved streets, and in the quiet endurance of those long excluded from the formal economy—exemplifying dynamics formulated in Lewisian development economics, such as the Harris-Todaro model of rural-to-urban labor migration.

Despite being labeled a slum at the time, Sitio Paz defied the bleak and destitute image I had anticipated. Many families owned mobile phones, ate three meals a day, and some had karaoke machines, shopped at malls, or used taxis. My two-story host family's *Ate* (sister) worked as a government employee, maintaining a stable livelihood. Like many Filipinos, residents cited "intangible resources" such as family ties and friendships within the community as key sources of happiness. They also reported that the material aspects of their living conditions had steadily improved.

These realities challenged the assumptions I had brought with me. My curiosity about this contradiction led me to a conversation with a *barangay kagawad*, a local official. When I asked what had driven the improvements in living standards, she turned to me with a knowing look and, referring to me by my nickname, said: "Justin, see? One great factor is definitely education."

The *kagawad* recounted success stories of locals who had pursued schooling and secured more stable livelihoods—some of them, fortunately, aided by NGOs. Yet many children still dropped out—not by choice, but due to financial constraints and family obligations. Her slow, low-toned, yet warm voice carried the weight of lived experience, lending eloquent validation to the development theories I had studied. That encounter left a lasting impression, sparking my initial curiosity about the intersection of education and poverty.

From January 2017, I was fortunate to return to the Philippines for a research stay until the same month of 2020. Dispatched as an overseas research fellow by the Institute of Developing Economies (IDE-JETRO), I worked as a visiting research fellow and senior lecturer at the University of the Philippines Diliman in Metro Manila, enabling me to conduct fieldwork more extensively. This time, I focused on rural areas, including the island province of Marinduque, allowing me to experience both urban and rural life. Early in my fieldwork, I frequently heard a striking phrase from local adults: "*Eh tamad kasi ang mga lalaki, masipag naman ang mga babae*"—"You see, because boys are lazy, while girls are diligent."

At first, this characterization seemed convincing, aligning with the trend of male students disengaging from education. Yet, I began to question whether it stemmed from a stereotype shaped by traditional gender norms. Were all boys inherently lazy, while all girls were diligent? Clearly, that could not be the case. This simplistic narrative, while reflecting common local beliefs, may also mask deeper structural issues. If boys are perceived as lazy, how is this idea socially constructed? What socioeconomic forces drive this perception? This reflection, like my encounter in Sitio Paz, became another defining moment in my research. It prompted me to explore broader mechanisms behind boys' disengagement or girls' growing engagement in education—analyzing these patterns through a microeconomic lens on intergroup heterogeneity in human capital formation.

These early observations convinced me that educational outcomes could not be fully understood through individual choices alone. Rather, they are embedded in broader structural conditions—including poverty, family roles, and school institutions—that shape the opportunities and constraints different social groups face. This led me to consider the concept of intergroup heterogeneity, referring to the patterned differences in how social groups—in this book, most centrally gender groups—respond on average to the same structural conditions. While this book emphasizes gendered patterns, such group-level differences may also emerge by class, region, or cultural background. Importantly, intergroup heterogeneity does not negate the reality of individual diversity; instead, it draws attention to the ways in which group-level tendencies often reflect structurally conditioned responses rather than essential traits.

This book delves into these issues, locally referred to as the "boys' crisis" in education, exploring how structural and socioeconomic factors underlie this phenomenon. Despite the Philippines' early achievements in gender equality and its relatively advanced implementation of universal primary education, recent trends indicate that male students are increasingly disengaging from school. This phenomenon is not unique to the Philippines; similar patterns have emerged in other lower-income countries across Asia and Africa. Using the Philippines as a case study, this book examines whether this issue should be understood not simply as a reversed gender disparity but as one embedded in deeper structural factors.

Through empirical research conducted across Luzon, Visayas, and Mindanao, this book explores the socioeconomic and institutional backgrounds shaping boys' disengagement while girls remain more engaged. It focuses on three key themes: (1) poverty and educational continuity; (2) family dynamics, including gendered household roles and intergenerational relations; and (3) school environments, including teacher biases and peer influences.

Ultimately, this book challenges the simplistic notion of reversed gender disparity by introducing the concept of economics of the reversal, emphasizing the complex, structural factors at play. Rather than reducing this phenomenon to a simple gender inversion within a zero-sum framework, the concept explores the economic, social, normative, and institutional factors that shape the pattern. In this concept, "reversal" is used in more than one sense—across gender patterns in schooling, over time when short-term payoffs overshadow long-term returns, and across domains where boys' schooling disadvantage coexists with women's disadvantage in the labor market. It is not a single, across-the-board reversal; patterns vary by domain, cohort, and context. Building on this framing, the book investigates how poverty, family dynamics, and school environments influence, both directly and indirectly, the decision-making processes of both boys and girls, shaping their educational trajectories. These forces together generate intergroup heterogeneity in educational attainment, resisting simple binary categories of privilege and disadvantage. By applying an economic and interdisciplinary perspective, grounded in both quantitative and qualitative methods, the book moves beyond conventional gender inequality discourse to explore how structural forces shape educational outcomes for all genders in multifaceted, context-dependent ways. I hope this book will offer insights not only to social scientists such as economists and development researchers but also to educators, policymakers, and others engaged in development issues and beyond the thematic, regional, and spatial borders.

Throughout this journey, I have been constantly reminded of the responsibility that comes with researching communities whose lived realities are far removed from my own. This book is not only an academic endeavor, but also a modest attempt to reciprocate the openness and trust extended to me by the children, families, and local leaders I met in the field.

The following chapters are based on the author's previously published or publicly circulated research, including peer-reviewed journal articles and working papers. All chapters have been thoroughly reorganized and revised to form a coherent monograph. These prior publications are acknowledged with appropriate permissions or under open access licenses granted by the respective publishers. I would like to express my sincere gratitude to them here. Specifically:

Chapter 2: Okabe, Masayoshi. "Gender-Preferential Intergenerational Patterns in Primary Educational Attainment: An Econometric Approach to a Case in Rural Mindanao, the Philippines." *International Journal of Educational Development* 46: 125–142, 2016.

Chapter 3: Okabe, Masayoshi. "Empirical Analysis of the Continuity of Sequential Demands for Education in a Rural Philippines: Gender and Parent–Child Relations." *Asian Studies* 63, no. 1: 1–26, 2017. [Japanese]

Chapters 4–5: Okabe, Masayoshi. "Unintended Effect of Mothers' Labor Force Participation on Child Time Allocations under Family Dynamics in Rural Philippines." *Review of Economics of the Household*: 1–53, 2025. https://doi.org/10.1007/s11150-024-09758-x.

Chapter 6: Okabe, Masayoshi. "Boys' Underperformance, Teacher Scoring Bias and Unbalanced Teacher Market in Rural Philippines." *Journal of Development Studies* 61, no. 1: 40–62, 2025.

Chapter 7: Okabe, Masayoshi. "'Under-Performing' or Resilient Filipino Boys in Education? Listening to Students' and Adults' Perspectives and Backgrounds: A Western Visayas Case." IDE Discussion Paper (unpublished working paper) 705, 2018.

Appendix Chapters A–B: Okabe, Masayoshi. "Inferences and Descriptive Analyses on Education, Livelihoods, and Rural Poverty through Fieldwork and Tailored Household Survey in Marinduque, the Philippines." IDE Discussion Paper Series (unpublished working paper) 754, 2019.

Tokyo, Japan Masayoshi Okabe

Acknowledgments

The development of this book has greatly benefited from the support of numerous scholars and institutions across disciplines and organizations. First and foremost, I extend my deepest gratitude to the professors at the University of Tokyo (UTokyo) who have guided me since my graduate studies. Above all, I am profoundly grateful to Professor Toru Nakanishi, Professor Emeritus of UTokyo and my academic supervisor, whose mentorship shaped the foundation of my research and scholarly direction. I remain equally indebted to my co-advisors, Professors Yasuyuki Sawada, Yuichi Sekiya, Yuto Kitamura, and Ryuichi Tanaka, whose insights from economics, education, area studies, and beyond were essential to both formulating and empirically examining my hypotheses, and whose incisive guidance and encouragement have left a lasting impact. Beyond my formal advisory team, I am deeply thankful to Professors Waka Aoyama and Hiroyuki Ukeda, whose warm support through heartfelt encouragement in various difficult moments and reminders of the importance of local engagement provided enduring reassurance and inspiration.

I am deeply grateful to the Institute of Developing Economies (IDE-JETRO) and the University of the Philippines Diliman (UP Diliman), whose support for my overseas research fellowship in the Philippines was vital to this project. I owe special thanks to my former senior colleagues—Dr. Tomohiro Machikita (currently at Kyoto University), Dr. Seiro Ito (Senior Researcher, IDE-JETRO), and Dr. Takeshi Kawanaka (currently at Asia University)—who served as my official research mentors and provided invaluable guidance throughout. I also wish to thank Mr. Shigeki Nomura, former Director-General of IDE-JETRO, whose leadership and support as my department head were instrumental.

My sincere appreciation also goes to my hosting colleagues, who have also been my dear friends, at UP Diliman, just to name a few: Dr. Maragtas S. V. Amante, former Professor at the School of Labor and Industrial Relations (SOLAIR) and former Vice President of the UP System, and Dr. Ronahlee A. Asuncion and Dr. Melisa R. Serrano, the former and current Deans of SOLAIR, respectively. Dr. Amante and Dr. Asuncion graciously hosted me as a visiting research fellow and senior lecturer from 2017 to 2020, and Dr. Serrano has continued this support by hosting me in a new capacity as a visiting professor since 2024. I am also deeply grateful for the frequent and invaluable discussions with my SOLAIR faculty "roommates," Dr. Emily C. Cabegin and Assistant Professor Mary Leian M. Pasumbal, and a "queen" of SOLAIR, Dr. Rebecca S. Gaddi as well as College Secretary Dr. Verna Dinah Q. Viajar, among other members of the SOLAIR community. Additionally, I extend my appreciation to my former and current institutions, Kyoritsu Women's University (KWU) and Saitama University (SU), for their academic and logistical support during various stages of this project. I am likewise thankful to my colleagues—both faculty and administrative staff—at IDE-JETRO, UP Diliman, KWU, and SU for their encouragement and assistance.

This book also humbly serves as my *taos-pusong pagpapahayag ng utang na loob*—heartfelt expression of deep gratitude—for the people and communities of Marinduque and Antique, where much of the fieldwork for this project was carried out. I am especially grateful to Mrs. Lolita Natal and Mr. Delfin Natal, Jr. from Gasan, Marinduque, and Mr. Raymund Gumboc from Pandan, Antique. I also extend my deep gratitude to the children and families who generously shared their stories, aspirations, and daily realities. Without their openness and trust, this book would not have been possible.

I also owe a deep debt of gratitude to the many local residents who participated in my fieldwork and to the barangay and municipal officials who extended their cooperation. In particular, I thank Dr. Homer L. Montejo of Marinduque State College for reviewing my research instruments and assisting in coordination efforts, as well as his students and local assistant members from Barangay Masiga who supported the research. I am likewise grateful to the field assistants in Antique who worked with Mr. Gumboc and played a critical role in the success of the project on-site. I wish to express my appreciation as well to the officials from barangay offices, municipal halls, provincial governments, and national agencies who provided briefings and shared insights on education, local governance, poverty alleviation, and labor and employment policies. Their cooperation and openness enriched my understanding of the institutional landscape that underpins this book.

I also wish to acknowledge the organizations that generously provided data for the empirical analysis in this book, including the International Food Policy Research Institute (IFPRI), the Philippine Statistics Authority, and various offices of the Department of Education and the Department of Social Welfare and Development in the Philippines. Additionally, I thank the many scholars and participants at academic conferences where I presented parts of this research. I am also grateful for the many conversations shared with fellow *young* scholars over meals and drinks at *Trellis*, *Dampa sa Timog*, and other familiar spots in Metro Manila. These informal yet intellectually stimulating exchanges have provided both camaraderie and critical perspectives along the way. Furthermore, my special thanks go to Assistant Professor Maria Cynthia Barriga (Hitotsubashi University) and Dr. Eri Kitada (Tokyo College) for their thoughtful feedback and suggestions, drawn from diverse disciplinary backgrounds.

I am also grateful to Professors Akiko Kamogawa (Waseda University), Mina Hattori (Nagoya University), Kazuo Kuroda (Waseda University), Makoto Ichikawa (Rikkyo University), and all other members of the RGG KAKENHI project team and participants in the TUMSAT International Workshop, whose shared focus on the reversed gender gap has fostered collaborative insights. I also thank Professor Yuji Utsumi (Nagoya University) for his thoughtful exchanges on this theme. I am indebted to Professor Atsushi Kato (Waseda University) for his heartfelt encouragement and detailed, constructive comments on parts of this study.

From Springer Nature, I extend my sincere appreciation to Dr. Makoto Yano, the editor of the *Economics, Law, and Institutions in Asia Pacific* book series, as well as the two anonymous reviewers whose insightful feedback helped refine this work. I am also immensely grateful to Ms. Juno Kawakami, the handling editor, for her efficient and resourceful editorial service and to her colleagues at Springer Nature for their editorial assistance throughout the publication process.

This work was supported by generous funding from the Japan Society for the Promotion of Science (JSPS) (Grant Nos. 20K22248, 22K13394), the Toyota Foundation (Grant No. D16-R-0798), the IDE-JETRO Overseas Research Fellowship, and faculty research budgets from KWU and SU.

As reflected above, in completing this book I have been privileged to draw intellectual and moral support from a wealth of individuals and organizations. I also wish to express my gratitude to many others to whom I am equally indebted but could not name individually due to space constraints. Any remaining errors are my own. Finally, I dedicate this book to my mother, Yoko, and my entire family, with deep gratitude for their love and unwavering belief in my work.

Tokyo, Japan Masayoshi Okabe

Contents

Part I Introduction

1 Reversed Gender Disparity in Education: International Comparisons and Philippine Focus 3
1 Introduction 4
1.1 Emerging "Boys' Disengagement from Education" 4
1.2 Merely a Transient Issue Accompanying Economic Development? 6
2 Motivations: The Philippines as the Focal Case Country 7
2.1 Background: Experienced "Setback" from the Beginning of the Millennium 7
2.2 "Boys' Crisis": International Comparison 8
2.3 A Philippine Puzzle? Intranational Comparison 13
2.4 "Boys' Crisis" Worsening Over Time: Increasingly Pressing 17
3 Conceptual Framework 18
3.1 Essentialism and "Essentialistic" Perspectives 18
3.2 Socioeconomic Perspectives 19
3.3 Economics of the Reversal 23
4 Approaches and Structure 23
5 Data Sources and Data Types Used 27
6 Summary: Framing the Agenda 28
References 29

Part II Family Dynamics and Poverty

2 ***Fathers to Sons?*—Gendered Delays in Schooling, Intergenerational Dynamics, and Institutional Change in Primary Education: Findings from Bukidnon, Northern Mindanao** 37
1 Introduction 37
2 Research Framework 40
2.1 Repetitions, Gender Disparity, and Internal Efficiency in Education 40
2.2 Motivations 41
3 Dataset and Surveyed Area 42
3.1 Bukidnon Panel Data Survey 42
3.2 Sample Description 43
4 Outline of Education in the Research Site 44
4.1 Nationwide Situation Around the Study Period 44
4.2 Educational Situations in Bukidnon Around the Study Period 45
5 Empirical Analyses 50
5.1 Dependent Variable: Years of Delay 50
5.2 Regression Model 51
5.3 Descriptive Statistics 54
5.4 Estimation Method 55
5.5 Further Explorations and Robustness Checks 56
6 Results 58
6.1 Individual Backgrounds 58
6.2 Family Backgrounds 58
6.3 Supply-Side Policies and Interventions 70
6.4 The Results with Robustness Checks 70
7 Conclusion 81
References 83

3 ***Mothers to Daughters?*—Gendered Continuity in Educational Demand Beyond Primary Education: Findings from Bukidnon, Northern Mindanao** 87
1 Introduction 88
2 Conceptual Framework 89
2.1 Sequential Continuity of Educational Demand 89
2.2 Theoretical Underpinnings and Implications 90
3 Data 90
3.1 Bukidnon Panel Data Survey 90
3.2 Individual Characteristics 91
3.3 Household Characteristics 93

4 Empirical Analysis ... 94
4.1 Sequential Decision Continuum ... 94
4.2 Probabilistic Framework ... 95
4.3 Modeling Sequential Continuity of Educational Demand ... 96
5 Results ... 98
5.1 Individual Characteristics ... 98
5.2 Same-Sex Intergenerational Influence on Educational Demand Continuity ... 102
5.3 Household Characteristics and Regional Backgrounds ... 102
5.4 Discussions ... 103
6 Conclusion ... 107
Appendix ... 109
References ... 110

4 *Mothers to Sons?*—Maternal Labor Force Participation, Child Time Allocations, and Boys' Educational Disengagement: Evidence from Marinduque, MIMAROPA, Southern Luzon ... 113
1 Introduction ... 113
2 Conceptual Framework ... 115
2.1 Trinity of Education, Labor, and Leisure ... 115
2.2 Gendered Impacts of MLFP on Child Education ... 117
3 Data ... 118
3.1 Research Site and Data Collection in Marinduque ... 118
3.2 Data Collection and Time-Use Survey ... 119
3.3 Methodological Innovations in Time-Use Analysis ... 121
3.4 Defining "Pro-Educational" Child Time-Allocation Patterns ... 123
4 Empirical Analysis ... 130
4.1 Formulation ... 130
4.2 Estimations ... 130
4.3 Summary Statistics ... 133
5 Results ... 136
5.1 Gender Disparity in Child Pro-Educational Time-Allocation Pattern ... 136
5.2 Effect of MLFP on Child Pro-Educational Time-Allocation Patterns ... 147
5.3 Discussion of Two Mechanisms ... 148
5.4 Tests of the Validity of IV ... 150
6 Conclusions ... 153
Appendix ... 154
References ... 156

5 *Families to Mothers*?—Poverty-Driven Maternal Labor, Extended Family's Potential for Support, and Boys' Educational Disengagement: Further Investigation in Marinduque, MIMAROPA, Southern Luzon ... 163
1 Introduction ... 163
2 Conceptual Framework ... 164
3 Data and Methods ... 166
3.1 Determinants of MLFP ... 166
3.2 Time Allocation and Extended Family Setting ... 166
3.3 Methods ... 167
3.4 Summary Statistics ... 167
4 Empirical Analysis ... 170
4.1 Joint Estimation of Determinants of Parental Labor Force Participation ... 170
4.2 Analysis on the Potential of Extended Family Offsetting the Unintended Effect of MLFP ... 171
5 Results ... 172
5.1 Determinants of Parental Labor Force Participation ... 172
5.2 Extended Family Setting ... 174
5.3 Test of the Validity of IV ... 181
5.4 Further Exploration of Dual Burden ... 182
6 Conclusions ... 187
References ... 188

Part III School Environment and Poverty

6 *Teachers to Boys?*—Scoring Bias, Stereotypes, and the Teacher Market in Rural Philippines: A Natural Experiment in Marinduque, MIMAROPA, Southern Luzon ... 193
1 Introduction ... 193
2 Setting ... 196
3 Data ... 197
3.1 Data Outline and Research Site ... 197
3.2 Descriptive Statistics ... 198
3.3 Two Scores on Report Cards and National Achievement Test ... 201
3.4 RC–NAT Score Differences with Multiple Hypothesis Tests ... 202
4 Empirical Analysis ... 204
4.1 Benchmark Model ... 204
4.2 Identification Strategy with Two-Score Difference Estimations ... 207
4.3 Female Teacher Gender Ratios at the School Level ... 208

5 Results 210
5.1 Male Effect on the Benchmark Model 210
5.2 Male Effect on Two-Score Difference Estimations 214
5.3 The Female Teacher Gender Ratios and Likelihood of Teacher–Student Gender (Mis)match 214
6 Mediation Discussion 217
6.1 On Tracking of the National Achievement Test Scores 217
6.2 On the Possibility of Alternative Mechanisms 218
7 Conclusions 222
References 224

7 *Peers to Boys?—Fed-Up na sa Barkada*—Resilience Amid Schooling Disengagement: A Qualitative Inquiry into a Case in Antique, Western Visayas 229
1 Introduction 230
2 Literature Review 232
3 Outlines of Research Site and Survey 234
4 Survey and Case School Outlines 237
5 Results and Observations on the Backgrounds of Dropouts 238
5.1 Economic Hindrances: Even Traveling Across the Sea to Negros Island 239
5.2 Personal Dispositions or Noncognitive Skills in Learning 239
5.3 Negative Experiences: Physical and Mental 240
5.4 Parents' Reactions to Their Sons' Dropping Out 240
6 Discussion: Back to School—Exploring the Pathways and Motivations 241
6.1 Awakening 241
6.2 Barkadahan: Social Bonds and Educational Challenges 242
7 Conclusion 243
References 245

Part IV Conclusions

8 Reconsidering the Economics of "Reversal": Toward Human Development for All 251
1 Introduction 251
2 Structuring Role of Poverty in Educational Disengagement 253
2.1 Pathways from Poverty to Disengagement: Institutional and Economic Mechanisms 253
2.2 Econocultural Norms: A Preliminary Note on a Bargain About Long-Term Loss for Short-Term Gain 253
3 Family Dynamics and Boys' Disengagement from Education 256
3.1 Intergenerational Dynamics: Parent–Child Nexus in Education 256
3.2 Mothers' Labor Force Participation and Its Impact on Family Dynamics 257

3.3 Maternal Dual Burden in Family Dynamics: Rural and Cultural Contexts 257
4 School Environment and Boys' Disengagement from Education 259
4.1 School Environment Matters 259
4.2 Exposure to Augmentation 260
4.3 Resilience, Social Network, and Role Models 261
5 Questioning the "Reversed" Gender Disparity 263
5.1 Reconsidering the "Reversal": Empirical Nuances 263
5.2 Consolidating What We Have Learned: A Conceptual Framework of This Book's Perspective 264
6 Epilogue: In Lieu of a Conventional Conclusion 266
6.1 Structural Disparities and Policy Imperatives 266
6.2 Methodological Reflections and Future Directions 267
References 269

Appendices 273

Index 311

About the Author

Masayoshi Okabe is an associate professor of development economics at the Graduate School of Humanities and Social Sciences, Saitama University, Japan, and is concurrently a visiting professor at the School of Labor and Industrial Relations (SOLAIR), University of the Philippines Diliman (UP Diliman), Philippines. He earned his Doctor of Philosophy from the University of Tokyo in 2019. His scholarly interests include human capital investment, poverty alleviation, socioeconomic informality and informal institutions, intrahousehold resource allocation, discrimination and prejudice, the education-to-labor-market nexus, educational policy reforms, Southeast Asian area studies, and Philippine area studies. Prior to his current positions, Dr. Okabe was affiliated with the Institute of Developing Economies, Japan External Trade Organization (IDE-JETRO) (2011–2020) and served as a visiting research fellow at SOLAIR, UP Diliman (2017–2020), a senior lecturer at UP Diliman's College of Education (2018) and at SOLAIR (2019), and an assistant and then associate professor at the Faculty of International Studies, Kyoritsu Women's University (2020–2024). He has served on the editorial board of *The Asian Studies*, Japan Association for Asian Studies (JAAS), since 2021, and was an assistant editor and assistant book-review editor for *The Developing Economies*, Wiley, on behalf of IDE-JETRO, from 2013 to 2017.

Part I
Introduction

Chapter 1
Reversed Gender Disparity in Education: International Comparisons and Philippine Focus

Abstract This book investigates the reversal of gender disparity in education, a phenomenon in which boys, particularly from poorer rural households, are increasingly falling behind girls in schooling outcomes. This trend contradicts global development narratives that continue to prioritize girls' education, often portraying them as the default disadvantaged group. Challenging the adequacy of such a zero-sum framing, the book introduces the concept of the "economics of the reversal." This perspective examines how gendered educational outcomes emerge from the interaction of household decision-making, comparative advantages, and socially embedded constraints. Using multi-scalar empirical analysis based on national datasets, original survey data, and qualitative fieldwork in three rural provinces of the Philippines, the book explores how both structural factors and cultural expectations contribute to boys' educational disengagement. Rather than simply documenting this trend, it uses the reversal as a critical lens through which to reconsider assumptions embedded in global education and development discourse. The case of the Philippines, a country often internationally recognized as having the highest level of gender equality in Asia, offers a compelling setting to explore how gender, poverty, and education interact in complex and context-specific ways.

Keywords Reversed gender disparity in education · Boys' educational disengagement · Intrahousehold dynamics · Economics of the reversal · structural constraints · Scarring

> So let us wage a global struggle against illiteracy, poverty and terrorism and let us pick up our books and pens. They are our most powerful weapons.
>
> ——*Malala Yousafzai, at the UN Youth Assembly, New York, July 12, 2013*

M. Okabe, *Economics of the Reversal in Gender Disparities in Education and Development*, Economics, Law, and Institutions in Asia Pacific,
https://doi.org/10.1007/978-981-96-9271-2_1

1 Introduction

1.1 Emerging "Boys' Disengagement from Education"

Education is one of the most practical means for transferring wealth to the next generation in developing countries as well as in developed ones. As such, it has long been recognized as central to development and poverty reduction efforts (Heyneman and Stern 2015). For instance, in analyzing the East Asian Miracle—a period of remarkable economic growth and poverty reduction in the region—the World Bank highlighted the critical role of education, alongside the complementary relationship between market forces and government policies, in driving this progress (World Bank 1993: 43–46). Over the past quarter century, developing and emerging countries have made significant strides in increasing children's access to basic education. The importance of education in alleviating poverty and promoting holistic development cannot be overstated (Heyneman and Stern 2015; Snowdon 2015).

However, despite the anticipated benefits, there remains an issue of insufficient demand for education in these regions (Maholmes and King 2012). The fulfillment of educational needs further varies not only at the individual level but also across different social groups and strata. This disparity persists despite a substantial body of literature demonstrating the positive impact of education on development in developing countries. It is therefore important to explore the intergroup heterogeneity—why some groups receive more education than others and why some receive less. Therefore, the pursuit of inclusive human capital development has traditionally drawn attention to gender, race, class, strata, religion, and more (Dee 2005; Duflo 2012; Riegle-Crumb and Humphries 2012).

This book primarily examines gender disparity as a form of such intergroup heterogeneity in the pursuit of education. Traditionally, the field has focused on the disadvantages faced by females in accessing and benefiting from development. Overcoming female underrepresentation in education has long been a subject of concern in socioeconomic development research, alongside other factors of impoverishment in other sectors (Dee 2005; Duflo 2012; Riegle-Crumb and Humphries 2012; Sen 2002). Consequently, international educational development and cooperation have predominantly targeted girls' and women's education in developing countries to address gender disparities (Tembon and Fort 2008; Unterhalter 2010; Nguyen and Scripter 2013). The Dakar Framework for Action, established in 2000, set goals to "eliminate gender disparities in elementary and secondary education by 2005, and achieve gender equality in education by 2015, with a focus on ensuring girls' full and equal access to and achievement in basic education of good quality" (UNESCO 2000, p. 8). Similarly, Goals 2 and 3 of the Millennium Development Goals (MDGs), launched in 2000, emphasized these objectives.

Since then, international efforts have continued to focus on gender-specific educational issues, particularly in developing countries' contexts where male dominance prevails (Herz et al. 1991; Kabeer 2001; King and Hill 1993; Psacharopoulos and Woodhall 1985; Psacharopoulos 1994; Unterhalter 2010). The centrality of addressing challenges related to girls' and women's education remains paramount, even in the current pursuit of the Sustainable Development Goals (SDGs), which succeeded the MDGs in 2015. The logic of prioritizing girls in educational policy, originally institutionalized in the MDGs, was further carried over into the Sustainable Development Goals (SDGs). Although the SDGs expanded the framework to address broader forms of inequality and inclusion, the implicit gender narrative—framing girls as the persistently disadvantaged—has remained largely unchanged.

In this context, it is notable that girls' education has recently improved in some parts of developing countries. For example, Bangladesh and Cambodia, which were often classified as low-income countries in the past, have made significant progress. Government interventions, such as affirmative action programs like stipends for female students, have increased the number of girls enrolled in school and encouraged them to pursue longer periods of education (Asadullah and Chaudhury 2009; Filmer and Schady 2008; Fuwa 2001; Khandker et al. 2003; Xu et al. 2022; Zimmermann and Williams 2016). These efforts have led to not only higher enrollment rates but also improved gender parity in education.

While addressing inequalities against females is essential, reversed gender disparity in education is emerging globally (Bertrand and Pan 2013; Carlana 2019; Cornwell et al. 2013; Fortin et al. 2015; Goldin et al. 2006; Hannum and Buchmann 2005; Husain and Millimet 2009; Klasen 2002; Lavy 2008; Lavy and Sand 2018; Nguyen et al. 2022; Terrier 2020; Welmond and Gregory 2021). Recently, certain developing regions are experiencing the reversal in gender disparities in education, with boys lagging behind girls. This trend is pronounced in some low- and lower-middle-income countries, such as Kenya, Tanzania, and Uganda in sub-Saharan Africa, and the Philippines and Lao People's Democratic Republic in Asia (Asadullah and Chaudhury 2009; Buhl-Wiggers et al. 2021; Jha et al. 2012; UNESCO 2022; Randall and Anderson 1999; Welmond and Gregory 2021; Yamauchi and Tiongco 2013; Zimmermann and Williams 2016).

In response, international organizations, including the United Nations Girls' Education Initiative (UNGEI), the World Bank, and UNESCO, have highlighted this phenomenon under terms such as "boys' underperformance in education," "educational underachievement among boys and men," and "boys' disengagement from education" (UNGEI 2012; Welmond and Gregory 2021; UNESCO 2022). The UNGEI report identifies the Philippines, Thailand, Malaysia, and Mongolia as case studies for examining boys' underperformance in education. Additionally, Jha et al. (2012) note that similar issues are emerging in sub-Saharan Africa, which has traditionally been viewed as a region with predominant male dominance. In some Latin American and Caribbean countries, boys also underperform compared to girls (Kitamura 2015; Randall and Anderson 1999).

This reversal raises the question of whether it can be optimistically interpreted as a sign of positive progress for girls, who have historically faced significant barriers to educational opportunities. However, this situation is complex and cannot be universally assessed across all regions. On one hand, there is less research on the specific challenges faced by male children compared to the well-documented barriers for females (UNGEI 2012). Studies on boys' educational issues are still developing, as these challenges are considered "a more complex phenomenon than female disadvantages," compounded by the fact that males generally enjoy "higher social and economic positioning" and "privileging within the family" (Jha et al. 2012: 12).

Yet, on the other hand, a disadvantage for boys does not necessarily translate into an advantage for girls (UNGEI 2012: 7). The emergence of male underachievement in human capital accumulation poses a potential obstacle not only to boys' personal development but also to women's advancement (Miralao 2008). Weaver-Hightower (2003) notes that the focus on girls' education was predominant "until recently" (i.e., the late 1990s to early 2000s), with a shift towards examining boys' education beginning in the mid-1990s, particularly in advanced or industrialized economies like the United States (Weaver-Hightower 2003: 472). Similarly, Heyneman and Stern (2015) identify male disadvantages in educational output and performance in developed, industrial, or democratic countries, such as OECD member states. They suggest that this reversal of gender bias may soon become a critical issue in international education development. Thus, the concerns raised by international organizations align with these earlier discussions.

1.2 *Merely a Transient Issue Accompanying Economic Development?*

The aforementioned reports by international organizations provide valuable macro-level insights through cross-country analyses, uncovering patterns behind the reversed gender disparity in education across various countries. For instance, the World Bank identifies one pattern in gender gaps in enrollment and completion rates in relation to national income levels (Welmond and Gregory 2021).

According to Welmond and Gregory (2021: 5–8), male disadvantages compared to females in these indices follow a U-shaped pattern relative to countries' per capita GDP. Specifically, during middle-income stages, lower male indices are more common, while at poorer income levels, female children are more likely to experience conventional gender disparities against them. In other words, the reversed gender disparity appears most closely associated with middle-income levels, marking a transition from a low-income situation at a macro level. Conversely, female disadvantage is linked to poorer income levels. This U-shaped pattern suggests that these disparities are followed by a phase of improvement as economic development progresses and national income levels rise.

If the reversed gender disparity corresponds to the bottom of the U-shaped curve, can we assume this reversal as a transitional issue that will eventually be resolved with poverty alleviations and economic development? Interestingly, these international agency reports are cautious in generalizations or unification of answers. They unanimously advocate for "in-depth" country-specific studies that focus on local microenvironments, such as labor markets and educational systems, as well as local social norms. They also emphasize the need for applied research that considers social strata and geographic diversity (UNGEI 2012; Welmond and Gregory 2021; UNESCO 2022).

The key points commonly advocated in these reports, which this book is also sharing, can be summarized as follows:

1. A reversed gender disparity in education has recently emerged in developing countries, including parts of traditionally male-dominated regions in Asia and the Pacific, the Middle East, Latin America and the Caribbean, and Sub-Saharan Africa.
2. Cross-country observations indicate that in middle-income countries, boys' disengagement from education is more pronounced, while conventional patterns of disparity unfavorable to girls are more prevalent in poorer, lower-income stages. At the household economics level, however, poverty is also strongly associated with this reversed disparity in various ways.
3. In addition to income levels, other factors such as labor market institutions, social norms, gender-role identities, geographic and social strata diversities, school environments (including curricula, classroom climates, and student-teacher interactions), teacher capacity building, and variations in public policies on development and education, are also expected to play a role. However, empirical investigations and evidence on these factors remain insufficient.
4. Therefore, academia and governments need to study and identify the political, economic, social, and cultural factors contributing to these disparities. These factors are highly context-dependent, necessitating country-specific studies rather than general approaches.
5. Boys are not a homogeneous group, and addressing boys' disadvantages in education does not necessarily result in disadvantages for girls. The situation is not a zero-sum game; addressing boys' issues can also benefit girls within broader social contexts.

2 Motivations: The Philippines as the Focal Case Country

In response to the aforementioned emerging needs, this book aims at providing an in-depth country study by focusing on the Philippines, exploring and examining the factors behind the reversal of gender patterns in education. The Philippines presents several unique characteristics that motivate the research covered in this book.

2.1 *Background: Experienced "Setback" from the Beginning of the Millennium*

During the 1980s, the Philippines was already praised for achieving a relatively high standard of educational attainment compared to other developing countries (Symaco 2013; Tomas 2013). In the 1990s, aligning with the international movement toward Education for All (EFA), the country continuously expanded and improved its elementary education system, making it free and compulsory under the new constitution drafted in 1986 and ratified in 1987 during Corazon Aquino's administration (Tanodra 2003; Tomas 2013). However, from that point onward, enrollment rates worsened even as other developing countries saw improvements under the EFA initiative (Symaco 2013). For example, the country's cohort survival rates in public elementary and secondary education barely increased during the 1990s compared to the previous decade (Balisacan 2003: 289). This highlights a stark contrast with the positive praise received.

Caoli-Rodriguez (2007) and David et al. (2009) noted that educational attainment in the Philippines began to experience a "stagnation" or even a "setback" over the two decades starting from 1990. This was in stark contrast to other developing countries, which were improving basic education under the EFA scheme during the same period. They emphasized the need for empirical studies to examine the background and current situation of educational underachievement among boys and men. Without such research, repetition and dropout rates may remain high, and the educational system could suffer from issues with internal efficiency despite high initial enrollment rates. Considerations beyond enrollment rates are now necessary. Indeed, David et al. (2009) highlighted that the decline in enrollment rates and low educational attainment were more severe among boys and men than among girls and women. Learning performance and scores on national academic achievement tests also demonstrate clear gender disparities, unfavorable for boys (David et al. 2009). Therefore, it is reasonable to assume that the noted instability in national educational attainment and boys' underachievement in education are connected.

In sum, local researchers had already recognized the link between the country's "setback" in securing education for all and boys' disengagement from education around the beginning of the millennium. This concern became so prevalent that it was discussed in Filipino social science and political circles under the expression "boys' crisis" (Miralao 2008). This term aligns with later problem-settings identified by the aforementioned international agencies, such as "boys' underperformance in education," "educational underachievement among boys and men," and "boys' disengagement from education" (UNGEI 2012; Welmond and Gregory 2021; UNESCO 2022).

2.2 "Boys' Crisis": International Comparison

To assess the Philippines' position regarding boys' underperformance in education compared to other countries, the Gender Parity Index (GPI) is a valuable tool for cross-country comparisons. The GPI is widely used to measure gender parity not only in education but across various international contexts.[1] It is important to note, however, that the GPI does not capture qualitative aspects of gender disparities.

The GPI is calculated using the formula:

$$\text{GPI} = \frac{\text{Female rate}}{\text{Male rate}}.$$

A GPI value of 1.0 indicates parity, meaning that the rates for males and females are equal. A GPI greater than 1.0 signifies that the female rate exceeds the male rate, while a GPI less than 1.0 indicates that the female rate is lower than the male rate.

For example, if the GPI for enrollment rates at various educational levels is less than 1.0, it suggests that males have better access to education compared to females. Conversely, a GPI greater than 1.0 indicates that females have better access to education. A GPI of 1.0 signifies equal enrollment rates for both genders.[2] This section analyzes regional and country-specific GPI data to explore international trends in developing regions, including the Philippines, and provides a comparative analysis to position the Philippines relative to its neighboring countries.

The analysis focuses on basic education, with GPIs based on net enrollment rates (NERs) illustrated in line graphs. These graphs depict the Philippines alongside regional averages for developing countries in East Asia and the Pacific, Latin America, South and West Asia, and Sub-Saharan Africa.[3] Figures 1 and 2 present the GPIs for elementary and secondary education levels, respectively. Due to variations in data availability, the year ranges in these figures differ.

According to Fig. 1, developing countries have generally achieved gender parity in elementary education over the past three decades. The most notable improvements are observed in West and South Asia, largely attributed to significant advancements in girls' education in Bangladesh (Asadullah and Chaudhury 2009; Khandker et al. 2003). East Asia and the Pacific, as well as Latin America, also demonstrate gender parity at the elementary level. Sub-Saharan Africa, while showing progress, still lags behind in achieving full parity. Overall, developing countries exhibit a consistent trend towards gender parity in elementary education.

In contrast, Fig. 2 reveals greater regional variation in GPIs for secondary education. The average GPI for developing countries has fluctuated between 0.90 and 0.95 over the past two decades. Sub-Saharan Africa consistently reports a GPI of 0.90 or lower. East Asia and the Pacific, starting from a GPI of 0.93, has made substantial progress towards gender parity. West and South Asia, initially at a low GPI of 0.78, have achieved significant improvement in gender parity, similar to the trends

[1] For terminological differences between gender parity and gender equality, see Chisamya et al. (2012).

[2] Technically, according to UNESCO (2022: 30), gender parity is considered achieved when the GPI falls within the range of 0.97 to 1.03, rather than being exactly 1.0.

[3] Note that comparisons based on NERs are unaffected by the relative sex ratios within a country's population. Therefore, the validity of the following discussions remains intact, even if the sex ratio in a country's population is significantly skewed towards one gender.

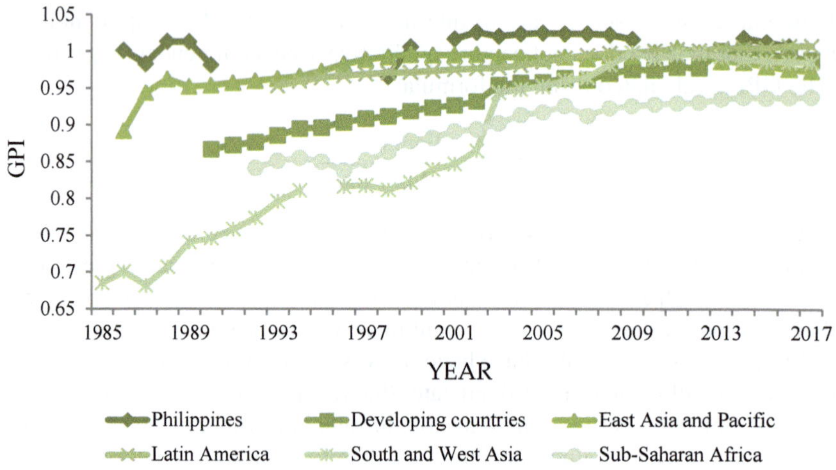

Fig. 1 Gender Parity Index (GPI) for Net Enrollment Rates (NER) in Elementary Education, by regions. *Note* Indicators more recent than those within the specified year ranges were not available at the time of this writing. *Source* Author's calculations based on UIS Stat

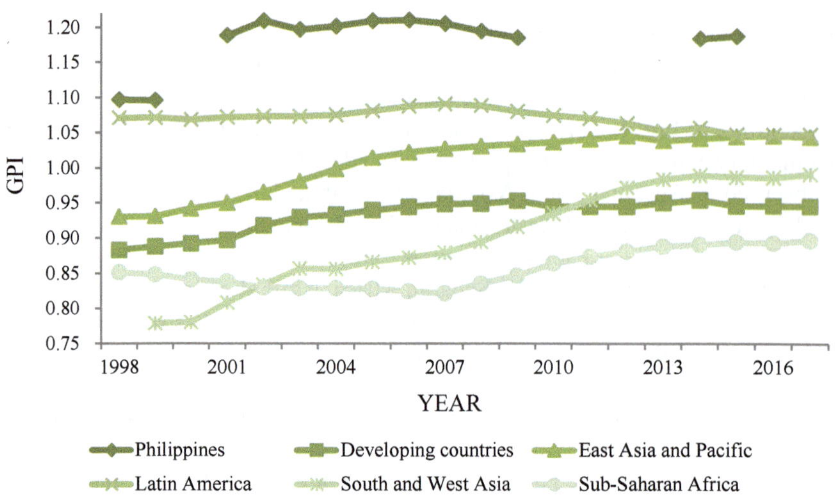

Fig. 2 Gender Parity Index (GPI) for Net Enrollment Rates (NERs) in Secondary Education, by regions. *Note* Indicators more recent than those within the specified year ranges were not available at the time of this writing. *Source* Author's calculations based on UIS Stat

observed in elementary education. In contrast, Latin America's GPI peaked at nearly 1.10 around 2007 and has remained above 1.05 since then.

Overall, secondary education reveals two distinct patterns of gender disparity: girls' underperformance in Sub-Saharan Africa and generally across developing countries (with Sub-Saharan Africa contributing to the lower average GPI), and boys' underperformance in Latin America. East Asia and the Pacific, as well as West and South Asia, appear to be achieving gender parity in secondary education as of 2017, despite previous disparities in the latter region. However, it is important to note that these trends may not necessarily continue in the future.

Here, we place the Philippines within the broader context of developing regions. In elementary education, the Philippines has generally maintained a GPI of no less than 1.0, as illustrated in Fig. 1. In secondary education, the Philippines' exceptional performance is even more evident. As shown in Fig. 2, the Philippines' GPI has consistently been around 1.20. This is notably higher than the GPI of the second-ranked region, Latin America, which is approximately 1.05. In alignment with trends in net NERs, the GPI for out-of-school children and out-of-school youths (OOSC/OOSY) further underscores this pattern (Fig. 3). Across most developing countries, both low- and middle-income, Fig. 3 reveals that more girls than boys leave school during elementary and secondary education. In East Asia and the Pacific, as well as in Latin America and the Caribbean, there are slightly more male OOSC/OOSYs compared to females. However, the Philippines stands out with the lowest GPIs, a situation that appears to be deteriorating in recent years. Additionally, female students in the Philippines are reported to achieve better academic performance than their male counterparts (Yamauchi and Tiongco 2013).

To compare the Philippines with its regional counterparts, Figs. 4 and 5 present the GPIs for elementary and secondary education, respectively. These figures include Southeast Asian countries such as Thailand, Indonesia, Malaysia, Cambodia, Laos, and Myanmar. Singapore and Vietnam are not included due to the unavailability of data from the same source. The trends observed in Figs. 4 and 5 are consistent with those depicted in Figs. 1 and 2: (i) gender disparity is minimal in elementary

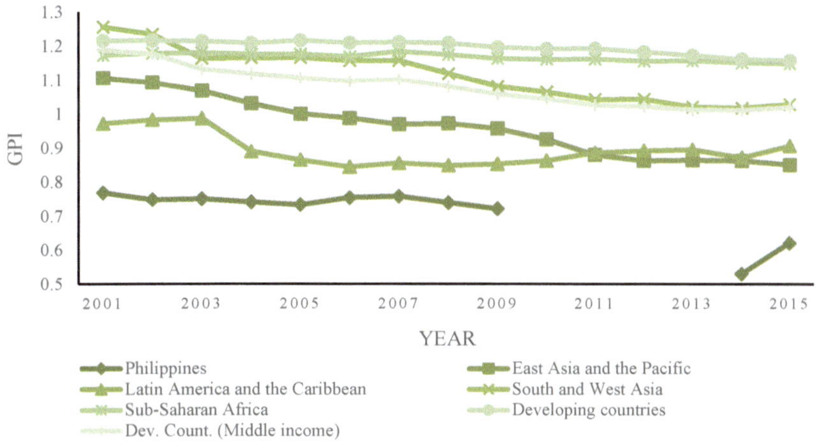

Fig. 3 Gender Parity Index (GPI) for Out-of-School Rates for Children and Youth, Elementary and Secondary School Age, by regions. *Note* Indicators more recent than those within the specified year ranges were not available at the time of this writing. *Source* Author's calculations based on UIS Stat

education across these countries, and (ii) there is a greater cross-country gender disparity in secondary education.

Cambodia and Laos have made substantial progress towards gender parity in both elementary and secondary education. These countries, having started with low GPIs, indicate that the observed improvements reflect increased access to education for

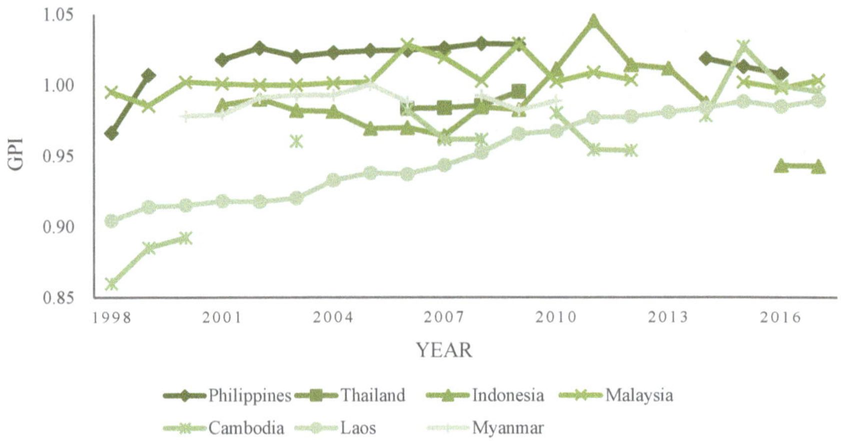

Fig. 4 Gender Parity Index (GPI), NER, Elementary, Comparison with Neighboring Countries of the Philippines. *Notes*: (1) Indicators more recent than the year ranges in the figure were not available at the time of this writing. (2) Singaporean and Vietnamese data are not available with the same data source. *Source* Author's calculations based on the UIS Stat

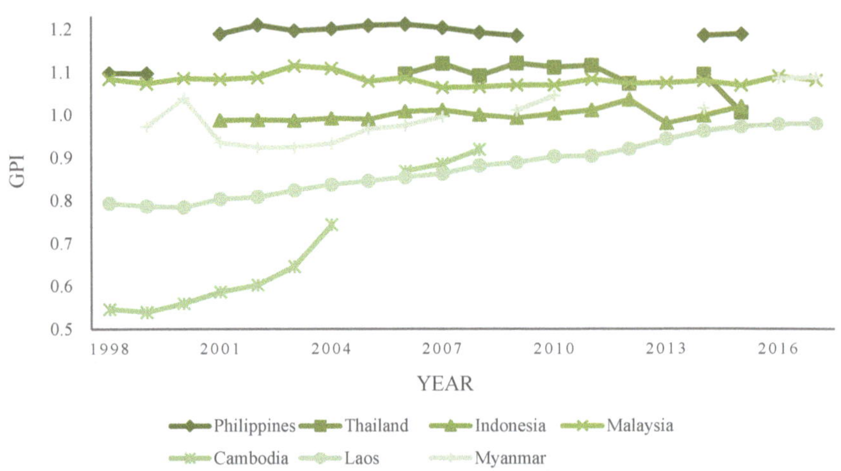

Fig. 5 Gender Parity Index (GPI), NER, Secondary, Comparison with Neighboring Countries of the Philippines. *Notes* (1) Indicators more recent than the year ranges in the figure were not available at the time of this writing. (2) Singaporean and Vietnamese data are not available with the same data source. *Source* Author's calculations based on the UIS Stat

girls rather than declines among boys. This suggests a significant catch-up effect among girls in these countries. In Cambodia, for instance, government initiatives, including affirmative action programs such as stipend schemes for female students, have played a crucial role in this progress (Zimmermann and Williams 2016).

Indonesia and Myanmar occupy an intermediate position, where gender parity is being progressively achieved. These countries show a steady improvement in gender parity, although they have not reached the levels observed in the leading countries. In contrast, Thailand and Malaysia demonstrate trends akin to those of the Philippines, as indicated by the GPIs. The Philippines distinguishes itself within the Southeast Asian region with GPIs approximately 10% higher than those of Thailand and Malaysia, which rank second. This high GPI underscores the Philippines' notable position in terms of gender parity in education relative to its regional peers.

Although the region-level disaggregated GPIs presented in Figs. 1 and 2 do not capture the full heterogeneity within the region, the country-specific comparisons in Figs. 4 and 5 highlight significant cross-country variation. Southeast Asia appears to be in an intermediate position where educational underperformance among boys or girls is less pronounced than in previous years. Nonetheless, the region exhibits patterns that align with broader international trends.

In the context of the Philippines, gender disparity in education has traditionally been regarded as less severe or even equal, especially when focusing exclusively on female students (Fuwa 2014). However, the international and regional comparisons of the GPI discussed in this section reveal a stark contrast to the perception of the Philippines as a gender-equal country. When considering the "boys' crisis" perspective (Miralao 2008), the reality shows a significant crisis affecting boys. This evidence underscores a pronounced imbalance that challenges the notion of gender parity.

2.3 A Philippine Puzzle? Intranational Comparison

According to the U-shaped relationship between cross-country income levels and boys' educational disadvantage discussed in Sect. 1.2, boys' underperformance in education is generally less pronounced in poorer regions and countries. However, this underperformance becomes more pronounced as income levels increase, following the alleged U-shaped curve. In this context, it is straightforward to see that gender disparity patterns in Sub-Saharan Africa typically disadvantage girls compared to higher-income regions like East Asia and the Pacific and Latin America. Similarly, within Southeast Asia, Laos shows a gender disparity that disadvantages girls relative to its wealthier counterparts. However, the fact that Thailand and Indonesia are considered wealthier than the Philippines suggests that the U-shaped relationship may not always hold consistently.[4]

This inconsistency is apparent in intranational comparisons within the Philippines. Unlike the cross-country pattern observed, boys' underperformance in education is more pronounced among poorer segments of the population compared to their wealthier counterparts, which contradicts the cross-country U-shaped relationship. This section explores this notable discrepancy through two dimensions: urban versus rural and high-income versus low-income comparisons. The conclusion emphasizes the importance of an in-depth focus on poorer households and rural regions, which this book adopts as its research approach, instead of country-representative large-scale studies.[5]

2.3.1 Urban–Rural Comparisons

In the Philippines, Metro Manila (Luzon Island), Metro Cebu (Cebu Island), and Metro Davao (Mindanao Island) are the country's major metropolitan areas. These regions are highly industrialized and populous, serving as the economic, social, and political centers of the country. Beyond these metropolises, there are several other urban centers scattered throughout the country.[6] Particularly in Luzon Island, regions such as Central Luzon and CALABARZON are evolving into suburban areas surrounding Metro Manila, with several political and economic centers.[7]

In simple terms, regions farther from Luzon Island tend to be more rural and less industrially and economically developed. There also appears to be a corresponding pattern of gender disparity in education based on proximity to urban centers or rural areas. Figure 6 presents two types of information: the NERs for both male and female students at the secondary level and the standardized gender parity ratios to zero by region. These ratios are calculated as:

$$\frac{\text{Male NER} - \text{Female NER}}{\text{NER of both males and females}},$$

[4] Notably, it is unclear if cross-country observations consistently guarantee both that each country will experience a reversed gender parity pattern as it develops and that this reversal will ease as the country progresses through its own time-series transitions.

[5] This statement does not imply that this book undervalues the necessity and importance of nationally representative studies. Combining rural case studies, as this book does, with nationally representative studies will be crucial in future approaches. However, this single-authored book focuses mainly on the former.

[6] Such as Baguio City (northern Luzon); Iloilo City and Bacolod City (Western Visayas); Cagayan de Oro City (northern Mindanao); Zamboanga City (western Mindanao); and General Santos City (southern Mindanao), among others.

[7] Such as Angeles City (Pampanga Province); Antipolo City (Rizal Province); Batangas City (Batangas Province); Clark Freeport and Special Economic Zone (Pampanga and Tarlac Provinces); Imus City (Cavite Province); Malolos City (Bulacan Province); and Subic Bay Freeport Zone (Zambales and Bataan Provinces), among others.

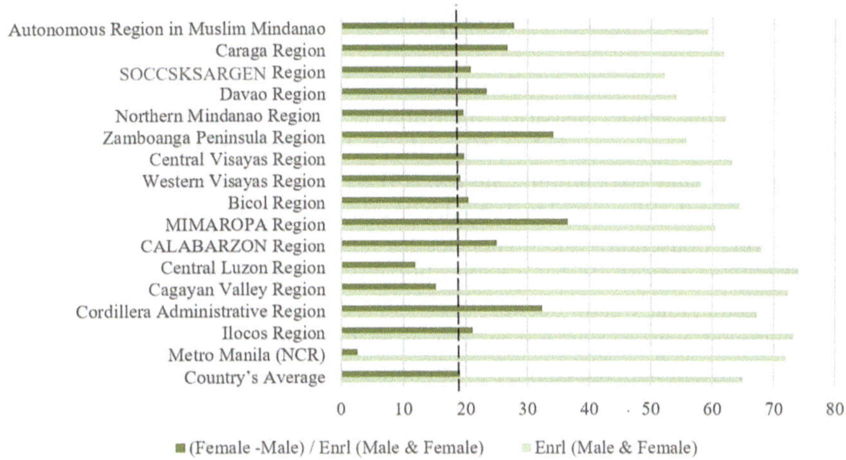

Fig. 6 Philippine Intranational Gender Disparities in NER (%), Secondary Level, by Regions. *Note* "(Female–Male)/Enrl(Male & Female)" means the proportion of differences of female-to-male net enrollment rates (NERs) over the total NERs of both males and females. "Enrl(Male & Female)" means the total NERs of both males and females. *Source* Author's calculations using PSA (2017a, 2021)

using the recent nationally representative education-related data from the *Functional Literacy, Education, and Mass Media Survey* (FLEMMS) (PSA 2017a, 2021). A standardized ratio of zero indicates gender parity in enrollment rates, corresponding to GPI 1.0.

NERs for both boys and girls are generally higher in Luzon Island (including Metro Manila, Ilocos Region, Cordillera Administrative Region (CAR), Cagayan Valley Region, Central Luzon Region, and CALABARZON Region) compared to other regions in the country. This is expected, given that Luzon Island is likely wealthier in terms of economic and industrial development compared to other regions.

However, the pattern of gender disparity in education differs from the pattern of NERs. The average gender disparity ratio in the country is around 20%, meaning that female students are enrolled at a rate 1.20 times that of male students in the same cohort. This aligns with the Philippine GPI observed in the international comparisons presented in Fig. 2 of the previous subsection. Metro Manila exhibits only a marginal gender disparity, whether favoring males or females, and other regions in Luzon also show smaller gender disparities compared to regions outside Luzon. Conversely, regions such as MIMAROPA, Zamboanga Peninsula, Caraga, and the Autonomous Region for Muslim Mindanao (ARMM; succeeded in 2019 by the Bangsamoro Autonomous Region in Muslim Mindanao, BARMM) show higher gender disparity ratios unfavorable to males. These observations indicate that both low enrollment rates and high gender disparity against boys are more prevalent in rural areas or regions outside Luzon compared to urban centers or regions within Luzon.

2.3.2 Household-Wealth-Level Comparisons

A similar pattern is observed in household wealth-level comparisons nationwide. Figure 7 presents gender disparity, measured as female-to-male NERs by wealth index deciles, using merged data from the Labor Force Survey (LFS) and the Family Income and Expenditure Survey (FIES) (PSA 2017b, 2018). This figure categorizes household wealth levels by deciles nationwide, with lower deciles representing poorer households and higher deciles representing wealthier ones. Positive percentage gaps (shown as bar graphs) indicate that male access to education is disadvantaged at that wealth decile.

The national average percentage, shown on the rightmost side of the graph, is positive, consistent with the country's GPI being above 1.0, as confirmed in previous sections. However, this national average does not account for variations across household wealth levels. When examining gender disparity by household wealth deciles, a clear pattern emerges; larger gender gaps unfavorable to male children are evident among poorer households. Only the wealthiest decile ("d10") shows a negative percentage, indicating that more male children are enrolled compared to females. The remaining nine deciles exhibit positive percentage gaps, with the size of these gaps increasing as households become poorer (toward "d1"). In other words, boys from poorer households lag behind girls in educational attainment, particularly beyond elementary education. It is noteworthy that intranational household wealth-level comparisons reveal a monotonically decreasing trend, in contrast to the U-shaped curve observed at the cross-country level.

Fig. 7 Philippine Intranational Female-to-Male Disparity in NERs (%), Secondary Level, by Household Wealth Index Deciles. *Note* The horizontal axis stands for wealth index deciles: the "d1" is the poorest group (1st) and the "d10" is the richest in the country. A bar is 0 when male and female net enrollment rates are equal. If a bar graph is over (below) 0, it means fewer (more) male children are enrolling than their female counterparts. *Source* Author's calculations using PSA (2017b, 2018)

In summary, boys' underperformance in education is more pronounced in rural areas and among poorer households than in urban areas and among wealthier households. This finding presents a puzzle in the Philippines, differing from international comparisons, which generally show that girls face educational disadvantages in poorer countries and regions. Therefore, it is reiterated that this book adopts an approach focusing selectively on rural areas and poverty through empirical case studies.

2.4 *"Boys' Crisis" Worsening Over Time: Increasingly Pressing*

In addition to comparisons based on degrees of rurality and wealth, there appears to be an intergenerationally expanding gap in educational attainment between Filipino men and women over time. Figure 8 illustrates this expanding gap across generations. The Gender Parity Index (GPI) at two literacy levels is calculated and visualized in line graphs: (i) "level 0," referring to illiteracy, and (ii) "level 4," equivalent to the literacy level of secondary school graduates (PSA 2017a).

The gender disparity in educational attainment has become more pronounced over time. For the age cohort 60–64 (the oldest generation in the sample), the GPIs for both literacy levels were the same, indicating minimal gender difference at those levels. However, from this oldest generation onward, the GPI of "level 4" has increased in subsequent generations, reaching 1.3 in the youngest cohort. In contrast, the GPI of "level 0" has decreased from older to younger generations, down to approximately 0.5 in the youngest generation. In other words, today, (i) there are 1.3 times as many women with at least a secondary education level of literacy compared to their male

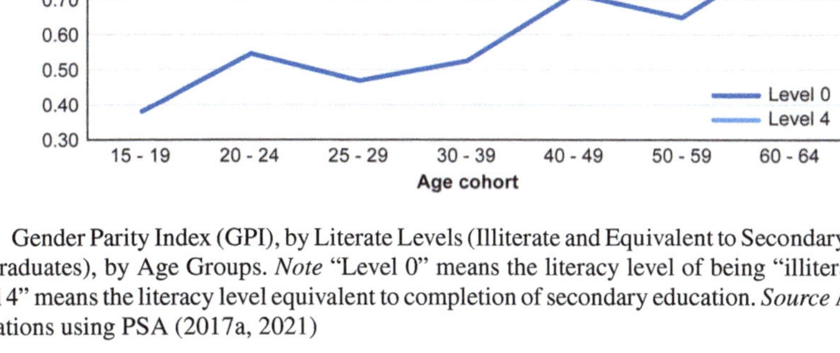

Fig. 8 Gender Parity Index (GPI), by Literate Levels (Illiterate and Equivalent to Secondary Education Graduates), by Age Groups. *Note* "Level 0" means the literacy level of being "illiterate" and "Level 4" means the literacy level equivalent to completion of secondary education. *Source* Author's calculations using PSA (2017a, 2021)

Table 1 Gender Equity in Education in the Philippines (2022) by Educational Level

Educational level	Female	Male	Female/Male
Enrolment in primary education (%)	96.60	97.28	0.99
Enrolment in secondary education (%)	93.91	85.88	1.09
Enrolment in tertiary education (%)	41.22	30.17	1.37

Source World Economic Forum (2022, p. 292)

counterparts, while (ii) there are around twice as many men with the lowest literacy level compared to their female counterparts. (iii) Initially, this gender disparity was minimal among the oldest generation but has become significantly more pronounced among younger generations.

This increasing severity of educational underachievement among boys in younger generations underscores that the issue is not merely transient. Instead, it has evolved into a persistent societal challenge that is intensifying over time. The growing disparity highlights the urgent need for both academic and policy responses. Addressing this issue is critical to ensuring equitable opportunities for human development and promoting broader social and economic development (Table 1).

3 Conceptual Framework

This section briefly reviews existing literature on boys' underperformance in education, identifying gaps that this book will address, while detailed literature reviews are provided in later chapters. It presents two main perspectives: essentialistic and socioeconomic, establishing the conceptual framework. The essentialistic view sees boys' underperformance as an inherent and unchangeable consequence of gender differences, while the socioeconomic perspective focuses on modifiable factors within varying socioeconomic conditions. The latter offers a more actionable approach, as it identifies determinants that could potentially improve educational outcomes for boys. Then, this study presents the third perspective, economics of the reversal.

3.1 Essentialism and "Essentialistic" Perspectives

While this book does not adopt an essentialistic perspective, it is important to discuss it briefly because such a view still shapes how boys' underperformance is understood in everyday discourse. The essentialistic perspective, though rarely directly embraced in social sciences beyond psychology, considers issues as consequences of inherent traits or internal natures, such as those attributed to men and women. This view aligns with fields like neuroscience, genetics, and physiology, which link sexual differences in behavior, perception, and attitudes to brain structure and hormones (Pease and

Pease 2001; Baron-Cohen 2004). For example, it might explain differences in skills, abilities, and interests as rooted in physiological factors. While this book does not extensively explore medical sciences, it notes the prevalence of essentialistic views in the Philippines, where boys are often seen as less serious or responsible in their learning compared to girls, perceived as more prone to truancy or vice (Bouis et al. 1998).

Even without explicitly invoking essentialism, attributing boys' educational issues merely to the impact of past women's movements reflects causality oversimplified by essentialism. This perspective suggests that increased gender equality in education, spurred by women's movements, is the root cause of observed disparities and that boys' underperformance will naturally balance out over time. However, this book argues against the notion that boys' underperformance is merely a temporary phase related to improvements in women's status. Miralao (2008) highlights that while women's activism has advanced gender equality, boys' underachievement remains a significant concern. They warn that if unaddressed, today's young women may face the burden of dealing with underachieving male relatives in various aspects of life. Therefore, even if viewed through an essentialistic lens, boys' educational issues demand social and practical solutions.

3.2 *Socioeconomic Perspectives*

In contrast to essentialistic views—which explain gender disparities in education as the natural result of biological or immutable traits—socioeconomic perspectives emphasize the role of structural, behavioral, and contextual factors in shaping educational outcomes. These perspectives offer more actionable insights, as they identify conditions and mechanisms that can be altered through policy or intervention.

This section introduces key theoretical approaches that locate boys' underperformance within broader socioeconomic frameworks. While the following review is necessarily brief, a more detailed discussion will be presented in subsequent chapters.

3.2.1 Human Capital Theory

Gender inequalities in education can be initially understood through the lens of economic status, particularly employment. This idea is rooted in human capital theory (Becker 1962, 1964; Snowdon 2015), which posits that individual investment in education is driven by anticipated future gains in labor markets. According to this theory, individuals invest in schooling up to the point where the expected, present-discounted marginal benefit of an additional year equals its marginal cost (including foregone earnings). Yet, as discussed in previous sections, in emerging low- and middle-income settings an apparent "reverse" pattern has increasingly been observed: girls attain more schooling than boys. Despite this, female labor-force participation rates and wage rates are generally lower than men's globally, including in these settings. These disparities help explain gender-differentiated schooling patterns. Human capital theory suggests that higher returns to education for women (or men) drive them to seek more education, but choices also depend on differential costs and outside options: adolescent boys often face readily available, cash-paying informal jobs (e.g., construction, transport, farm piecework), raising the shadow price of attendance, whereas girls may perceive stronger non-pecuniary and expectation-based returns (safety, school climate, credential value in public-sector hiring or marriage) (Kabeer 2001; Chiappori et al. 2009; Duflo 2012).

However, the foundational human capital theory assumes a market with perfect information and no friction or failures. In theory, education should be an attractive investment, even if current affordability is an issue. The theory implies that individuals can borrow from credit markets at given market interest rates to cover educational costs, but in practice borrowing is limited and risk-priced, so liquidity constraints bind and the opportunity cost of schooling can be higher for boys when immediate earnings are available (Deaton 1997; de Janvry and Sadoulet 2021). Empirical studies support this, showing that returns on education often exceed credit market interest rates, particularly at lower education levels and in developing regions (Psacharopoulos 1994; Psacharopoulos and Patrinos 2004, 2018). Taking these frictions into account helps reconcile higher female attainment with lower female wages and yields a testable implication for the analyses that follow: where demand for adolescent male labor is stronger, dropout should rise more steeply for boys than for girls, conditional on school quality (Buhl-Wiggers et al. 2021; Randall and Anderson 1999).

3.2.2 Dynamics of Poverty

The dynamics of poverty are crucial in understanding gender differentiations in education. Market failures are more prevalent in developing countries than in advanced economies (de Janvry and Sadoulet 2021). Crucially, poverty is not static: households experience idiosyncratic and covariate income shocks and strong seasonality, and where credit and insurance markets are thin, they smooth consumption by adjusting children's time first—absences and reduced study effort become the buffer (Deaton 1997; Hulme and Shepherd 2003; de Janvry and Sadoulet 2021; Maholmes and King 2012). Transition grades impose lumpy costs (fees, uniforms, transport) that create liquidity thresholds; if these bind near periods of peak local labor demand, temporary absences can turn into withdrawal (King and Hill 1993; Buhl-Wiggers et al. 2021; Filmer and Schady 2008; Khandker et al. 2003). When household income from parents is insufficient, children may need to work instead of attending school, especially as they reach physical maturity (Torres 2011). Even short interruptions can lower achievement, reduce expected returns, and raise the subjective cost of re-entry, generating path dependence (hysteresis) and persistent adverse (scarring) effects that make dropout more likely at the next decision point (Andrew 2014; DiPrete and Eirich 2006; Maholmes and King 2012). Even without pressing children into labor, poorer parents may withdraw them from school earlier than wealthier families, so that identical wage returns can still produce gender-divergent schooling choices once shocks, seasonality, and liquidity thresholds are accounted for.

3.2.3 New and Old Regime in Family Economics

Family economics also explores why women increasingly invest in education compared to men. Scholars in this field have examined the relationship between pre-marriage human capital investment and its impact on post-marital gains, focusing on spousal roles and intrahousehold coordination. Chiappori et al. (2009) investigated this issue, concluding that as labor-market returns to education rise, reduced home production demands, and weaker traditional labor division norms, women are more likely to invest in education.

Education is a form of human capital investment, with implications for household consumption and labor coordination. The theory proposes two regimes: the "old" and the "new." In the "old" regime, women spent more time on home production, leading to lower labor market wages and returns to schooling. In contrast, the "new" regime allows women more time for market work, increasing wage gains and educational returns. Technological innovations that reduce labor-intensive household chores and lower fertility rates are key factors in this transition (Greenwood et al. 2005; Albanesi and Olivetti 2009).

3.2.4 Inter-Gender Comparative Advantage of Employability by Sectors

Inter-gender comparative advantages in employability influence educational investment gaps between men and women. Comparative advantages are evident between agricultural and non-agricultural occupations (Estudillo et al. 2009). In developing countries, agricultural jobs are becoming less profitable compared to non-agricultural jobs. Farming often requires physical strength, and some sons from farming households may perceive agricultural work as their future occupation, even if they underperform academically.

Conversely, women have a comparative advantage in non-agricultural sectors (Estudillo and Otsuka 2016). Non-agricultural jobs generally offer higher returns on education and greater social status compared to agricultural jobs. The physical differences between males and females shape these comparative advantages. Recent developments in non-agricultural sectors, especially in rural areas, highlight why women are increasingly motivated to pursue education compared to their male counterparts.

3.2.5 Parental Egalitarianism

In rural areas of the Philippines, observations reveal parental behaviors that reflect a form of egalitarianism. Parents often prioritize passing land to their sons as a bequest, which serves as a productive asset for continuing farming practices (Estudillo et al. 2001a, b; Quisumbing 1994). This allocation of land is rooted in the comparative advantage that men have in agricultural work, while women are more likely to excel in non-agricultural sectors. As a result, sons are expected to inherit the land and carry on the farming tradition, whereas daughters are not considered for this bequest.

In response to this differential treatment, parents invest more in their daughters' education as a form of compensation. This investment aims to balance the opportunities for wealth transfer between sons and daughters, thereby reflecting a pattern of parental egalitarianism (Estudillo et al. 2001a, b; Quisumbing 1994). By enhancing their daughters' human capital, parents seek to equalize the disparities in future prospects that arise from the land inheritance system.

This pattern of investment in daughters' education can also be linked to the "pro-girl" bias observed in intrahousehold consumption (Fuwa 2014). In this context, girls are often given more support for education-related expenses, such as transportation fares. This preferential treatment underscores the parents' attempt to provide educational opportunities that compensate for the lack of land inheritance, ensuring that daughters have better prospects in sectors where women are increasingly gaining comparative advantages.

3.2.6 Unfavorable Labor Market Characteristics for Women

Aside from the micro intrahousehold situations noted above that may motivate girls to pursue more education, an empirical analysis exploiting subnational variation within the Philippines finds that parental investment responds to anticipated gender wage penalties in the Philippine labor market, raising incentives for greater female human capital accumulation, so that women can achieve parity with their male counterparts in the labor market (Yamauchi and Tiongco 2013). This mechanism is consistent with evidence of gender wage penalties against women. According to their study, the Philippine labor market is not gender-equal; rather, it continues to exhibit conventional bias against women, as in other developing countries. Wage penalties for women also persist even after controlling for other factors. Philippine researchers such as Asuncion (2018) and Serrano and Certeza (2014) also reach similar conclusions.

However, while compelling, this "uncompensation" or wage-penalty mechanism is so general and so widely observed across countries that it cannot by itself explain why boys' lag is particularly pronounced in the Philippines (as well as in the regions and countries discussed above). Alongside this "uncompensation" or penalty–returns framework, therefore, this book examines further mechanisms underlying the scale and persistence of boys' lag; the following sections take up these issues.[8]

[8] Gender wage penalties against women are widely documented across countries worldwide, not only in the Philippines or in Asian and other developing economies; thus, the "uncompensation" (penalty–returns) logic is general rather than country- or region-specific. At the same time, even where higher female attainment improves promotion prospects, recognition of credentials is

3.3 *Economics of the Reversal*

In this book, I propose a third perspective that I refer to as the "economics of the reversal." This framework builds on the socioeconomic view and emphasizes how structural constraints embedded in local socioeconomic contexts shape dynamic interactions between family strategies, labor markets, and educational incentives and how temporary shocks can leave scarring effects (Andrew 2014; DiPrete and Eirich 2006), which, in interaction with these constraints, can lead to apparent gender reversals in schooling outcomes in specific settings. It neither assumes essentialist accounts of gender nor treats social disadvantage as unidirectional; instead, it focuses on a form of hysteresis dynamic, in which seemingly rational short-run choices, often shaped by gendered opportunity structures, can produce persistent shifts in schooling patterns, such as the underperformance of boys in rural areas. Here, the "reversal" is used as an analytical lens rather than a claim of complete inversion, a single across-the-board reversal in all domains, or a zero-sum account. It is deliberately multivalent; Chapter 8 (Conclusion) develops its layered senses across group patterns, time horizons, and institutional domains, while here it is introduced only to orient the analyses that follow. This lens guides the empirical chapters that follow.

4 Approaches and Structure

Through the integrated framework of economics of the reversal, this book empirically investigates the mechanisms that give rise to the reversed gender disparity in education. It particularly examines how poverty, often considered a background condition, is in fact actively embedded in and refracted through the domains of family and school. Rather than treating poverty, family dynamics, and school environment as separate or additive factors, the book conceptualizes poverty as a cross-cutting structural force that shapes how families and institutions respond to constraints. These responses, in turn, produce intergroup heterogeneity in gendered educational outcomes.

By this, the book refers to patterned differences in how particular social groups—most centrally gender in this study, though potentially also including class, region, or religion in general (though not within the book's analytical scope)—tend to respond, on average, to a given variable under shared structural conditions such as poverty, institutional bias, or cultural expectations.

This conceptualization of intergroup heterogeneity does not imply that all individuals within a group behave uniformly, nor does it rest on essentialist assumptions about group identity. On the contrary, the book fully acknowledges that individual

---

uneven across organizations and sociocultural settings, so returns to schooling are heterogeneous. Accordingly, the same wage-penalty channel can either raise or depress girls' (or boys') schooling across settings, depending on the appropriability of returns, access to female- and male-leaning employment, and the tightness of constraints (mobility, safety, liquidity).

variation—what may be called *intra*group heterogeneity—is both real and significant. For example, while this book empirically traces the average trend of boys being more likely than girls to disengage from education in the focal country of the Philippines, it also recognizes that many boys remain diligent and high-achieving at the individual level—and that some girls likewise disengage from education. Let it be underscored that intergroup heterogeneity, as used here, is thus compatible with such individual variation; it draws attention to the ways in which group-level tendencies often emerge from structurally conditioned patterns, rather than innate differences.

The concept is particularly important in this book because it enables a structural reading of what might otherwise appear to be personal or familial choices. It provides a lens to examine how gendered disparities—especially those that seem "reversed" in educational settings—are neither random nor merely cultural, but are linked to how social groups systematically navigate poverty, labor markets, family roles, and schooling environments. The chapters that follow explore these patterned responses not to flatten individual experience, but to contextualize it within broader socioeconomic forces.

As noted by Deaton (1997: 223), gender bias in intrahousehold resource allocation is a critical factor underlying such disparities. While the primary axis of this heterogeneity concerns the disparity between male and female students, this is further complicated by intrafamily role dynamics (such as differences in influence between mothers and fathers), variations in school environments, and local peer cultures—including within- and out-of-school affiliations—that jointly shape schooling trajectories. Ultimately, the book interrogates whether the observed reversal truly signals a shift in gendered advantage or reflects deeper recursive inequalities shaped by persistent poverty and institutional bias.

This book is organized into four parts. Following this introductory chapter (Part I), the remaining three parts present the core empirical analyses and findings.

Parts II and III focus on empirical studies conducted in rural areas of the Philippines, which are essential for understanding boys' underperformance in education. The geographical coverage of these studies includes all three island groups of the Philippine archipelago, with one distinct rural province studied from each group, yielding a total of three different provinces: Luzon (Marinduque Province, MIMAROPA Region or Region IV-B), Visayas (Antique Province, Western Visayas or Region VI), and Mindanao (Bukidnon Province, Northern Mindanao Region or Region X), shown in Fig. 9. Studies in Marinduque are addressed in both Parts II and III, while the studies in Bukidnon are discussed in Part II, and the study in Antique is covered in Part III.

Part II: Family Dynamics and Poverty examines how family-level dynamics, shaped by poverty, influence educational outcomes. Chapter 2 investigates the internal efficiency of education by analyzing the determinants of delays in compulsory elementary education and explores gender-based educational patterns and their implications for intergenerational educational attainment in rural Mindanao. Chapter 3 extends the analysis from Chap. 2 to include the continuity of educational demand not only at the elementary level but also at the secondary and tertiary levels, using the same data from rural Mindanao. It particularly emphasizes the long-term

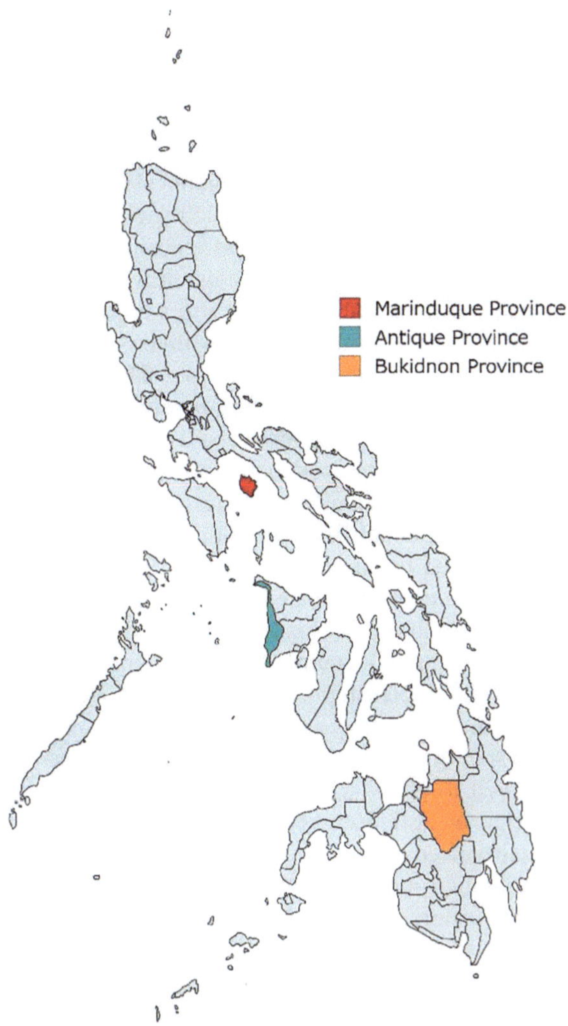

Fig. 9 Focal Provinces in the Philippines. *Source* Created using MapChart

influence of maternal education on daughters' schooling continuity, reflecting the formation of gendered intergenerational patterns. This chapter analyzes how educational demand persists across generations and the relationship between parental and child education levels through a sequential discrete choice analysis. These chapters emphasize the same-sex parent-to-child nexus of educational attainment, noting a stronger connection between mothers and daughters compared to fathers and sons. This dynamic suggests the formation of a virtuous cycle as a form of hysteresis in which highly educated mothers are more likely to have highly educated daughters—a pattern less evident among their male counterparts. The household data used in these chapters were collected during 1984–1985 and 2003 by the International

Food Policy Research Institute (IFPRI) in the United States and Xavier University's Research Institute for Mindanao Culture (RIMCU) in the Philippines.

Chapters 4 and 5 build on the theme of the mother-driven family dynamics using original primary data I collected in another rural province, Marinduque, during my three-year stay in the Philippines from 2017 to 2020. Chapter 4 examines the impact of such family dynamics on boys' underperformance, including time allocation and maternal labor force participation (MLFP) in rural Philippine households. It begins by confirming MLFP as a positive outcome of past progress in women's human capital. Then, using time-use surveys for children, it identifies that working mothers' MLFP status contributes to a scarring, widening gender disparity in pro-educational behaviors of children, with sons exhibiting poorer pro-educational behaviors compared to daughters. However, Chap. 5 also finds that this MLFP effect is unintended and reflects complex family dynamics, leading to sons spending less time on pro-educational activities. This unintended aspect of the MLFP effect is explored through an examination of the maternal dual burden as it interacts with poverty-structured family dynamics, as detailed in the data analysis.

Part III: School Environment and Poverty investigates how school environments, shaped by structural poverty, contribute to the gendered challenges experienced by students. Chapter 6, utilizing the same primary data as Chaps. 4 and 5, explores how in-school biases—identified through comparisons between blind and non-blind scoring—contribute to augmenting boys' underperformance that scars them. This chapter highlights how the school environment acts as a driving force behind the expanding reversed gender disparity. It examines how long-standing social stereotypes—such as boys being perceived as lazy and less inclined to study compared to girls—translate into scoring biases that disadvantage male students. The chapter also discusses background factors contributing to this bias, including the unbalanced teacher market in the Philippines and gender-segmented local labor opportunities in rural settings, among others.

Furthermore, Chap. 7 delves into the challenges faced by high school students using another set of primary fieldwork data I collected in the province of Antique, Western Visayas. This chapter is based on interviews and interactive discussions with students, school principals, and teachers. It explores gender patterns in education and highlights unique cases of male students who have struggled with continuous schooling. Specifically, the chapter examines instances of resilience among those who have successfully returned to high school despite significant obstacles. By identifying the barriers that keep Filipino boys out of school and presenting a contrasting image of "resilient" boys that counteract scarring, it offers a nuanced perspective on male students' educational journeys, incorporating the concept of *barkadahan*, a local term referring to peer groups. In addition, Chap. 7 challenges the prevailing modernist notion of a linear trajectory of progress in formal education, by illustrating the resilience demonstrated by the case students that softens path-dependent dynamics.

Part IV: Conclusion re-examines the overarching themes and key findings of this book, with Chap. 8 critically reassessing whether the observed reversal in gender disparities in education constitutes a genuine shift. Instead of treating boys' educational underperformance as a simple reversal of conventional gender norms, this chapter probes its structural roots and broader implications, including the potential for recursive gendered disadvantages affecting both boys and girls. It situates the pattern within locally embedded dynamics interacting with short-term rational choices under long-run structural conditions of adverse incorporation, and frames the "reversal" as multivalent—across gender, intertemporal, and post-school domains—not a zero-sum outcome. It accordingly suggests a need to rethink how inequality is conceptualized in development discourse and to consider structural, non-zero-sum responses. The chapter also proposes directions for future research and policy, grounded in an interdisciplinary, integrative, and context-sensitive framework.

Finally, **Appendix Chapters A and B** provide supplementary information about the research sites, socioeconomic contexts, and details about the sample children and households in Marinduque, on which the data in Parts II and III are based. The inclusion of these appendices reflects the fact that this province has been less frequently documented in the relevant development literature compared to the others.

5 Data Sources and Data Types Used

For the approaches described in the previous section, data are a crucial academic asset. The choice of data coverage, including population and sample, is also critical. This book integrates data from various sources (Table 2). Data from international organizations include cross-country data provided by the UNESCO Institute for Statistics (UIS) Stat and the World Development Indicators, which are widely utilized throughout this book. Data from the Philippine government are categorized into two types: (1) aggregated data, such as national census, statistical yearbooks, educational data, and regional development reports, and (2) raw data, such as the Annual Poverty Indicators Survey (APIS), LFS, and FIES. International organization data are mainly aggregated because they derive from the governments of each country. In contrast, national government data include both aggregated and raw data, with nationally aggregated data coming from original surveys. These data sources are used extensively in this book to validate and analyze international trends and nationally representative information from large-scale household surveys conducted in the Philippines.

In Parts II and III, raw household data from two sources are primarily used: one from third-sector research institutes and the other from my own primary data. The former data, from the IFPRI and RIMCU, were collected in Bukidnon Province. The latter data are from my own collections, which include household surveys and interviews conducted in Marinduque Province.

Aside from my primary data, the other data are publicly accessible. Data from international organizations are mostly available online. Aggregated data from the national government can be accessed through the relevant statistics office's website.

Table 2 Data Classification, by Sources

	Data Source	Aggregated Data or Raw Data?	Organizations of Example	Primary Data?	Mainly Used Part(s)	Open to the public?
1	International organizations	Aggregated data	UNESCO, World Bank	No	I, II, III, App.	Yes
2	National government	Both	PSA, DepEd, MinDA	Yes*	I, II, III, App.	Yes†
		Raw data	DepEd (confidential administrative data)	Yes*	III	No
3	Third-sector research institutes	Raw data	IFPRI, RIMCU	Yes*	II	Yes†
4	Author's primary data	Raw data	Tailored household survey, Fieldwork	Yes	II, III, App.	No

*Not original data from the author's collection
†Authorized requests for data are required
Note PSA = Philippine Statistics Authority. DepEd = Philippine Department of Education. MinDA = Mindanao Development Authority. IFPRI = International Food Policy Research Institute. RIMCU = Research Institute for Mindanao Culture, Xavier University. App. = Appendix Chapters
Source Author's classification

IFPRI data are not available online without data requests, but similar studies using these data are available in the literature (see Chaps. 2 and 3).

Conversely, my primary data collected in Marinduque Province is not publicly accessible due to the nature of primary data. Additionally, Marinduque has been less studied compared to other regions in the Philippines such as those in Luzon Island. To address this gap, I provide supplementary information about the sampling process and local livelihoods in Marinduque in Appendix Chapters A and B. Confidential administrative data collected through cooperation with the Department of Education (DepEd) of the Government of the Philippines in 2018–2019 are also included in the data analysis in Chap. 6.

6 Summary: Framing the Agenda

This introductory chapter has presented the central puzzle that motivates this book: the apparent reversal of gender disparity in education, particularly pronounced among rural, poorer households in the Philippines, where poverty itself becomes an embedded, structural force influencing gendered educational outcomes. By juxtaposing international trends with intranational patterns, and essentialist interpretations with socioeconomic ones, the chapter has questioned the adequacy of prevailing narratives that frame girls as the default disadvantaged group, as if gender equity were a zero-sum game. Instead, it draws attention to the mutually constitutive relationship between the experiences, constraints, and opportunities of both sexes—suggesting that gendered disadvantage cannot be fully understood without considering how the positioning of one group shapes and is shaped by the other.

Rather than asserting that one gender is inherently more disadvantaged than the other, this book emphasizes the economics of the reversal, exploring how structural forces such as poverty, family dynamics, and school environments contribute to gendered educational outcomes. This perspective moves beyond a single-axis, zero-sum logic of gender advantage or disadvantage. It instead seeks to understand how individuals and groups make decisions and allocate resources under conditions of varying comparative advantages and constraints—where such decisions may be rational from the perspective of households at one stage, yet are shaped, both explicitly and implicitly, by socially constructed norms and institutional arrangements. In doing so, the book aims to capture the dynamic, context-dependent ways in which gendered positions shift across domains such as education, labor, and parenting or childrearing. In this framing, the "economics" of the reversal refers not only to material incentives or utility maximization, but to the broader logics of decision-making, opportunity structures, and institutional constraints that shape gendered educational outcomes.

The chapters that follow investigate this puzzle through multi-scalar empirical analysis, including original quantitative and qualitative data based on fieldwork conducted by the author as well as publicly available data. In doing so, this book seeks to advance a more situated and disaggregated understanding of educational inequality; one that attends to within-country heterogeneity, intergenerational stratification, and the lived experiences of youth in both school and family environments. The agenda framed here is not merely to document the educational disengagement of boys, but to consider what such disengagement reveals about the assumptions embedded in regional and global development discourse. In this sense, the reversal becomes both an empirical anomaly to be explained and an analytical vantage point from which to rethink gender, education, and development, particularly through the focal case of the Philippines, which is often internationally recognized as achieving the highest level of gender equality in Asia.

As subsequent chapters will demonstrate, explaining the reversed gender disparity requires looking beyond enrollment statistics to the deeper economic, social, institutional (both formal and informal), and intergenerational forces that shape educational decision-making. A broader reconsideration of what such a "reversal" signifies is taken up in the concluding chapter.

References

Albanesi S, Olivetti C (2009) Production, market production and the gender wage gap: Incentives and expectations. Rev Econ Dyn 12(1):80–107. http://dx.doi.org/10.1016/j.red.2008.08.001

Andrew M (2014) The scarring effects of primary-grade retention? A study of cumulative advantage in the educational career. Social Forces 93(2):653–685. https://doi.org/10.1093/sf/sou074

Asadullah MN, Chaudhury N (2009) Reverse gender gap in schooling in Bangladesh: insights from urban and rural households. J Dev Stud 45(8):1360–1380. https://doi.org/10.1080/00220380902935824

Asuncion RA (2018) Aging societies and gender mainstreaming in the Philippines. In: Why Asia must up female workforce participation: women hold the key to growing productivity in a sustainable way, as aging shrinks workforces, by Asian Productivity Organization (APO). APO, Tokyo. https://doi.org/10.61145/DOGT5393

Balisacan AM (2003) The Philippine economy: development, policies, and challenges. Ateneo de Manila University Press, Quezon City

Baron-Cohen S (2004) The essential difference: men, women and the extreme male brain. Penguin Books, London

Becker GS (1962) Investment in human capital: a theoretical analysis. J Polit Econ 70(5):9–49. http://dx.doi.org/10.1086/258724

Becker GS (1964) Human capital: a theoretical and empirical analysis, with special reference to education, 3rd edn. University of Chicago Press, Chicago. https://doi.org/10.7208/chicago/9780226041223.001.0001

Bertrand M, Pan J (2013) The trouble with boys: social influences and the gender gap in disruptive behavior. Am Econ J Appl Econ 5(1):32–64. https://doi.org/10.1257/app.5.1.32

Buhl-Wiggers J, Jones S, Thornton R (2021) Boys lagging behind: unpacking gender differences in academic achievement across East Africa. Int J Educ Dev 83:102382. https://doi.org/10.1016/j.ijedudev.2021.102382

Bouis HE, Palabrica-Costello M, Solon O, Westbrook D, Limbo AB (1998) Gender equality and investments in adolescents in the rural Philippines. International Food Policy Research Institute, Washington, DC. https://doi.org/10.2499/0896291111rr108

Caoli-Rodriguez R (2007) The Philippines country case study. Country Profile Prepared for the Education for All Global Monitoring Report 2008: Education for All by 2015: Will We Make It? United Nations Educational, Scientific and Cultural Organization (UNESCO), Paris

Carlana M (2019) Implicit stereotypes: evidence from teachers' gender bias. Quart J Econ 134(3):1163–1224. https://doi.org/10.1093/qje/qjz008

Chiappori P-A, Iyigun M, Weiss Y (2009) Investment in schooling and the marriage market. Am Econ Rev 99(5):1689–1713. https://doi.org/10.1257/aer.99.5.1689

Chisamya G, DeJaeghere J, Kendall N, Aziz Khan M (2012) Gender and education for all: progress and problems in achieving gender equity. Int J Educ Dev 32:743–755. https://doi.org/10.1016/j.ijedudev.2011.10.004

Cornwell C, Mustard DB, Van Parys J (2013) Noncognitive skills and the gender disparities in test scores and teacher assessments: evidence from primary school. J Hum Resour 48(1):236–264. https://doi.org/10.3368/jhr.48.1.236

David, CC, Albert, JRG, Carreon-Monterola, SL (2009) In pursuit of sex parity: are girls becoming more educated than boys? Policy Notes PN2009-005. PIDS, Quezon City

David CC, Albert JRG, Vizmanos JFV (2017) Sustainable Development Goal 5: How does the Philippines fare on gender equality? Research Paper Series 2018-04. Philippine Institute for Development Studies (PIDS), Quezon City

Deaton A (1997) The analysis of household surveys: a microeconometric approach to development policy. World Bank, Washington, DC

Dee TS (2005) A teacher like me: does race, ethnicity, or gender matter? Am Econ Rev 95(2):158–165. https://doi.org/10.1257/000282805774670446

DiPrete TA, Eirich GM (2006) Cumulative advantage as a mechanism for inequality: A review of theoretical and empirical developments. Annual Rev Sociology 32(1):271–297. https://doi.org/10.1146/annurev.soc.32.061604.123127

de Janvry A, Sadoulet E (2021) Development economics: theory and practice, 2nd edn. Routledge, Abingdon. https://doi.org/10.4324/9781003024545

Duflo E (2012) Women empowerment and economic development. J Econ Lit 50(4):1051–1079. https://doi.org/10.1257/jel.50.4.1051

Estudillo JP, Quisumbing A, Otsuka K (2001a) Gender differences in land inheritance and schooling investment in the Rural Philippines. Land Econ 77(1):130–143. https://doi.org/10.2307/3146985
Estudillo JP, Quisumbing A, Otsuka K (2001b) Gender differences in land inheritance, schooling and lifetime income: evidence from the Rural Philippines. J Dev Stud 37(4):23–48. https://doi.org/10.1080/00220380412331322031
Estudillo JP, Sawada Y, Otsuka K (2009) Income dynamics, schooling investment, and poverty reduction in Philippine villages, 1985–2004. In: Otsuka K, Estudillo JP, Sawada Y (eds) Rural poverty and income dynamics in Asia and Africa. Routledge, New York. https://doi.org/10.4324/9780203885055-7
Estudillo JP, Otsuka K (2016) Moving out of poverty: an inquiry into inclusive growth in Asia. Routledge, New York. https://doi.org/10.4324/9781315673547
Filmer D, Schady N (2008) Getting girls into school: evidence from a scholarship program in Cambodia. Econ Dev Cult Change 56(3):581–617. https://doi.org/10.1086/533548
Fortin NM, Oreopoulos P, Phipps S (2015) Leaving boys behind: gender disparities in high academic achievement. J Hum Resour 50(3):549–79. https://doi.org/10.3368/jhr.50.3.549
Fuwa N (2001) The net impact of the female secondary school stipend program in Bangladesh. MPRA Paper 23402. University Library of Munich
Fuwa N (2014) Pro-girl bias in intra-household allocation in the Rural Philippines. Rev Dev Econ 18(4):727–740. https://doi.org/10.1111/rode.12115
Goldin C, Katz LF, Kuziemko I (2006) The homecoming of American college women: the reversal of the college gender gap. J Econ Perspect 20(4):133–56. https://doi.org/10.1257/jep.20.4.133
Greenwood J, Seshadri A, Yorukoglu M (2005) Engines of liberation. Rev Econ Stud 72(1):109–133. https://doi.org/10.1111/0034-6527.00326
Hannum E, Buchmann C (2005) Global educational expansion and socio-economic development: an assessment of findings from the social sciences. World Dev 33(3):333–354. https://doi.org/10.1016/j.worlddev.2004.10.001
Herz B, Subbarao K, Habib M, Raney L (1991) Letting girls learn promising approaches in primary and secondary education. World Bank Discussion Paper, WDP133. World Bank, Washington, DC
Heyneman S, Stern J (2015). Development and education. In: Pauline D, Humble S, Counihan C (eds) Handbook of international development and education. Edward Elgar, Cheltenham. https://doi.org/10.4337/9781783473540.00010
Hulme D, Shepherd A (2003) Conceptualizing chronic poverty. World Dev 31(3):403–423. https://doi.org/10.1016/S0305-750X(02)00222-X
Husain M, Millimet DL (2009) The mythical 'boy crisis'? Econ Educ Rev 28(1):38–48. https://doi.org/10.1016/j.econedurev.2007.11.002
Jha J, Bakshi S, Faria EM (2012) Understanding and challenging boys' disadvantage in secondary education in developing countries. Background paper prepared for the Education for All Global Monitoring Report 2012. UNESCO, Paris
Kabeer N (2001) The power to choose: Bangladeshi women and labour market decisions in London and Dhaka. Verso Press and Sage Publications, London and New Delhi
Khandker S, Pitt M, Fuwa N (2003) Subsidy to promote girls' secondary education: the female stipend program in Bangladesh. MPRA Paper 23688, University Library of Munich, Munich
King E, Hill A (1993) Women's education in developing countries: barriers, benefits, and policies. World Bank, Washington, DC
Kitamura Y (2015) The scope of international educational development studies (Kokusai kyōiku kaihatsu no kenkyū shatei). Toshindo Press, Tokyo [Japanese]
Klasen S (2002) Low schooling for girls, slower growth for all? Cross-country evidence on the effect of gender inequality in education on economic development. World Bank Econ Rev 16(3):345–373. https://doi.org/10.1093/wber/lhf004
Lavy V (2008) Do gender stereotypes reduce girls' or boys' human capital outcomes? Evidence from a natural experiment. J Public Econ 92(10–11):2083–2105. https://doi.org/10.1016/j.jpubeco.2008.02.009

Lavy V, Sand E (2018) On the origins of gender gaps in human capital: short- and long-term consequences of teachers' biases. J Public Econ 167:263–279. https://doi.org/10.1016/j.jpubeco.2018.09.007
Maholmes V, King R (eds) (2012) The Oxford handbook of poverty and child development. Oxford University Press, Oxford. https://doi.org/10.1093/oxfordhb/9780199769100.001.0001
Miralao VA (2008) Towards post-feminism in Philippine education. In: Bernardo A (ed) The paradox of Philippine education and education reform: social scientific perspectives. Philippine Social Science Council, Quezon City
Nguyen JT, Scripter C (2013) Educational access and opportunity–gender. In: Ness D, Lin C-L (eds) International education: an encyclopedia of contemporary issues and systems, vol 1. Routledge, Oxford, pp 74–77
Nguyen HT, Brinkman S, Le Thu H, Zubrick SR, Mitrou F (2022) Gender Differences in time allocation contribute to differences in developmental outcomes in children and adolescents. Econ Educ Rev 89:102270. https://doi.org/10.1016/j.econedurev.2022.102270
Pease A, Pease B (2001) Why men don't listen and women can't read maps: how we're different and what to do about it. Orion Book, London
Philippine Statistics Authority (PSA) (2017a) Functional literacy, education, and mass media survey 2013. Philippine Statistics Authority, Manila
Philippine Statistics Authority (PSA) (2017b) Labor Force Survey 2015. Philippine Statistics Authority, Manila
Philippine Statistics Authority (PSA) (2018) Family Income and Expenditure Survey 2015. Philippine Statistics Authority, Manila
Philippine Statistics Authority (PSA) (2021) Functional literacy, education, and mass media survey 2019. Philippine Statistics Authority, Manila
Psacharopoulos G (1994) Returns to investment in education: a global update. World Dev 22(9):1325–1343. https://doi.org/10.1016/0305-750X(94)90007-8
Psacharopoulos G, Patrinos HA (2004) Returns to investment in education: a further update. Educ Econ 12(2):111–134. https://doi.org/10.1080/0964529042000239140
Psacharopoulos G, Patrinos HA (2018) Returns to investment in education: a decennial review of the global literature. Educ Econ 26(5):1–14. https://doi.org/10.1080/09645292.2018.1484426
Psacharopoulos G, Woodhall M (1985) Education for development: an analysis of investment choices. Oxford University Press, New York
Quisumbing AR (1994) Intergenerational transfers in Philippine rice villages: gender differences in traditional inheritance customs. J Dev Econ 43(2):167–195. https://doi.org/10.1016/0304-3878(94)90003-5
Randall L, Anderson MR (eds) (1999) Schooling for success: preventing repetition and dropout in Latin American primary schools. M. E. Sharpe, New York
Riegle-Crumb C, Humphries M (2012) Exploring bias in math teachers' perceptions of students' ability by gender and race/ethnicity. Gend Soc 26(2):290–322. https://doi.org/10.1177/0891243211434614
Sen A (2002) More than 100 million women are missing. In: Naffine N (ed) Gender and justice. Palgrave Macmillan, London, pp 1–12
Serrano MR, Certeza RA (2014) Gender, unions and collective bargaining in the Philippines: issues and critical factors. In: Scherrer C (ed) Labor and globalization, vol. 4. Rainer Hampp Verlag, Munich
Snowdon B (2015) The role of human capital in economic development. In: Pauline D, Humble S, Counihan C (eds) Handbook of international development and education. Edward Elgar, Cheltenham. https://doi.org/10.4337/9781783473540.00011
Symaco LP (2013) The Philippines: education issues and challenges. In: Symaco LP (ed) Education in South-East Asia. Bloomsbury, New York. https://doi.org/10.5040/9781472544469.ch-010
Tanodra EQ (2003) Philippine educational system. Verh Educational Enterprise, Quezon City

Tembon M, Lucia F (2008) Girls' education in the 21st century: gender equality, empowerment, and economic growth. World Bank, Washington, DC. http://documents.worldbank.org/curated/en/511381468138604385

Terrier C (2020) Boys lag behind: how teachers' gender biases affect student achievement. Econ Educ Rev 77:101981. https://doi.org/10.1016/j.econedurev.2020.101981

Torres A (2011) Analysis on why boys do poorly: Philippines case study [Mimeo]. United Nations Girls' Education Initiatives

Tomas CB (2013) The Philippines: East Asia. In: Ness D, Lin C-L (eds) International education: an encyclopedia of contemporary issues and systems, vol. 2. Routledge, Oxford

United Nations Educational, Scientific and Cultural Organization (UNESCO) (2000) Dakar Framework for Action. UNESCO, Paris

United Nations Educational, Scientific and Cultural Organization (UNESCO) (2022) Leave No Child Behind: Global Report on Boys' Disengagement from Education. UNESCO, Paris. https://doi.org/10.54675/BDLL3314

United Nations Girls' Education Initiative (UNGEI) (2012) Why are boys under-performing in education? Gender analysis of four Asia-Pacific countries. https://www.unicef.org/eapro/report_why_are_boys_underperforming_FINAL.pdf. Accessed June 2, 2017

Unterhalter E (2010) Partnership, participation, and power for gender equality in education. Paper Prepared as part of the work of the committee overseeing the planning for UNGEI's E4 conference: Engendering Empowerment: Education and Equality, Dakar, May 17–20

Weaver-Hightower M (2003) The 'boy turn' in research on gender and education. Rev Educ Res 73(4):471–498. https://doi.org/10.3102/00346543073004471

Welmond MJ, Gregory L (2021) Educational underachievement among boys and men. World Bank, Washington, DC

World Bank (1993) The East Asian miracle: economic growth and public policy. Oxford University Press, New York

Xu S, Shonchoy AS, Fujii T (2022) Assessing gender parity in intrahousehold allocation of educational resources: evidence from Bangladesh. World Dev 151:105730. https://doi.org/10.1016/j.worlddev.2021.105730

Yamauchi F, Tiongco M (2013) Why women are progressive in education? Gender disparities in human capital, labor markets, and family arrangement in the Philippines. Econ Educ Rev 32:196–206. https://doi.org/10.1016/j.econedurev.2012.09.003

Zimmermann T, Williams JH (2016) Parents' educational expectations, their determinants, and consequences in explaining students' dropout in an area in Cambodia. In: Kitamura Y, Edwards Jr. DB, Sitha C, Williams JH (eds) The political economy of schooling in Cambodia: issues of quality and equity. Palgrave Macmillan, Hampshire. https://doi.org/10.1057/9781137456007_7

Part II
Family Dynamics and Poverty

Chapter 2
Fathers to Sons?—Gendered Delays in Schooling, Intergenerational Dynamics, and Institutional Change in Primary Education: Findings from Bukidnon, Northern Mindanao

Abstract This chapter examines delays in primary education as a measure of educational inefficiency, focusing on gender disparities and intergenerational dynamics in a rural Philippine case. Based on household survey data from Bukidnon Province, the study finds that boys are more likely to experience greater delays in primary education compared to girls. Parental education plays a critical role, with higher maternal education reducing delays regardless of the child's gender, while paternal education has a stronger impact specifically on boys. However, fathers generally have lower educational attainment than mothers, a disparity carried over to a similar gap between sons and daughters, perpetuating a vicious cycle. The analysis also highlights the effect of supply-side institutional changes, particularly an earlier school entrance age, on reducing delays. Female students benefit more significantly from this policy, showing greater progress toward minimal delays compared to their male counterparts. While household poverty exacerbates delays for both genders, cultural and contextual factors in rural Bukidnon further shape these patterns, where socioeconomic constraints and family dynamics interact in complex ways. The findings underscore the need for gender-sensitive educational policies to address the unique challenges faced by boys and girls, with attention to intergenerational and gendered dynamics in education.

Keywords Intergenerational transmission of education · Schooling delay · Parental education impact · School entry age policy · Bukidnon · Mindanao

1 Introduction

Schooling attainment, often measured as the total years of education completed, is a widely used metric for assessing individual and societal progress in education. However, this measure alone does not capture inefficiencies within education systems that hinder optimal outcomes. One critical inefficiency is schooling delays (Cortes

This chapter builds on Okabe (2016).

M. Okabe, *Economics of the Reversal in Gender Disparities in Education and Development*, Economics, Law, and Institutions in Asia Pacific,
https://doi.org/10.1007/978-981-96-9271-2_2

2015), defined as the gap between children's actual grades and their ideal grades based on their age and the school system. Delays in schooling highlight challenges related to access and progression, but they also provide a lens to evaluate the internal efficiency of education systems—a concept rooted in pedagogical perspectives.

Reducing delays is crucial not only for improving system-level efficiency but also for minimizing long-term negative outcomes for individuals. Economists have emphasized that delays in education postpone the accumulation of human capital during critical developmental periods, leading to dynamic and compounding losses in lifetime earnings and welfare (Angrist and Krueger 1991; Glewwe and Jacoby 1995; Mayer and Knutson 1999). These dual perspectives—educational and economic—underscore the importance of addressing schooling delays as part of broader efforts to enhance educational outcomes. Within this dynamic framework, early grade repetition and delayed entry—particularly at the primary level—can leave scarring effects that depress subsequent continuation probabilities, conditional on prior achievement (Andrew 2014). In other words, early within-cohort advantage or disadvantage can trigger cumulative processes that widen inequality within and across groups (DiPrete and Eirich 2006). These dynamics are consistent with a form of hysteresis—a concept more familiar in macroeconomics (Dutt 2023) but applied here to schooling behavior in a microeconomic context—built into the schooling trajectories of students who experience delay due to delayed entry and/or grade repetition. The time period covered in this chapter corresponds to the beginning of the century when the "setback" in basic education began to be experienced in the Philippines, as discussed in Sect. 2.1 of Chapter 1 (Balisacan 2003: 289; Caoli-Rodriguez 2007; David et al. 2009). We use rural Mindanao case as one of the highly disadvantaged areas during that time in the Philippines in terms of educational attainment, even at the compulsory level.

A unique advantage of delay analysis lies in its normative nature, as it measures deviations from the *ideal* grade level noted above. This makes it particularly suitable for analyzing primary education, which in the Philippines is compulsory as is in most of countries. The compulsory nature of primary education establishes a clear benchmark for assessing delays, offering valuable insights into the system's internal efficiency. However, this approach becomes less applicable to non-compulsory stages of education, where progression and participation are more influenced by additional factors such as individual choice and economic constraints. For this reason, the analytical framework and method used in this chapter are expanded in Chapter 3 to address the complexities of post-primary education. Readers are encouraged to refer to Chapter 3 for a discussion on how the framework evolves to accommodate these differences.

This chapter serves as the starting point for **Part II: Family Dynamics and Poverty**, which explores how economic constraints and family structures influence educational outcomes and boys' educational disengagement in the Philippines. As the first empirical chapter, it establishes a foundation for understanding the interplay between individual-and household-level factors and institutional dynamics in shaping schooling attainment and delays. Insights gained here are further developed in subsequent chapters, which expand the analysis to post-primary education and other aspects of family dynamics, such as maternal labor force participation and extended family support.

In Bukidnon Province, Northern Mindanao, delays in primary education are pervasive, reflecting broader regional trends of educational disadvantage. These delays are shaped by household-level factors, such as parental education and poverty, as well as supply-side constraints, including inadequate school infrastructure and teacher shortages (Glewwe and Kremer 2006). Literature has consistently shown that household poverty affected by parental education plays a key role for child education (Behrman et al. 1999; Quisumbing and McNiven 2010). Poverty has potential for further exacerbating delays by limiting household resources available for education, such as fees, transportation, and learning materials (Filmer and Pritchett 2001). These dynamics highlight the complex interplay between socioeconomic constraints, intergenerational influences, and institutional factors in shaping educational outcomes (Behrman et al. 1999; Filmer and Pritchett 2001).

Institutional factors play a critical role in mitigating or exacerbating schooling delays. Policies that adjust school entrance ages or improve teacher training and availability can significantly impact educational progression, particularly in rural settings where systemic challenges are acute (Mayer and Knutson 1999; Lincove and Painter 2006). In past studies, the effects of such an earlier entrance age on educational outcomes have yielded mixed findings, with no clear consensus reached (Katz 2000; Lincove and Painter 2006; Mayer and Knutson 1999) The dataset used in this chapter provides a unique opportunity to analyze the effects of such institutional changes, as it includes cohorts both before and after the 1995 nationwide policy change in school entrance age, which was also applied in Bukidnon Province. This adjustment specifically targeted primary education, establishing a uniform standard for entry ages across the country. The inclusion of these cohorts allows for an examination of how such reforms influence schooling delays and attainment, offering valuable insights into the broader implications of institutional reforms. By incorporating this perspective, the analysis not only addresses household and socioeconomic factors but also evaluates the role of policy-driven changes in shaping educational outcomes.

By integrating an analysis of both gender and intergenerational factors, this chapter sets the stage for the subsequent chapters in **Part II**, which further explore how family dynamics, economic constraints, and institutional factors intersect to shape educational demand and outcomes.

The remainder of this chapter is structured as follows: Sect. 2 outlines the research framework, while Sect. 3 discusses the dataset and surveyed area. Section 4 provides an overview of the Philippine education system and specific conditions in Bukidnon. Section 5 explains the empirical analysis, and Sect. 6 presents the results along with robustness checks. Finally, Sect. 7 concludes the study.

2 Research Framework

2.1 Repetitions, Gender Disparity, and Internal Efficiency in Education

The school enrollment ratio in the Philippines has been relatively high compared to other developing countries. However, such high enrollment rates do not necessarily indicate efficiency (Balisacan 2003). As discussed in Sect. 2.1 of Chapter 1, access to education in the Philippines has faced setbacks (Caoli-Rodriguez 2007). Repetition and dropout rates contribute to discrepancies in educational progress among groups. Literature examining the determinants of delays in education in developing countries includes studies by Randall and Anderson (1999) on Latin American countries, Glewwe and Jacoby (1995) on poverty and nutrition in Ghana, Nishimura et al. (2008) on the relationship between household income, education expenditures, family-wide education level, and universal elementary education policy in Uganda, and Miwa (2008) on poverty and malnutrition in Cambodia.

However, Philippine-centric case studies using a quantitative approach are scarce. Bouis et al. (1998) conducted anthropological surveys and interviews with barangay leaders and adults, many of whom were also parents. A *barangay* is the smallest local government unit in the Philippines. According to their research, interviewees cited the dropout problem as a reason for delays in schooling and noted that boys and men are more likely to experience it. This type of research is useful for explaining qualitative or descriptive reasons for the phenomenon. Interviewees attributed the male bias in dropout frequency to boys being perceived as less responsible and prone to "vices" such as drinking, as well as being overly fond of "roaming around" and "playing with their *barkada*"[1] (a Filipino term for a group of friends) (Bouis et al. 1998: 22).[2]They did not cite economic reasons, such as the need to work or help on the farm, as primary causes for dropping out. Instead, reasons included being "sick," "ashamed," "a slow learner," having "lost interest in schooling," "playing hooky from school," being "influenced by his *barkada*," "not liking school and teachers," and "playing too much" (Bouis et al. 1998: 22–23). The survey revealed that parents did not want their children to work or believe it would help them if their children left school. Instead, it suggests that dropouts occur due to perceptual reasons, such as parents or children losing interest in school and parents attributing the boys' dispositions as a cause.

[1] *Barkada* refers to a close-knit group of friends, often sharing strong social bonds and spending time together regularly. It is sometimes translated as a "peer group" or "circle of friends," reflecting the importance of social connections in Filipino culture. Chapter 7 further explores *barkada* and education.

[2] Bouis et al. (1998: 22) suggest an economic rationale where boys in rural settings may have more opportunities for employment or income-generating activities, which could motivate them to leave school as soon as they find a job. Additionally, boys may perceive schooling as having a lower payoff, as they often expect to become farmers, a profession that requires less formal education. This perspective is consistent with economic theories, as discussed by Chang (2014: chap. 10).

As discussed in Sect. 3 in Chapter 1, it is important to quantitatively examine the associated socioeconomic factors before attributing dropout rates solely to personal dispositions. This consideration is influenced by another context within the sociology of education in developing countries. While it has long been assumed that school characteristics significantly impact educational outcomes, there has been a recent reconsideration of the larger role played by student- and household-specific characteristics (Huang 2010).[3]

2.2 Motivations

The literature review has identified that girls are more educated than boys in the Philippines, and some have rationalized the background of this disparity. This study focuses on limited geographic coverage and unitary treatment of parents that are found in the literature reviewed. With regard to geographic coverage, Takayama et al. (2010), analyzing rural poverty dynamics from a statistical approach, utilized evidence from Mindanao Island, which is a less-examined and relatively underdeveloped area in the country.[4] Those authors rationalized education as one of the key factors to eliminate poverty; however, education, as a factor, is less studied in Mindanao Island compared with that in Luzon Island.

As for the unitary treatment of parental decisions, recent perspectives focus more on differential patterns by parents' genders. Relatively little is known about such patterns, which potentially determine children's differentiation in educational attainment, compared to parental income. Bevis and Barrett (2015) expressed simply but eloquently that education was a normal good in a sampled area in rural Philippines, analyzing intergenerational income elasticity. In Bukidnon Province, the elasticity between parental income and child education is examined as part of their analyses; doubling parental income during childhood predicts 1.6 and 1.3 years of additional education for girls and boys, respectively (Bevis and Barrett 2015).[5]

In theory, family dynamics such as intergenerational or parent–child relations in human capital investment are critical in shaping gender differentiations, as parental expectations and perceptions toward children are not identical across child genders.

[3] According to Huang (2010), this concept is referred to as the HL (Heyneman-Loxley) effect. In the Philippine context, using data from Cebu, Huang (2010) provides further insight into student-level factors by revisiting the HL effect. Although this analysis does not follow the education production function approach, the insights offered are valuable for understanding the roles of supply- and demand-side attributes.

[4] Nakanishi (2001) notes that, unlike the rice-cropping regions predominantly found in Luzon Island, non-rice-cropping regions benefited less from the Green Revolution. This disparity created a qualitative difference between Luzon regions (particularly Central Luzon) and other areas where rice cropping is less prevalent. According to Nakanishi's classification, the study area, Bukidnon, falls under the category of a non-rice-cropping region because corn cropping is dominant.

[5] Yet, they did not detect a statistically significant greater effect for either daughters or sons explicitly but noted that the point estimate for daughters was "far more precisely estimated" than that for sons (Bevis and Barrett 2015: 240).

In addition, in the parent–child relations, parenting also varies by child and parental genders in the educational context (Alderman and King 1998; Gorman-Smith et al. 2012; Bhagowati 2014). It is thus probable that parental education is also an important predictor in the same manner as elasticity of their income varies depending on child genders, but it has not yet been explicitly examined about intergenerational factors or parent-child relations regarding their educational attainment.

3 Dataset and Surveyed Area[6]

3.1 Bukidnon Panel Data Survey

This study utilizes the Bukidnon Panel Data Survey (BPDS); specifically, this paper makes use of the 2003/04 data set (IFPRI 2008). The BPDS is a household survey conducted in Bukidnon Province, Northern Mindanao Region (Region X), the Philippines (Fig. 1).[7] Regarding Bukidnon Province and the purposes and designs of their surveys, the information is described in detail by Bouis and Haddad (1990) and McNiven and Quisumbing (2007). According to these, the survey was conducted by the IFPRI and RIMCU. The first survey in 1984–1985 was intended to gather information on food and nonfood expenditures, agricultural production, and other socioeconomic attributes. The survey sampled 29 communities from the southern half of the landlocked province of Bukidnon. Around 20 years after the first survey was conducted, the 2003 and 2004 rounds were conducted. The data cover topics similar to those in the 1984/5 survey.

The original survey aimed to examine agricultural commercialization effects on consumption, expenditure, nutrition, and household welfare. Bouis and Haddad (1990) published the study related to these dimensions. According to the summarized information by Bouis and Haddad, Bukidnon Province saw the opening of the sugar mill company, called Bukidnon Sugar Company (BUSCO), in 1977. This establishment provided local farmers with the option to commercialize their farms by switching from subsistence corn production to commercial sugar production. Those farmers' choices were reported to depend on their proximities to the sugar mill. The initial sample started with 510 households, and 448 households were interviewed through in all the survey rounds in the BPDS.

Bouis and Haddad (1990), the original case study, examined the effects of the mentioned shift from subsistence to commercial mode of agricultural production that followed the BUSCO sugar mill construction. Then in 1992, out of the original 448 households, 352 were re-interviewed as part of a subsequent study that focused on adolescents (Bouis et al. 1998). This 1992 survey included only one round of data collection and used a condensed survey instrument. Furthermore, this 1992 survey

[6] This section is shared with the next Chap. 3.

[7] For basic information on the survey, see also Bouis and Haddad (1990) and McNiven and Quisumbing (2007).

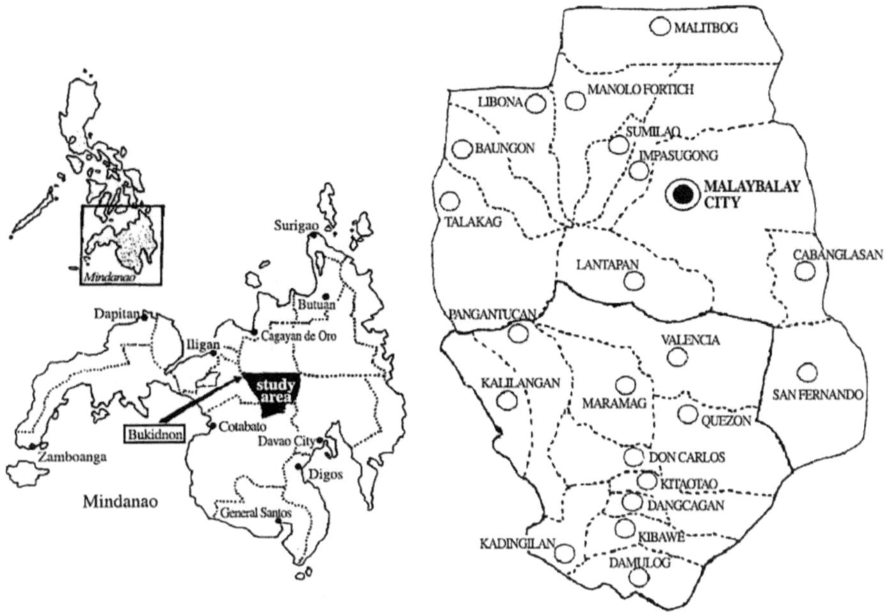

Fig. 1 Map of Study Area, Bukidnon Province. *Source* Takayama et al. (2010: Fig. 1) with the author's and journal's permissions

is not open for public use while the raw data of 1984 and 2003 rounds are open and available if made a formal request to IFPRI.

3.2 Sample Description

The BPDS contains data subsets arranged by topic such as household demographics, agricultural production, education, income, assets, and shocks, among others. By topic, its subsamples differ slightly or considerably across subsets; e.g., the women's reproduction-history subset contains data from adult women and the education subset contains data on children, whereas the basic unit of analysis is the household head or the household itself (see also McNiven and Quisumbing 2007).

In order to focus on elementary educational attainment, the education subset is used as master data. This subset comprises all co-resident children in all surveyed households and it contains information on education such as highest grade completed of those individuals in that sample. The dataset for regression analysis is formed by merging other subsets into the master data, so that it contains individual-level, household-level, and region-specific variables as explained. To observe gender-related heterogeneity, all children, regardless of gender, are, in principle, selected. Children's ages range from school age to above (i.e., adult, or too old), as long as they are children of the household head and his/her spouse. From this sample of "children," the sample for analysis is further chosen as described below.

First, the education data subset indicates whether the child attended school within the past 12 months (regardless of age). In order to avoid including "non-eligible" or "too-old" children (contextually including adults) into the sample for analysis, a restriction is imposed regarding age in the regressions, i.e., ages must be older than six and younger than 12 (see also Eq. (1)) and its explanation). However, if this restriction is applied simply by rule, children whose ages are older than expected but who are nevertheless in the elementary education stage being sampled, might be excluded.

Second, hence, to avoid this possibility, children who attended school within the past 12 months are included in the sample even if they seem to be "over-age." The sample therefore contains "over-age" children. Ideally, households should have been asked directly whether the child currently attended school but were not in practice. Accordingly, the author utilized these two criteria of restrictions to choose the sample children. As shown in descriptive statistics (Table 3), the number of children included in the sample is 327.

4 Outline of Education in the Research Site[8]

4.1 Nationwide Situation Around the Study Period

During the study period from 1984–2003, the formal and basic education in the Philippines followed a 6-4-4 system: six years for elementary-, four years for secondary-, and four years (in general) for tertiary-level education,[9,10] (Table 1). Children used to enter elementary schools mostly at age seven, but this changed to age six in 1995 (Ichikawa 1999: 252).

The 1987 Philippine Constitution established educational policies, reaffirming that elementary education should be free and compulsory. Secondary education also became free through the Free Public Secondary Act of 1988. In line with the Education for All (EFA) initiative, the Philippines developed its own EFA Philippine Plan of Action for 1991–2000. The Department of Education (DepEd) introduced the Schools First Initiative to enhance school improvement through community-based management and established the Basic Education Sector Reform Agenda to promote continuous improvement in basic education.

---

[8] This section is shared with the next Chap. 3.

[9] This was the case during the years when the data were gathered. Since 2012, however, the Philippines has established a K–12 program. For details, see Okabe (2018).

[10] Note that the old 6–4 system is applied in this chapter and the next, while the 6–4–2 system (referred to as the "K–12 program") is used from Chap. 4 onward.

Table 1 The Philippine School System during the Study Period

Level / Age	~6	6	7	8	9	10	11	12	13	14	15	16	17~
Kindergarten	✔												
Elementary		(✔)	✔	✔	✔	✔	✔	✔					
Secondary								(✔)	✔	✔	✔	✔	
Tertiary												(✔)	✔

Note Parentheses indicate the age of enrollment one year earlier due to government policy changes in 1995 and afterward compared to pre-1995. After 1995, the entrance age was moved earlier by one year at each level

Source Author's creation based on Okabe (2018)

Table 2 Final Educational Attainment, Bukidnon Province, 2000 (%)

Level of Education	All	Male	Female
Elementary	53.90	56.65	50.97
Secondary	22.63	20.91	24.46
College-degree holder	1.82	1.40	2.27

Source NSO (2003)

4.2 *Educational Situations in Bukidnon Around the Study Period*

According to the census data from the then National Statistics Office (NSO),[11] the proportion of people aged five years or older who attended or graduated from elementary education was approximately 53.90% (56.65% for males and 50.97% for females). For secondary education, the proportion was 22.63% (20.91% for males and 24.46% for females), and for degree holders, it was 1.82% (1.40% for males and 2.27% for females) in 2000 (NSO 2003, see Table 2). Women had higher proportions in all educational categories compared to men. These figures include adults who completed their education at the elementary or secondary level. The proportions of the school-age population are illustrated in Figs. 2 and 3. The proportion of elementary school-aged children was in the high 80s%, peaking at 95% for age 11. For secondary school-aged children, the proportion was in the mid-40s%, peaking at 50% for age 16. The gender pattern shows higher educational attainment for women at all levels.

To examine the completion rates of Grades 5 and 6 (the final two years of elementary education), see Fig. 4. This figure indicates that while a significant number of students continue elementary education beyond the typical age for secondary school entry, this number decreases with age. Notably, the proportions of males and females switch at ages 13–14. Females generally advance through elementary grades faster than males, even those with schooling delays.

[11] Currently, the NSO has been merged into the PSA.

Table 3 Descriptive Statistics

Variables	Descriptions	Mean	Standard Deviation
Dependent variable:			
ΔA	years of schooling delay	1.08	1.17
A_2	years of schooling completed	2.72	1.87
Independent variables:			
Individual characteristics (X_1):			
Age	age	9.76	2.41
Sqage	squared age	101.01	48.18
D_g	1 if girl	0.52	0.50
BMI	BMI	15.44	1.94
D_Ilonggo†	1 if speaking Ilonggo as first language	0.01	0.11
D_Ilokano†	1 if speaking Ilokano as first language	0.01	0.08
D_Waray†	1 if speaking Waray as first language	0.01	0.08
PW	Years ago when paid work began	0.13	0.63
PW×*D_g*	*PW*×*D_g*	0.05	0.40
Household characteristics (X_2):			
Numson	number of sons	2.85	1.93
Numdau	number of daughters	2.44	1.72
Numson×*D_g*	*Numson*×*D_g*	1.25	1.77
Numdau×*D_g*	*Numdau*×*D_g*	1.52	1.86
D_Wshock	1 if experienced weather shock	0.53	0.50
D_Wshock×*D_g*	*D_Wshock*×*D_g*	0.30	0.46
D_Mshock	1 if experienced military-presence shock	0.02	0.13
D_Mshock×*D_g*	*D_Mshock*×*D_g*	0.02	0.12
Sav	1 if household has a savings account	0.24	0.94
Sav×*D_g*	*Sav*×*D_g*	0.17	0.84
D_Refu	1 if hh head experienced refused of credit	0.19	0.39
D_Refu×*D_g*	*D_Refu*×*D_g*	0.10	0.30
SC	social capital (no. of persons)	1.97	1.24
Fated	years of schooling of father	6.86	3.38
Momed	years of schooling of mother	7.56	3.03
Fated×*D_g*	*Fated*×*D_g*	3.71	4.40
Momed×*D_g*	*Momed*×*D_g*	4.04	4.48

(continued)

Table 3 (continued)

Variables	Descriptions	Mean	Standard Deviation
Fat_ab‡	1 if household head lives away from household	0.00	0.06
Mom_ab‡	1 if household spouse lives away from household	0.00	0.06
Income:			
log *Y*	log per capita income	7.48	2.56
log $Y \times D\_g$	log $Y \times D\_g$	4.04	4.24
log R	log per capita remittance	3.55	2.89
log $R \times D\_g$	log $R \times D\_g$	1.86	2.78
Asset:			
OL	Owned land (ha)	90.81	171.18
TL	Rented-in land (ha)	108.84	139.71
$OL \times D\_g$	Owned land $\times D\_g$	62.80	152.21
$TL \times D\_g$	Rented-in land $\times$ D_g	56.81	128.10
D_mot	1 if having motorbike	0.16	0.36
D_car	1 if having car	0.03	0.17
D_nonelec	1 if non-electrified house	0.31	0.47
D_nopipe	1 if non-piped water	0.51	0.50
Supply-side school variables (*S*)			
Inst_change	1 if generation that benefitted from institutional change of entrance age to primary schools	0.98	0.15
D_Snack	1 if received school snack	0.32	0.47
D_Lunch	1 if received school lunch	0.18	0.39
No. of observations = 327 (except the number of ΔA's observations 326)			

†Reference of the dummies is the category of speaking Cebuano or Tagalog
‡In the household where each of parent lives away there are only boys, so gender-interactions with these variables are not used
Source Author's calculation by IFPRI (2008)

The Philippine Human Development Index Report 2000 provides an overview of Bukidnon's educational situation, comparing it with other provinces. At that time, Bukidnon was among the ten lowest-ranked provinces in terms of basic educational attainment (National Statistical Coordination Board (NSCB) 2002). The lowest-ranked province was Sulu, followed by Sarangani, Maguindanao, and Bukidnon. Bukidnon's rank dropped from 64 in 1994 to 76 in 1997, improving slightly to 74 in 2000 (NSCB 2002: 17). This decline should be viewed in the context of its previous stable position. Additionally, cohort survival rates (Fig. 5) and dropout rates (Fig. 6) highlight Bukidnon's consistently low educational attainment compared to other regions.

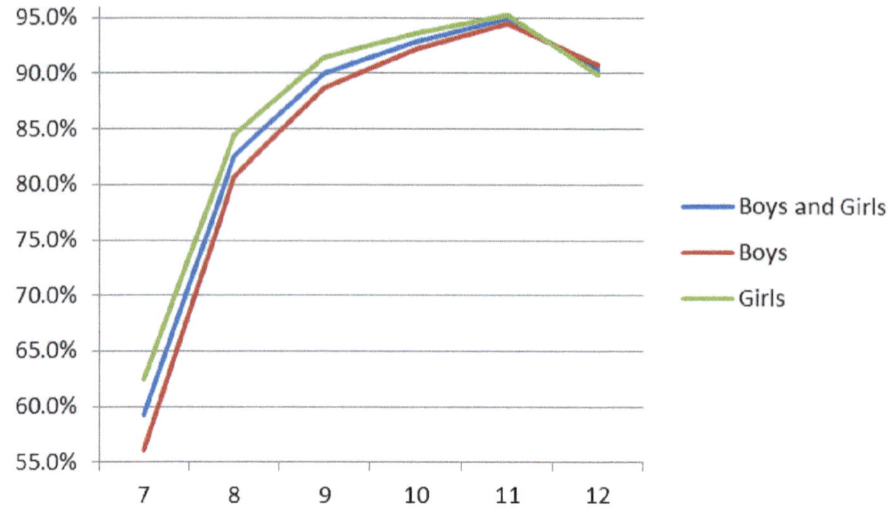

Fig. 2 Proportion of Elementary-level Enrolled Population, Bukidnon, 2000. *Source* Author's calculation based on NSO (2003)

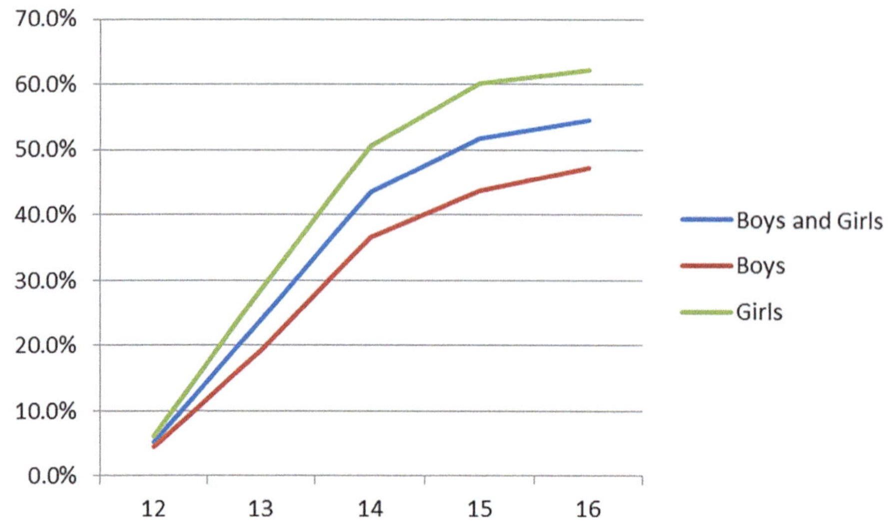

Fig. 3 Proportion of Secondary-Education Enrolled Population, Bukidnon, 2000. *Source* Author's calculation based on NSO (2003)

Nationwide, many regions improved access to education in response to international policies prioritizing education. However, the data suggest that Bukidnon has fallen behind other regions. Mesa (2007) ranked Bukidnon among the lowest in terms of average years of education and inequality, and similar trends are seen in survival and dropout rates (Figs. 5 and 6).

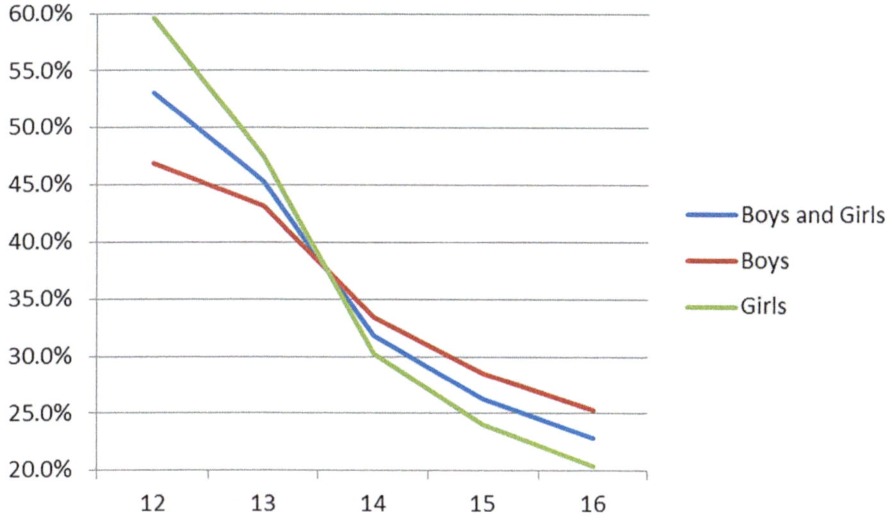

Fig. 4 Proportion of Population Completed Grades 5–6 in Elementary Education, Bukidnon, 2000. *Source* Author's calculation based on NSO (2003)

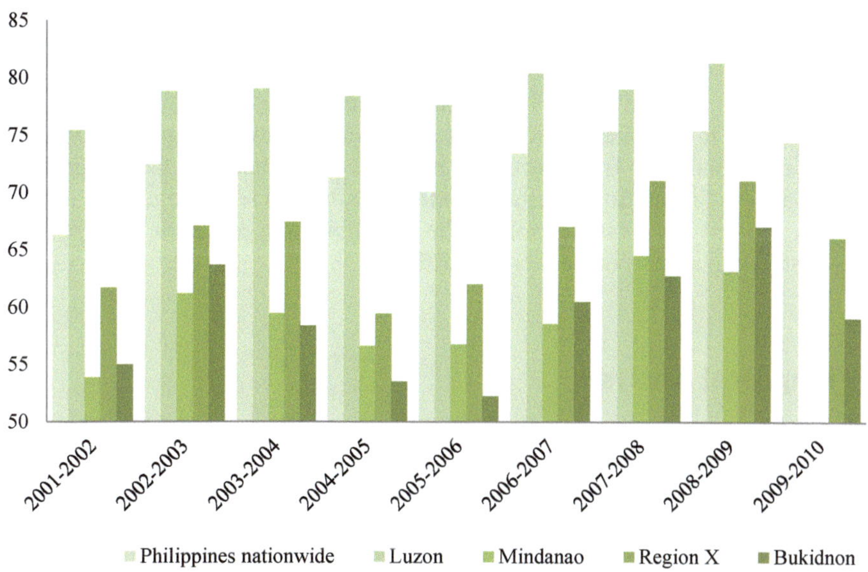

Fig. 5 Cohort Survival Rate by Region, Elementary Education, the Philippines. *Note* Data not available for Luzon and Mindanao in 2009–2010. *Source* Author's calculation based on Mindanao Development Authority

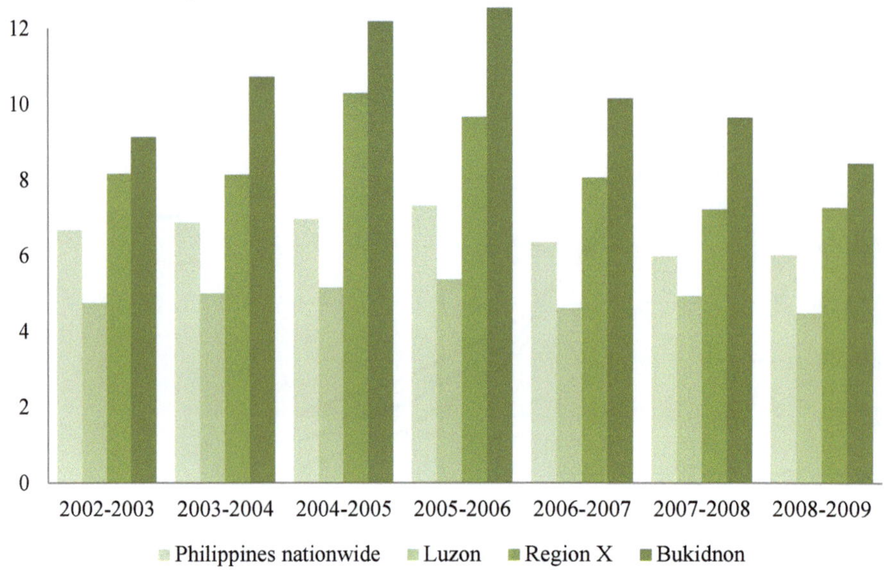

Fig. 6 Dropout Rate by Region, Elementary Education, the Philippines (%). *Source* Author's calculation based on Mindanao Development Authority

In Mindanao, Sulu Province ranks poorly in human development and educational attainment due to long-standing conflict, violence, and poverty. Bukidnon, located in Northern Mindanao, is less affected by these issues but still faces significant educational challenges. To understand the factors affecting schooling, more detailed analyses are needed. This study explores the determinants of educational inefficiency, particularly with a focus on gender disparities.

5 Empirical Analyses

5.1 Dependent Variable: Years of Delay

To determine the association between individual- and household-level characteristics as well as region-specific effects, we construct a regression model. Let the number of years of delay in elementary education experienced by a student i be denoted as ΔA_i. This is defined as:

$$\Delta A_i = \begin{cases} A_{1i} - A_{2i,} & \text{if } 6 \leq Age_i \leq 12, \\ (A_{1i} - A_{2i}) + (Age_i - 12), & \text{if } Age_i = 13, \\ (A_{1i} - A_{2i}) + (Age_i - 13), & \text{if } Age_i \geq 14, \end{cases} \tag{1}$$

where A_{1i} is the ideal year of schooling calculated from Age_i, the student i's age; and A_{2i} is the real year of schooling when the research was conducted.[12] The case of no delay in schooling means $A_{1i} = A_{2i}$ and $\Delta A_i = 0$.

Here, by the way, we need to ask ourselves a normative question before calculating ΔA. In the Philippines, education is made compulsory only at the elementary level by the 1987 Constitution. No other educational stage is mandatory, although public secondary education is free (in principle). Considering the norm of MDGs and SDGs, ideally, all children are expected to complete elementary education; however, in principle, the secondary education and beyond is neither compulsory nor a legal duty for all people even in developed countries. In this sense, the sample in the delay analysis is restricted to those students who did not complete the elementary level at the timing of data collection. Usually, children are expected to enter elementary schools at the age of six. Ideally, students completed Grade 1 at the age of seven and accordingly Grade 6 at the age of 13 at the end of elementary education, and Grade 10 at the age of 17 when secondary education is completed (note again that this discussion is applied to the data collection timing prior to the K–12 Program with 6–4–2–4 system implemented in 2011 and made law in 2013). Because the sample already includes those aged older than 13, the difference between age 13 and the student's actual age is first adjusted for those students. Figure 7 is a histogram of ΔA_i by age and by gender. Strikingly, though a few, those high-school-age children who were still enrolled in elementary schools are observed.

5.2 *Regression Model*

Let us assume the functional relation $A(\cdot)$ of ΔA_i as:

$$\Delta A_i = A(\mathbf{X}_{1i}, \mathbf{X}_{2i}, \mathbf{S}_i),$$

where $\mathbf{X}_1$ is a vector of students' individual characteristics and attributes, including a gender dummy variable taking the value of one if the student i is a girl and zero otherwise; $\mathbf{X}_2$ is a vector of the characteristics and attributes of the student's household and family; $\mathbf{S}$ is a vector of supply-side school variables. Then, we derive the multiple regression models as:

[12] As explained in Sect. 4.1 in this chapter, children formerly entered elementary schools at age seven, but this changed to age six in 1995 (Ichikawa 1999; Tomas 2013). The Philippine Department of Education (DepEd) directed that children who are six years old before the commencement of classes at the beginning of June are eligible to enroll in Grade 1 of elementary school (for details, see http://www.deped.gov.ph/orders?f[0]=field_classification%3A224). The construction of the variable *Age* considered the circumstance: The age data of children are their age at the time of data collection in the fall of 2003 (IFPRI 2008). It thus means that, for example, children who were five years old when schools opened (who were thus not eligible to enroll then) and turned six before the data collection were reported as six years old despite being one-year younger. Therefore, to adjust this gap, one year is subtracted for the children born during the period between them in terms of school age.

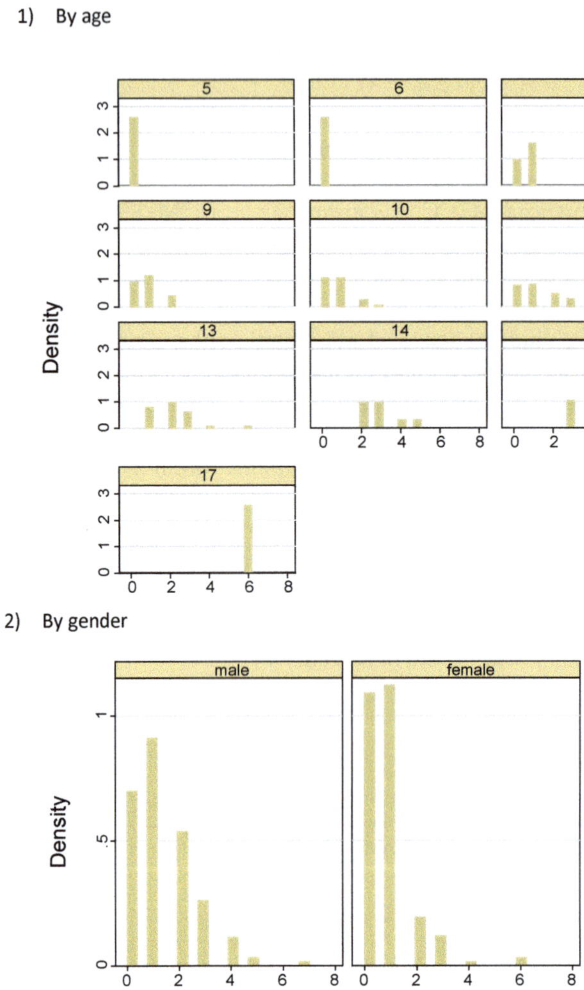

Fig. 7 Distribution of Delayed Years in Elementary Education (Horizontal axis: years of delay; Vertical axis: density). *Source* Author's calculation by IFPRI (2008)

$$\Delta A_i = \beta_0 + \mathbf{X}_{1i}\boldsymbol{\beta}_1 + \mathbf{X}_{2i}\boldsymbol{\beta}_2 + \mathbf{S}_i\boldsymbol{\delta} + \eta + \varepsilon_i, \qquad (2)$$

where β_0 is an intercept, and $\boldsymbol{\beta}_1$, $\boldsymbol{\beta}_2$, and $\boldsymbol{\delta}$ are the coefficients to be estimated. The error term u_i is divided into two terms: η for a region-specific effect for unobserved regional heterogeneity and ε_i as an idiosyncratic disturbance term, that is, $\eta + \varepsilon_i$.

For $\mathbf{X}_{1i}$, the following characteristics and attributes of students are used: age and age square; a dummy variable taking the value of one if female; a dummy of minority language taking the value of one if speaking a language other than Filipino (the national language of the Philippines) or Cebuano (the lingua franca in

Northern Mindanao); student's nutrition status proxied by body mass index (BMI); the student's period of child labor experience taking zero if none; and some interaction terms with the female dummy.

For $\mathbf{X}_{2i}$, the following characteristics and attributes of households are used: number of brothers and/or sisters; two kinds of shock-experience dummies that take a value of one if shocks caused by weather and military presence were experienced, respectively; a dummy variable of savings account holder taking the value of one if the household has at least one savings account; a dummy of credit constraints[13]; the size of social network[14]; parental education; and the dummy variables representing father and mother living away from the household, respectively.[15] Furthermore, income variables are introduced. Since income variables have a potentiality of econometrically endogenous property, the asset variables are introduced instead of income variables. They include the information on the owned and rented-in land; the dummy variables of taking a value of one if the household has bikes and cars, respectively; and the dummy variables taking a value of one if the household is non-electrified and has no running water. Some of these variables, in addition, interacted with the gender dummy.

Finally, the supply-side (i.e., school-related) variables are ideally required in the estimation. Due to the very purpose of the BPDS not primarily for educational research, little information is available. Yet, for $\mathbf{S}_i$, the following information is used: The dummy variable indicating whether the student has benefited from the national policy of one-year change in the elementary-school entrance age; and the indicators of school-lunch and school-snack provisions.

The entrance-age change is assumed such a policy effect as in the policy change in elementary-education entrance age. Children who entered elementary school in or after 1995 are thought to have benefitted from the change in all years of elementary education. Examining this allows us to learn whether such an educational system change can contribute to students' educational attainment (Mayer and Knutson 1999). It also enables us to examine if the delays in education are detected even after the policy change of entrance age is controlled for. In addition, the municipality-specific effect, η, is also added to a set of independent variables in hope of controlling for unobserved location-specific heterogeneity.

---

[13] This dummy variable takes a value of one if the household head has been both refused credit by moneylenders and is unable to borrow needed funds from other moneylenders or from the household head's relatives.

[14] Social network is regarded here as the number of friends and acquaintances upon whom the household head can rely in an emergency.

[15] This information should be related to the gender patterns of association between parents' and children's education. Furthermore, the sample contained few households in which the head and/or spouse live away, and children belonging to those households are all boys. Therefore, the heterogeneity of this variable in relation to gender cannot be tested since interaction terms cannot be formed.

5.3 Descriptive Statistics

Before talking about the regression analysis and estimation, let us confirm the basic information from the descriptive statistics (Table 3). On average, the children in the sample have a 1.1-year size of delay and completed 2.7 years of schooling. The average age of sample is 9.8 years old. In the sample, 52% of the sample is female and so 48% are male. No more than 2 or 3% of the children in the sample speak languages other than Tagalog-Filipino or Cebuano. Those languages observed in the sample are Ilonggo, Ilokano, and Waray. Ilonggo, also called Hiligaynon, is spoken in Western Visayas (mainly in Iloilo in Panay Island) and Waray is in Eastern Visayas (in Samar Island and parts of Leyte Island). These two are classified as Visayan language, to which Cebuano is classified as well. In contrast, Ilokano (also spelled Ilocano) is spoken in northern Luzon Island, mainly in Ilocos Region. Thus, Ilokano is linguistically far to Cebuano in contrast to the similarity under the Visayan languages between Ilonggo/Waray and Cebuano. Interestingly, despite the geographic distance from , a few Ilocano people had migrated to some parts of Mindanao and their descendants live there to date.

As for child labor, the children in the sample, on average, have experienced labor for 0.13 years. Each household has on average 2–3 sons and daughters, respectively. About a half of households in the sample has experienced a negative shock, one-quarter of households have a saving account, and one-fifth of households have experienced that their demands for credit was not satisfied. The size of the social network (which includes friends, relatives, and acquaintances upon whom the interviewed adults think their household can rely) is on average two people.

Regarding parental education level, the average level of paternal education is elementary-school level plus one additional year of secondary education and that of maternal education is around one year longer than paternal. Few households have both the head and spouse no longer living together. This could reflect the Philippines' religious background as a devoutly Christian country (exceptional in Southeast Asia), where divorce is religiously and culturally taboo. The studied area, Bukidnon, is a Christianity-prevalent region although located in Mindanao Island.

For income variables, the log of per capita income and the log of per capita remittance received are used for estimation, and asset variable statistics, in turn, show that mobile facilities such as motorbikes and cars are a type of rare asset that is seemingly not affordable for average households. One-third and one-half of households are not electrified and do not have water pipe inside the house, respectively. Households in the sample present some typical characteristics of rural poverty.

Finally, regarding the supply-side (school-side) variables, approximately 97% of children belong to the generation benefiting from the one-year institutional change in elementary school entrance-age. As that change was implemented in 1995, children born six years previously to 1995 (i.e., born in or after 1989) have benefited. In summary, the large part of sample is in the benefiting generation, whereas a few overage students are not. If the coefficient of this variable is significant even when other age-related variables are controlled together, the policy effects of the entrance-age change can be examined in one direction. As for school-food provisions, it is reported that around 32.1% of sample students have received some snacks and 18.0% have been provided with some lunch from schools. The number of those who have been provided some lunch is smaller than the case of snacks. Such provisions of foods particularly with the poor are expected to affect favorably the enrollment even before waiting for the larger-scale and more cost-demanding stipend and scholarship programs such as conditional cash transfer programs, and thus those indicators are assumed to be positively significant.

5.4 Estimation Method

Generally, to estimate the regression model such as in Eq. (2), the ordinary least squares (OLS) method is used. Theoretically, however, the dependent variable, ΔA, does not take a value smaller than zero. In other words, ΔA is censored at the value of zero ($\Delta A \geq 0$) or is considered a limited dependent variable. Therefore, estimation of Eq. (2) by OLS may be inappropriate. The econometric background is that the least-square method assumes linearity, but with a censored dependent variable, the linearity assumption is violated, which can cause a downward bias in OLS estimators (Amemiya 1985: 362). Alternatively, a standard method is Tobit model, which can be classified into five types (Amemiya 1985: chap. 10).[16] This study utilizes what Amemiya classified as the Type I Tobit model because the independent variables are observed even when a dependent variable takes the value of zero. The model is rewritten as below by introducing a latent variable.

First, let the latent variable of ΔA be denoted as ΔA^*, and that is regressed by the same set of independent variables as in Eq. (2):

$$\Delta A_i^* = \beta_0 + \boldsymbol{X}_{1i}\boldsymbol{\beta}_1 + \boldsymbol{X}_{2i}\boldsymbol{\beta}_2 + \boldsymbol{S}_i\boldsymbol{\delta} + \eta + \varepsilon_i. \tag{3}$$

In this setting, the true dependent variable ΔA is equal to ΔA^* if ΔA^* takes a nonnegative value and otherwise is equal to zero if ΔA^* takes a negative value including the value of zero. For the Type I Tobit model, the estimation follows the maximum likelihood (ML) method. The Tobit model is written as follows:

$$\Delta A_i = \begin{cases} \Delta A_i^*, & \text{if } \Delta A_i^* > 0, \\ 0, & \text{if } \Delta A_i^* \leq 0. \end{cases} \tag{4}$$

[16] For example, Type I Tobit is used for a censored model whereas Type II is used for a selection model. See Amemiya (1985: ch. 10) for details.

5.5 Further Explorations and Robustness Checks

To explore the results, the interaction terms of gender dummy variable with other selected individual and household characteristics are added as discussed before. This provides us with a more detailed comparison of the magnitude of and relation to each gender with respect to other independent characteristics variables. For a robustness check, not only the ΔA but also the years of schooling completed, i.e., A_2, are used as the dependent variables.[17] In addition, the following arrangements are made to further robustness checks.

5.5.1 Application of Count Data Framework—Poisson Regression

By considering the statistical form of distribution of the dependent variable, another regression model is introduced. It is a Poisson model. The distribution form of dependent variable ΔA_i appears to take on integer numbers beginning from the value of zero, such as 0, 1, 2, ..., and to have a high density in accordance with the value of zero (Fig. 7). For this type of dependent variable, the Poisson model rather than the Tobit model can be appropriate in terms of the property of count data. Thus, the model is termed "the count data model" and assumes that the dependent variable follows the Poisson distribution:

$$\Pr(\Delta A = a) = \frac{\exp(-\mu)\mu^a}{a!}, \text{ where } a = 0, 1, 2, \cdots, \tag{5}$$

where μ in Eq. (5) is the intensity term. Under the Poisson distribution, we have the following property called the equidispersion property of the Poisson distribution (Cameron and Trivedi 2005):

$$\mathrm{E}(\Delta A) = \mu$$

$$\mathrm{V}(\Delta A) = \mu$$

From the equidispersion property, the Poisson model can be expressed as:

$$\mu_i = \exp(\mathbf{X}_i\boldsymbol{\beta}_P), \quad i = 1, 2, \ldots, \tag{6}$$

where $\mathbf{X}_i\boldsymbol{\beta}_P$ is the linear combination of the same regressors as in Eqs. (2) and (3) with coefficients newly estimated specifically for the new model.[18] The most natural

[17] It is noted that the dependent variable ΔA is calculated based on A_2 and age (*age*) as in Eq. (1). In this sense, it is not that surprising even if the estimators of ΔA and A_2 are qualitatively similar each other, although there may be a case where nonlinear specifications matter between the equations of two dependent variables.

[18] Identically, regression equation (6) can also be written as $\ln\mu_i = \mathbf{X}_i\boldsymbol{\beta}_P$.

estimator is ML. The maximization problem of the log-likelihood function is:

$$\max_{\boldsymbol{\beta_P}} \ln L = \sum_{i=1} \left(\Delta A_i \mathbf{X}_i \boldsymbol{\beta_P} - \exp(\mathbf{X}_i \boldsymbol{\beta_P}) - \ln \Delta A_i!\right). \tag{7}$$

The Poisson MLE, $\widehat{\boldsymbol{\beta_P}}$, is the solution corresponding to the first-order condition for maximum likelihood:

$$\frac{\partial \ln L}{\partial \boldsymbol{\beta_P}} = \sum_{i=1} (\Delta A_i - \exp(\mathbf{X}_i \boldsymbol{\beta_P}))\boldsymbol{X}_i = 0.$$

Although the interpretation of the coefficients estimated in linear models is the marginal numerical effect in accordance with a one-unit change in the corresponding independent variable, the Poisson model is, like other limited dependent-variable models such as Tobit, so nonlinear that we cannot interpret the coefficients in the same way. The values shown in Table 5 are only the coefficients and do not include the marginal effects. Here, similar to the Tobit estimation, only the statistical significance, signs (negative or positive), and magnitude relations are informative.

Unlike the assumptions made under Tobit estimation, Poisson estimations are considered more sensitive to minor increases and decreases in a set of regressors if the dependent variable comprises count data. Indeed, the histogram of the dependent variable shows that the distribution is localized in ΔA's value of zero and in the area of smaller integer numbers. Then, using the Poisson estimation, we will check (1) the eligibility of the utilized Poisson regression model by the chi-square (χ^2) test with its null hypothesis H_0: the dependent variable, ΔA, follows the Poisson distribution, and (2) whether the result produced by the Tobit estimation is qualitatively similar to the result yielded by the Poisson estimation.

5.5.2 Estimation with a Household-Specific Effect to Control for Some Household-Level Unobserved Heterogeneity

In turn, a household-specific effect is also added in the estimation model in hope of mitigating the possibility of omitted-variable bias and to take into account unobserved heterogeneity (e.g., household-specific but slight difference of data collection timing). The model is now rewritten with additional term ν_H as:

$$\Delta A_i = \beta_{H0} + \mathbf{X}_{1i}\boldsymbol{\beta}_{\mathbf{H}1} + \mathbf{X}_{2i}\boldsymbol{\beta}_{\mathbf{H}2} + \mathbf{S}_i\boldsymbol{\delta}_{\mathbf{H}} + \nu_H + \eta_H + \epsilon_i, \tag{8}$$

where β_{Hk} $(k = 0, 1, 2)$ and $\boldsymbol{\delta}_{\mathbf{H}}$ are the newly estimated coefficients and η_H is the region-specific effect. The error term in the Tobit model is now divided: ν_H is a term of household-specific effects, and ϵ_i is an idiosyncratic error term. Due to the incidental parameter problem, nonlinear estimations such as Tobit and Poisson ML estimations are no longer usable. Hence, the linear regression model is applied. The standard errors utilized are the household-cluster standard errors. After taking these steps, whether or not the results yielded by the estimation with household-specific effects are qualitatively the same as that yielded by the estimation without these effects, i.e., Eqs. (3) and (4), is examined.

6 Results

Let us begin by confirming the results shown in Table 4, corresponding to the Tobit model, which is the benchmark model. Interpretations are based on the association with the main dependent variable, the delay in education unless otherwise indicated.

6.1 Individual Backgrounds

The variable of age is not statistically significant in relation to the dependent variable of delays in schooling but it is positively and statistically significant in terms of the dependent variable of years completed, and the age square (Age^2) is negatively and statistically significant in relation to the years of education completed. This means that $\frac{\partial \Delta A_i}{\partial (Age_i)} > 0$ and $\frac{\partial^2 \Delta A_i}{\partial (Age_i)^2} < 0$, implying that years completed increase as age increases and at the same time the marginal increase in years completed is declining. The purpose of the age variable inclusion in the models is to control for age effects in the first place. The BMI variable is statistically negatively significant to the years of educational delay and positively significant to the years of education completed as well, albeit controlling for age: It may show the possibility that the BMI is a proxy of nonage attributes such as health and nutrition and associates positively with educational attainment.

As hypothesized regarding gender variables, girls complete more years of education and experience fewer delays in schooling than their boy counterparts [cf. gender effect alone isolated, see the specifications shown in the columns (3)–(4) and (7)–(8)]. Though the models' coefficients including interaction terms of gender with other variables [the specifications in columns (1)–(2) and (5)–(6)] became insignificant with regard to an isolated gender dummy variable, the effect is thought to be diluted by other gender interaction terms.

6.2 Family Backgrounds

Among the shock dummy variables, the military-shock dummy shows a positive association with delays in schooling and a negative association with the number of school years completed. Its interaction terms with the gender dummy report the same

Table 4 Result of Delay Analysis (Tobit estimation)

Variables	Dependent Variable = ΔA				Dependent Variable = A_2			
	w/ Gender Interaction		w/o Gender Interaction		w/ Gender Interaction		w/o Gender Interaction	
	(1)	(2)	(3)	(4)	(5)	(6)	(7)	(8)
Individual characteristics (X_1):								
Age	0.22	0.30	0.15	0.19	1.50	1.52	1.62	1.62
	[0.23]	[0.23]	[0.24]	[0.23]	[0.24]***	[0.24]***	[0.24]***	[0.24]***
Sqage	0.01	0.00	0.01	0.01	−0.04	−0.04	−0.04	−0.04
	[0.01]	[0.01]	[0.01]	[0.01]	[0.01]***	[0.01]***	[0.01]***	[0.01]***
D_g	−0.29	−0.62	−0.47	−0.44	0.28	0.75	0.39	0.36
	[0.68]	[0.61]	[0.14]***	[0.14]***	[0.55]	[0.50]	[0.12]***	[0.12]***
BMI	−0.12	−0.09	−0.11	−0.09	0.10	0.09	0.10	0.09
	[0.05]**	[0.04]**	[0.04]**	[0.04]**	[0.03]***	[0.03]***	[0.03]***	[0.03]***
D_Ilonggo	−0.03	0.03	0.16	0.37	−0.05	−0.13	−0.07	−0.20
	[0.58]	[0.58]	[0.58]	[0.59]	[0.34]	[0.32]	[0.30]	[0.31]
D_Ilokano	0.72	0.41	0.67	0.46	−0.55	−0.24	−0.48	−0.26
	[0.72]	[0.71]	[0.71]	[0.72]	[0.61]	[0.61]	[0.61]	[0.61]
D_Waray	0.04	−0.25	−0.13	−0.27	0.14	0.55	0.32	0.55
	[0.43]	[0.44]	[0.42]	[0.44]	[0.29]	[0.33]*	[0.29]	[0.33]*
PW	0.05	0.05	0.22	0.23	−0.06	−0.03	−0.20	−0.19
	[0.14]	[0.13]	[0.12]*	[0.12]*	[0.13]	[0.12]	[0.11]*	[0.12]*
PW × D_g	0.38	0.45			−0.35	−0.40		
	[0.18]**	[0.16]***			[0.16]**	[0.15]***		

(continued)

Table 4 (continued)

Variables	Dependent Variable = ΔA				Dependent Variable = A_2			
	w/ Gender Interaction		w/o Gender Interaction		w/ Gender Interaction		w/o Gender Interaction	
	(1)	(2)	(3)	(4)	(5)	(6)	(7)	(8)
Household characteristics (X_2):								
Numson	0.06	0.05	0.03	0.04	−0.04	−0.03	−0.03	−0.04
	[0.05]	[0.05]	[0.04]	[0.04]	[0.04]	[0.05]	[0.03]	[0.03]
Numdau	0.05	0.07	0.06	0.06	−0.02	−0.04	−0.02	−0.03
	[0.07]	[0.06]	[0.05]	[0.04]	[0.06]	[0.05]	[0.04]	[0.04]
Numson × *D_g*	−0.07	−0.02			0.02	−0.02		
	[0.07]	[0.08]			[0.06]	[0.06]		
Numdau × *D_g*	0.00	−0.04			0.00	0.01		
	[0.09]	[0.08]			[0.07]	[0.07]		
D_Wshock	0.01	0.03	0.10	0.10	−0.02	−0.04	−0.07	−0.08
	[0.20]	[0.20]	[0.14]	[0.14]	[0.18]	[0.17]	[0.12]	[0.11]
D_Wshock × *D_g*	0.15	0.16			−0.11	−0.13		
	[0.27]	[0.27]			[0.22]	[0.22]		
D_Mshock	0.14	0.12	0.39	0.55	0.21	0.20	−0.27	−0.41
	[0.38]	[0.42]	[0.30]	[0.27]**	[0.29]	[0.33]	[0.24]	[0.23]*
D_Mshockf × *D_g*	0.30	0.28			−0.59	−0.69		
	[0.51]	[0.47]			[0.40]	[0.37]*		

(continued)

Table 4 (continued)

Variables	Dependent Variable = ΔA				Dependent Variable = A_2			
	w/ Gender Interaction		w/o Gender Interaction		w/ Gender Interaction		w/o Gender Interaction	
	(1)	(2)	(3)	(4)	(5)	(6)	(7)	(8)
Sav	−0.02	0.00	−0.10	−0.05	0.13	0.12	0.04	−0.01
	[0.17]	[0.14]	[0.08]	[0.09]	[0.15]	[0.12]	[0.06]	[0.06]
Sav × *D_g*	−0.11	−0.09			−0.10	−0.14		
	[0.19]	[0.17]			[0.16]	[0.12]		
D_Refu	0.26	0.19	0.33	0.37	−0.12	−0.03	−0.20	−0.19
	[0.24]	[0.24]	[0.19]*	[0.20]*	[0.22]	[0.22]	[0.17]	[0.18]
D_Refu × *D_g*	0.12	0.27			−0.13	−0.20		
	[0.35]	[0.36]			[0.32]	[0.32]		
SC	−0.11	−0.10	−0.09	−0.10	0.04	0.03	0.03	0.03
	[0.05]**	[0.05]**	[0.05]*	[0.05]**	[0.03]	[0.03]	[0.03]	[0.03]
Fated	−0.10	−0.11	−0.04	−0.04	0.08	0.09	0.02	0.02
	[0.04]**	[0.04]***	[0.02]*	[0.02]*	[0.03]**	[0.03]***	[0.02]	[0.02]
Momed	−0.04	−0.04	−0.07	−0.07	0.04	0.03	0.07	0.07
	[0.04]	[0.05]	[0.03]**	[0.03]**	[0.04]	[0.04]	[0.02]***	[0.02]***
Fated × *D_g*	0.11	0.13			−0.10	−0.11		
	[0.05]**	[0.05]**			[0.04]**	[0.04]***		
Momed × *D_g*	−0.04	−0.06			0.03	0.04		
	[0.06]	[0.06]			[0.05]	[0.05]		
Fat_ab	0.76	0.33	0.37	0.33	-0.63	-0.24	-0.29	-0.22
	[0.42]*	[0.30]	[0.38]	[0.30]	[0.35]*	[0.25]	[0.31]	[0.25]

(continued)

Table 4 (continued)

Variables	Dependent Variable = ΔA				Dependent Variable = A_2			
	w/ Gender Interaction		w/o Gender Interaction		w/ Gender Interaction		w/o Gender Interaction	
	(1)	(2)	(3)	(4)	(5)	(6)	(7)	(8)
Mom_ab	-0.33	-0.63	-0.20	-0.25	-0.08	0.11	0.40	0.50
	[0.71]	[0.54]	[0.41]	[0.38]	[0.65]	[0.45]	[0.29]	[0.29]*
log Y	0.05		0.01		-0.05		-0.01	
	[0.03]		[0.03]		[0.03]*		[0.02]	
log Y×D_g	-0.11				0.10			
	[0.05]**				[0.04]**			
log *R*	−0.0115		0.0154		0.0036		−0.0089	
	[0.03]		[0.03]		[0.03]		[0.02]	
log *R* × *D_g*	0.0648				−0.0303			
	[0.05]				[0.04]			
OL		0		0.0002		−0.0008		−0.0003
		[0.00]		[0.00]		[0.00]		[0.00]
TL		0.0006		−0.0008		−0.0011		0.0001
		[0.00]		[0.00]		[0.00]		[0.00]
OL × *D_g*		0.0001				0.0008		
		[0.00]				[0.00]		
TL × *D_g*		−0.0027				0.0018		
		[0.00]**				[0.00]**		
D_mot		−0.3007		−0.3378		0.2645		0.2674
		[0.22]		[0.21]		[0.18]		[0.17]

(continued)

Table 4 (continued)

Variables	Dependent Variable = ΔA				Dependent Variable = A_2			
	w/ Gender Interaction		w/o Gender Interaction		w/ Gender Interaction		w/o Gender Interaction	
	(1)	(2)	(3)	(4)	(5)	(6)	(7)	(8)
D_car		−0.5433		−0.3677		0.322		0.2587
		[0.40]		[0.41]		[0.25]		[0.26]
D_noelec		0.0657		0.0379		−0.2043		−0.1569
		[0.17]		[0.17]		[0.14]		[0.14]
D_nopipe		0.138		0.1145		−0.0642		−0.0722
		[0.15]		[0.16]		[0.13]		[0.13]
Supply-side school variables:								
Inst_change	−1.4216	−1.3609	−1.2767	−1.2227	1.8814	1.8503	1.7695	1.7146
	[0.55]**	[0.57]**	[0.61]**	[0.62]**	[0.55]***	[0.55]***	[0.59]***	[0.58]***
D_Snack	−0.3133	−0.3235	−0.3583	−0.358	0.2395	0.2301	0.2726	0.2619
	[0.16]*	[0.16]**	[0.16]**	[0.16]**	[0.13]*	[0.13]*	[0.13]**	[0.13]**
D_Lunch	−0.4589	−0.4089	−0.4687	−0.4542	0.2744	0.1796	0.2732	0.2221
	[0.21]**	[0.22]*	[0.20]**	[0.21]**	[0.15]*	[0.17]	[0.15]*	[0.16]
Region-specific effect	Yes	Yes	Yes	Yes	Yes	Yes	Yes	Yes
Intercept	2.5503	1.9221	2.6136	2.3332	−12.8514	−12.9161	−13.2605	−13.0531
	[1.41]*	[1.39]	[1.36]*	[1.36]*	[1.32]***	[1.35]***	[1.29]***	[1.35]***
Σ-constant	1.0075	0.9961	1.0412	1.0305	0.8647	0.8578	0.8922	0.8823
	[0.06]***	[0.06]***	[0.06]***	[0.06]***	[0.05]***	[0.05]***	[0.05]***	[0.05]***
Pseudo R^2	0.2581	0.2683	0.2417	0.2496	0.4206	0.4251	0.4073	0.4129
Log-likelihood	−374.318	−369.155	−382.601	−378.608	−383.789	−380.798	−392.644	−388.891
No. of observations	326	326	326	326	327	327	327	327

*$p < 0.10$; **$p < 0.05$; ***$p < 0.01$
Notes Robust standard errors are in brackets
Source Author's calculation by IFPRI (2008)

Table 5 Result of Delay Analysis (Poisson estimation)

Variables	Dependent Variable = ΔA				Dependent Variable = A_2			
	w/ Gender Interaction		w/o Gender Interaction		w/ Gender Interaction		w/o Gender Interaction	
	(1)	(2)	(3)	(4)	(5)	(6)	(7)	(8)
Individual characteristics (X_1):								
Age	0.50	0.54	0.41	0.41	1.34	1.36	1.37	1.37
	[0.16]***	[0.15]***	[0.16]**	[0.16]***	[0.13]***	[0.13]***	[0.13]***	[0.13]***
Sqage	−0.01	−0.02	−0.01	−0.01	−0.05	−0.05	−0.05	−0.05
	[0.01]*	[0.01]**	[0.01]	[0.01]	[0.01]***	[0.01]***	[0.01]***	[0.01]***
D_g	0.07	−0.56	−0.35	−0.34	0.11	0.25	0.15	0.13
	[0.48]	[0.41]	[0.09]***	[0.10]***	[0.19]	[0.17]	[0.04]***	[0.04]***
BMI	−0.08	−0.06	−0.06	−0.05	0.03	0.03	0.03	0.03
	[0.03]**	[0.03]**	[0.03]**	[0.03]*	[0.01]***	[0.01]***	[0.01]***	[0.01]***
D_Ilonggo	−0.16	−0.03	0.04	0.19	−0.04	−0.07	0.03	0.00
	[0.54]	[0.51]	[0.51]	[0.50]	[0.17]	[0.14]	[0.09]	[0.10]
D_Ilokano	0.52	0.29	0.50	0.32	−0.19	−0.07	−0.18	−0.09
	[0.48]	[0.48]	[0.48]	[0.48]	[0.18]	[0.18]	[0.19]	[0.19]
D_Waray	0.01	−0.14	−0.03	−0.04	0.02	0.20	0.09	0.20
	[0.29]	[0.28]	[0.26]	[0.27]	[0.11]	[0.13]	[0.11]	[0.13]
PW	−0.01	−0.01	0.07	0.07	0.00	0.01	−0.03	−0.03
	[0.06]	[0.05]	[0.05]	[0.06]	[0.04]	[0.03]	[0.03]	[0.03]
$PW \times D\_g$	0.20	0.24			−0.07	−0.09		
	[0.08]**	[0.08]***			[0.06]	[0.06]		

(continued)

Table 5 (continued)

Variables	Dependent Variable = ΔA				Dependent Variable = A_2			
	w/ Gender Interaction		w/o Gender Interaction		w/ Gender Interaction		w/o Gender Interaction	
	(1)	(2)	(3)	(4)	(5)	(6)	(7)	(8)
Household characteristics (X_2):								
Numson	0.03	0.01	0.01	0.01	−0.01	−0.01	−0.01	0.00
	[0.03]	[0.03]	[0.02]	[0.02]	[0.01]	[0.02]	[0.01]	[0.01]
Numdau	0.04	0.04	0.04	0.04	−0.01	−0.02	−0.01	−0.02
	[0.04]	[0.03]	[0.03]	[0.03]	[0.02]	[0.02]	[0.01]	[0.01]
Numson × *D_g*	−0.02	0.02			0.02	0.01		
	[0.05]	[0.05]			[0.02]	[0.02]		
Numson × *D_g*	0.00	−0.01			−0.01	−0.01		
	[0.06]	[0.05]			[0.02]	[0.02]		
D_Wshock	0.01	0.00	0.08	0.06	−0.02	−0.03	−0.04	−0.05
	[0.12]	[0.12]	[0.10]	[0.09]	[0.06]	[0.06]	[0.04]	[0.04]
D_Wshock × *D_g*	0.19	0.22			−0.03	−0.02		
	[0.18]	[0.18]			[0.08]	[0.07]		
D_Mshock	−0.03	0.09	0.13	0.19	0.14	0.13	−0.09	−0.12
	[0.27]	[0.28]	[0.19]	[0.19]	[0.11]	[0.13]	[0.08]	[0.08]
D_Mshock × *D_g*	0.23	0.13			−0.26	−0.26		
	[0.33]	[0.33]			[0.14]*	[0.15]*		

(continued)

Table 5 (continued)

Variables	Dependent Variable = ΔA				Dependent Variable = A_2			
	w/ Gender Interaction		w/o Gender Interaction		w/ Gender Interaction		w/o Gender Interaction	
	(1)	(2)	(3)	(4)	(5)	(6)	(7)	(8)
Sav	−0.05	−0.04	−0.12	−0.09	0.07	0.08	0.01	−0.01
	[0.14]	[0.11]	[0.08]	[0.08]	[0.08]	[0.06]	[0.02]	[0.02]
Sav × *D_g*	−0.10	−0.07			−0.07	−0.09		
	[0.17]	[0.14]			[0.08]	[0.07]		
D_Refu	0.14	0.11	0.17	0.21	−0.04	−0.02	−0.05	−0.05
	[0.14]	[0.14]	[0.12]	[0.13]	[0.08]	[0.08]	[0.06]	[0.06]
D_Refu × *D_g*	0.08	0.15			−0.05	−0.05		
	[0.22]	[0.24]			[0.11]	[0.11]		
SC	−0.09	−0.09	−0.07	−0.07	0.02	0.02	0.02	0.02
	[0.04]**	[0.04]**	[0.04]*	[0.04]*	[0.01]**	[0.01]*	[0.01]*	[0.01]*
Fated	−0.05	−0.07	−0.03	−0.03	0.03	0.03	0.01	0.01
	[0.02]**	[0.02]***	[0.02]*	[0.02]**	[0.01]**	[0.01]***	[0.01]*	[0.01]*
Momed	−0.03	−0.03	−0.05	−0.05	0.01	0.01	0.02	0.02
	[0.03]	[0.03]	[0.02]**	[0.02]**	[0.01]	[0.01]	[0.01]**	[0.01]**
Fated × *D_g*	0.06	0.09			−0.03	−0.03		
	[0.03]**	[0.03]***			[0.01]**	[0.01]**		
Momed × *D_g*	−0.05	−0.05			0.01	0.01		
	[0.04]	[0.04]			[0.02]	[0.02]		
Fat_ab	0.62	0.30	0.41	0.36	-0.25	-0.14	-0.17	-0.13
	[0.28]**	[0.18]*	[0.25]	[0.11]*	[0.12]**	[0.09]	[0.11]	[0.09]

(continued)

Table 5 (continued)

Variables	Dependent Variable = ΔA				Dependent Variable = A_2			
	w/ Gender Interaction		w/o Gender Interaction		w/ Gender Interaction		w/o Gender Interaction	
	(1)	(2)	(3)	(4)	(5)	(6)	(7)	(8)
Mom_ab	-0.30	-0.43	-0.02	-0.09	-0.13	0.17	0.17	0.15
	[0.56]	[0.44]	[0.34]	[0.33]	[0.34]	[0.24]	[0.09]*	[0.09]
log *Y*	0.03		0.01		−0.02		−0.01	
	[0.02]		[0.02]		[0.01]*		[0.01]	
log *Y* × *D_g*	−0.08				0.03			
	[0.04]**				[0.02]**			
log *R*	−0.0013		0.0071		−0.0035		−0.0038	
	[0.02]		[0.02]		[0.01]		[0.01]	
log *R* × *D_g*	0.0329				−0.0052			
	[0.03]				[0.01]			
OL		0.0003		0.0003		−0.0002		−0.0001
		[0.00]		[0.00]		[0.00]		[0.00]
TL		0.0005		−0.0003		−0.0003		0.0001
		[0.00]		[0.00]		[0.00]		[0.00]
OL × *D_g*		−0.0002				0.0002		
		[0.00]				[0.00]		
TL × *D_g*		−0.0018				0.0005		
		[0.00]**				[0.00]		
D_mot		−0.2547		−0.2611		0.0351		0.0363
		[0.17]		[0.17]		[0.06]		[0.06]

(continued)

Table 5 (continued)

Variables	Dependent Variable = ΔA				Dependent Variable = A_2			
	w/ Gender Interaction		w/o Gender Interaction		w/ Gender Interaction		w/o Gender Interaction	
	(1)	(2)	(3)	(4)	(5)	(6)	(7)	(8)
D_car		−0.2492		−0.084		0.1678		0.1308
		[0.37]		[0.39]		[0.10]*		[0.09]
D_noelec		0.0863		0.0289		−0.0829		−0.0793
		[0.10]		[0.10]		[0.05]*		[0.05]*
D_nopipe		0.1081		0.1106		−0.0425		−0.0419
		[0.10]		[0.11]		[0.04]		[0.04]
Supply-side school variables:								
Inst_change	−0.4342	−0.3932	−0.3048	−0.2459	−0.0089	−0.0146	−0.0343	−0.0593
	[0.20]**	[0.21]*	[0.20]	[0.21]	[0.16]	[0.17]	[0.17]	[0.17]
D_Snack	−0.2361	−0.2076	−0.2306	−0.2368	0.0952	0.0816	0.0975	0.0922
	[0.11]**	[0.12]*	[0.11]**	[0.12]**	[0.04]**	[0.04]*	[0.04]**	[0.04]**
D_Lunch	−0.3562	−0.2887	−0.3713	−0.3346	0.1545	0.1232	0.1523	0.1358
	[0.13]***	[0.14]**	[0.13]***	[0.14]**	[0.06]***	[0.06]**	[0.05]***	[0.06]**
Region-specific effect	Yes	Yes	Yes	Yes	Yes	Yes	Yes	Yes
Intercept	−1.3556	−1.568	−1.1412	−1.2007	−8.1269	−8.2241	−8.245	−8.2366
	[0.94]	[0.90]*	[0.93]	[0.93]	[0.66]***	[0.66]***	[0.65]***	[0.65]***
Goodness of fit: Pr > χ^2	0.997	0.998	0.997	0.997	1.000	1.000	1.000	1.000
H_0: Dependent variable ~ Poisson								
Pseudo R^2	0.2393	0.2449	0.2286	0.233	0.301	0.3023	0.2979	0.2996
Log-likelihood	−346.825	−344.272	−351.735	−349.725	−468.263	−467.444	−470.345	−469.256
No. of observations	326	326	326	326	327	327	327	327

*$p < 0.10$; **$p < 0.05$; ***$p < 0.01$
Notes Robust standard errors are in brackets
Source Author's calculation by IFPRI (2008)

association with regard to the number of education years completed. It implies that the influence of shock status is related to schooling variables albeit at a relatively weak level of statistical significance (more than 5%). Next, credit constraints, indicated by loan refusal experience, show the expected unfavorable association with educational delays. The social network variable shows that larger networks are associated with fewer delays but not associated with schooling completed.

Next, let us examine parents' educational attainment levels. First, the maternal education level negatively influences schooling delays and positively impacts the completed years of schooling in the estimation without gender interaction terms. This relation is favorable for child education. The paternal education level shows a similar result to that of mothers with the child delays in education. Yet, the parental education alone is statistically more robust in maternal education level than in paternal. In addition, although paternal education level itself is statistically negative to the delay and positively significant to the completed years of schooling, the interaction terms of paternal education with the girl dummy variable show the opposite relation when we refer to the results in the specifications (1)–(2) and (5)–(6), where their interaction terms on the children's gender dummy are added.

These findings indicate that the level of paternal education preferentially and favorably influences the level of his same-gender children, that is, sons, because the magnitude of interaction is larger than that on paternal education alone. In contrast, maternal education alone is negatively significant in terms of the delay in schooling and positively significant in relation to number of school years completed [in the specifications shown in the columns (3)–(4) and (7)–(8)]. However, in models with interaction terms, both maternal education itself and its interaction terms with the girl dummy are insignificant. It implies that, unlike paternal education, maternal education equally influences children regardless of their gender. As shown, when the effect of fathers living away is positively associated with the delay in education and negatively associated with the years completed, the results of parental education levels are consistently robust even after controlling for the absence of the father/mother.

The income variables do not alone show significant results [columns (3) and (7)] whereas the coefficients of their interaction term with child gender present favorable for girls' education [columns (1) and (5)]. In turn, the explanation power of asset variables is little whereas the rented-in land variable possibly implies a girl-friendly association with educational attainment. One background is that the provisions of elementary level of education, to which we are focusing here, was made free. Hence, probably, the income effect is expected to be more serious when we cover the secondary level of education onward (for further on this, see the discussion on estimated negative predictors of the probabilities to enter high schools and colleges in the next chapter).

6.3 Supply-Side Policies and Interventions

The entrance-age change policy has a negative and significant impact on delays in education and a positive and significant impact on the number of years completed. These results indicate that, even after controlling for age-related characteristics, students who benefited from the policy were able to complete more years of education while experiencing fewer delays. This finding is notable, as it reveals that accelerating the entrance age to elementary school by just one year has a positive impact on the educational attainment of those who benefited compared to those who did not (Mayer and Knutson 1999).

During early educational stages, there has been ongoing debate about the effects of an earlier entrance age on educational outcomes, with mixed findings and no clear consensus (Katz 2000; Lincove and Painter 2006; Mayer and Knutson 1999). Our findings, however, suggest that the policy positively influences educational efficiency by reducing delays.

In addition, the provision of school snacks and lunches also exerts similarly favorable impacts on educational attainment, regardless of the dependent variable—whether delays or the number of years completed. Similar to the entrance-age change policy, even after controlling for other characteristics, students who had access to school food provisions were more likely to complete more years of education and experience fewer delays.

6.4 The Results with Robustness Checks

6.4.1 Consideration of Count Data

As already noted in subsections 5.5 of Sect. 5, the Poisson model is additionally estimated, and its results are shown in Table 5. Before confirming the estimators, it is necessary to assess the goodness of fit to determine whether Poisson modeling is appropriate for the count data. The null hypothesis states that the dependent variable statistically follows the Poisson distribution, and the chi-square test does not reject this hypothesis at any conventional levels of statistical significance. Therefore, the Poisson model is deemed suitable for this analysis.[19] Compared to the results in Table 4, the statistical significance levels, the signs of the coefficients, and the magnitude relations in Table 5 remain largely consistent. Even with the Poisson model, the findings are quantitatively similar to those derived from the Tobit model. However, several key differences between the two models are noteworthy.

[19] The Poisson model's goodness of fit is statistically tested. The chi-square test under the null hypothesis that the dependent variable(s) follow a Poisson distribution shows that the reported $\Pr > \chi^2$ values for all models in Table 5 exceed conventional significance levels, i.e., we fail to reject the null hypothesis. Thus, the Poisson model fits the data well. See Table 5.

First, the age variable (*Age*) is statistically positively significant, while the squared age variable (*Sqage*) is negatively significant in relation to both the years delayed and years completed. This indicates that older students tend to experience delays more frequently, but they also attain more years of education, although the rate of increase diminishes with age. Second, the dummy variable for fathers living away from the household is more robustly and positively significant with respect to the number of delay years, and negatively significant in relation to the number of years completed, whereas the dummy variable for mothers living away does not exhibit robust significance. This suggests that fathers living away from the household is unfavorably associated with educational attainment in terms of both delayed years and completed years. Third, the interaction terms between income variables and the girl dummy become more statistically significant, while some asset variables, such as car ownership and household electrification, also emerge as significant in relation to the number of years completed. This finding reinforces the idea that economic affordability plays a crucial role, as indicated by the explanatory power of both income and asset variables, which were introduced to mitigate the potential endogeneity of income with educational outcomes.

In conclusion, these differences between the Poisson and Tobit models are not contradictory but instead reinforce the results obtained in the benchmark analysis. The Poisson regression highlights the importance of factors such as age, parental presence, and economic conditions in shaping educational attainment.

6.4.2 Consideration of Further Possible Household-Specific Heterogeneity

Further to the Poisson estimation using additional covariates, we estimated the model by including a household-specific effect term, isolating it from the error term u. The results, shown in Table 6, remain largely consistent with both the benchmark and Poisson estimations, with a few notable differences. First, the dummy variable for speaking Ilokano (D_{Ilokano}) becomes positively significant for years delayed and negatively significant for years completed, suggesting a potential disadvantage in educational progression for Ilokano speakers. Second, positive significance emerges for the weather shock dummy (D_{Wshock}) regarding years delayed and for the military shock dummy (D_{Mshock}) for both dependent variables, with military shocks appearing particularly unfavorable for girls. Third, social capital (*SC*) becomes insignificant for both dependent variables, indicating a reduced role in explaining educational outcomes. Fourth, while the dummy for father's absence (*Fat_ab*) remains significant, its robustness decreases compared to the Poisson estimators. Lastly, the interaction term between log per capita income and the gender dummy ($\log Y \times D_g$) becomes insignificant, whereas the interaction term between log per capita remittance and the gender dummy ($\log R \times D_g$) becomes negatively significant for years completed, though not for years delayed.

Table 6 Result of Delay Analysis (Linear regression, household-specific effect)

Variables	Dependent Variable = ΔA				Dependent Variable = A_2			
	w/ Gender Interaction		w/o Gender Interaction		w/ Gender Interaction		w/o Gender Interaction	
	(1)	(2)	(3)	(4)	(5)	(6)	(7)	(8)
Individual characteristics (X_1):								
Age	−0.18	−0.14	−0.21	−0.21	0.83	0.80	0.86	0.86
	[0.14]	[0.14]	[0.14]	[0.14]	[0.15]***	[0.16]***	[0.16]***	[0.16]***
Sqage	0.02	0.02	0.02	0.02	0.00	0.00	−0.01	0.00
	[0.01]***	[0.01]**	[0.01]***	[0.01]***	[0.01]	[0.01]	[0.01]	[0.01]
D_g	−0.51	−0.53	−0.31	−0.30	0.47	0.59	0.29	0.27
	[0.45]	[0.43]	[0.09]***	[0.09]***	[0.47]	[0.44]	[0.10]***	[0.10]***
BMI	−0.07	−0.06	−0.07	−0.06	0.09	0.08	0.09	0.08
	[0.03]**	[0.03]*	[0.03]**	[0.03]**	[0.03]***	[0.03]***	[0.03]***	[0.03]***
D_Ilonggo	−0.15	−0.16	−0.09	−0.03	−0.02	−0.03	−0.03	−0.10
	[0.24]	[0.25]	[0.21]	[0.21]	[0.25]	[0.26]	[0.21]	[0.21]
D_Ilokano	0.47	0.38	0.44	0.35	−0.45	−0.29	−0.42	−0.26
	[0.18]**	[0.19]**	[0.18]**	[0.19]*	[0.20]**	[0.21]	[0.20]**	[0.21]
D_Waray	0.09	−0.09	−0.09	−0.19	−0.01	0.18	0.18	0.28
	[0.25]	[0.30]	[0.26]	[0.31]	[0.25]	[0.31]	[0.26]	[0.31]
PW	0.07	0.07	0.21	0.22	−0.08	−0.08	−0.23	−0.23
	[0.14]	[0.14]	[0.11]*	[0.11]*	[0.14]	[0.14]	[0.12]**	[0.12]*
PW × *D_g*	0.34	0.36			−0.38	−0.40		
	[0.19]*	[0.18]**			[0.19]**	[0.18]**		

(continued)

Table 6 (continued)

Variables	Dependent Variable = ΔA				Dependent Variable = A_2			
	w/ Gender Interaction		w/o Gender Interaction		w/ Gender Interaction		w/o Gender Interaction	
	(1)	(2)	(3)	(4)	(5)	(6)	(7)	(8)
Household characteristics (X_2):								
Numson	0.04	0.04	0.03	0.03	−0.03	−0.03	−0.03	−0.03
	[0.05]	[0.05]	[0.03]	[0.03]	[0.05]	[0.05]	[0.03]	[0.03]
Numdau	0.04	0.05	0.03	0.03	−0.03	−0.05	−0.02	−0.03
	[0.06]	[0.05]	[0.04]	[0.04]	[0.06]	[0.05]	[0.04]	[0.04]
Numson × *D_g*	−0.02	−0.01			0.00	−0.01		
	[0.06]	[0.06]			[0.05]	[0.06]		
Numdau × *D_g*	−0.02	−0.05			0.02	0.04		
	[0.06]	[0.06]			[0.06]	[0.06]		
D_Wshock	0.11	0.12	0.17	0.18	−0.09	−0.09	−0.13	−0.14
	[0.16]	[0.16]	[0.11]	[0.11]*	[0.17]	[0.17]	[0.12]	[0.11]
D_Wshock × *D_g*	0.05	0.09			−0.04	−0.09		
	[0.18]	[0.18]			[0.18]	[0.19]		
D_Mshock	0.13	−0.06	0.29	0.37	−0.04	0.09	−0.34	−0.46
	[0.22]	[0.29]	[0.23]	[0.20]*	[0.24]	[0.31]	[0.24]	[0.21]**
D_Mshock × *D_g*	0.18	0.38			−0.36	−0.57		
	[0.27]	[0.28]			[0.26]	[0.29]**		

(continued)

Table 6 (continued)

Variables	Dependent Variable = ΔA				Dependent Variable = A_2			
	w/ Gender Interaction		w/o Gender Interaction		w/ Gender Interaction		w/o Gender Interaction	
	(1)	(2)	(3)	(4)	(5)	(6)	(7)	(8)
Sav	−0.03	−0.02	−0.04	−0.02	0.09	0.07	0.03	0.00
	[0.10]	[0.09]	[0.04]	[0.05]	[0.16]	[0.14]	[0.06]	[0.06]
Sav × *D_g*	−0.04	−0.01			−0.06	−0.07		
	[0.11]	[0.10]			[0.17]	[0.15]		
D_Refu	0.18	0.12	0.22	0.23	−0.19	−0.12	−0.23	−0.24
	[0.21]	[0.21]	[0.16]	[0.17]	[0.21]	[0.22]	[0.17]	[0.19]
D_Refu × *D_g*	0.05	0.11			−0.03	−0.11		
	[0.27]	[0.27]			[0.26]	[0.27]		
SC	−0.03	−0.03	−0.03	−0.03	0.03	0.02	0.03	0.03
	[0.03]	[0.03]	[0.03]	[0.03]	[0.03]	[0.03]	[0.03]	[0.03]
Fated	−0.08	−0.08	−0.03	−0.03	0.08	0.08	0.03	0.03
	[0.03]**	[0.03]**	[0.02]*	[0.02]*	[0.03]**	[0.03]**	[0.02]	[0.02]
Momed	−0.03	−0.03	−0.05	−0.04	0.04	0.04	0.06	0.06
	[0.04]	[0.04]	[0.02]*	[0.02]*	[0.04]	[0.04]	[0.02]***	[0.03]**
Fated × *D_g*	0.08	0.08			−0.08	−0.09		
	[0.03]**	[0.03]**			[0.03]**	[0.04]**		
Momed × *D_g*	−0.02	−0.03			0.03	0.03		
	[0.04]	[0.04]			[0.04]	[0.04]		
Fat_ab	0.63	0.33	0.43	0.38	-0.56	-0.24	-0.30	-0.27
	[0.32]**	[0.24]	[0.29]	[0.24]	[0.33]*	[0.23]	[0.29]	[0.24]

(continued)

Table 6 (continued)

Variables	Dependent Variable = $\varDelta A$				Dependent Variable = A_2			
	w/ Gender Interaction		w/o Gender Interaction		w/ Gender Interaction		w/o Gender Interaction	
	(1)	(2)	(3)	(4)	(5)	(6)	(7)	(8)
Mom_ab	-0.29	-0.47	-0.39	-0.40	-0.01	0.30	0.43	0.52
	[0.47]	[0.39]	[0.24]	[0.24]*	[0.66]	[0.58]	[0.28]	[0.29]*
log Y	0.03		0.01		-0.03		-0.01	
	[0.02]		[0.02]		[0.03]		[0.02]	
log $Y \times D\_g$	-0.04				0.06			
	[0.03]				[0.04]			
log R	-0.01		0.01		0.02		-0.01	
	[0.03]		[0.02]		[0.03]		[0.02]	
log $R \times D\_g$	0.0486				−0.0556			
	[0.03]				[0.03]*			
OL		0		0.0002		0		−0.0001
		[0.00]		[0.00]		[0.00]		[0.00]
TL		0.0005		−0.0002		−0.0004		0.0002
		[0.00]		[0.00]		[0.00]		[0.00]
$OL \times D\_g$		0.0003				−0.0002		
		[0.00]				[0.00]		
$TL \times D\_g$		−0.0012				0.0011		
		[0.00]				[0.00]		
D_mot		−0.1476		−0.151		0.2091		0.2104
		[0.17]		[0.16]		[0.19]		[0.18]

(continued)

Table 6 (continued)

Variables	Dependent Variable = ΔA				Dependent Variable = A_2			
	w/ Gender Interaction		w/o Gender Interaction		w/ Gender Interaction		w/o Gender Interaction	
	(1)	(2)	(3)	(4)	(5)	(6)	(7)	(8)
D_car		−0.2477		−0.1829		0.2767		0.2305
		[0.20]		[0.22]		[0.22]		[0.24]
D_noelec		0.0688		0.0549		−0.0825		−0.062
		[0.14]		[0.14]		[0.15]		[0.15]
D_nopipe		0.0628		0.0551		−0.1001		−0.0955
		[0.12]		[0.13]		[0.13]		[0.14]
Supply-side school variables:								
Inst_change	−1.132	−1.0873	−0.9557	−0.9015	2.2709	2.2429	2.092	2.0584
	[0.58]*	[0.60]*	[0.66]	[0.67]	[0.56]***	[0.59]***	[0.64]***	[0.65]***
D_Snack	−0.2536	−0.2815	−0.3082	−0.3095	0.2532	0.2668	0.3082	0.2965
	[0.12]**	[0.13]**	[0.13]**	[0.13]**	[0.13]*	[0.14]*	[0.13]**	[0.14]**
D_Lunch	−0.2917	−0.2746	−0.3023	−0.2947	0.265	0.2146	0.2636	0.2343
	[0.15]*	[0.16]*	[0.15]*	[0.16]*	[0.16]	[0.18]	[0.17]	[0.18]
Household-specific effect	Yes	Yes	Yes	Yes	Yes	Yes	Yes	Yes
Region-specific effect	Yes	Yes	Yes	Yes	Yes	Yes	Yes	Yes
Intercept	3.9381	3.5642	3.7179	3.6492	−9.7103	−9.3471	−9.4809	−9.3194
	[1.04]***	[1.06]***	[0.96]***	[0.99]***	[1.08]***	[1.13]***	[1.02]***	[1.08]***
Pseudo R^2								
Log-likelihood								
No. of observations	326	326	326	326	327	327	327	327

*$p < 0.10$, **$p < 0.05$, ***$p < 0.01$
Notes Standard errors (household clustered) are in brackets
Source Author's calculation by IFPRI (2008)

These results imply several key points. Although the indicator for speaking a minor language remained insignificant in previous estimations, it may still unfavorably affect educational attainment. Additionally, both weather and military shocks are associated with delays in education, with military shocks having a stronger negative impact on girls. The diminished significance of social capital suggests that its explanatory power is weaker in this model. Moreover, while father's absence remains a significant factor, its influence appears less robust. Finally, the inconsistent correlation between income and educational attainment, along with the significance of remittances, highlights the complex role of economic factors. Despite these differences, the results overall reinforce the findings from the robustness checks, particularly regarding intergenerational gender-preferential patterns.

6.4.3 Consideration of the Zero-Inflated Data

The consideration of count data by the Poisson model is here further expanded given the distribution form of the delayed years in education. According to Fig. 7, the distribution form of delayed years in education not only shows the count-data feature but also has spikes in density in the observed values of 0 and 1 year. Hence, the distribution form of the dependent variable looks zero-inflated.

To address both count-data and such zero-inflated data features, the Zero-Inflated Poisson (ZIP) model is additionally employed for a further robustness check of the estimators in this Subsection. The ZIP model is different from the Poisson model in that the ZIP model considers the two-step processes (Cameron and Trivedi 2005: 600–601). First, the binary process of the dependent variable as to whether it takes a value of 0 or 1 is estimated. This binary process, i.e., the zero-inflation process, is estimated in the logit (or probit) manner, where the ZIP model uses specific regressor(s) for estimating this binary process in the logit manner. Second, after these, the ZIP model follows the count-data regression similar to the Poisson model when the binary process takes on a value of 1. The result of ZIP-model estimation is shown in Table 7. This table newly reports the logit coefficients for the variable predicting the excess zeros. Table 7 reports the case of dependent variable as ΔA only, because A_2 does not look zero-inflated. As the logit-step regressors, *Inst_change* and its gender interaction with *D_g* (i.e., *Inst_change* $\times$ *D_g*) are used.

The ZIP-model estimation first confirms that the coefficients estimated are almost robustly and qualitatively identical to the previous estimators in other econometric estimations shown in Tables 4, 5, and 6. The only difference, though statistically significant at 10% level, is that in column (3), the coefficient of *sav* is negative, meaning that students, regardless of male or female, from households that have a saving account are more likely to experience shorter delays in education than otherwise. Other variables, including the variables about gender-preferential intergenerational relations between students and their parents, show the same qualitative results.

The merit of the ZIP model is, as noted, that we obtain the binary-process logit estimators of the dependent variable taking on a zero or non-zero value. The zero

Table 7 Result of Delay Analysis (Zero-Inflated Poisson Model)

Variables	Dependent Variable = ΔA			
	w/ Gender Interaction		w/o Gender Interaction	
	(1)	(2)	(3)	(4)
Individual characteristics ($\boldsymbol{X}_1$):				
Age	0.42	0.47	0.33	0.34
	[0.13]***	[0.13]***	[0.13]**	[0.13]***
Sqage	−0.01	−0.01	−0.01	−0.01
	[0.01]	[0.01]**	[0.01]	[0.01]
D_g	0.07	−0.50	−0.37	−0.35
	[0.50]	[0.43]	[0.09]***	[0.09]***
BMI	−0.07	−0.05	−0.06	−0.05
	[0.03]**	[0.03]*	[0.03]**	[0.03]*
D_Ilonggo	−0.15	0.00	0.00	0.19
	[0.55]	[0.52]	[0.52]	[0.50]
D_Ilokano	0.50	0.26	0.48	0.30
	[0.54]	[0.53]	[0.53]	[0.53]
D_Waray	0.08	−0.12	0.02	−0.03
	[0.30]	[0.29]	[0.28]	[0.28]
PW	0.02	0.01	0.08	0.08
	[0.05]	[0.05]	[0.05]*	[0.05]
PW × *D_g*	0.17	0.23		
	[0.08]**	[0.08]***		
Household characteristics ($\boldsymbol{X}_2$):				
Numson	0.03	0.02	0.01	0.02
	[0.03]	[0.03]	[0.02]	[0.02]
Numdau	0.03	0.04	0.03	0.04
	[0.04]	[0.03]	[0.03]	[0.03]
Numson × *D_g*	−0.03	0.02		
	[0.05]	[0.05]		
Numson × *D_g*	0.01	−0.01		
	[0.06]	[0.06]		
D_Wshock	0.03	0.01	0.08	0.07
	[0.12]	[0.12]	[0.10]	[0.09]
D_Wshock × *D_g*	0.16	0.20		
	[0.19]	[0.19]		
D_Mshock	0.12	0.21	0.25	0.32
	[0.27]	[0.29]	[0.20]	[0.19]*
D_Mshockf × *D_g*	0.20	0.12		

(continued)

Table 7 (continued)

Variables	Dependent Variable = ΔA			
	w/ Gender Interaction		w/o Gender Interaction	
	(1)	(2)	(3)	(4)
	[0.34]	[0.35]		
Sav	−0.10	−0.10	−0.14	−0.11
	[0.14]	[0.11]	[0.08]*	[0.08]
Sav × *D_g*	−0.05	−0.01		
	[0.18]	[0.15]		
D_Refu	0.15	0.12	0.18	0.21
	[0.15]	[0.14]	[0.12]	[0.13]
D_Refu × *D_g*	0.07	0.14		
	[0.22]	[0.23]		
SC	−0.10	−0.09	−0.08	−0.08
	[0.04]**	[0.04]**	[0.04]*	[0.04]**
Fated	−0.05	−0.07	−0.03	−0.04
	[0.02]**	[0.02]***	[0.02]*	[0.02]**
Momed	−0.03	−0.02	−0.05	−0.05
	[0.03]	[0.03]	[0.02]**	[0.02]**
Fated × *D_g*	0.06	0.08		
	[0.03]*	[0.03]**		
Momed × *D_g*	−0.05	−0.05		
	[0.04]	[0.04]		
Fat_ab	0.59	0.29	0.37	0.32
	[0.29]**	[0.18]	[0.26]	[0.18]*
Mom_ab	0.01	−0.12	0.13	0.07
	[0.59]	[0.45]	[0.35]	[0.34]
log *Y*	0.04		0.02	
	[0.03]		[0.02]	
log *Y* × *D_g*	−0.09			
	[0.04]**			
log *R*	0.00		0.01	
	[0.02]		[0.02]	
log *R* × *D_g*	0.04			
	[0.03]			
OL		0.00		0.00
		[0.00]		[0.00]

(continued)

Table 7 (continued)

Variables	Dependent Variable = ΔA			
	w/ Gender Interaction		w/o Gender Interaction	
	(1)	(2)	(3)	(4)
TL		0.00		0.00
		[0.00]		[0.00]
OL × *D_g*		0.00		
		[0.00]		
TL × *D_g*		0.00		
		[0.00]***		
D_mot		−0.28		−0.29
		[0.18]		[0.17]*
D_car		−0.27		−0.07
		[0.37]		[0.39]
D_noelec		0.11		0.06
		[0.10]		[0.10]
D_nopipe		0.11		0.10
		[0.11]		[0.11]
Supply-side school variables:				
Inst_change	−0.40	−0.37	−0.25	−0.20
	[0.22]*	[0.22]*	[0.20]	[0.21]
D_Snack	−0.24	−0.22	−0.24	−0.25
	[0.11]**	[0.12]*	[0.11]**	[0.12]**
D_Lunch	−0.39	−0.31	−0.39	−0.35
	[0.14]***	[0.15]**	[0.13]***	[0.14]**
Region-specific effect	Yes	Yes	Yes	Yes
Inflate:				
Inst_change	−4.45	−7.96	−4.44	−5.85
	[0.48]***	[0.49]***	[0.44]***	[0.45]***
Inst_change × *D_g*	16.28	15.19	17.85	18.58
	[0.78]***	[0.78]***	[0.75]***	[0.75]***
Intercept	−0.92	−1.13	−0.65	−0.71
	[0.79]	[0.77]	[0.77]	[0.79]
Log-likelihood	−350.04	−347.01	−354.44	−352.31
No. of observations	326	326	326	326

*$p < 0.10$, **$p < 0.05$, ***$p < 0.01$
Notes Robust standard errors are in brackets
Source Author's calculation by IFPRI (2008)

value of dependent value indicates the status of having no delays in education. The supply-side policy variable, *Inst_change*, predicts both the binary and count processes. According to the coefficient of *Inst_change* alone and the coefficients of *Inst_change* and *Inst_change* × *D_g* in the row of "inflate," such a policy change in earlier entrance age to elementary schools still has the mitigating effect of delayed years in the count process. Yet, there is gender-specific heterogeneity in the binary process. In the row of "inflation," the coefficient of *Inst_change* alone is negative but that of the interaction term *Inst_change* × *D_g* is positive, and the magnitude of the latter is larger than that of the former (i.e., with a particularly pronounced effect among female students).

In short, students in the beneficiary cohorts of this policy change, which shifted the entrance age to one year earlier, are generally more likely to experience shorter delays in education. Moreover, female students in these cohorts tend to respond more positively to achieving no delays under the policy change compared to their male counterparts. It is noteworthy that the policy-change variable effectively predicts the zero-inflated spike in the dependent variable, particularly highlighting the gender heterogeneity in its effects. Given the noted ongoing nature of the debate in Sect. 6.3 about the effects of an earlier entrance age on educational outcomes, this additional finding on the gendered difference in reducing delays deserves further attention (Katz 2000; Lincove and Painter 2006; Mayer and Knutson 1999).

7 Conclusion

This chapter has primarily focused on the intergenerational nexus between child gender and parental educational attainment. The results across various specifications and estimations reveal that significant gender-specific patterns persist, even after controlling for individual, household, region-specific, and supply-side characteristics. One of the main findings is that girls are less likely to experience delays in elementary education and are likely to attain more years of schooling compared to their male counterparts. This finding is robust across both dependent variables: the number of delay years and the years completed. It highlights the educational disadvantages faced by boys relative to girls, aligning with existing literature (Illo 1997; Bouis et al. 1998; David et al. 2009; Bhagowati 2014, among others). These disadvantages for boys are evident even at the elementary level of education.

Parental education presents an additional dimension to these gendered patterns. Mothers' educational levels positively influence both sons and daughters, whereas fathers' educational levels preferentially benefit sons. In the Philippines, where fathers are traditionally regarded as breadwinners and are expected to provide economic stability (see also Chaps. 4 and 5), their influence on household dynamics and the father–son association warrants attention (Gorman-Smith et al. 2012).[20] The positive intergenerational correlation between fathers' and sons' educational attainment suggests that sons who inherit lower educational levels from their fathers may face similar constraints when they eventually take on the breadwinner role in the next generation. This dynamic underscores the importance of addressing the educational disadvantages of boys in the present generation, as it has implications for their ability to fulfill societal expectations as future fathers and household heads. Encouraging a positive father–son dynamic could help mitigate boys' educational disadvantages over generations. If the paternal effect proves to be greater than the maternal one, the current gender gap unfavorable to boys could potentially be reduced. However, further analysis is needed to quantitatively compare the magnitudes of maternal and paternal effects.

Supply-side characteristics are also of great importance. This study adds evidence to the literature on how supply-side services improve students' educational progress. The 1995 policy change in elementary school entrance age in the Philippines has had a robustly favorable effect on educational attainment, regardless of the dependent variables analyzed, even after controlling for timing- and age-related factors. Additionally, according to the ZIP model, female students are more responsive to this policy change, tending to experience fewer delays under the new policy than male students. These gender-heterogeneous responses to an educational policy change offer new insights for policymakers, not only in the Philippines but also in other countries (Katz 2000; Lincove and Painter 2006; Mayer and Knutson 1999). The provisions of school snacks and lunches, which are expected to help students remain enrolled and reduce delays in education, are also found to have a positive and significant impact.

As for household-affordability or shock-related characteristics, these appear to be less of an obstacle in elementary education due to its free and compulsory nature. However, exploring secondary and higher education is essential to understand whether similar patterns hold across different educational stages. These questions motivate the next chapter, which expands the framework to analyze gender-specific continuities and disparities in secondary and tertiary education.

Despite these contributions, this chapter acknowledges certain limitations and highlights avenues for future research. First, the delay analysis used here is normative and applies specifically to elementary education, where clear standards exist for measuring delays. Extending this framework to secondary and tertiary education requires different approaches that account for the less structured nature of progression

---

[20] Although this is beyond the scope of this chapter, the following points provide additional context. McKay and Lucero-Prisno III (2012) highlight the father's increased control over household decisions in cases where the mother is absent, such as when she works abroad. While gender equality is often considered relatively advanced in the Philippines, Bhagowati (2014) argues that elements of "male chauvinism" persist, which may become more pronounced in the mother's absence. This dynamic potentially reinforces traditional breadwinner roles, with fathers assuming greater authority. In addition to economic and pedagogical perspectives, Tomas (2013) underscores the psychological role of fathers in children's development, emphasizing its qualitative distinction from mothers' influence. Chapters 4 and 5 further explore mothers' dual roles as primary child caregivers and supplementary breadwinners.

at these levels, an issue the next chapter seeks to address. Second, while this study infers intergenerational dynamics, it does not account for other potential influencing factors, such as cultural norms or specific economic shocks. Future research should integrate these elements to provide a more comprehensive understanding of gendered educational patterns, perspectives that Chapters 4 and 5 explore in their respective contexts. Third, this study focuses on a specific region in the Philippines. Although the findings provide valuable insights, caution is needed in generalizing these results to other regions or countries with differing socioeconomic contexts.

In summary, this study highlights the unique intergenerational dynamics in the Philippines, where a "female-favorable" gender-preferential pattern in educational attainment stands in contrast to trends in many other developing countries. In the literature, this phenomenon has been attributed to a reflection of gendered comparative advantages in labor markets or inheritance systems (Estudillo et al. 2001, 2008; Mapa 2021; Quisumbing 1994; Yamauchi and Tiongco 2013). The father–son intergenerational nexus in education identified in this study offers another important complementary perspective for addressing gender inequalities in education over generations. Future research should explore how these intergenerational dynamics extend to higher educational stages, where new gendered patterns may emerge due to differing socioeconomic and cultural contexts. Building on these findings, the next chapter expands the analysis to secondary and tertiary education, focusing on how gender-specific continuities and disparities evolve beyond elementary education.

References

Alderman H, King EM (1998) Gender differences in parental investment in education. Struct Chang Econ Dyn 9:453–468. https://doi.org/10.1016/S0954-349X(98)00040-X

Amemiya T (1985) Advanced econometrics. Basil Blackwell, Oxford

Andrew M (2014) The scarring effects of primary-grade retention? A study of cumulative advantage in the educational career. Social Forces 93(2):653–685. https://doi.org/10.1093/sf/sou074

Angrist JD, Krueger AB (1991) Does compulsory school attendance affect schooling and earnings? Quart J Econ 106(4):979–1014. https://doi.org/10.2307/2937954

Balisacan AM (2003) The Philippine economy: Development, policies, and challenges. Ateneo de Manila University Press, Quezon City

Behrman JR, Foster AD, Rosenzweig MR, Vashishtha P (1999) Women's schooling, home teaching, and economic growth. J Polit Econ 107(4):682–714. https://doi.org/10.1086/250075

Bevis LEM, Barrett CB (2015) Decomposing intergenerational income elasticity: The gender-differentiated contribution of capital transmission in rural Philippines. World Dev 74:233–252. https://doi.org/10.1016/j.worlddev.2015.04.010

Bhagowati SK (2014) Women in Southeast Asia. New Century Publications, New Delhi

Bouis HE, Haddad LJ (1990) Agricultural commercialization, nutrition, and the rural poor: A study of Philippine farm households. Lynne Rienner, Boulder and London

Bouis HE, Palabrica-Costello M, Solon O, Westbrook D, Limbo AB (1998) Gender equality and investments in adolescents in the rural Philippines. International Food Policy Research Institute, Washington, DC. https://doi.org/10.2499/0896291111rr108

Cameron AC, Trivedi PK (2005) Microeconometrics: Methods and applications. Cambridge University Press, New York. https://doi.org/10.1017/CBO9780511811241

Caoli-Rodriguez R (2007) The Philippines country case study. Country Profile Prepared for the Education for All Global Monitoring Report 2008: Education for All by 2015: Will We Make It? United Nations Educational, Scientific and Cultural Organization (UNESCO), Paris
Chang HJ (2014) Economics: The user's guide. Pelican, London
Cortes P (2015) The feminization of international migration and its effects on the children left behind: Evidence from the Philippines. World Dev 65:62–78. https://doi.org/10.1016/j.worlddev.2013.10.021
David CC, Albert JRG, Carreon-Monterola SL (2009) In pursuit of sex parity: Are girls becoming more educated than boys? Policy Notes PN2009-005. PIDS, Quezon City
DiPrete TA, Eirich GM (2006) Cumulative advantage as a mechanism for inequality: A review of theoretical and empirical developments. Annual Rev Sociology 32(1):271–297. https://doi.org/10.1146/annurev.soc.32.061604.123127
Dutt AK (2023) Hysteresis and path dependence in economic analysis: formalizations causes and implications. Rev Keynesian Econ 11(4):435–459. https://doi.org/10.4337/roke.2023.04.01
Estudillo JP, Quisumbing A, Otsuka K (2001) Gender differences in land inheritance, schooling and lifetime income: Evidence from the rural Philippines. J Dev Stud 37(4):23–48. https://doi.org/10.1080/00220380412331322031
Estudillo JP, Sawada Y, Otsuka K (2008) Poverty and income dynamics in Philippine Villages 1985–2004. Rev Dev Econ 12:877–890. https://doi.org/10.1111/j.1467-9361.2008.00458.x
Filmer D, Pritchett LH (2001) Estimating wealth effects without expenditure data—or tears: An application to educational enrollments in states of India. Demography 38(1):115–132. https://doi.org/10.1353/dem.2001.0003
Glewwe P, Jacoby HG (1995) An economic analysis of delayed primary school enrollment in a low-income country: The role of early childhood nutrition. Rev Econ Stat 77(1):156–169. https://doi.org/10.2307/2110001
Glewwe P, Kremer M (2006) Schools, teachers, and education outcomes in developing countries. Handbook Econ Educ 2:945–1017. https://doi.org/10.1016/S1574-0692(06)02016-2
Gorman-Smith D, Hunt EG, Robertson D (2012) Fatherhood and fathering among low-income and minority men. In: King R, Maholmes V (eds) Oxford handbook of poverty and child development. Oxford University Press, Oxford
Huang FL (2010) The role of socioeconomic status and school quality in the Philippines: Revisiting the Heyneman-Loxley effect. Int J Educ Dev 30(3):288–296. https://doi.org/10.1016/j.ijedudev.2009.10.001
Ichikawa M (1999) Public education and religion in the Philippines: Its establishment and development process (*Firipin no kō kyōiku to shūkyō: Seiritsu to tenkai katei*). Tōshindō Press, Tokyo [Japanese]
Illo JFI (1997) Women in the Philippines. Asian Development Bank, Mandaluyong City
International Food Policy Research Institute (IFPRI) (2000) Philippines Cash Cropping Project, Southern Bukidnon Province, 1984–1985 (Datasets). IFPRI, Washington, DC
International Food Policy Research Institute (IFPRI) (2008) Philippines: Bukidnon Panel Survey, 2003–2004 (Datasets). IFPRI, Washington, DC
Katz LG (2000) Academic redshirting and young children. Office of Educational Research and Improvement, Washington, DC
Lincove JA, Painter G (2006) Does the age that children start kindergarten matter? Evidence of long-term educational and social outcomes. Educ Eval Policy Anal 28(2):153–179. https://doi.org/10.3102/01623737028002153
Mapa DS (2021) Working children and child labor situation. Reference Number 2021-484. Philippine Statistics Authority
Mayer SE, Knutson D (1999) Does the timing of school affect how much children learn? In: Mayer SE, Peterson PE (eds) Earning and learning: how schools matter. Russell Sage Foundation, New York, pp 79–102

McKay S, Lucero-Prisno III DE (2012) Masculinities Afloat: Filipino seafarers and the situational performance of manhood. In: Ford M, Lyons L (eds) Men and masculinities in Southeast Asia. Routledge, Oxford
McNiven S, Quisumbing AR (2007) Introduction to the 2003/4 rounds of the Bukidnon Panel Survey. IFPRI, Washington, DC
Mesa EP (2007) Measuring Education Inequality in the Philippines. Discussion Paper 2007, no. 04. School of Economics, University of the Philippines, Quezon City
Miwa K (2008) Child health and school enrolment and delayed enrolment in Rural Cambodia (*Kambojia nōson ni okeru kodomo no kenkō to shūgaku, nyūgaku chien*). Asian Economies (*Azia Keizai*) 49(9):2–21 (in Japanese)
Nakanishi T (2001) Two-class system in economic development: the Philippines (*Firipin no nikaisō shakai to minshu shugi: Chūkansō no seichō niyoru henka no kanōsei*). In: Sato Y (ed) Economic and Social Policies in Newly Democratized Countries (*Shinkō minshu shugi koku no keizai, shakai seisaku*). Institute of Developing Economies (in Japanese), Chiba
National Statistical Coordination Board (NSCB) (2002) Report on the 2000 Philippine Human Development Index. NSCB, Makati
National Statistics Office (NSO) (2003) 2000 Census of Population and Housing. Report No. 2-19 J (Bukidnon) Volume I: Demographic and Housing Characteristics. NSO, Manila
National Statistics Office (NSO) (various years) Census of Population and Housing. National Statistics Office (currently, Philippine Statistics Authority), Quezon City
Nishimura M, Yamano T, Sasaoka Y (2008) Impacts of the universal primary education policy on educational attainment and private costs in rural Uganda. Int J Educ Dev 28(2):161–175. https://doi.org/10.1016/j.ijedudev.2006.09.017
Okabe M (2016) Gender-preferential intergenerational patterns in primary educational attainment: An econometric approach to a case in Rural Mindanao, The Philippines. Int J Educ Dev 46:125–142. https://doi.org/10.1016/j.ijedudev.2015.10.006
Okabe M (2018) 'K to 12' program as a national HRD to develop the workforce. Philippine J Labor Ind Relat 35(1–2):124–140. https://www.journals.upd.edu.ph/index.php/pjlir/article/view/7449
Quisumbing AR (1994) Intergenerational transfers in Philippine rice villages. Gender differences in traditional inheritance customs. J Dev Econ 43(2):167–195. https://doi.org/10.1016/0304-3878(94)90003-5
Quisumbing AR, McNiven S (2010) Moving forward, looking back: The impact of migration and remittances on assets, consumption, and credit constraints in the Rural Philippines. J Dev Stud 46(1):91–113. https://doi.org/10.1080/00220380903197960
Randall L, Anderson MR (eds) (1999) Schooling for success: Preventing repetition and dropout in Latin American primary schools. M. E. Sharpe, New York
Takayama N, Fuwa N, Yurugi T (2010) The role of non-agricultural sectors in rural poverty reduction: A case study in Mindanao, Philippines. Japan J Southeast Asian Stud (*Tōnan azia kenkyū*) 48(1):46–73 [Japanese]. https://doi.org/10.20495/tak.48.1_46
Tomas CB (2013) The Philippines: East Asia. In: Ness D, Lin C-L (eds) International education: An encyclopedia of contemporary issues and systems, vol. 2. Routledge, Oxford
Yamauchi F, Tiongco M (2013) Why women are progressive in education? Gender disparities in human capital, labor markets, and family arrangement in the Philippines. Econ Educ Rev 32:196–206. https://doi.org/10.1016/j.econedurev.2012.09.003

Chapter 3
Mothers to Daughters?—Gendered Continuity in Educational Demand Beyond Primary Education: Findings from Bukidnon, Northern Mindanao

Abstract This chapter explores factors affecting the continuity of educational demand in Bukidnon, rural Mindanao, using an agricultural socioeconomic survey. The analysis indicates that educational demand is more consistent when advancing to higher levels and less so when stopping at lower levels. The study's key contribution is its examination of gender-specific educational patterns: (i) Boys' education is more closely linked to their fathers' education at the primary level as discussed in Chapter 2; however, (ii) the association between mothers' and children's education is notably stronger, particularly for daughters at secondary and tertiary levels. This suggests that higher maternal education significantly enhances daughters' educational attainment compared to sons. This chapter also considers the impact of non-agricultural livelihoods and bilateral descent on these gendered patterns. Interruptions in educational continuity due to income shocks occur at stage-entry points, not only at graduation points. Income constraints play a crucial role in determining access to the next level of education rather than in the completion of the previous level. This finding aligns with existing literature emphasizing the need to address financial barriers, particularly in rural areas. The study concludes that income-related obstacles vary across educational stages, indicating a need for further investigation into these dynamics.

Keywords Sequential educational progression · Continuity of educational demand · Stage-specific decision-making · Intergenerational education dynamics · Mother–Daughter educational associations

---

This chapter is adapted from Okabe (2017) and has been substantially translated and restructured for inclusion in this volume.

M. Okabe, *Economics of the Reversal in Gender Disparities in Education and Development*, Economics, Law, and Institutions in Asia Pacific,
https://doi.org/10.1007/978-981-96-9271-2_3

1 Introduction

Building on the findings of Chapter 2, this chapter extends the analysis of educational inefficiency to explore the continuity of educational demand across primary, secondary, and tertiary levels. Chapter 2 focused on delays in primary education, a stage where compulsory education allows for the systematic evaluation of internal inefficiency. Delays in primary education were calculated as the gap between the ideal grade based on a student's age and the actual grade attained, reflecting a normative framework tied to the structure of compulsory schooling. This normative nature of delay measures makes them suitable for assessing inefficiencies in primary education, where universal progression is expected (Glewwe and Jacoby 1995; Hanushek et al. 2008). However, such an approach is less applicable to post-compulsory education, where progression depends more on individual choices, household dynamics, and broader socioeconomic factors (Cameron and Heckman 2001).

To address these complexities, this chapter adopts an extended perspective by employing a sequential framework to analyze decision-making across multiple educational stages. This framework captures the sequential, dynamic nature of educational progression by focusing on stage-specific decisions, such as enrollment, continuation, completion, and cessation, and examining the conditional probabilities associated with each stage (Behrman and Knowles 1999). Because being enrolled raises the utility of remaining enrolled, a one-period spell of failure or cessation can leave scarring that raises the threshold for recovery or re-entry in subsequent stages (Andrew 2014; DiPrete and Eirich 2006). This approach provides insights into the scarring as a barrier to persistence and the determinants of dropout, particularly in the context of family dynamics, socioeconomic conditions, and gender disparities. With this, an intriguing additional finding is revealed: while Chapter 2 highlighted the positive correlation between fathers' and sons' educational attainment, this dynamic is gradually supplanted by a robust correlation between mothers' and daughters' attainment at higher educational stages, consistent with other findings on gendered intergenerational dynamics (Quisumbing 1994; Behrman 1997). In doing so, this chapter elaborates the "reversal" in gender disparity not merely as boys' disadvantage, but as a patterned intergenerational advantage for daughters, particularly when supported by maternal education.

This chapter also examines the concept of continuity of educational demand as a crucial aspect beyond traditional measures such as years of schooling or binary enrollment status. Low continuity of demand refers to situations where students, often facing decisions leading to cessations, either drop out temporarily or permanently withdraw from education. These discontinuities, often categorized as out-of-school children (OOSC) or out-of-school youth (OOSY) problems, reflect inefficiencies in the education system, leading to significant losses in individual lifetime welfare and human capital accumulation (Caoli-Rodriguez 2007; Glewwe and Jacoby 1995; Symaco 2013).[1]

[1] Note that this chapter, adopting such a continuation-or-cessation framework, analytically treats the school system as a linear, irreversible progression, where cessation is regarded as a source of

The continuity of educational demand has broader implications for human capital formation and social equity. In the Philippine context, while initial progress has been made in achieving near-universal enrollment in primary education, significant challenges remain in retaining students through secondary and tertiary stages (Caoli-Rodriguez 2007; Symaco 2013). Rural areas like Bukidnon Province face severe barriers, including poverty, limited access to secondary and tertiary education, and cultural norms that shape educational decisions differently for boys and girls (Quisumbing and McNiven 2006). These factors contribute to persistent OOSC/OOSY rates and underscore the importance of assessing not just enrollment but also the persistence of educational demand.

By analyzing the continuity of educational demand, this chapter provides a nuanced understanding of intermediate stages in educational trajectories, enabling the identification of persistence and dropout patterns that cannot be captured by focusing solely on final educational attainment (Cameron and Heckman 2001). This approach is critical for designing interventions that address scarring barriers to educational persistence at specific stages, improving overall human capital outcomes and reducing inequality.

The remainder of this chapter is structured as follows: Sect. 2 outlines the conceptual framework, highlighting the sequential nature of educational decisions. Section 3 describes the dataset and study area, while Sect. 4 presents the empirical model and variables. Section 5 discusses the results, and Sect. 6 concludes with policy implications. The Appendix to this chapter provides technical notes for reference.

2 Conceptual Framework

2.1 Sequential Continuity of Educational Demand

Educational demand can be conceptualized as a sequential process, where each stage—enrollment, continuation, and completion—represents a distinct decision point influenced by socioeconomic, cultural, and institutional factors (Cameron and Heckman 2001). For example, the decision to enroll in primary education is often shaped by access to schools and basic household resources, while progression to secondary or tertiary education depends on perceived returns to education and the various opportunity costs of attending school.

Sequential analysis offers distinct advantages over aggregate or one-stage approaches such as those focusing solely on cumulative years of schooling or

---

inefficiency (see also Chapter 2). While this approach offers the advantage of comprehensively analyzing the sequential decisions that sustain educational demand, it may also impose a limitation by narrowing perspectives on the flexibility of formal education. In this regard, a later chapter explores alternative perspectives that challenge this efficiency- and progressivism-based notion. Specifically, Chapter 7 examines the case of dropped-out students who demonstrate resilience, prompting a reconsideration of linear and irreversible pathways in educational trajectories.

highest educational attainment. By modeling each stage as a discrete choice, this framework captures the conditional probabilities associated with transitions between stages, revealing insights into the barriers to persistence and determinants of dropout (Behrman and Knowles 1999). These insights are particularly relevant in contexts like rural Bukidnon Province, where structural barriers and cultural norms play a significant role in educational behavior and decisions.

2.2 Theoretical Underpinnings and Implications

The sequential framework aligns with theories of dynamic optimization, where individuals make stage-specific decisions based on perceived costs and benefits at each juncture (Cameron and Heckman 2001; Glewwe and Jacoby 1995). Educational discontinuities represent inefficiencies in this process, leading to human capital losses and perpetuating socioeconomic inequalities across generations (Heckman et al. 2006). For example, early dropout not only reduces individual earning potential but also hinders long-term social mobility (Glewwe and Jacoby 1995).

Gender disparities also play a crucial role in shaping educational trajectories. Cultural and economic constraints disproportionately affect boys at lower educational levels and girls at higher levels (Grant and Behrman 2010; Boudet et al. 2013). In rural settings, these disparities are exacerbated by limited access to quality education, reinforcing cycles of inequality (Estudillo et al. 2008, 2009). The findings in this chapter emphasize the need for policies that address these scarring barriers through targeted interventions, such as scholarships and conditional cash transfers, which can improve continuity in education across stages.

3 Data

3.1 Bukidnon Panel Data Survey

Following the data and methods outlined in Chapter 2, this chapter utilizes the Bukidnon Panel Data Survey (BPDS) dataset (IFPRI 2000, 2008). For further details about Bukidnon Province and the survey methodology, refer to Sects. 3–4 in Chapter 2 and Bouis and Haddad (1990). The BPDS comprises sub-datasets organized by research topics, such as basic household demographics (e.g., gender, age), education, agricultural production, loan refusal, and consumption expenditure. Of these, two education-related sub-datasets are particularly relevant: one focuses on short-term educational information for children, while the other provides long-term educational backgrounds covering both juveniles and adults (Quisumbing and McNiven 2006).

In this chapter, the analysis primarily relies on the long-term educational sub-dataset, which includes information spanning primary to tertiary levels and incorporates data on adults. This sub-dataset forms the core of the analysis. Additional sub-datasets, containing socioeconomic variables such as gender, age, and loan refusal experiences, were merged using household and individual identifiers (IFPRI 2008). To capture retrospective information about adults' educational histories, data from the 1984–85 survey (IFPRI 2000) were also integrated. As a result, the final dataset is tailored to address the specific research objectives of this chapter.

Yet, it is worth noting some limitations of the dataset. First, as mentioned in Chapter 2, the BPDS survey was conducted exclusively in the southern part of Bukidnon Province, leaving the northern regions unrepresented. Second, the process of merging sub-datasets introduced missing values. Despite these issues, the BPDS remains a unique and valuable resource for analyzing long-term educational data at the micro level, especially since it was not originally designed for educational research. Recognizing these limitations is essential for ensuring accurate interpretations and avoiding overgeneralization of the findings.

3.2 *Individual Characteristics*

Table 1 summarizes the descriptive statistics for the dependent and independent variables. A female dummy variable shows that females are more likely than males to attain higher levels of education, particularly beyond secondary school. For instance, while women account for 44% of the sample at the stage of entry to primary education ($S = 1$), their share increases to 51% at the stage of entry to secondary education ($S = 3$). The mean age of individuals in the sample is approximately 20 years, reflecting a mix of children and adults, which is a distinguishing approach in this chapter from Chapter 2.

Language variables indicate that, in addition to Filipino (the national language) and Cebuano (the lingua franca in Northern Mindanao or Region X), 1–3% of individuals speak Ilonggo or Ivatan. Ilonggo is primarily spoken in Iloilo City in the Western Visayas Region, while Ivatan is native to Batanes Province, located between the Philippines and Taiwan, making it geographically distant from Mindanao Island. The presence of Ivatan, even if only a few individuals, in Bukidnon is likely due to historical migration patterns. Economic opportunities, such as agricultural labor, and family or community networks may have led Ivatan speakers to settle in the region.[2]

[2] Indeed, it has been documented that internal migration in the Philippines during the early- to mid-twentieth century was characterized by either rural-to-urban movement or the southward migration of Roman Catholics to agricultural settlements on the island of Mindanao (Keely 1973: 179–180; Slater 1977: 35). Migration from Batanes to Bukidnon, a predominantly Christian province in Northern Mindanao (Region X) in contrast to the Muslim-majority regions of southwestern Mindanao, may have been driven by the search for "kinder environments" in Mindanao, in contrast to the "rugged, rocky, and windswept" conditions of Batanes (Slater 1977: 36). Although they represent

Table 1 Descriptive statistics (mean values, by S stage)

Variables	$S = 1$	$S = 2$	$S = 3$	$S = 4$	$S = 5$
Dependent variable: $\Pr(S = j \mid S \geq j)$	0.97	0.67	0.85	0.54	0.51
Independent variables:					
Individual characteristics:					
Female dummy (=1)	0.44	0.45	0.48	0.51	0.52
Age	20.08	20.31	23.34	22.76	26.15
Age squared	461.22	467.76	589.50	556.50	718.28
Ilonggo-speaking indicator (=1)	0.03	0.03	0.03	0.03	0.02
Ivatan-speaking indicator (=1)	0.01	0.01	#	#	#
Generation indicator: 40 or over	#	0.01	0.02	0.01	0.02
Generation indicator: 35–39	0.04	0.04	0.05	0.04	0.06
Generation indicator: 30–34	#	0.08	0.12	0.10	0.19
Generation indicator: 25–29	0.13	0.13	0.22	0.23	0.26
Generation indicator: 20–24	0.29	0.29	0.30	0.31	0.35
Generation indicator: 15–19	0.21	0.22	0.23	#	#
Household characteristics:					
Father's education	6.07	6.10	6.90	7.13	8.23
Mother's education	7.04	7.06	8.01	8.28	9.22
Number of brothers	3.16	3.12	2.61	2.65	2.16
Number of sisters	2.51	2.49	2.22	2.29	1.95
Per capita agricultural income (month)	1227.82	1218.02	1188.66	969.83	807.68
Per capita non-agricultural income (month)	257.10	254.96	265.62	292.48	423.08
Per capita net total income (year)	13,275.26	12,867.97	17,490.48	18,948.79	25,644.80
Shock experience indicator: Weather shock	#	0.37	0.37	#	0.36
Shock experience indicator: Military presence	#	0.01	0.01	#	#
Indicator: Household member with a disability	#	0.03	0.02	#	#
Indicator: experience of loan refusal	0.21	0.21	0.19	0.18	0.14
Social network size	1.95	1.96	2.04	2.05	2.09
No. of Observation	971	944	755	641	403

Notes:

1. # excluded from the set of independent variables due to multicollinearity diagnostics.
2. The dependent variable, S, represents the educational stages as shown in Fig. 1. Specifically, $S = 1$ and $S = 2$ denote the stages of entrance to and completion of primary education, $S = 3$ and $S = 4$ denote the stages of entrance to and completion of secondary education, and $S = 5$ denotes the stage of entrance to tertiary education, respectively.

Source Author's calculations using IFPRI (2000, 2008).

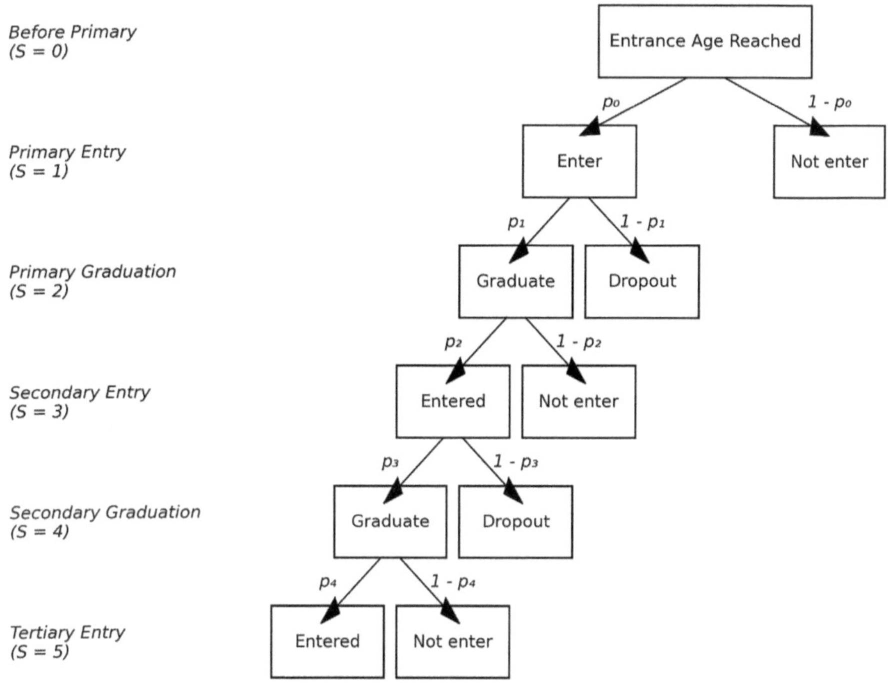

Fig. 1 Tree diagram of educational decisions (*Source* Author's creation)

Cohort dummy variables, which serve as proxies for generational differences, are included with the reference category being individuals "younger than 15." These variables facilitate an examination of generational shifts in educational attainment while accounting for age differences.

3.3 *Household Characteristics*

The analysis incorporates several household-level variables, including parental education levels, number of siblings, income, shock experiences (dummy variable), credit constraints (dummy variable), and social network size.[3] Parental education levels are primarily drawn from the 2003 data. However, in cases where decisions regarding education were likely made before 1985, as inferred from the age of

only 1–3% of the sample, their presence interestingly highlights the diverse migration-related and linguistic landscapes of the Philippines.

[3] Information on credit constraints and the social network size was not available from the 1984/85 data. As a second-best approach, data from 2003 were used as proxies for these characteristics, assuming they reflect conditions prior to 1985. However, this assumption should be interpreted with caution, particularly in cases where the events occurred significantly earlier.

children, parental education levels are sourced from the 1984–85 dataset. Notably, mothers generally exhibit higher educational attainment than fathers, with an average gap of one year across all educational stages. This disparity widens as individuals progress to higher educational levels (i.e., as $S = j$ increases).

The number of siblings is inversely correlated with educational progression, suggesting that families with fewer children are more likely to achieve higher educational levels. This pattern aligns with the expectation that limited household resources for education are often allocated competitively among siblings, favoring fewer children. Such dynamics are consistent with the "quantity-quality trade-off" theory in family economics, where larger family sizes dilute parental resources, leading to reduced investments in each child's education (Becker and Lewis 1973; Black et al. 2005).

Household income variables exhibit notable variations across sequential educational levels. While agricultural income decreases at higher educational levels, an inverse relationship is observed for non-agricultural and total income. This suggests that households with members achieving higher educational levels rely less on agricultural income and more on non-agricultural sources. This pattern aligns with well-documented dynamics of rural economic transformation in the Philippines, where the non-agricultural sector increasingly supports household incomes (Bouis and Haddad 1990; Estudillo et al. 2008, 2009; Estudillo and Otsuka 2016; Takayama et al. 2010; Quisumbing and McNiven 2006, 2010).

Experiencing shocks is captured by a dummy variable, which equals one if the household encountered a significant shock in the past five years. Credit constraints are indicated by a dummy variable that equals one if the household was denied credit when requested. The data reveal that credit constraints become less common at higher educational stages. Conversely, social network size increases with educational attainment, suggesting that social capital may play a role in supporting further education.

4 Empirical Analysis

4.1 Sequential Decision Continuum

We begin with the assumption that the continuity of educational demand can be understood as a series of sequential decisions made by students and their parents. Based on this framework, Fig. 1 illustrates a tree diagram depicting the probabilistic decisions at each educational stage ($S = j$).

At the initial stage ($S = 0$), children who reach the eligible age for primary school face two options: enrolling (p_0) or not enrolling ($1 - p_0$). If they do not enroll, it is assumed that educational demand ceases at this point (the same applies to the subsequent stages). For those who do enroll ($S = 1$), the next decision concerns completing and graduating from primary school ($S = 2$, with probability p_1) or not ($1 - p_1$).

Students who successfully complete primary school ($S = 2$) then decide whether to enter secondary school ($S = 3$, with probability p_2) or not ($1 - p_2$). Subsequently, those enrolled in secondary school face the decision to complete and graduate ($S = 4$, with probability p_3) or not ($1 - p_3$). Finally, students who graduate from secondary school may choose to enter tertiary education ($S = 5$, with probability p_4), as shown in Fig. 1.

The final stage of progression in this framework, tertiary enrollment ($S = 5$), is the endpoint of this analysis. The decision to exclude the next stage ($S = 6$, tertiary graduation) is due to limitations in the BPDS data, which does not specify whether individuals have completed a bachelor's degree or equivalent. While tertiary education typically requires two to four years for standard programs and even longer for specialized fields such as medicine or engineering, the data lacks information about institution types, majors, or completion statuses. Thus, this analysis focuses on progression up to tertiary enrollment ($S = 5$).

4.2 Probabilistic Framework

For observed individuals, the dependent variable in this model is the probability of reaching a specific educational stage ($S = j$) for individual i. For example, the probability of entering primary school ($S = 1$) is $\Pr(S = 1) = p_0$. The probability of completing primary school ($S = 2$) is expressed using the chain rule of conditional probability as

$$\Pr(S = 2) = \Pr(S = 2|S = 1) \cdot \Pr(S = 1) = p_1 p_0.$$

More generally, the probability of reaching stage $S = y$ is expressed as:

$$\begin{aligned}&\Pr(S = y) = \Pr(S = y|S = y - 1) \cdot \Pr(S = y - 1|S = y - 2) \cdot \cdots \cdot \\ &\Pr(S = 1|S = 0) \cdot \Pr(S = 0) \quad \text{where } \Pr(S = 0) \equiv 1,\end{aligned}$$

which simplifies to:

$$\Pr(S = y) = \prod_{j=0}^{y-1} p_j \qquad \text{where } y = 1, 2, \cdots, 5. \tag{1}$$

This sequential framework ensures that progression to any stage ($S = y$, where $y \in j$) is contingent upon the successful completion of all preceding stages ($S = y - 1, y - 2, \ldots, 1$). For instance, needless to say, students cannot proceed to tertiary education without first completing both primary and secondary education, except in rare cases involving grade skipping or accelerated advancement based on merit.

4.3 Modeling Sequential Continuity of Educational Demand

To model this sequential decision-making process, we employ a sequential logit model as outlined by Winkelmann and Boes (2009), Weiler (1986), and Buis (2010).[4] This modeling approach is particularly suitable for analyzing stage-specific probabilities in educational progression because it explicitly accounts for the conditional nature of decisions across stages. Moreover, it models the sequential process by conditioning on prior stages; region fixed effects can be included. Stage-specific idiosyncratic errors are assumed independent across stages and individuals; later stages are observed only conditional on earlier ones, so the observed outcomes across stages are not independent. No cross-stage (cross-equation) error correlation is modeled (unless additional random effects are introduced).

In the previous section, the probabilities of progression at each stage were expressed as p_j. These probabilities can be further modeled using a logistic function, allowing for the incorporation of stage-specific explanatory variables and regional unobserved heterogeneity. In this framework, the conditional probability at stage $S = j$ given $S \geq j$ is expressed as:

$$\Pr(S_i = j \mid S_i \geq j, \mathbf{X}_i; \theta) = \Lambda\big(\alpha_j + \mathbf{X}_i\beta_j\big) \tag{2}$$

where α_j represents a stage-specific constant, $\mathbf{X}_i\beta_j$ denotes the linear combination of the individual i's explanatory variables with estimated coefficients, and $\Lambda(\cdot)$ is the logistic (transformation) function. The logistic function is defined as:

$$\Lambda(z) = \frac{\exp(z)}{1 + \exp(z)}. \tag{3}$$

Letting j represent the current stage under consideration ($S = j$), while k iterates over all preceding stages ($k = 0, 1, \ldots, j - 1$) to account for cumulative conditions, the joint probability of observing an individual at a specific stage $S = j$ can then be written as:

[4] Another model, such as the nested logit model or the full information maximum likelihood (FIML) model, could also have been employed, offering greater flexibility due to its relaxed assumptions (Sawada and Lokshin 2009). Similarly, the discrete dynamic choice model (Cameron and Heckman 2001) could have been another alternative, as it accounts for dynamic decision-making processes over time. However, both approaches require more detailed stage-specific or dynamic information than was available in the current dataset (Ben-Akiva and Lerman 1985). Consequently, the sequential logit model was deemed more appropriate for this analysis, given the limited variables specific to each decision-making stage.

$$\Pr(S_i = j|\mathbf{X}_i,\ \theta) = \Pr(S_i = j|S_i \geq j, \mathbf{X}_i,\ \theta) \cdot \prod_{k=0}^{j-1} [1 - \Pr(S_i = k|S_i \geq k, \mathbf{X}_i,\ \theta)]. \tag{4}$$

This formulation simplifies to:

$$\Pr(S_i = j|\mathbf{X}_i,\ \theta) = \Lambda\big(\gamma_{0,j} + \mathbf{X}_i\gamma_j + \omega\big) \cdot \prod_{k=0}^{j-1} \big[1 - \Lambda\big(\gamma_{0,k} + \mathbf{X}_i\gamma_k + \omega\big)\big]. \tag{5}$$

where $\gamma_{0,j}$ is the stage-specific constant, $\mathbf{X}_i\gamma_j$ is the linear combination of the individual i's explanatory variables at stage j with the coefficients estimated, and ω accounts for regional heterogeneity. The term $\Lambda\big(\gamma_{0,j} + \mathbf{X}_i\gamma_j + \omega\big)$ corresponds to the conditional probability p_j at stage j introduced earlier, now expressed as a logistic function of explanatory variables and regional heterogeneity. The parameter vector $\theta = \big(\gamma_{0,j},\ \gamma_j, \omega\big)$ captures the stage-specific effects.[5] This formulation ensures that the conditional probability at each stage is influenced by the cumulative effects of all previous stages.

The dependent variable in this model is the probability $\Pr(S_i = j)$, which represents the likelihood that individual i reaches or completes a specific educational stage j. These probabilities are defined for both enrollment and completion at various levels of education. For primary and secondary education, $\Pr(S_i = 1)$ and $\Pr(S_i = 3)$ correspond to the probabilities of enrollment, while $\Pr(S_i = 2)$ and $\Pr(S_i = 4)$ represent the probabilities of completing and graduating at the respective levels. For tertiary education, $\Pr(S_i = 5)$ indicates the probability of enrollment. This framework ensures that the dependent variable reflects the sequential nature of educational progression, where the probability at each stage is contingent upon the successful completion of all preceding stages. By focusing on $\Pr(S_i = j)$ as the outcome of interest, the model captures not only the progression but also the transitions between educational stages, providing a comprehensive understanding of the factors influencing educational demand.

The sequential logit model incorporates these dependencies and estimates the joint probabilities using the maximum likelihood method.[6] Unlike single-stage logit models that treat stages independently, the sequential logit conditions on prior outcomes and models stage-specific conditional probabilities; it does not by itself model cross-equation error correlations unless additional random effects or multivariate structures are introduced, and stage-specific equations can include region

[5] The parameters γ_{0j} and γ_j represent log-odds coefficients. Given that the estimations are based on a sequential logit model, it is often convenient to interpret $\exp(\gamma)$ as odds ratios. In either case, the signs and significance levels of the estimated coefficients are critical for interpreting the results.

[6] For further precise discussions on the estimation process and methodological details, see the Appendix to this chapter.

fixed effects. This provides a comprehensive understanding of the barriers and facilitators of educational demand continuity, as depicted in Fig. 1. This figure visually represents the stages of educational progression, including enrollment, graduation, and dropout, and serves as a foundational reference for interpreting the model's structure.

5 Results

5.1 Individual Characteristics

As shown in Table 2, the parameters are estimated across ten specifications, corresponding to $S_i = 1, \cdots, 5$, with two variations: one including interaction terms between the female dummy and other variables, and the other excluding them. In specifications (1), (2), (3), (4), (7), and (8), age is found to have a significantly positive association, while age squared has a significantly negative association with the outcomes. This suggests that older individuals are more likely to have enrolled in and graduated from primary school, as well as to have graduated from secondary school, compared to younger individuals. However, this positive effect diminishes as age increases, reflecting the diminishing returns of age.

The coefficients for cohort dummies, serving as proxies for generational effects, are larger in magnitude than those for age-related variables in specifications (1)–(4). This implies that, even after accounting for individual age, the continuity of educational demand for primary and secondary education has improved over time.

Regarding the female dummy, the results indicate that, controlling for other variables, females are more likely to complete primary education and progress from entering primary or secondary education to graduating from the respective levels, compared to their male counterparts. However, for tertiary education entry, the coefficient is not statistically significant, even though the descriptive statistics show that there are slightly more women in the subsample of those who at least entered tertiary education.[7]

Interpretations of the specifications that include interaction terms between the female dummy and other variables are discussed in the next subsection.

[7] This finding is somewhat inconsistent with recent trends in the Philippines, where female enrollment in tertiary education surpasses male enrollment (Miralao 2008). A possible explanation is that, unlike the nationwide trend (more pronounced in urban centers, though), the uptake of tertiary education among women in an agriculture-dominated province such as Bukidnon during the periods of 1984–85 and 2003, reflecting around the last fifteen years of the last century, could be relatively limited.

Table 2 Results of Sequential Logit Analysis on Educational Demand Continuity (Dependent Variable: $\Pr(S = j|S \geq j)$)

Stages (j)	S = 1		S = 2		S = 3		S = 4		S = 5	
Independent variables:	(1)	(2)	(3)	(4)	(5)	(6)	(7)	(8)	(9)	(10)
Individual characteristics:										
Female dummy (=1)	−0.74	0.38	1.33	1.09	−2.74	0.72	−0.81	0.43	−2.82	0.02
	[−0.48]	[0.64]	[1.54]	[5.04]***	[−1.90]*	[2.79]***	[−0.77]	[1.94]*	[−1.75]*	[0.07]
Age	2.01	1.97	1.49	1.48	0.07	0.14	2.12	2.13	0.29	0.42
	[4.70]***	[4.77]***	[3.15]***	[3.23]***	[0.22]	[0.46]	[7.50]***	[7.57]***	[0.59]	[0.88]
Age squared	−0.04	−0.03	−0.03	−0.03	0.00	−0.01	−0.04	−0.04	−0.01	−0.01
	[−4.59]***	[−4.66]***	[−2.11]**	[−2.15]**	[−0.72]	[−1.05]	[−6.23]***	[−6.28]***	[−0.60]	[−0.80]
Generation indicator: 35–39	−11.17	−10.62	−1.77	−1.72	1.27	1.55	−1.15	−1.36	−2.02	−2.41
	[−3.76]***	[−3.77]***	[−0.46]	[−0.45]	[0.62]	[0.74]	[−0.64]	[−0.76]	[−1.19]	[−1.42]
Generation indicator: 30–34	#	#	−4.06	−3.98	0.40	0.78	−2.73	−2.81	−0.53	−1.02
			[−1.85]*	[−1.84]*	[0.22]	[0.43]	[−2.48]**	[−2.58]**	[−0.41]	[−0.80]
Generation indicator: 25–29	−13.15	−12.72	−4.20	−4.12	0.72	0.95	−2.44	−2.52	−0.74	−1.14
	[−3.72]***	[−3.69]***	[−3.71]***	[−3.67]***	[0.47]	[0.61]	[−3.20]***	[−3.32]***	[−0.72]	[−1.16]
Generation indicator: 24–20	−11.04	−10.76	−2.29	−2.23	0.26	0.29	−0.66	−0.74	−0.28	−0.50
	[−3.61]***	[−3.58]***	[−2.67]***	[−2.65]***	[0.22]	[0.25]	[−1.40]	[−1.59]	[−0.42]	[−0.80]

(continued)

Table 2 (continued)

Stages (*j*)	S = 1		S = 2		S = 3		S = 4		S = 5	
Independent variables:	(1)	(2)	(3)	(4)	(5)	(6)	(7)	(8)	(9)	(10)
Generation indicator: 15–19	−5.62	−5.34	0.52	0.55	0.53	0.54				
	[−2.55]**	[−2.43]**	[0.85]	[0.92]	[0.62]	[0.68]				
Household characteristics:										
Father's education	−0.01	0.15	0.33	0.09	0.51	0.09	0.19	0.04	0.51	0.09
	[−0.04]	[1.32]	[2.50]**	[2.03]**	[3.12]***	[1.53]	[1.50]	[1.05]	[3.20]***	[1.97]**
Mother's education	−0.15	−0.01	0.24	0.40	−0.43	0.41	−0.09	0.19	−0.42	0.17
	[−0.54]	[−0.13]	[1.68]*	[7.71]***	[−2.18]**	[5.85]***	[−0.65]	[3.69]***	[−2.21]**	[2.53]**
Female × Father's education	0.10		−0.18		−0.30		−0.10		−0.27	
	[0.47]		[−2.09]**		[−2.77]***		[−1.32]		[−2.82]***	
Female × Mother's education	0.12		0.12		0.64		0.20		0.42	
	[0.64]		[1.30]		[4.20]***		[2.06]***		[3.03]***	
Female × Number of Brothers	0.12		0.04		0.31		−0.04		0.44	
	[0.49]		[0.42]		[1.52]		[−0.32]		[2.60]***	
Number of Brothers	−0.62	−0.44	−0.06	0.01	−0.22	0.18	0.20	0.14	−0.32	0.22
	[−1.71]*	[−3.04]***	[−0.36]	[0.17]	[−0.91]	[2.43]**	[1.18]	[2.62]***	[−1.35]	[2.91]***
Number of sisters	0.26	0.02	0.33	0.25	−0.04	0.18	−0.14	0.12	0.03	0.23
	[0.82]	[0.14]	[1.89]*	[4.01]***	[−0.19]	[2.38]**	[−0.71]	[1.78]*	[0.12]	[2.73]***

(continued)

Table 2 (continued)

Stages (*j*)	S = 1		S = 2		S = 3		S = 4		S = 5	
Independent variables:	(1)	(2)	(3)	(4)	(5)	(6)	(7)	(8)	(9)	(10)
Per capita net total income	Minus	minus	zero	zero	plus	plus	zero	zero	plus	plus
	[−2.26]**	[−2.56]**	[0.18]	[0.12]	[2.14]**	[2.40]**	[0.95]	[0.95]	[2.10]**	[2.11]**
Indicator: household member with a disability	#	#	−1.02	−0.92	−0.43	−0.41	#	#	#	#
			[−1.97]**	[−1.79]*	[−0.49]	[−0.45]				
Region-specific effect:	Yes	Yes	Yes	Yes	Yes	Yes	Yes	Yes	Yes	Yes
Constant	−8.80	−10.15	−21.20	−20.77	1.45	−3.85	−28.01	−29.68	−2.77	−7.96
	[−2.53]**	[−3.53]***	[−5.10]***	[−5.19]***	[0.36]	[−1.13]	[−7.65]***	[−8.71]***	[−0.42]	[−1.36]
Log likelihood	−59.06	−59.80	−321.14	−323.30	−221.04	−234.45	−296.44	−299.20	−218.21	−229.44
No. of Observations	971	971	944	944	755	755	641	641	403	403

*$p < 0.10$; ** $p < 0.05$; ***$p < 0.01$

Notes: 1. The reported coefficients are odds ratios, and the numbers in brackets are *z*-statistics calculated using heteroscedasticity-robust standard errors
2. Coefficients for independent variables included in the equations but not statistically significant are omitted from the table. These variables include: Ilonggo-speaking indicator (=1), Ivatan-speaking indicator (=1), generation indicator (age 40 or over), Female × Number of sisters, shock experience indicators (Weather shock; Military presence), indicator for experience of loan refusal, and social network size.

Source Author's estimation using IFPRI (2000; 2008)

5.2 Same-Sex Intergenerational Influence on Educational Demand Continuity

The educational levels of parents, with the exception of the stage of primary-level entry, exhibit a significantly positive association with children's educational outcomes. Notably, the educational attainment of mothers becomes increasingly significant beyond the stage of primary-level entry. Between fathers and mothers, the coefficients for mothers' education are consistently larger in magnitude, highlighting their greater influence on children's educational progression. Interestingly, the probability of entry into tertiary education is not significantly explained by individual characteristics such as age and generation dummy variables, suggesting that household factors, such as parental education, play a more substantial role in determining college entry. While fathers' education remains relevant, mothers' education emerges as a statistically stronger predictor of children's educational attainment across generations.

The results from specifications that include interaction terms with the female dummy variable further reveal a same-sex preferential nexus between parents and children. Specifically, the negative coefficient for the interaction term "*Female* × *Fathers' education*" indicates a preferential association between fathers and sons. This finding aligns with the results presented in Chapter 2. However, an additional observation unique to this chapter is the identification of a similar same-sex preferential nexus between mothers and daughters, which was not detected in the delay analysis limited to primary education in Chapter 2.

Moreover, the coefficients for "*Female* × *Mothers' education*" are larger in magnitude than those for "Mothers' education" alone. This suggests that in the study villages of Bukidnon Province, both father–son and mother–daughter preferential associations are present regarding educational attainment. Furthermore, the mother–daughter nexus appears to exhibit a stronger influence, as evidenced by the larger coefficient magnitudes.

5.3 Household Characteristics and Regional Backgrounds

The results for household characteristics reveal notable differences in the impact of siblings on educational outcomes. The number of brothers is significantly negatively associated with primary-level entry ($S = 1$) but does not exhibit a consistent relationship at higher educational stages. In contrast, the number of sisters shows a significantly positive association, with the level of significance increasing as the educational stage progresses. The interaction term between the number of brothers and the female dummy suggests that women with more brothers are more likely to enter tertiary education ($S = 5$) than those with fewer brothers. However, a similar relationship with the number of sisters is not clearly observed.

Regarding income variables, an interesting pattern emerges. Income is significant at the stages of educational entry (i.e., $S = 1, 3, 5$) but becomes insignificant at the stages of graduation or completion (i.e., $S = 2, 4$). However, recalling the information in the descriptive statistics (in Sect. 3.3 and Table 1) reconfirms that the mean values of per capita non-agricultural and net incomes are higher as the stage $S = j$ increase. These findings suggest that household income plays a heterogeneous role across different stages, particularly influencing the decision at entering higher levels of education rather than at completing the current level.

Similarly, the shock experience indicator, which captures households where members experienced impairments, is associated with a slightly lower probability of graduating from primary education ($S = 2$) among affected households. However, this variable appears inconsistent and lacks robustness, as it was omitted from the analysis due to multicollinearity diagnostics. Moreover, regional-specific effects based on residential areas are consistently controlled for across all specifications. This demonstrates that even when location-specific unobserved factors, along with individual and household characteristics, are accounted for, the aforementioned findings remain robust.

5.4 Discussions

5.4.1 Gendered Intergenerational Continuity in Education

The analyses in this chapter reveal that the continuity of women's educational demand is robust across both econometric regression analyses using the IFPRI dataset (Table 2) as well as the descriptive statistics (Table 1). While Quisumbing and McNiven (2006) previously examined educational levels by gender in Bukidnon Province using bar graphs, this study strengthens their findings by providing an econometric foundation. The results indicate that parental education levels and same-sex parent–child education associations play a significant role. Specifically, intergenerational associations are evident not only between fathers and sons but also between mothers and daughters. While the father–son association identified in Chapter 2 is consistent with these findings, the current analysis uniquely highlights the predictive strength of the mother–daughter nexus in educational continuity.

This finding represents a significant contribution of this chapter compared to Chapter 2 and existing literature. This chapter suggests that highly educated women who later become mothers are more likely to influence their daughters' educational outcomes than their sons'. If this pattern continues, the observed gendered differences in education may persist intergenerationally. These same-sex intergenerational associations favoring women have critical implications for policies aiming to reduce gender disparities in education. Chapters 4–5 delve further into relevant perspectives to this, using another rural Philippine case.

Moreover, the parent–child educational associations strengthen as the educational stages advance, from primary to secondary and from secondary to tertiary levels. This indicates that the educational attainment of one generation is likely to be transmitted to the next, even when controlling for the female dummy variable. However, this dynamic poses a risk of reinforcing intergenerational educational inequality if left unaddressed. For instance, if fathers generally have lower educational levels than mothers and same-sex intergenerational associations are particularly pronounced in the mother–daughter relationship, policies must be designed to address boys' educational needs, considering broader societal and economic contexts. While international educational cooperation has predominantly focused on promoting girls' education, this study suggests a complementary agenda that proactively addresses men's issues (Cornwall et al. 2011), by integrating traditional approaches aimed at supporting women's empowerment.

In summary, gender differentiation in educational attainment is not uniform. Daughters with highly educated mothers are more likely to achieve higher education themselves, while sons with highly educated fathers exhibit a similar tendency. However, the mother-to-daughter association is quantitatively stronger than the father-to-son association, though the latter remains statistically significant. Overall, intergenerational educational transfers appear to be stronger for women than for men.

Lastly, while this study focuses on Mindanao Island, which is often associated with Islamic culture, the provinces of Northern Mindanao (Region X), including Bukidnon, are majority Christian, in contrast to the western and southern regions of the island. This regional variation underscores the importance of considering specific societal, economic, cultural, and religious contexts in future analyses. For instance, although beyond the scope of the current study, it is noteworthy that even in madrasahs within the Autonomous Region in Muslim Mindanao (ARMM),[8] Western Mindanao, women's educational attainment has been reported to surpass men's (Miralao 2008). Expanding the study to Muslim-majority areas within Mindanao in future would provide comparative insights and enhance the applicability of analytical frameworks to subnational diversity.

5.4.2 Understanding Bukidnon's Gendered Educational Dynamics: Local and Sociocultural Contexts

The intergenerational link in educational levels between mothers and daughters warrants closer examination. How does this connection compare to the father–son relationship? Two interpretations provide insight: the first examines the industrial context of Bukidnon Province through a review of relevant literature, and the second considers socio-anthropological studies that highlight unique aspects of Bukidnon compared to other regions in the Philippines. While the following discussion of sociocultural dynamics is hypothetical, it offers valuable perspectives for interpreting the quantitative results.

(1) **Industrial Context in Mindanao Regions**

---

[8] The former ARMM was replaced in 2019 by a new autonomous political entity, the Bangsamoro Autonomous Region in Muslim Mindanao (BARMM).

As discussed in Sect. 3 of Chapter 2, the Mindanao regions, including Bukidnon Province, differ significantly from Central Luzon in terms of agricultural practices, a topic more frequently documented for Central Luzon in past studies (Estudillo et al. 2008, 2009; Estudillo and Otsuka 2016; Takayama et al. 2010; Quisumbing and McNiven 2006). Central Luzon, renowned for its rice farming, experienced transformative benefits from the Green Revolution. In contrast, Bukidnon Province, with its reliance on corn farming and limited rice cultivation, did not undergo comparable agricultural modernization (Nakanishi 2001).

Bukidnon's economic landscape has been shaped by several key factors. First, the development of non-agricultural sectors and associated employment opportunities has been relatively limited compared to regions like Central Luzon. Second, the local sugarcane industry, a significant part of Bukidnon's economy, has faced fluctuations in international sugar prices (Takayama et al. 2010). Third, corn farming, the predominant agricultural activity in Bukidnon, has not achieved the same levels of yield increases or technological advancements as rice farming in Luzon. Finally, although non-agricultural sectors are essential for poverty reduction and socioeconomic development (Estudillo et al. 2008, 2009; Estudillo and Otsuka 2016), these sectors' growth in Bukidnon during the BPDS period was limited (Bouis and Haddad 1990; Takayama et al. 2010). Consequently, both employment and job opportunities outside agriculture were predominantly in public-sector roles, such as teaching and civil service, rather than in the private sector (Takayama et al. 2010).[9]

These economic conditions may help explain households' tendency in Bukidnon to prioritize daughters' education over sons'. Daughters are more likely to pursue higher education and secure public sector jobs requiring formal qualifications, such as teaching and civil-service roles,[10] while sons are often expected to continue agricultural work, which typically requires less formal education. This dynamic underscores Bukidnon's dependence on the public sector as a primary source of employment outside agriculture, contrasting sharply with the growth of private service sectors in Luzon.

(2) Sociocultural Context in Bukidnon Province

Sociocultural contexts of Bukidnon offer further insights into the observed mother–daughter educational nexus. Social anthropology provides valuable insights

[9] Recent developments in non-agricultural sectors, including a shift toward high-value crops (HVCs) as an emerging trend, are noteworthy (Estudillo and Otsuka 2016: 87). This contrasts with the earlier periods, such as those of Bouis and Haddad (1990), who analyzed data from 1984–85; Bouis et al. (1998), who used non-public ethnographic data from 1992; and Quisumbing and McNiven (2006) and Takayama et al. (2010), who based their findings on 2003 data. More recently, HVC yields have risen both within and beyond Luzon, extending into the Visayas. HVCs include high-value fruits (e.g., mangoes, papayas), vegetables (e.g., lettuce, *ampalaya* [bitter gourd]), horticultural products (e.g., orchids, roses, ornamental plants), and aquaculture products (e.g., shrimp, fish). This shift towards HVCs represents a form of crop diversification. However, whether this trend has extended across Mindanao regions, including Bukidnon, remains under-researched. Bouis and Haddad (1990) indicated that Bukidnon historically served as a central region for sugar production and fruit cultivation, with significant foreign capital involvement.

[10] This perspective is related to Chapter 6.

into kinship structures and genealogical settings. Research on Southeast Asian societies highlights the Philippines as relatively unique due to its bilateral kinship system, where genealogies are traced through both maternal and paternal lines, and property is inherited equally (Kikuchi 1980; Ofstedal et al. 1999).

However, Sudo (1989) documented that Bukidnon society had matrilineal tendencies, rather than patrilineal or bilateral (Sudo 1989: 17).[11] Matrilineal societies, where descent and inheritance are traced through the maternal line, are relatively uncommon worldwide. According to Sudo (1989: 14), the complex structures in matrilineality, where male authority and managerial roles tended to be weaker than in patrilineal societies, were susceptible to erosion due to influences from surrounding patrilineal groups, population increases, and the spread of the cash economy. In matrilineal contexts, decision-making authority and intrafamilial bargaining power are more closely associated with female family members, and kinship and descent are reckoned through the female line.

While it is essential to avoid overgeneralizing anthropological findings, we treat the foregoing ethnographic observations as contextual background that may shape intrahousehold resource allocation and power dynamics, particularly between fathers and mothers and between sons and daughters, rather than as a province-wide or time-invariant classification. Given that the regional heterogeneity term ω in the sequential discrete choice analysis absorbs unobserved contextual differences, we interpret the observed mother–daughter association as consistent with (but not necessarily identified as caused by) such kinship-related norms.[12]

5.4.3 Barriers to Educational Continuity: Income Constraints and Transition Dynamics

The sequential discrete choice analysis reveals that the probabilities of enrolling in primary education and progressing to secondary education are relatively high. Most individuals are likely to enroll in primary education, which is compulsory and tuition-free, and subsequently transition to secondary education upon graduating from the primary level. This indicates that "graduation from the previous stage" and "entry into the next stage" are generally contiguous processes.

However, the analysis also demonstrates that income variables play a significant role in influencing the decision to "enter" the next educational stage (enrollment

[11] It is important to note that Sudo's (1989) geographic mapping identified matrilineal tendencies in specific localities within Bukidnon Province; it should not be read as a uniform, province-wide, or contemporary classification, nor does it extend to other provinces such as Marinduque Province (the focus of Chapters 4–6) and Antique Province (discussed in Chapter 7) in this book.

[12] It is important to acknowledge that contemporary anthropologists caution against conflating everyday-life practices with deeper anthropological structures, such as matrilineality. While matrilineal systems may provide valuable context, directly attributing econometric findings—such as the positive intergenerational association between daughters and mothers observed in this chapter—to those structures is unwarranted without additional evidence. A more nuanced interdisciplinary approach would be needed to fully probe these complexities.

and progression), rather than to "graduate" from the current stage. This highlights the heterogeneous impact of income across educational stages, with a particularly strong effect observed during transitions to higher education levels. In other words, the continuity of educational demand tends to fluctuate or decline at these critical entry points, where economically disadvantaged individuals and households often encounter income and credit constraints when investing in human capital (de Janvry and Sadoulet 2021; Lochner and Monge-Naranjo 2012; Heckman et al. 2006). These findings emphasize the enduring importance of financial support and stipends, particularly for economically marginalized households, in sustaining continuity in educational demand.

6 Conclusion

This chapter extends the findings of Chapter 2 by focusing on the continuity of educational demand across primary, secondary, and tertiary stages. It offers extended insights into how intergenerational and gendered dynamics shape educational progression in Bukidnon Province, highlighting the importance of interventions tailored to local socioeconomic conditions. Expanding on this foundation, this chapter identifies a nuanced pattern of intergenerational educational associations. While Chapter 2 emphasized the father–son association, this chapter demonstrates that the mother–daughter nexus is even stronger, particularly at higher educational stages. This finding has significant policy implications. It highlights the importance of tailoring educational support to address both boys' underperformance and girls' educational progression in rural, resource-constrained settings. For example, while promoting girls' education remains critical, additional interventions targeting boys' education, particularly in the context of intergenerational dynamics, play a pivotal role in achieving greater equity (DiPrete and Eirich 2006).

The observed educational dynamics are deeply intertwined with Bukidnon's economic and sociocultural contexts. Economically, Bukidnon's reliance on agriculture, particularly corn farming and the sugarcane industry, contrasts sharply with the more developed non-agricultural sectors in regions like Central Luzon (Takayama et al. 2010). Limited industrial and service sector growth in Bukidnon has historically limited economic diversification and the returns from human capital investments (Estudillo et al. 2008, 2009; Nakanishi 2001; Quisumbing and McNiven 2006). These have influenced educational priorities within households. They appear to prioritize daughters' education as a pathway to public-sector employment, such as teaching and civil service, which requires higher levels of formal education. In contrast, sons are often expected to continue in agricultural work, which demands less formal education. This gendered investment pattern reflects Bukidnon's economic structure and contrasts with the dynamics observed in more urbanized or more agricultural regions.

The sequential discrete choice analysis further reveals that income constraints disproportionately affect transitions between educational stages. While enrolling in primary education and progressing to secondary education are relatively common due to free tuition and compulsory policies, income constraints emerge as critical barriers at transition points to higher education levels (Lochner and Monge-Naranjo 2012; Heckman et al. 2006). These findings underscore the importance of targeted financial interventions, such as scholarships and conditional cash transfers, to support educational continuity for economically disadvantaged households.

These findings suggest that educational investments targeting female students beyond secondary school may contribute not only to individual attainment, but also to a structural pattern of intergenerational continuity (DiPrete and Eirich 2006). In many rural contexts, where institutional resources are limited, supporting girls' transitions to higher education remains an important and legitimate priority. Mothers with higher levels of education function as transmitters of aspiration, especially for daughters, potentially reinforcing a positive trajectory of female educational mobility. At the same time, in the context of boys' lags, this dynamic may also exacerbate boys' marginalization in households lacking sufficient maternal educational capital. Accordingly, gender-responsive policies should be designed not only to support successful pathways but also to identify and address points of exclusion, at which educational continuity fails to take root.

Taken together with the findings from Chapter 2, which revealed how boys in the same region face significant delays in educational progression, this chapter illustrates a structural asymmetry in gendered educational trajectories. While boys are more likely to fall behind or drop out at critical junctures, girls—particularly those with educated mothers—are positioned to continue their schooling across stages. This asymmetry is not incidental but socially and institutionally embedded, suggesting that gendered educational outcomes are not merely individual but structurally patterned within family dynamics and policy environments.

Despite its contributions, this study is not without limitations. Specifically, the data derived from IFPRI surveys conducted in 1984–85 and 2003 may not fully capture contemporary trends in educational and socioeconomic dynamics. Additionally, individual-level data on school attendance, study habits, and detailed school-related factors were limited. Future research is expected to incorporate more recent primary and administrative datasets to address these gaps and provide a more comprehensive understanding of educational demand continuity. In this regard, the subsequent chapters (Chapters 4 onward) address these perspectives through their respective approaches and focal points, using more recent and primary data-based sources.

In conclusion, this chapter has revealed how intergenerational influences, economic constraints, and local contexts jointly shape gendered educational trajectories in Bukidnon. These insights contribute to the broader understanding of how reversal patterns are sustained and how targeted policy interventions can promote educational equity in structurally disadvantaged regions, by addressing a form of hysteresis (Dutt 2023) whereby early disadvantage triggers cumulative (dis)advantage, leading to greater and more persistent inequality within and across groups over time (DiPrete and Eirich 2006).

Appendix

This appendix provides an overview of the maximum likelihood estimation (MLE) method used for the sequential logit model in this study, building on the methodologies outlined in Winkelmann and Boes (2009) and Buis (2010). As described in the main sections, this sequential logit framework models educational continuation as a series of conditional decisions, reflecting the reality that students must pass through each stage before advancing to the next. Each logit function estimates the likelihood of continuing at a specific stage, conditional on having completed the previous one.

In this framework, the probability of an individual being at stage $S_i = j$, given $S_i \geq j$, is expressed using a logistic function. The conditional probability is defined as:

$$\Pr\left(S_i = j \mid S_i \geq j, \mathbf{X}_i; \theta\right) = \frac{\exp\left(\gamma_{0,j} + \mathbf{X}_i\gamma_j + \omega\right)}{1 + \exp\left(\gamma_{0,j} + \mathbf{X}_i\gamma_j + \omega\right)},$$

where $\gamma_{0,j}$ represents the stage-specific constant; $\mathbf{X}_i\gamma_j$ is the linear combination of explanatory variables $\mathbf{X}_i$ at stage j; ω accounts for location-specific heterogeneity; and $\theta = \left(\gamma_{0,j}, \gamma_j\right)$ is the vector of all stage-specific parameters.

The likelihood function for the entire sample is constructed as the product of the conditional probabilities for all individuals across all stages. This is expressed as:

$$L(\theta) = \prod_{i=1}^{N}\prod_{j=1}^{5} \Pr(S_i = j|S_i \geq j, \mathbf{X}_i; \theta)^{y_{ij}},$$

where $y_{ij} = 1$ if individual i is at stage j and $y_{ij} = 0$ otherwise; and N denotes the total number of individuals in the sample. By taking the natural logarithm of this likelihood function, the log-likelihood function is derived as:

$$\ln L(\theta) = \sum_{i=1}^{N}\sum_{j=1}^{5} y_{ij} \ln \Pr(S_i = j|S_i \geq j, \mathbf{X}_i; \theta).$$

To estimate the parameters θ, the log-likelihood function is maximized numerically. This process involves iterative methods such as the Newton–Raphson algorithm. The gradient of the log-likelihood function with respect to θ is computed as:

$$\frac{\partial \ln L(\theta)}{\partial \theta} = \sum_{i=1}^{N}\sum_{j=1}^{5} \frac{\partial \ln \Pr(S_i = j|S_i \geq j, \mathbf{X}_i; \theta)}{\partial \theta}.$$

The Hessian matrix, $\mathbf{H}(\theta)$, representing the second derivative of the log-likelihood function, is expressed as:

$$\mathbf{H}(\theta) = \frac{\partial^2 \ln L(\theta)}{\partial\theta\partial\theta^T}.$$

Using the gradient and Hessian, the Newton–Raphson algorithm updates the parameter estimates iteratively. The parameter vector at iteration $t + 1$ is updated as[13]:

$$\theta^{(t+1)} = \theta^{(t)} - \mathbf{H}^{-1}\left(\theta^{(t)}\right) \cdot \frac{\partial \ln L\left(\theta^{(t)}\right)}{\partial\theta}.$$

The process continues until convergence is achieved, which is determined by the magnitude of the gradient approaching zero or the change in parameter estimates falling below a predefined threshold. The final estimates of θ provide the stage-specific coefficients and other model parameters that best fit the observed data within the sequential logit framework.

This estimation approach is particularly well-suited for analyzing sequential dependencies in educational decision-making. By accounting for the conditional probabilities at each stage, the sequential logit model enables a detailed understanding of the factors influencing progression and dropout decisions at multiple educational stages in the model of this chapter.

References

Andrew M (2014) The scarring effects of primary-grade retention? A study of cumulative advantage in the educational career. Social Forces 93(2):653–685. https://doi.org/10.1093/sf/sou074

Becker GS, Lewis HG (1973) On the interaction between the quantity and quality of children. J Polit Econ 81(2):S279–S288. https://doi.org/10.1086/260166

Behrman JR (1997) Mother's schooling and child education: a survey. Penn Institute for Economic Research (PIER) Working Paper No. 97–025. PA: PIER, University of Pennsylvania

Behrman JR, Knowles JC (1999) Household income and child schooling in Vietnam. World Bank Econ Rev 13(2):211–256. https://doi.org/10.1093/wber/13.2.211

Ben-Akiva M, Lerman SR (1985) Discrete choice analysis: Theory and application to travel demand. MIT Press, Cambridge, MA

Black SE, Devereux PJ, Salvanes KG (2005) The more the Merrier? The effect of family size and birth order on children's education. Quart J Econ 120(2):669–700. https://doi.org/10.1093/qje/120.2.669

Boudet AMM, Petesch P, Turk C, Thumala A (2013) On norms and agency: Conversations about gender equality with women and men in 20 countries. Directions in development: human development. World Bank, Washington, DC. https://doi.org/10.1596/978-0-8213-9862-3

Bouis HE, Haddad LJ (1990) Agricultural commercialization, nutrition, and the rural poor: a study of Philippine farm households. Lynne Rienner, Boulder and London

Bouis HE, Palabrica-Costello M, Solon O, Westbrook D, Limbo AB (1998) Gender equality and investments in adolescents in the rural Philippines. International Food Policy Research Institute, Washington, DC

13 The parentheses around t in $\theta^{(t)}$ clarify that t denotes the iteration index, not an exponent.

Buis M (2010) Inequality of educational outcome and inequality of educational opportunity in the Netherlands during the 20th century. Faculty of Social Sciences, University of Amsterdam, Amsterdam

Cameron SV, Heckman JJ (2001) The dynamics of educational attainment for Black, Hispanic, and White Males. J Polit Econ 109(3):455–499. http://dx.doi.org/10.1086/321014

Caoli-Rodriguez R (2007) "The Philippines country case study", Country profile prepared for the education for all global monitoring report 2008: education for all by 2015: will we make it? United Nations Educational, Scientific and Cultural Organization, Paris

Cornwall A, Edström J, Greig A (eds) (2011) Men and development: Politicising masculinities. Zed Books Ltd., New York

de Janvry A, Sadoulet E (2021) Development economics: Theory and practice, 2nd edn. Routledge, Abingdon. https://doi.org/10.4324/9781003024545

DiPrete TA, Eirich GM (2006) Cumulative advantage as a mechanism for inequality: A review of theoretical and empirical developments. Annual Rev Sociology 32(1):271–297. https://doi.org/10.1146/annurev.soc.32.061604.123127

Dutt AK (2023) Hysteresis and path dependence in economic analysis: formalizations causes and implications. Rev Keynesian Econ 11(4):435–459. https://doi.org/10.4337/roke.2023.04.01

Estudillo JP, Otsuka K (2016) Moving out of poverty: An inquiry into inclusive growth in Asia. Routledge, New York. https://doi.org/10.4324/9781315673547

Estudillo JP, Sawada Y, Otsuka K (2008) Poverty and income dynamics in Philippine Villages 1985–2004. Rev Dev Econ 12(4):877–890. https://doi.org/10.1111/j.1467-9361.2008.00458.x

Estudillo JP, Sawada Y, Otsuka K (2009) Income dynamics, schooling investment, and poverty reduction in Philippine villages, 1985–2004. In Otsuka K, Estudillo JP, Sawada Y (eds) Rural poverty and income dynamics in Asia and Africa. Routledge, New York, pp 22–46. https://doi.org/10.4324/9780203885055-7

Glewwe P, Jacoby HG (1995) An economic analysis of delayed primary school enrollment in a low-income country: The role of early childhood nutrition. Rev Econ Stat 77(1):156–169. https://doi.org/10.2307/2110001

Grant MJ, Behrman JR (2010) Gender gaps in educational attainment in less developed countries. Popul Dev Rev 36(1):71–89. https://doi.org/10.1111/j.1728-4457.2010.00318.x

Hanushek EA, Victor L, Hitomi K (2008) Do students care about school quality? Determinants of dropout behavior in developing countries. J Hum Cap 2(1):69–105. https://doi.org/10.1086/529446

Heckman JJ, Lochner L, Todd P (2006) Earnings functions, rates of return, and treatment effects: The Mincer equation and beyond. In Hanushek EA, Welch F (eds) Handbook of the economics of education 1. Elsevier, Amsterdam, pp 307–458. https://doi.org/10.1016/S1574-0692(06)01007-5

International Food Policy Research Institute (IFPRI) (2000) Philippines cash cropping project, Southern Bukidnon Province, 1984–1985 (Datasets). IFPRI, Washington, DC

International Food Policy Research Institute (IFPRI) (2008) Philippines: Bukidnon panel survey, 2003–2004 (datasets). IFPRI, Washington, DC

Keely CB. (1973) Philippine migration: Internal movements and emigration to the United States. Int Migr Rev 7(2):177–187. https://doi.org/10.1177/019791837300700204

Kikuchi Y (1980) Social anthropology of the Philippines (*Firipin no shakai zinruigaku*). Keibundo Press, Tokyo (in Japanese)

Lochner L, Monge-Naranjo A (2012) Credit constraints in education. Annual Rev Econ 4(1):225–256. https://doi.org/10.1146/annurev-economics-080511-110920

Miralao VA (2008) Towards post-feminism in Philippine education. In Bernado A (ed) The paradox of Philippine education and education reform: Social scientific perspectives. Philippine Social Science Council, Quezon City

Nakanishi T (2001) Two-class system in economic development: The Philippines (Firipin no nikaisō shakai to minshu shugi: Chūkansō no seichō niyoru henka no kanōsei). In Sato Y (ed) Economic

and social policies in newly democratized countries (*Shinkō minshu shugi koku no keizai, shakai seisaku*). Institute of Developing Economies, Chiba (in Japanese)
Okabe M (2017) Empirical analysis of the continuity of sequential demands for education in a rural Philippines: Gender and parent–child relations. (Firipin mindanao nōsonbu niwokeru kyōikujuyō no jizokusei nikansuru shakaikeizai bunseki: jendā to kyōiku suijun no sedaikankankei ni chakumoku shite.) Asian Stud 63(1):1–26. [Japanese] https://doi.org/10.11479/asianstudies.63.1_1
Ofstedal MB, Knodel J, Chayovan N (1999) Intergenerational support and gender: A comparison of four Asian countries. Asian J Soc Sci 27(2):21–41. https://doi.org/10.1163/030382499X00039
Okabe M (2018) 'K to 12' Program as a national HRD to develop the workforce. Philippine J Labor Ind Relat 35(1–2):124–140. https://www.journals.upd.edu.ph/index.php/pjlir/article/view/7449
Quisumbing AR (1994) Intergenerational transfers in Philippine rice villages: Gender differences in traditional inheritance customs. J Dev Econ 43(2):167–195. https://doi.org/10.1016/0304-3878(94)90003-5
Quisumbing AR, McNiven S (2006) Migration and rural-urban continuum: Evidence from Bukidnon, Philippines. Philippine J Dev 33(1–2):1–43
Quisumbing AR, McNiven S (2010) Moving forward, looking back: The impact of migration and remittances on assets, consumption, and credit constraints in the rural Philippines. J Dev Stud 46(1):91–113. https://doi.org/10.1080/00220380903197960
Sawada Y, Lokshin M (2009) Obstacles to school progression in rural Pakistan: An analysis of gender and sibling rivalry using field survey data. J Dev Econ 88(2):335–347. https://doi.org/10.1016/j.jdeveco.2008.03.002
Slater PB (1977) Nodal migration regions of the Philippines. Philippine Statistician 26(3–4):35–41
Sudo K (1989) The structure in matrilineal societies (Bokei shakai no kozō). Kinokuniya Shoten Press, Tokyo (in Japanese)
Symaco LP (2013) The Philippines: education issues and challenges. In Symaco LP (ed) Education in South-East Asia, Bloomsbury New York, pp 191–212. https://doi.org/10.5040/9781472544469.ch-010
Takayama N, Fuwa N, Yurugi T (2010) The role of non-agricultural sectors in rural poverty reduction: A case study in Mindanao, Philippines. Japanese J Southeast Asian Stud 48(1):46–73 [Japanese]. https://doi.org/10.20495/tak.48.1_46
Weiler W (1986) A sequential logit model of the access effects of higher education institutions. Econ Educ Rev 5(1):49–55. https://doi.org/10.1016/0272-7757(86)90162-7
Winkelmann R, Boes S (2009) Analysis of microdata, 2nd edn. Springer-Verlag, Berlin

Chapter 4
Mothers to Sons?—Maternal Labor Force Participation, Child Time Allocations, and Boys' Educational Disengagement: Evidence from Marinduque, MIMAROPA, Southern Luzon

Abstract This chapter examines how mothers' labor force participation (MLFP) affects pro-educational child time allocation patterns, focusing on boys' educational disengagement, using evidence from Marinduque Province. Using time-use data collected from rural households, the study explores MLFP as a contributing factor to gender disparities in children's pro-educational time allocation. To identify the causal effect of MLFP, the analysis leverages exogenous changes in the regional labor market as an instrumental variable. The unintended effect of MLFP, defined in this study as its differential impact on boys' and girls' time allocation patterns, is explored through two mechanisms: first, a "role model" effect, where daughters emulate the occupational stability of formally employed mothers, often tied to higher educational qualifications; and second, reduced maternal supervision, which disproportionately affects boys, leading to diminished engagement in pro-educational activities. These findings illuminate how mothers' employment reshapes gendered patterns in children's pro-educational time use under conditions of poverty. By analyzing the unintended consequences of MLFP on children's time allocation patterns, this chapter offers critical insights for addressing gender disparities in pro-educational engagement through family dynamics.

Keywords Child time use · Daily activities · Mothers' labor force participation · Role model · Supervision

1 Introduction

The preceding chapters have explored gendered patterns in educational attainment, revealing significant parent–child intergenerational linkages and gender disparities. Chapter 2 highlighted that boys in Bukidnon experienced substantial delays in educational progression compared to girls, with these delays strongly linked to fathers'

This chapter is adapted from part of Okabe (2025).

M. Okabe, *Economics of the Reversal in Gender Disparities in Education and Development*, Economics, Law, and Institutions in Asia Pacific,
https://doi.org/10.1007/978-981-96-9271-2_4

lower educational attainment. This father–son linkage raises concerns about the intergenerational persistence of educational inefficiencies without targeted policy interventions. Chapter 3 extended this analysis to higher levels of education, revealing that maternal influence becomes increasingly prominent for daughters as they progress through secondary and tertiary education stages. This finding aligns with broader evidence on the significance of maternal education in shaping children's outcomes, particularly for girls.

Building on these insights, this chapter delves further into such family dynamics by examining how mothers' labor force participation (MLFP) influences children's allocation of time to educational activities. The analysis sheds light on household-level mechanisms that contribute to gendered disparities in educational time use, offering a more nuanced understanding of these dynamics. Past studies have shown that MLFP is both a necessity for income generation and a response to shifting gender norms in many low- and middle-income countries (Blau and Kahn 2007; Jensen 2012). While maternal employment often provides critical financial support for households, it can also reshape intrahousehold dynamics, redistributing responsibilities among family members. For both sons and daughters, these shifts may increase their involvement in household chores or income-generating tasks, which in turn can reduce the time they devote to schooling and study (Basu et al. 2010; Glick 2008).

Having said that, the growing participation of women in the labor force, especially in developing countries, is often regarded as a positive outcome of female empowerment and socioeconomic progress (ADB 2020; Blundell et al. 2016; Cabegin and Gaddi 2019; Duflo 2012). However, despite the growing relevance of MLFP, its implications for children's education remain complex and contested due partly to the background stated in the last paragraph. Some studies indicate that MLFP can positively affect children's academic performance through increased household income, while others suggest negative consequences, such as reduced parental supervision (Afridi et al. 2016; Bianchi and Milkie 2010; Bertrand and Pan 2013; Cawley and Liu 2007; Cortes 2015; Ermisch and Francesconi 2013; Goldin 1995; Grootaert and Kanbur 1995; McKenzie and Rapoport 2011; Meyerhoefer and Chen 2011; Nazier and Ezzat 2022; Sawada et al. 2006).

This chapter focuses on how MLFP shapes child time-allocation patterns in a rural Philippine context, with particular attention to the gendered implications of these patterns on educational outcomes. Existing literature has established the importance of time use in determining educational outcomes, with time spent on learning activities correlating positively with academic performance (Ahn and Yoo 2022; Larson and Verma 1999; McHale et al. 2001). However, fewer studies have examined the relationship between MLFP and children's time use in developing countries (Esquivel et al. 2008; Field et al. 2023; Hirway 2010; Lloyd et al. 2008; Nazier and Ezzat 2022; Nguyen et al. 2022; Williams et al. 2016).

Our study reveals that MLFP exacerbates a gendered gap in time-allocation patterns between sons and daughters, based on original data collected in rural villages in the Philippines. For instance, boys may spend more time on leisure activities and less on studying, while girls are more likely to devote their time to homework and other educational tasks. This chapter explores how this "unintended" effect of

MLFP—defined in this study as the differential impacts on boys' and girls' pro-educational time allocation patterns—reflects how maternal employment is shaped by existing gender norms. In comparison, fathers' labor force participation (FLFP) also influences children's time use, but the results indicate that it has a less pronounced effect compared to MLFP.

The unintended effect of MLFP is analyzed through two mechanisms: (1) a "role model" effect, where daughters emulate the occupational stability of formally employed mothers with higher educational qualifications, and (2) reduced maternal supervision, which disproportionately impacts boys, reducing their engagement in pro-educational activities. These findings illuminate how mothers' employment reshapes gendered patterns in children's pro-educational time use under conditions of poverty.

This study leverages primary data collected from Marinduque, a province in the MIMAROPA region of the Philippines, to provide a granular understanding of how MLFP influences child time-allocation patterns. By utilizing original time-use surveys and household interviews, this analysis offers unique insights beyond those provided by publicly available datasets, such as the IFPRI dataset used in earlier chapters. It seeks to uncover household-level mechanisms that contribute to broader gendered educational disparities (Ilahi, 2010).

The structure of the chapter is as follows: Sect. 2 reviews the conceptual framework. Section 3 details the data collection process and defines "pro-educational" time allocation among children. Section 4 introduces the empirical model, estimation methods, and identification strategy. Section 5 presents and discusses the findings. Finally, Sect. 6 concludes by discussing the policy implications of these findings, including recommendations for mitigating gendered disparities in educational outcomes, and outlines potential directions for future research.

2 Conceptual Framework

2.1 Trinity of Education, Labor, and Leisure

In developing countries, children's daily lives are shaped by the competing demands of education, labor, and leisure. This trinity reflects the allocation of time and resources within households, heavily influenced by socioeconomic conditions such as household poverty and cultural norms (Bouis et al. 1998; Estudillo et al. 2001, 2008; Fuwa 2014; Mapa 2021; Quisumbing 1994; Torres 2011; Yamauchi and Tiongco 2013). The time required for education often conflicts with the economic necessity of labor and the social preference for leisure, particularly among boys (Larson and Verma 1999). Some studies suggest stereotypical views of boys as lazy and girls as diligent (Bouis et al. 1998; UNGEI 2012; Torres 2011), making it essential to examine pro-educational behavior from children's perspectives.

Boys in developing countries frequently face a precarious balance between these three domains. Time-use studies have shown that boys allocate more time to labor and leisure activities than girls, whose time is disproportionately spent on household chores *and/or* studying (McHale et al. 2001; Williams et al. 2016). This imbalance is often exacerbated by poverty, which necessitates children's participation in income-generating activities, and by cultural expectations that frame boys as future breadwinners (Nguyen et al. 2022). Within this context, MLFP acts as a critical yet complex variable that influences how children navigate the trinity of education, labor, and leisure.

In economic studies, families are often viewed as adult-governed units where children are not central to decision-making (Browning et al. 2014; Deaton 1997, Chap. 4; Eswaran 2014), leading to assumptions that educational investments are primarily adult-driven. However, empirical studies show that children are key contributors to their own human capital investment. For instance, children in Mexico develop subjective expectations about their education (Attanasio and Kaufmann 2009, 2014), and in the US, children's time investments influence their test scores more than their mothers' (Del Boca et al. 2017). Time is a critical resource for education, and students' time investments strongly affect educational outcomes (Williams et al. 2016; Nguyen et al. 2022; Xu et al. 2022).

Thus far, time-use studies have been conducted in economics, sociology, and related social sciences. Existing time-use surveys are concentrated mainly on developed countries, and their central interest is time allocations of adults about work (either paid or unpaid [care] work), rather than juveniles (Dinkelman and Ngai 2022; Esquivel et al. 2008; Field et al. 2023; Lloyd et al. 2008; Nazier and Ezzat 2022; Nguyen et al. 2022; Williams et al. 2016). It reflects motivations to recalculate and reevaluate values added by unpaid and domestic work primarily contributed by women to impute into the system of national accounts (Boserup 1970; Cabegin and Gaddi 2019; Chen et al. 2005; Dong and An 2015; Esquivel et al. 2008; Nazier and Ezzat 2022). The literature emphasizes the limited time-use surveys in developing countries, particularly among school-aged adolescents (Esquivel et al. 2008; Lloyd et al. 2008; Seymour et al. 2020; Sharma and Bisht 2022).

One characteristic that distinguishes developing countries from developed countries is the higher extent to which children engage in labor activities that compete with education. As children become physically mature, it is common for them to be considered not only as students but also as labor-force members (Estudillo et al. 2001; Torres 2011; Quisumbing 1994). Child labor and education are often seen as being in a tradeoff, with working children allocating time to labor at the expense of education (Acosta 2011; Alcaraz et al. 2012; Beegle et al. 2009; Borga 2019; Edmonds and Shrestha 2014; Heady 2003; Bai and Wang 2020; Patrinos and Psacharopoulos 1997; Psacharopoulos 1997; Ravallion and Wodon 2000; Reggio 2011).

However, some studies question this direct tradeoff. For example, Ravallion and Wodon (2000) show that while a school-fee subsidy increased school attendance in

Bangladesh, it did not proportionally reduce working time.[1] Similarly, Fuwa et al. (2006) and Kurosaki et al. (2006) find no clear inverse relationship between child labor and school enrolment in India, highlighting the need to consider leisure time explicitly in time-allocation studies. Sociologists also pay special attention to leisure time (Jacobs et al. 2004). From the literature, one study shares a similar motivation as ours (Pörtner 2016) and acknowledges the importance of leisure among child time allocations. However, their measure passively captures residual leisure time amid schooling and labor activities. We capture leisure time more explicitly and incorporate it with the time spent on education to provide a "pro-educational" time-allocation pattern in the gender-comparison framework (see Sects. 3.3 and 3.4).

2.2 *Gendered Impacts of MLFP on Child Education*

MLFP has become increasingly prevalent in many developing countries, driven by both economic necessity and shifts in gender norms (Duflo 2012; Jensen 2012). Since the last century, female labor force participation rates have recently grown in some developing countries in Asia and the Pacific, which is viewed as a positive consequence of female empowerment and development, as introduced in the introduction section. While MLFP can enhance household income and improve access to educational resources, it also reshapes family dynamics in ways that have gendered consequences for children's time allocation (Afridi et al. 2016; Bertrand and Pan 2013). Therefore, the impact of increasing MLFP on children's well-being has become a matter of public concern (Antman 2013: 296).

The literature presents, however, a mixed and sometimes inconclusive picture regarding the effects of MLFP on child welfare, with some showing positive impacts and others suggesting negative ones; additionally, some find only minor associations (Afridi et al. 2016; Antman 2013; Cawley and Liu 2007; Cortes 2015; Ermisch and Francesconi 2013; Fertig et al. 2009; Grootaert and Kanbur 1995; Grootaert and Patrinos 1999, 2002; Haveman and Wolfe 1995; Le and Nguyen 2020; Meyerhoefer and Chen 2011; Nazier and Ezzat 2022; Nankinga et al. 2019; Shajan and Sumalatha 2022; Sawada et al. 2006). Notably, the introduction of child gender combinations further adds complexity to these findings (Grootaert and Kanbur 1995: 192; Parish and Willis 1993; Sawada et al. 2006; Strauss and Thomas 1995: 1990).

The varying results from the literature can be attributed to the emphasis placed on either MLFP's positive influence of increasing household income or the negative influence of maternal absence. The former suggests that the additional earnings positively contribute to child well-being, whereas the latter posits that working parents have less time to spend with their children, which can have detrimental

[1] The subsidy certainly "reduced the incidence of child labor," but "the reduction in the incidence of child labour [sic] by boys (girls) represents" only "about one quarter (eighth) of the increase in their school enrolment rate." The authors interpreted this to mean that parents valued their children's leisure time (Ravallion and Wodon 2000: C173).

effects (Antman 2011; Bertrand and Pan 2013; Cawley and Liu 2007; Desai and Devaki 1994; Grootaert and Kanbur 1995: 192; Nankinga et al. 2019; Parreñas 2007; Rubiano-Matulevich and Viollaz 2019; Sayer et al. 2004; Yang 2008). The negative consequences of MLFP can also be attributed to the substitution of household chores with children when their mothers work (Afridi et al. 2016; Fuwa et al. 2012; Sawada et al. 2006). In addition, Bertrand and Pan (2013) highlight the importance of parental involvement, particularly for male children during their adolescent years. Therefore, this study investigates the impact of MLFP on child time allocation patterns while considering the income contributed by working mothers. By controlling for the income, we can better understand the specific effects of MLFP on children's daily activities.

For boys, MLFP often results in an increase in their autonomy and in reduced mothers' supervision, leading to a greater likelihood of spending time on leisure activities or labor at the expense of studying (Cortes 2015; Esquivel et al. 2008). This trend reinforces existing stereotypes about boys' lower academic engagement and contributes to widening gender disparities in educational outcomes (UNGEI 2012; Torres 2011). Conversely, girls are typically expected to assume additional household responsibilities in the absence of maternal supervision, limiting their time for education but also fostering higher levels of academic diligence in some cases (Nguyen et al. 2022; Hirway 2010). These consequences highlight that, while MLFP alleviates financial pressures, it often intensifies the caregiving and labor demands placed on children. This dynamic underscores the importance of examining how MLFP intersects with cultural norms and household structures to shape boys' and girls' educational trajectories.

3 Data[2]

3.1 Research Site and Data Collection in Marinduque

As discussed in Chap. 1, despite the countrywide indices, literature, and government reports shown there, the severity of "underperformance," "disengagement," or "crisis" of boys in the Philippines is more pronounced in rural provincial regions than in urban centers (Philippine Statistics Authority 2017, 2021). The country's average gender parity index for secondary education is nearly 1.2, which indicates that about 20% more female students than male students are enrolled at the secondary level. The urban–rural contrast indicates: Metro Manila (urban) has its low rate closest to zero while other rural and provincial regions have their lower rates like MIMAROPA, Zamboanga Peninsula, and Cordillera Administrative Regions, among others. Since the purpose of the study is not merely reiterating the existence of the boys' issue

[2] This Data section also serves as the corresponding information for Chap. 5.

per se but is exploring the background of it specifically through the child-time–MLFP nexus, this study opts for an in-depth case study focusing on rural areas, to complement the Philippine and international governments' nation-wide reports. The research site is located in the MIMAROPA Region.

The empirical analysis data were collected in Marinduque Province, located in the MIMAROPA Region of the Philippines (Fig. 1). This province is primarily rural and lacks any cities, and its economy is centered on agriculture and self-employment.[3] It is geographically distant from urban areas, including the national capital. To prepare for the pilot survey, the author visited the province from August to December 2017, staying in a village (called *barangay*[4]) to become acquainted with the locals and their various locations.[5]

To ensure that a representative sample was captured from municipalities with different economic levels, three of the province's six municipalities were selected: Boac (the provincial capital), Gasan, and Buenavista. The selection was made based on the recommendations of the officials at the Provincial Office, who qualified their socioeconomic ranges, noting that the remaining three municipalities were similar to those chosen. Boac represented the economically advanced municipality, Gasan represented the intermediate level, and Buenavista represented the disadvantaged level.

Next, three barangays were randomly sampled from each municipality. The community-based monitoring system (CBMS), a family registry, was utilized for this purpose, and the provincial and barangay offices granted permission to access the registry. Subsequently, households were randomly chosen from each barangay using the master list of households meeting the school-age children criterion, as provided by the CBMS.[6] As a result, our dataset encompasses 150 households with a total of 284 children. In exchange, our data collected unique information on children, as we explain in upcoming subsections, which is rarely gathered by large-scale samples or nationally representative surveys. The sample was proportionally adjusted based on the original populations of each barangay and municipality, according to the CBMS.

3.2 Data Collection and Time-Use Survey

The sample households were provided with self-administered survey questionnaires. Respondents answered for our questions in four categories (Table 1). Category (1) includes the children's names, genders, birthdays and birth years, birth order,

[3] For further socioeconomic details of Marinduque Province, see Appendix Chapter A.

[4] A "*barangay*" is the smallest administrative division in the Philippines, similar to villages in other countries.

[5] The pilot study was conducted with the cooperation of Marinduque State College's faculty and students to ensure the accuracy of the questionnaire. This included language checks and confirmation of the relevance of respondents prior to the main survey.

[6] At this stage prior to the main household survey, we did not set any criteria to distinguish children enrolled in schools from those not enrolled.

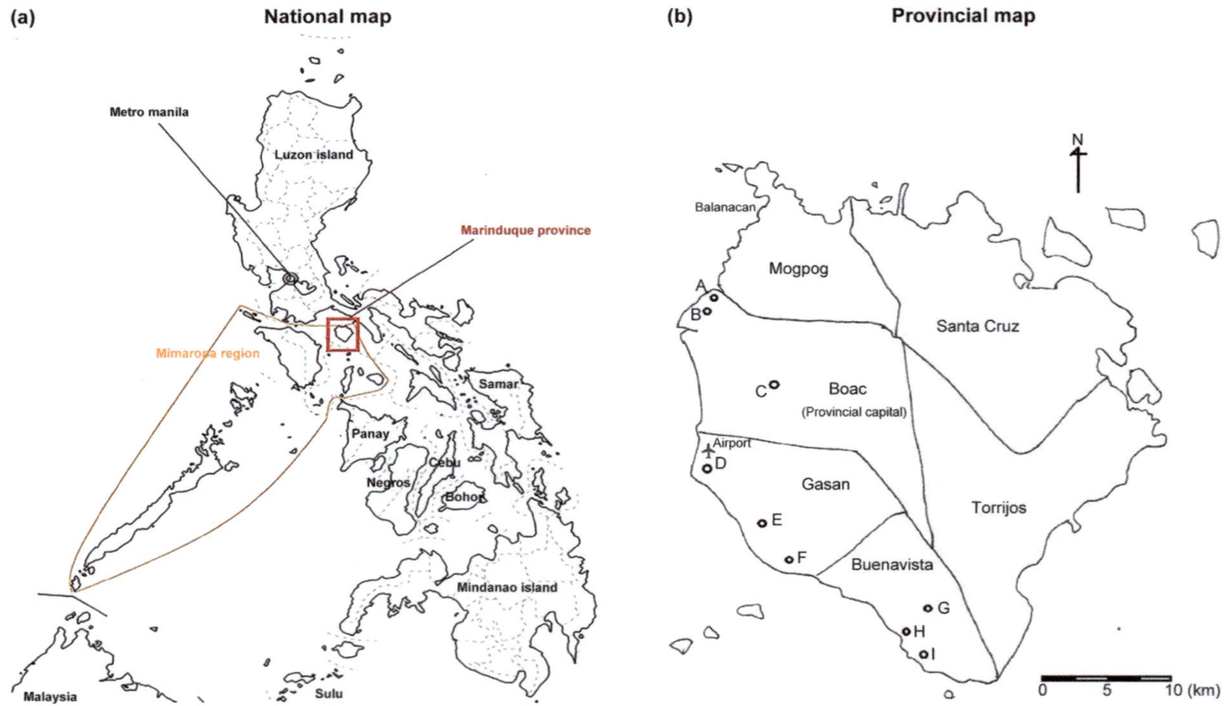

Fig. 1 Locations of research site. *Notes* Marinduque Province is part of the MIMAROPA Region, as shown in (a). The circles A–I in (b) represent the nine sampled *barangays*. *Source* Author's creation

Table 1 Collected information

Categories		Data collection method	About whom	Who answered?	Examples
(1)	Individual characteristics	Self-administered questionnaires	Children	Parents	Demographic profiles such as age, sex, birthday, number of siblings, birth order etc
(2)	Educational profiles	Self-administered questionnaires	Children	Parents/ Children	Enrolling status, school grade, school name, school type, academic scores etc
(3)	Household characteristics	Self-administered questionnaires	Parents and family structure	Parents	Demographic profiles, educational attainment, employment status, income, MLFP information etc
(4)	Child time-use	Self-administered diary-type questionnaires	Children	Children	Structured activities: sleeping, studying, schooling, labor, leisure, and unstructured activities (free descriptions)

Source Author

number of siblings, etc. Category (2) is of their enrolment status, school information, and educational performance as measured by the scores on their most recent semester's report cards. For category (3), the home address, contact information, demographic characteristics, educational, working, and earnings information of parents and other household members, including the MLFP status and mothers' earnings, were collected. Parents (primarily mothers) responded to questions in categories (1)–(3). Category (4) is explained in the next subsection.

3.3 Methodological Innovations in Time-Use Analysis

Time-use surveys in existing research on developing countries primarily set the surveyed periods in the past based on the timing of the research (Bouis et al. 1998; Esquivel et al. 2008; Lloyd et al. 2008; Sawada et al. 2006). This design is retrospective and relies on the memory of respondents. We also considered that respondents may have subconsciously altered their responses out of fear of being exposed, particularly to their parents. Accordingly, our survey design was influenced by Kudo et al.

(2019) to address the following issues.[7] First, our design avoids using a retrospective approach because respondents may not be confident in recalling how they spent their time, even just a few days prior, particularly based on honest reactions of our pilot-study-phase respondents. Second, the collected time-allocation variables are not posed in a discrete, categorical, or "yes–no" format, as has been the norm in previous research, but are numerically continuous.

The survey instructions included the following steps. First, diary-style questionnaire sheets were distributed to the children of respondents when their households were visited for the household questionnaire survey. Each respondent child was informed, both in writing and verbally, that the researcher merely wished to learn about their everyday activities and was not their teacher or monitor. We also emphasized that all of their personal information and responses would be immediately encoded into numeric and anonymous data so that no one could identify the respondents. Second, we collected completed forms in a week directly from respondents without showing them to their parents. Third, truthful responses were repeatedly emphasized to their parents, especially mothers, and they were urged not to view or censor the questionnaire sheets their children were keeping. Lastly, it was emphasized to both the respondent children and their parents that it made no difference whether they were or pretended to be family-oriented, diligent, studious, or hard-working, as we as researchers were not their teachers, supervisors, or authority figures.

As indicated by these steps, our time survey procedure was designed to be self-administered. Although this method is commonly used in higher income countries, it is often considered impractical in lower income countries due to the challenges posed by the social conditions, despite providing valuable and detailed information (Field et al. 2023: 4–5). In the absence of such surveys, researchers have relied on stylized survey questions that require individuals to aggregate their inputs over a specified period (Field et al. 2023: 5). However, according to Field et al.'s (2023) literature survey, the stylized survey question approach is susceptible to measurement errors (Kan and Pudney 2008) and social desirability biases (Kahneman et al. 2004). Hence, they may place a greater cognitive burden on the respondents than intended (Seymour et al. 2020). Nevertheless, we endeavored to overcome these conventional limitations when implementing our survey in a rural, developing context.

The collected information on time allocations includes education-related time, working time, and leisure time in addition to unstructured time. First, we compiled two time uses for education-related activities: time spent studying at home and time spent in school. The time spent in school is the period during which the student attended classes. The number of school-attending days was also included in the time use. Collecting these variables allows us to find the number of students who have left class early or who have arrived late to school for whatever reason.

For the working time, we were informed by our pilot-study participants that work by children in the basic-education stage is officially illegal in the Philippines. As a result, if children were asked directly and literally about their time engaged in labor or work, children and their parents would be concerned that they would be accused

[7] We referred to Kudo et al.'s (2019) preprint during our survey preparation in 2017.

of illegal activities.[8] Hence, we chose to link it to parental work and inquired about the time spent assisting their fathers' and mothers' jobs, respectively, based on the advice of our pilot-study participants that the collected time accurately reflected the durations of child labor.

The time information we collected as leisure includes time spent playing or in computer-game shops (CGS).[9] Leisure time can be theoretically divided into unstructured and structured activities (Lam and McHale 2015). Combining these classifications with the observations and suggestions from our pilot study, a semistructured questionnaire with free-form descriptions and numerical questions was designed. After collecting the survey responses, we examined the contents of each response individually. In every instance where we found inconsistent or incorrect responses regarding time spent on education, labor, and leisure, we asked the case respondents to report their correct responses via mobile phone or a second in-person interview.

Table 2 summarizes the mean values of the time-allocation variables. Most boys assist their fathers with their jobs, spend more time playing, and use CGS longer than their female counterparts. Girls study at home and assist with housework significantly longer, have fewer absences, and remain in school longer than their male counterparts. Girls are more likely to commit to their education and household duties, whereas boys are more likely to commit to helping their fathers with their jobs and playing outside.[10]

3.4 Defining "Pro-Educational" Child Time-Allocation Patterns

We compiled the most recent school report cards for Filipino, mathematics, English, science, social studies, music, arts, and physical and health education (MAPEH), and technology and livelihood education (TLE) at the individual level. In the Philippine education system, report card scores below 70 indicate "failures," with practical scores ranging from 70 to 100. Table 3 summarizes children's mean scores and z-scores, revealing distinct gender differences in educational performance. Female students consistently outperform male students across all subjects, including practice-based subjects such as MAPEH and TLE.

Using these individual-level school report card z-scores as the dependent variables, we conducted regression analyses where the independent variables were

[8] In a precise sense, the government distinguishes child labor from other child work and, following the International Labour Organization, defines child labor as "any work or economic activity performed by a child that subjects him/her to any form of exploitation or is harmful to his/her health and safety or physical, mental or psychosocial development" (DOLE, 2012). However, this study uses child labor and child work more broadly to compare time uses with educational activities.

[9] Collecting time spent in CGS also reflects the advice from participants in our pilot study that Filipino youth today are fond of CGS as part of leisure.

[10] For more detailed breakdowns of activities boys and girls engage in, refer to Table A.1 in Appendix to this chapter.

Table 2 Mean comparisons of time-allocation variables (weekly average)

Variables	Mean	(1) Of girls		(2) Of boys	(1) / (2)*
Sleeping time (mins.)	3610.8	3628.9	≈	3590.9	1.01
School-attended days†	4.3	4.7	>	3.9	1.21
Schooling time (mins.)	2114.9	2323.8	>	1884.2	1.23
Help father's job (mins.)	106.2	41.8	<<	177.2	0.24
Help mother's job (mins.)	73.5	73.6	≈	73.4	1.00
Help household chores (min.)	448.2	529.8	>	358.2	1.48
Studying time at home (mins.)	278.5	343.2	>	207	1.66
Playing time (mins.)	234.2	113.1	<<	367.8	0.31
Number of friends	2.6	1.7	<<	3.6	0.47
Time for computer-game shop usages	53.9	34.3	<<	75.6	0.45

Notes * "(1) / (2)" means the index of gender parity
† The total weekly days of attending school classes
Source Author's calculations

Table 3 Educational performance (seven subject scores on school report cards) by child gender

Subject	Obs	Overall		Male		Female		*z*-scores		
		Mean	Std. dev	Mean	Std. dev	Mean	Std. dev	Male (M)	Female (F)	Δ (F–M)
Filipino	275	83.18	5.32	81.15	4.95	84.99	4.98	−0.38	0.34	0.72
Math	274	81.88	4.84	80.45	4.63	83.16	4.67	−0.30	0.26	0.56
English	274	82.48	5.27	80.02	4.75	84.60	4.77	−0.47	0.40	0.87
Science	270	82.80	4.88	80.92	4.51	84.40	4.61	−0.39	0.33	0.72
Social Studies	259	83.44	4.67	81.67	4.48	85.02	4.26	−0.38	0.34	0.72
MAPEH	269	84.90	5.06	82.95	4.97	86.53	4.54	−0.38	0.32	0.71
TLE	240	84.67	5.12	82.89	5.14	86.13	4.65	−0.35	0.28	0.63

Note "MAPEH": Music, arts, and physical and health education. "TLE": Technical and livelihood education
Source Author's calculations

individual-level time-use variables, controlling for village and school dummy variables.[11] Table 4 presents the results in three panels: (a) both males and females combined, (b) only males, and (c) only females. These analyses explore the partial correlations between time-use patterns and educational performance across genders.

[11] In this subsection, before our main scope and analysis in Sect. 4, we confine ourselves to associations between child time use and test scores in Table 4. Still, it is reasonable to assume that correlated variables are related to each other in some capacity. Establishing causality is beyond the scope here and warrants a separate study.

Table 4 Partial correlations between time-allocation patterns and educational performance

Variables	Filipino	Math	English	Science	Social Studies	MAPEH	TLE
(a) Both Males and Females							
Sleeping	0.36	−0.29	−0.16	−0.08	0.01	0.29	0.48
	[0.32]	[0.32]	[0.33]	[0.34]	[0.36]	[0.34]	[0.37]
Education-related Activities							
Studying at home	1.05***	0.85**	0.79**	1.02***	1.06***	0.62	1.15***
	[0.39]	[0.34]	[0.37]	[0.35]	[0.39]	[0.40]	[0.38]
Schooling	−1.08	−0.27	−1.25	0.20	0.30	−0.15	0.50
	[0.68]	[0.67]	[0.63]	[0.62]	[0.63]	[0.67]	[0.91]
Attendance (in days)	0.69	0.51	1.10	0.37	1.13	0.54	−0.37
	[0.98]	[0.91]	[0.81]	[0.85]	[0.85]	[1.05]	[1.12]
Labor							
Helping with fathers' jobs	−0.75*	−0.86**	−0.96**	−1.06***	−0.76**	−0.50	−0.72
	[0.43]	[0.38]	[0.39]	[0.35]	[0.37]	[0.43]	[0.50]
Helping with mothers' jobs	−0.01	−0.03	0.34	0.57	0.16	−0.01	0.26
	[0.52]	[0.31]	[0.47]	[0.36]	[0.40]	[0.30]	[0.47]
Household chores	−0.15	−0.30	−0.18	−0.36	−0.35	−0.11	−0.24
	[0.37]	[0.35]	[0.41]	[0.36]	[0.35]	[0.40]	[0.39]
Leisure							
Playing	−1.19***	−0.82**	−0.84**	−0.64*	−0.94**	−0.99**	−1.52***
	[0.43]	[0.36]	[0.41]	[0.39]	[0.39]	[0.43]	[0.48]
Using computer-game shops	−0.30	−0.65*	−0.48	−0.30	−0.16	−0.38	−0.94**
	[0.34]	[0.35]	[0.33]	[0.31]	[0.42]	[0.42]	[0.39]

(continued)

Table 4 (continued)

Variables	Filipino	Math	English	Science	Social Studies	MAPEH	TLE
Constant	83.92***	78.12***	84.20***	84.14***	81.04***	77.08***	93.52***
	[3.58]	[2.60]	[3.15]	[1.90]	[2.38]	[3.16]	[1.77]
Regional effect	Yes	Yes	Yes	Yes	Yes	Yes	Yes
School effect	Yes	Yes	Yes	Yes	Yes	Yes	Yes
Adjusted R^2	0.17	0.15	0.18	0.15	0.16	0.14	0.18
No. of Observations	248	247	248	243	232	243	219
(b) Only males							
Variables	Filipino	Math	English	Science	Social Studies	MAPEH	TLE
Sleeping	−0.52	0.25	−0.41	−0.29	−0.70	−0.06	0.15
	[0.73]	[0.73]	[0.75]	[0.73]	[0.70]	[0.84]	[0.89]
Education-related Activities							
Studying at home	1.27**	1.72**	1.76**	1.68***	1.49**	1.31	1.62*
	[0.61]	[0.68]	[0.74]	[0.63]	[0.74]	[0.97]	[0.86]
Schooling	−2.31**	−1.47	−1.21	0.95	0.23	0.58	−0.46
	[0.89]	[0.97]	[0.84]	[0.84]	[0.87]	[0.88]	[1.71]
Attendance (in days)	−0.37	2.50	0.07	1.89	3.55***	−0.78	0.71
	[1.58]	[1.53]	[1.54]	[1.42]	[1.21]	[2.51]	[2.29]
Labor							
Helping with fathers' jobs	−0.81	−1.23**	−0.20	−0.44	−0.70	−0.21	−0.27
	[0.56]	[0.56]	[0.53]	[0.47]	[0.46]	[0.71]	[0.78]
Helping with mothers' jobs	−1.46	−0.29	−1.58	−0.17	0.51	−0.82	−0.99
	[1.26]	[0.50]	[0.97]	[0.79]	[1.09]	[0.73]	[1.18]

(continued)

Table 4 (continued)

Variables	Filipino	Math	English	Science	Social Studies	MAPEH	TLE
Household chores	−0.19	−1.39**	−0.48	−0.54	−1.19	−1.25	−0.02
	[0.77]	[0.67]	[0.82]	[0.63]	[0.76]	[0.81]	[1.19]
Leisure							
Playing	−1.30**	−0.26	−0.53	0.07	−0.30	−0.97	−1.54
	[0.56]	[0.53]	[0.57]	[0.59]	[0.56]	[0.73]	[1.00]
Using computer-game shops	0.11	−0.38	−0.41	0.14	−0.26	−0.08	−1.22**
	[0.44]	[0.40]	[0.45]	[0.42]	[0.50]	[0.53]	[0.60]
Constant	91.90***	79.52***	90.83***	83.91***	82.68***	78.41***	69.50***
	[7.35]	[3.90]	[5.68]	[3.34]	[6.67]	[4.06]	[7.99]
Regional effect	Yes	Yes	Yes	Yes	Yes	Yes	Yes
School effect	Yes	Yes	Yes	Yes	Yes	Yes	Yes
Adjusted R^2	0.25	0.23	0.14	0.15	0.21	0.04	0.06
No. of Observations	107	106	105	101	99	101	90
(c) Only females							
Variables	Filipino	Math	English	Science	Social Studies	MAPEH	TLE
Sleeping	0.98**	−0.12	0.12	0.27	0.70	0.76*	1.18**
	[0.40]	[0.38]	[0.39]	[0.43]	[0.48]	[0.41]	[0.46]
Education-related Activities							
Studying at home	0.99**	0.75	0.45	0.99**	1.02**	0.62	1.17***
	[0.48]	[0.46]	[0.51]	[0.47]	[0.46]	[0.45]	[0.43]
Schooling	0.24	1.80**	−1.31	0.24	1.84*	0.29	1.13
	[1.11]	[0.87]	[0.92]	[0.94]	[1.04]	[1.04]	[1.35]

(continued)

Table 4 (continued)

Variables	Filipino	Math	English	Science	Social Studies	MAPEH	TLE
Attendance (in days)	0.72	−1.26	1.39	0.08	−0.96	0.46	−0.78
	[1.21]	[1.16]	[1.13]	[1.18]	[1.19]	[1.18]	[1.46]
Labor							
Helping with fathers' jobs	1.88**	1.79*	0.68	0.44	1.46*	0.92	1.09
	[0.76]	[0.92]	[0.95]	[0.87]	[0.84]	[0.75]	[1.09]
Helping with mothers' jobs	−0.01	−0.18	0.30	0.47	0.01	−0.04	0.29
	[0.58]	[0.42]	[0.53]	[0.54]	[0.56]	[0.40]	[0.56]
Household chores	−0.36	−0.02	−0.53	−0.53	−0.30	0.10	−0.17
	[0.47]	[0.43]	[0.53]	[0.46]	[0.39]	[0.49]	[0.49]
Leisure							
Playing	−0.21	−1.56**	0.29	−0.61	−1.01	−0.54	−1.06
	[0.87]	[0.78]	[0.83]	[0.86]	[0.76]	[0.86]	[0.77]
Using computer-game shops	−1.16	−1.82**	0.10	−0.71	0.83	−1.03	−1.2
	[0.95]	[0.73]	[0.79]	[0.72]	[0.92]	[1.23]	[0.91]
Constant	91.72***	84.41***	89.67***	89.69***	82.88***	91.32***	78.20***
	[2.97]	[5.58]	[2.93]	[3.12]	[4.76]	[5.94]	[5.08]
Regional effect	Yes	Yes	Yes	Yes	Yes	Yes	Yes
School effect	Yes	Yes	Yes	Yes	Yes	Yes	Yes
Adjusted R^2	0.06	0.06	0.08	0.06	0.09	−0.02	0.16
No. of Observations	141	141	143	142	133	142	129

***$p < 0.01$; **$p < 0.05$; *$p < 0.10$

Notes Numbers in brackets are the small sample adjusted standard errors. Time-allocation variables are standardized into *z*-scores. "MAPEH": Music, arts, and physical and health education. "TLE": Technical and livelihood education

Source Author's calculations

When both males and females are analyzed together in panel (a), three key time-use variables show statistically significant correlations with educational performance: (1) studying at home (positive correlation), (2) helping fathers with their jobs (negative correlation), and (3) playing (negative correlation). More time spent studying at home is associated with higher academic scores, while more time spent playing or helping fathers with their jobs is associated with lower scores. These patterns are consistent across almost all school subjects, except for MAPEH, and align with previous studies such as Nguyen et al. (2022).[12]

Here, we define this time-allocation pattern as "pro-educational;" that is, a child's time-allocation pattern is pro-educational if either more time is allocated for studying at home or less time is allocated for playing or assisting fathers with their jobs. In the analysis, we focus mainly on these pro-educational time-use elements.

However, when the sample is divided into gender-specific subsamples, as shown in panels (b) and (c), some of the correlations observed in (a) become less pronounced. This suggests that gender alone holds significant explanatory power over time-use patterns, seemingly accounting for much of the observed gaps in educational outcomes between males and females. This strong explanatory power of a single variable—gender—is indeed important. Nonetheless, this study seeks to go beyond simply attributing differences in academic performance to gender itself. Instead, we focus on the specific time-use patterns associated with being male or female—such as boys spending more time playing, or girls dedicating more time to studying at home, for instance—that play a crucial role in shaping educational outcomes. Importantly, the results in (a) do not imply that all time-use activities are equally correlated with academic performance. Rather, it remains crucial that specific activities—studying at home, helping fathers with jobs, and playing—that show particularly strong correlations with educational outcomes, even if one argues that gender alone absorbs much of the variation.

While the focus of this paper is on these key pro-educational time uses, it is essential to recognize the significance of the results from (b) and (c). They suggest that the strong explanatory power of gender on educational gaps stems from these gendered time-allocation patterns, which are closely tied to pro-educational behaviors. This indicates that the observed differences between males and females in educational outcomes are not solely due to gender itself, but rather to the specific ways in which boys and girls allocate their time.

[12] Yet, the point estimate of the time studying at home for MAPEH and its relatively small standard error still imply a likely positive correlation.

4 Empirical Analysis

In the empirical analysis, we estimate time-allocation functions to determine the effect of the child gender variable on the prediction of educational time use. Through this, we are particularly interested in the effects of MLFP on the pro-educational time-use patterns.

4.1 Formulation

As shown in Table 2, we collected the time allocations for sleeping, studying at home, schooling, helping father's jobs, helping mothers' jobs, household chores, playing, and CGS. Denoting each activity as k, the estimated time-allocation function for t_{ki} is expressed as follows:

$$t_{ki} = \alpha_{1k}G_i + \alpha_{2k}MLFP_{ij} + \alpha_{3k}\left(G_i * MLFP_{ij}\right) + \mathbf{x_i}\beta_{\mathbf{1k}} + \mathbf{x_j}\beta_{\mathbf{2k}} + \omega_k + u_{ki}, \quad (1)$$

where the independent variables G_i and $MLFP_{ij}$ represent the gender dummy variable of child i, equal to zero if female and one if male, and the mother's labor force participation variable of the mother of child i within household j, taking zero if not participating in the labor force and one if participating, respectively. The ω_k are region- and school-level specific fixed effects of the barangay where each household lives and the schools where each child is enrolled. The vectors $\mathbf{x_i}$ and $\mathbf{x_j}$ represent the covariates of other individual characteristics of the child i and household characteristics of the household j of the child i, respectively. The term u_{ki} is a stochastic error term. In this study, we treat each child time-use category as an independent outcome variable, investigating the causal link between maternal labor force participation and each time-use category separately.

4.2 Estimations

In estimating time use, some previous studies have employed Tobit models, given that the dependent variable is often censored at zero (Nazier and Ezzat 2022). Other studies have used ordinary least squares (OLS) methods, arguing that OLS estimators of time use are generally unbiased, particularly over short periods of time (Cawley and Liu 2012: 354; Stewart 2013). Our time-use survey shares these fundamental principles. Additionally, as observed in migration studies (Antman 2013: 293–294), endogeneity concerns may arise in the relationship between MLFP and children's time use. For instance, if children spend more time helping with household chores, this may make it easier for their mothers to work outside the home. Conversely, if mothers are employed, children may spend more time playing and less time studying due to a lack of supervision. Thus, there is a potential bidirectional relationship between children's time use and MLFP. To address this issue, we employ the IV method.

For our study, we exploit an exogenous institutional change—the implementation of a minimum wage policy under the National Wages and Productivity Commission, via the MIMAROPA Regional Tripartite Wages and Productivity Board, within the Department of Labor and Employment (DOLE)—to construct the IV. Minimum wage changes affect labor market conditions, and research suggests that women in lower-income countries are often more sensitive to these changes than men. The policy change is considered exogenous, as it is not directly related to individual household characteristics (Faria and Sachsida 2012).

Before our field study, Republic Act (RA) No. 10361 (the Domestic Workers Act of 2013) established minimum wage levels for domestic workers, who make up a significant part of the local female labor force. The wage levels differed between chartered cities and first-class municipalities (PhP2,000) and other municipalities (PhP1,500).[13] Our survey covered municipalities in both categories: Boac, the provincial capital (a first-class municipality) and Gasan and Buenavista (other municipalities). Later, Wage Order No. RB-MIMAROPA-DW-01 (July 7, 2017) increased the minimum wage to PhP2,500 across the entire MIMAROPA region. This represented a significant increase of PhP500 to PhP1,000 over the RA 10361 baseline. Thus, all the municipalities in our survey experienced a post–July 2017 increase.

Next, we constructed a mothers' *revealed* wage trend indicator as our IV. We asked mothers to compare the wage trends between two time periods: from two years ago to one year ago (period (A) to (B) in Fig. 2), and from one year ago to the present (period (B) to (C) in Fig. 2). The IV takes a value of 1 only if the mother reported a consistent increase in wages over both time intervals, and 0 otherwise. This variable was constructed for both working and non-working mothers. Working mothers compared their actual monthly *average* wages across these periods,[14] while non-working mothers responded based on their perception and local knowledge of the wage trends in the specific occupational market they would potentially enter if they were to seek employment immediately.

We limited the IV taking 1 to cases where mothers reported a consistent wage increase across both periods (A) to (B) and (B) to (C) to ensure the robustness of

[13] These domestic workers include, but are not limited to, those in live-in or live-out arrangements for general house help, *yaya* (babysitter), cook, gardener, laundry person, or any domestic work in one household on an occupational basis (PIA MIMAROPA 2017). These occupations dominate the jobs of working mothers who reported that they were self-employed. Hence, the act covers a broad population of workers in the local context.

[14] In Filipino, it is "*karaniwang*" wage a month, which conveys the idea of a general, ordinary, average, or typical wage, excluding extreme events, though the language does not have an exact term corresponding literally to "average" in English.

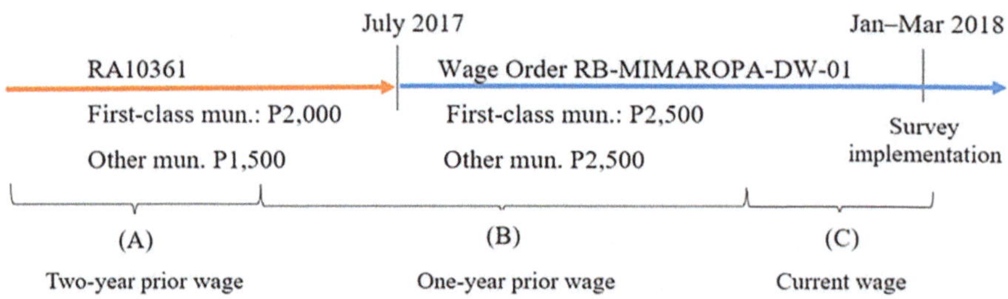

Fig. 2 Minimum wage change timings and time coverage of collected information. *Note* "mun." = municipalities

the indicator.[15] Since the IV partly relies on perceived trends (especially for non-working mothers), narrowing the definition to consistent increases over both periods strengthens the reliability of the indicator, mitigating potential bias from subjective perceptions or short-term fluctuations.

This approach aims to ensure respondent coverage for both working and non-working mothers. Given that the MLFP rate is around fifty percent, omitting half of the total sample of mothers would have incurred a significant cost otherwise. For non-working mothers, although their actual wages were not observed, they were able to respond based on their perception and local knowledge of the wage trends in the specific occupational market they would potentially enter if they sought employment. The exogenous institutional change in the minimum wage, which occurred between periods (A) and (B), and (B) and (C), allowed us to capture mothers' revealed wage trends, encompassing both pre- and post-implementation of the wage increase.

The assumption of exclusion restriction here is that the institutional change correlates with MLFP by influencing (or altering the perception of) the wage trend, which in turn affects the decision to participate in the labor market. However, this change should only indirectly affect children's time-use patterns through its influence on MLFP. The minimum wage policy is expected to shape mothers' decisions regarding labor force participation, but not directly influence how children allocate their time within the short period covered by our study.

In the regression analyses, we control for other confounding factors, such as household characteristics including their regional variations, when instrumenting MLFP. Additionally, as part of the robustness checks, we further validate the exclusion restriction by demonstrating that the IV is not directly correlated with the dependent variable (children's time-use patterns). These additional estimations, which provide evidence supporting the exclusion restriction, are presented in Sect. 5.

Now, following the two-step least squares method, we first obtain the fitted value of MLFP, $\widehat{MLFP}_{ij}$,using the IV, z_{ij}, which is used here but not included in the main

[15] The IV takes the value of 1 for 14% of the sample, representing mothers who reported consistent wage increases. Though this may seem like a small share, it is meaningful, especially considering the gradual nature of minimum wage policy changes in the Philippines. This raises another independent and interesting question about the beneficiaries' perceptions of the policy's impact and duration, warranting further studies.

equation. As noted above, the z_{ij} takes 1 if the wage trend answered by the mother of child i at the household j was increasing and 0 otherwise. Then, instead of $MLFP_{ij}$, the $\widehat{MLFP}_{ij}$ is used in the main equation as the following equation:

$$t_{ki} = \alpha_1 G_i + \alpha_2 \widehat{MLFP}_{ij} + \alpha_3\left(G_i * \widehat{MLFP}_{ij}\right) + \mathbf{x}_i \beta_1 + \mathbf{x}_j \beta_2 + \omega_k + u_{ki},$$
$$\widehat{MLFP}_{ij} = \widehat{\zeta}\, z_{ij} + \mathbf{x}_i \widehat{\eta}_1 + \mathbf{x}_j \widehat{\eta}_2. \tag{2}$$

We estimate Eq. (2) using the two-stage least squares (2SLS) model. Alongside the 2SLS estimators, we conduct statistical tests of the MLFP's exogeneity and the weak instrument in Sect. 4. The estimation does not treat the equations as a joint system but rather investigates each category separately, ensuring the validity of using a single instrument.

4.3 Summary Statistics[16]

Table 5 reports the summary statistics of the dependent and independent variables used in the upcoming regression analyses. Estimations are conducted separately for the full sample, which includes all children in the sample, and the restricted sample, which includes only enrolled children. This allows for a better understanding of the heterogeneity in leisure time between schoolchildren and out-of-school children. Therefore, the enrolment indicator (equal to 1 if a child is enrolled and 0 otherwise) is additionally controlled for in the full sample.

4.3.1 Dependent Variables: Child Time Uses

The dependent variables include the child's weekly time spent on various activities, such as sleeping, education (home study, schooling, and school attendance), labor (assisting fathers and mothers with their jobs and household chores), and leisure (playing and using computer-game shops (CGS)). The details of these time-use variables were discussed in Sect. 3.3 and outlined in Table 2. In the regression analyses, time-use variables are standardized into z-scores for ease of comparison.

4.3.2 Independent Variables

Individual Child Characteristics: The independent variables are categorized into three groups: (i) individual child characteristics, (ii) household characteristics, and (iii) school-related variables. In the total sample ($n = 274$), approximately 91% of

[16] This summary statistics subsection also serves as the corresponding information to this for Chap. 5.

Table 5 Summary statistics of variables

Variables	Full Sample ($n = 284$)		Enrolled Sample ($n = 258$)	
	Mean	Std. Dev	Mean	Std. Dev
Dependent variables:				
Time allocation, 7 days				
Sleeping	3610.23	435.94	3598.72	429.73
Studying at home	279.14	267.17	307.71	271.19
Schooling (in min)	2097.54	913.50	2307.52	663.46
Schooling (in days)	4.31	1.61	4.71	0.95
Helping with fathers' jobs	111.48	253.88	86.53	186.64
Helping with mothers' jobs	76.72	175.54	83.82	182.75
Household chores	447.04	367.75	450.72	365.22
Playing	228.65	308.90	198.99	291.19
Computer-game shops	54.30	131.46	48.15	103.17
Independent variables and covariates:				
Individual characteristics				
Enrolling (=1)	0.91	0.28	n.a	n.a
Male (=1)	0.46	0.50	0.41	0.49
Age	15.22	2.84	15.14	2.62
Lowly aspired child (=1)	0.10	0.29	0.05	0.22
Eldest (=1)	0.18	0.38	0.19	0.39
Youngest (=1)	0.21	0.41	0.20	0.40
Elder siblings	2.68	2.33	2.69	2.44
Younger siblings	1.80	1.45	1.77	1.38
Household characteristics				
FLFP indicator (=1 if father is working)	0.93	0.25	0.94	0.24
Father: Land-owner farmer (=1)	0.05	0.22	0.05	0.22
Father: Wage labor (=1)	0.13	0.33	0.13	0.33
Father: Self-employment (=1)	0.31	0.46	0.31	0.46
FLFP: Wage-increase indicator (=1 if increasing)	0.19	0.39	0.19	0.39
MLFP indicator (=1 if mother is working)	0.50	0.50	0.53	0.50
Mother: Land-owning farmer (=1)	0.01	0.08	0.01	0.09
Mother: Self-employment (=1)	0.35	0.48	0.38	0.49
MLFP: Wage-increase indicator (=1 if increasing) *	0.14	0.34	0.13	0.34
ln per capita income	6.97	1.05	7.08	1.02
per capita income	1871.68	2867.10	1952.46	2959.60
Income shares to non-parental household members' earnings (%)	0.14	0.24	0.13	0.24

(continued)

Table 5 (continued)

Variables	Full Sample		Enrolled Sample	
	($n = 284$)		($n = 258$)	
	Mean	Std. Dev	Mean	Std. Dev
Father's age	47.17	7.81	46.93	7.56
Mother's age	44.91	6.89	44.57	6.39
Father's education (=1 if college graduate)	0.11	0.31	0.12	0.33
Mother's education (=1 if college graduate)	0.14	0.35	0.14	0.35
Female headed (=1)	0.04	0.19	0.03	0.16
Separate father (=1)	0.13	0.34	0.13	0.34
Separate mother (=1)	0.09	0.29	0.09	0.28
Extended family (=1)	0.32	0.47	0.32	0.47
School variables				
Public school (=1)	n.a	n.a	0.90	0.29
Commuting time (mins., one-way)	n.a	n.a	18.72	14.63
Walking to schools (=1)	n.a	n.a	0.20	0.40
Distance (km, one-way)	n.a	n.a	3.58	5.07

* Instrument variable for MLFP

Note Dependent variables are standardized into z-scores in regression analyses for the comparison. FLFP and MLFP refer to fathers' and mothers' labor force participation, respectively

Source Author's calculations

children are enrolled in school ($n = 258$), while the remaining 9% are not. About 46% of the full sample and 41% of the enrolled sample are male, with the latter reflecting the reversed gender disparity. The average age of children in both samples is around 15, corresponding to high school age. The "low aspirations child" indicator is assigned a value of 1 if the parents' aspirations for their child's final educational attainment fall below the college level, which is the norm for most parents. In the full sample, 9.5% of children's parents aspire for them to achieve a secondary education or less, compared to 5% in the enrolled sample. Regarding demographic data such as birth order and number of siblings, the average number of siblings (including the respondent) is five to six in both samples, with little variation in demographic characteristics between the two samples.

MLFP and Other Controls at Household Characteristics. The summary statistics of the MLFP indicator show that, on average, the mothers of approximately half the children in our sample were working at the time of the survey and in the preceding six months (50% and 53% for the full and enrolled samples, respectively). These figures align with regional statistics (Cabegin and Gaddi 2019: 5). Two dummy variables provide additional information on occupation categories: land-owning farmers, accounting for approximately 2% of total working mothers (1% divided by the 50% MLFP rate), and self-employment, accounting for approximately 70% and 76% of total working mothers (35% and 38% divided by the 50% MLFP rate, respectively), with formal employment as the reference category.

For comparison, the FLFP rates are 93% and 94%, respectively. These higher rates for fathers reflect the sociocultural norm in rural areas, where fathers are considered the primary breadwinners (further discussed in Chap. 5). Similar to mothers, the paternal occupation categories are represented by dummy variables: land-owning farmers account for around 5% of total working fathers, wage laborers for around 13% (observed only among fathers in our data), and self-employed fathers make up approximately 31%, with formal employment as the reference category.

The mothers' wage-increasing trend indicator shows an upward trend for the mothers of 14% of children in the full sample and 13% in the enrolled sample over the past two years. Logarithmic per capita income is calculated based on the household's monthly average income over the past six months. Household size is higher in the enrolled sample than in the full sample. The income shares of non-parental household members account for 14% and 13% in the full and enrolled samples, respectively. A higher share of non-parental income suggests greater instability in the breadwinner roles of the father and/or mother, as the household relies on contributions from extended family members.

Fathers and mothers are, on average, in their mid-forties. Mothers have a higher average educational attainment than fathers: 14% of mothers and 10%-12% of fathers in both samples have completed tertiary education. The overwhelming majority of household heads are men (96% in the full sample, 97% in the enrolled sample), indicating that men dominate the breadwinner role. In approximately 13% of households, fathers live separately from other family members, while 9–10% of mothers live apart from their children.

School Variables. Among the enrolled students, 90% attend public schools, while 10% are in private institutions. Twenty percent of enrolled students walk to school, while the remaining 80% use some form of transportation (e.g., tricycles or jeepneys). The average one-way commute to school takes around 19 min. The average distance from home to school is 3.6 km, though this varies significantly depending on the child's educational level.

5 Results

5.1 Gender Disparity in Child Pro-Educational Time-Allocation Pattern

Regression estimations are presented in Table 6 for both the full and enrolled samples, with four specifications. Specifications [1] and [2] pertain to the full sample, where [1] includes no interaction terms with the boy indicator, while [2] introduces interaction terms between selected independent variables and the boy indicator. Specifications

Table 6 Determinants of child time-allocations: Full sample and enrolled sample

					Education							
Variables	Sleep				Studying at Home				Schooling			
	[1]	[2]	[3]	[4]	[1]	[2]	[3]	[4]	[1]	[2]	[3]	[4]
Boy indicator (=1)	0.00	−1.48**	−0.11	−0.77	−0.41***	1.13	−0.44***	−0.14	−0.16**	0.07	−0.17**	−0.54
	[0.11]	[0.75]	[0.12]	[0.57]	[0.12]	[0.70]	[0.14]	[0.72]	[0.08]	[0.49]	[0.08]	[0.34]
Enrolled school	−0.45	−1.33***			0.91***	1.61***			2.14***	2.26***		
	[0.29]	[0.47]			[0.18]	[0.40]			[0.14]	[0.30]		
Boy × Enrolled school		1.04*				−0.82*				−0.21		
		[0.56]				[0.42]				[0.34]		
Mothers' Labor Force Participation (MLFP)	−0.09	−0.21	0.00	0.02	0.81	1.71	1.15	2.07	0.62	1.00	0.26	0.59
	[0.56]	[0.84]	[0.51]	[0.81]	[0.77]	[1.21]	[0.81]	[1.28]	[0.48]	[0.73]	[0.47]	[0.70]
Boy × MLFP		0.10		−0.03		−1.71**		−1.97**		−0.84		−0.65
		[0.65]		[0.65]		[0.87]		[0.95]		[0.54]		[0.55]
Mother: Land-owner farmer	0.10	0.00	−0.33	−0.33	−1.12	−1.63	−1.05	−1.76	0.19	0.06	0.33	0.24
	[0.57]	[0.69]	[0.55]	[0.74]	[0.79]	[1.04]	[0.81]	[1.14]	[0.53]	[0.69]	[0.47]	[0.65]
Mother: Self-employed	0.41	0.37	0.31	0.27	−0.77	−1.35	−0.98*	−1.68*	−0.77**	−1.06*	−0.46	−0.77
	[0.46]	[0.64]	[0.42]	[0.63]	[0.59]	[0.90]	[0.58]	[0.94]	[0.36]	[0.56]	[0.33]	[0.53]

(continued)

Table 6 (continued)

					Education							
Variables	Sleep				Studying at Home				Schooling			
	[1]	[2]	[3]	[4]	[1]	[2]	[3]	[4]	[1]	[2]	[3]	[4]
Boy × Mother: Self-employed		0.10		0.06		1.23*		1.59**		0.59		0.46
		[0.49]		[0.50]		[0.67]		[0.74]		[0.47]		[0.46]
Fathers' Labor Force Participation (FLFP)	0.41	0.30	0.41	0.28	0.02	0.15	0.15	0.08	−0.09	−0.13	−0.02	−0.09
	[0.26]	[0.34]	[0.26]	[0.32]	[0.21]	[0.31]	[0.22]	[0.32]	[0.19]	[0.18]	[0.20]	[0.17]
Boy × FLFP		0.35		0.58		−0.57		0.03		0.08		0.45
		[0.45]		[0.55]		[0.45]		[0.65]		[0.31]		[0.34]
Father: Land-owner farmer	−0.03	0.21	0.17	0.13	−0.12	−0.40	−0.23	−0.39	−0.02	−0.31	0.24	−0.16
	[0.23]	[0.26]	[0.22]	[0.27]	[0.31]	[0.46]	[0.36]	[0.49]	[0.26]	[0.38]	[0.23]	[0.29]
Boy ×Father: Land-owner farmer		−0.46		0.07		0.71		0.82		0.64		0.94**
		[0.40]		[0.31]		[0.55]		[0.67]		[0.48]		[0.38]
Father: Wage labor	−0.59***	−0.47**	−0.53***	−0.55**	0.21	0.16	0.18	0.22	0.31***	0.38***	0.31**	0.31**
	[0.18]	[0.22]	[0.18]	[0.23]	[0.19]	[0.27]	[0.21]	[0.27]	[0.11]	[0.12]	[0.12]	[0.14]
Boy ×Father: Wage labor		−0.24		0.02		0.16		−0.03		−0.16		−0.15

(continued)

Table 6 (continued)

	Education											
Variables	Sleep				Studying at Home				Schooling			
	[1]	[2]	[3]	[4]	[1]	[2]	[3]	[4]	[1]	[2]	[3]	[4]
		[0.31]		[0.33]		[0.32]		[0.39]		[0.23]		[0.27]
Father: Self-employed	0.00	0.04	0.13	0.03	−0.20	−0.51*	−0.24	−0.51*	−0.08	−0.27*	−0.06	−0.29*
	[0.17]	[0.24]	[0.16]	[0.25]	[0.18]	[0.27]	[0.19]	[0.29]	[0.11]	[0.16]	[0.12]	[0.16]
Boy ×Father: Self-employed		−0.16		0.21		0.55*		0.39		0.34		0.42*
		[0.32]		[0.33]		[0.29]		[0.33]		[0.21]		[0.21]
Constants	0.15	1.02	0.15	0.21	−3.98***	−4.89***	−3.66***	−3.49***	−2.58***	−2.95***	0.03	0.1
	[0.88]	[0.99]	[1.00]	[1.06]	[0.88]	[1.03]	[1.07]	[1.06]	[0.64]	[0.69]	[0.74]	[0.76]
Other covariates:												
Individual and household characteristics	Yes	Yes	Yes	Yes	Yes	Yes	Yes	Yes	Yes	Yes	Yes	Yes
Region Dummies	Yes	Yes	Yes	Yes	Yes	Yes	Yes	Yes	Yes	Yes	Yes	Yes
Enumerator Dummies	Yes	Yes	Yes	Yes	Yes	Yes	Yes	Yes	Yes	Yes	Yes	Yes
School variables	No	No	Yes	Yes	No	No	Yes	Yes	No	No	Yes	Yes
R^2	0.22	0.24	0.24	0.25	0.23	0.24	0.13	0.12	0.61	0.62	0.30	0.36
No. of Observations	284	284	256	256	284	284	256	256	284	284	256	256

(continued)

Table 6 (continued)

Variables	Education			
	Attendance			
	[1]	[2]	[3]	[4]
Boy indicator (=1)	−0.07	0.26	−0.11	−0.39
	[0.07]	[0.38]	[0.08]	[0.34]
Enrolled school	2.73***	2.98***		
	[0.13]	[0.14]		
Boy × Enrolled school		−0.37		
		[0.23]		
Mothers' Labor Force Participation (MLFP)	0.48	0.74	0.51	0.82
	[0.44]	[0.67]	[0.44]	[0.66]
Boy × MLFP		−0.60		−0.68
		[0.49]		[0.51]
Mother: Land-owner farmer	0.33	0.23	0.32	0.10
	[0.46]	[0.60]	[0.42]	[0.58]
Mother: Self-employed	−0.48	−0.66	−0.45	−0.74
	[0.33]	[0.51]	[0.32]	[0.51]
Boy × Mother: Self-employed		0.43		0.54
		[0.42]		[0.43]
Fathers' Labor Force Participation (FLFP)	0.11	0.02	0.18	0.07
	[0.16]	[0.15]	[0.16]	[0.16]
Boy × FLFP		0.16		0.41
		[0.27]		[0.32]
Father: Land-owner farmer	−0.10	−0.16	0.01	−0.11

(continued)

Table 6 (continued)

	Education			
Variables	Attendance			
	[1]	[2]	[3]	[4]
	[0.20]	[0.31]	[0.17]	[0.23]
Boy ×Father: Land-owner farmer		0.16		0.26
		[0.35]		[0.33]
Father: Wage labor	0.00	−0.03	0.00	−0.04
	[0.09]	[0.10]	[0.10]	[0.11]
Boy ×Father: Wage labor		0.07		−0.02
		[0.21]		[0.24]
Father: Self-employed	−0.11	−0.15	−0.07	−0.19
	[0.10]	[0.15]	[0.10]	[0.15]
Boy ×Father: Self-employed		0.06		0.16
		[0.16]		[0.17]
Constants	−3.15***	−3.54***	−0.57	−0.45
	[0.47]	[0.49]	[0.57]	[0.62]
Other covariates:				
Individual and household characteristics	Yes	Yes	Yes	Yes
Region Dummies	Yes	Yes	Yes	Yes
Enumerator Dummies	Yes	Yes	Yes	Yes
School variables	No	No	Yes	Yes
R^2	0.73	0.73	0.19	0.19
No. of Observations	284	284	256	256

(continued)

Table 6 (continued)

	Labor and Chores											
Variables	Father's Job				Mother's Job				Household Chores			
	[1]	[2]	[3]	[4]	[1]	[2]	[3]	[4]	[1]	[2]	[3]	[4]
Boy indicator (=1)	0.46***	1.91	0.39***	0.81	0.00	−1.15	0.04	−0.26	−0.41***	−3.12***	−0.37***	−1.10*
	[0.11]	[1.20]	[0.10]	[0.54]	[0.12]	[0.82]	[0.12]	[0.82]	[0.13]	[0.85]	[0.12]	[0.60]
Enrolled school (=1)	−1.03**	0.00			−0.02	−0.58			−0.45*	−2.40***		
	[0.47]	[0.44]			[0.26]	[0.59]			[0.27]	[0.61]		
Boy × Enrolled school		−1.13*				0.64				2.24***		
		[0.68]				[0.66]				[0.65]		
Mothers' Labor Force Participation (MLFP)	−0.45	−0.90	−0.90*	−1.41*	−0.68	−1.91	−0.75	−1.90*	−1.03*	−1.43	−0.86	−1.22
	[0.51]	[0.86]	[0.49]	[0.84]	[0.69]	[1.17]	[0.68]	[1.07]	[0.57]	[0.92]	[0.60]	[0.93]
Boy × MLFP		0.61		0.80		1.85**		1.99**		0.73		0.73
		[0.68]		[0.66]		[0.87]		[0.83]		[0.76]		[0.77]
Mother: Land-owner farmer	0.67	0.75	0.51	0.86	0.74	1.38	0.84	1.71	1.09*	1.23	1.10**	1.49*
	[0.48]	[0.65]	[0.40]	[0.68]	[0.91]	[1.13]	[0.84]	[1.10]	[0.59]	[0.79]	[0.56]	[0.79]
Mother: Self-employed	0.40	0.82	0.65*	1.20*	1.24**	2.11**	1.26**	2.12***	0.83*	0.98	0.67	0.93
	[0.41]	[0.65]	[0.38]	[0.63]	[0.57]	[0.86]	[0.52]	[0.78]	[0.45]	[0.72]	[0.44]	[0.70]
Boy × Mother: Self-employed		−0.44		−0.82*		−1.31**		−1.44**		−0.50		−0.64
		[0.51]		[0.49]		[0.63]		[0.62]		[0.65]		[0.66]
Fathers' Labor Force Participation (FLFP)	−0.03	0.25	0.18	0.38	−0.19	−0.04	−0.25	−0.06	−0.22	−0.36	−0.36	−0.36

(continued)

Table 6 (continued)

	Labor and Chores											
Variables	Father's Job				Mother's Job				Household Chores			
	[1]	[2]	[3]	[4]	[1]	[2]	[3]	[4]	[1]	[2]	[3]	[4]
	[0.36]	[0.23]	[0.21]	[0.29]	[0.31]	[0.42]	[0.33]	[0.42]	[0.24]	[0.31]	[0.25]	[0.29]
Boy × FLFP		−0.34		−0.53		−0.05		−0.27		0.27		0.35
		[0.83]		[0.47]		[0.50]		[0.76]		[0.45]		[0.54]
Father: Land-owner farmer	−0.32	0.12	0.00	0.25	0.10	0.42	0.29	0.49	−0.01	0.05	0.08	0.00
	[0.23]	[0.26]	[0.19]	[0.26]	[0.34]	[0.48]	[0.38]	[0.51]	[0.26]	[0.38]	[0.24]	[0.31]
Boy ×Father: Land-owner farmer		−0.70*		−0.39		−0.57		−0.52		−0.30		−0.07
		[0.37]		[0.31]		[0.46]		[0.49]		[0.43]		[0.37]
Father: Wage labor	0.02	−0.05	0.11	−0.01	−0.06	−0.26	−0.12	−0.23	0.27	0.51**	0.40*	0.49**
	[0.19]	[0.15]	[0.16]	[0.17]	[0.20]	[0.22]	[0.22]	[0.25]	[0.21]	[0.24]	[0.21]	[0.25]
Boy ×Father: Wage labor		0.04		0.36		0.46		0.42		−0.35		0.05
		[0.40]		[0.29]		[0.30]		[0.33]		[0.34]		[0.35]
Father: Self-employed	0.13	−0.01	0.19	0.07	0.03	−0.05	−0.07	−0.02	0.21	0.38*	0.28*	0.42*
	[0.16]	[0.16]	[0.13]	[0.17]	[0.18]	[0.25]	[0.16]	[0.25]	[0.16]	[0.23]	[0.16]	[0.22]
Boy ×Father: Self-employed		0.29		0.35		0.34		0.12		−0.32		−0.24
		[0.27]		[0.24]		[0.28]		[0.27]		[0.27]		[0.27]

(continued)

Table 6 (continued)

	Labor and Chores											
Variables	Father's Job				Mother's Job				Household Chores			
	[1]	[2]	[3]	[4]	[1]	[2]	[3]	[4]	[1]	[2]	[3]	[4]
Constants	0.67	−0.04	−0.24	−0.09	−0.1	0.76	−0.12	−0.25	1.53*	3.31***	0.37	0.09
	[0.92]	[0.77]	[0.69]	[0.75]	[0.78]	[0.98]	[0.95]	[0.96]	[0.92]	[1.02]	[0.95]	[0.97]
Other covariates:												
Individual and household characteristics	Yes	Yes	Yes	Yes	Yes	Yes	Yes	Yes	Yes	Yes	Yes	Yes
Region Dummies	Yes	Yes	Yes	Yes	Yes	Yes	Yes	Yes	Yes	Yes	Yes	Yes
Enumerator Dummies	Yes	Yes	Yes	Yes	Yes	Yes	Yes	Yes	Yes	Yes	Yes	Yes
School variables	No	No	Yes	Yes	No	No	Yes	Yes	No	No	Yes	Yes
R^2	0.31	0.35	0.18	0.16	0.22	0.18	0.29	0.25	0.22	0.26	0.23	0.27
No. of Observations	284	284	256	256	284	284	256	256	284	284	256	256

	Leisure							
Variables	Playing				CGS			
	[1]	[2]	[3]	[4]	[1]	[2]	[3]	[4]
Boy indicator (=1)	0.68***	0.46	0.57***	0.50	0.25**	0.55	0.22**	0.84*
	[0.12]	[0.82]	[0.11]	[0.58]	[0.10]	[0.68]	[0.09]	[0.44]
Enrolled school (=1)	−0.71**	−0.19			−0.32	0.31		
	[0.30]	[0.32]			[0.48]	[0.38]		

(continued)

Table 6 (continued)

	Leisure							
Variables	Playing				CGS			
	[1]	[2]	[3]	[4]	[1]	[2]	[3]	[4]
Boy × Enrolled school		−0.66				−1.04*		
		[0.48]				[0.61]		
Mothers' Labor Force Participation (MLFP)	−1.67***	−2.96***	−1.13*	−1.90**	−1.25**	−2.16**	−0.57	−0.36
	[0.60]	[1.13]	[0.59]	[0.96]	[0.56]	[1.05]	[0.41]	[0.62]
Boy × MLFP		2.54***		1.91**		1.44		−0.29
		[0.87]		[0.78]		[0.91]		[0.50]
Mother: Land-owner farmer	0.48	1.32	0.37	1.07	2.45***	2.53**	1.27**	1.06
	[0.73]	[0.92]	[0.62]	[0.79]	[0.85]	[1.02]	[0.56]	[0.69]
Mother: Self-employed	1.31***	2.06**	0.84*	1.28*	1.08**	1.63**	0.58*	0.4
	[0.49]	[0.84]	[0.43]	[0.69]	[0.46]	[0.79]	[0.35]	[0.51]
Boy × Mother: Self-employed		−1.50**		−1.02*		−0.98		0.24
		[0.69]		[0.61]		[0.73]		[0.43]
Fathers' Labor Force Participation (FLFP)	−0.63**	−0.59	−0.68***	−0.63**	0.53**	0.50	0.47**	0.63***
	[0.27]	[0.43]	[0.26]	[0.29]	[0.25]	[0.35]	[0.20]	[0.18]
Boy × FLFP		0.31		−0.32		0.31		−0.35
		[0.55]		[0.57]		[0.58]		[0.42]
Father: Land-owner farmer	0.56*	0.57	0.16	0.25	−0.02	0.23	−0.01	0.06
	[0.33]	[0.44]	[0.27]	[0.29]	[0.27]	[0.41]	[0.28]	[0.33]

(continued)

Table 6 (continued)

Variables	Leisure							
	Playing				CGS			
	[1]	[2]	[3]	[4]	[1]	[2]	[3]	[4]
Boy ×Father: Land-owner farmer		0.06		−0.31		−0.76		−0.33
		[0.66]		[0.50]		[0.49]		[0.41]
Father: Wage labor	0.12	0.47**	0.08	0.50***	−0.30*	−0.05	−0.31**	−0.05
	[0.16]	[0.18]	[0.17]	[0.17]	[0.17]	[0.20]	[0.13]	[0.17]
Boy ×Father: Wage labor		−0.79**		−1.01***		−0.52		−0.64**
		[0.32]		[0.33]		[0.33]		[0.27]
Father: Self-employed	0.31**	0.65***	0.22	0.51**	0.14	0.19	0.01	0.05
	[0.15]	[0.25]	[0.13]	[0.20]	[0.19]	[0.20]	[0.12]	[0.14]
Boy ×Father: Self-employed		−0.52*		−0.46*		0.08		−0.17
		[0.30]		[0.27]		[0.36]		[0.28]
Constants	2.41***	2.43**	1.18	0.39	−0.62	−1.05	0.33	−0.09
	[0.81]	[0.99]	[0.79]	[0.91]	[0.82]	[0.97]	[0.74]	[0.74]
Other covariates:								
Individual and household characteristics	Yes	Yes	Yes	Yes	Yes	Yes	Yes	Yes
Region Dummies	Yes	Yes	Yes	Yes	Yes	Yes	Yes	Yes
Enumerator Dummies	Yes	Yes	Yes	Yes	Yes	Yes	Yes	Yes
School variables	No	No	Yes	Yes	No	No	Yes	Yes
R^2	0.22	0.15	0.29	0.32	0.12	0.02	0.15	0.21
No. of Observations	284	284	256	256	284	284	256	256

*** $p<0.01$; ** $p<0.05$; * $p<0.10$.
Notes Numbers in brackets are the small sample adjusted standard errors.
Source Author's calculations

[3] and [4] correspond to the enrolled sample, where [3] mirrors [1] and [4] mirrors [2], respectively.

Consistent with the descriptive statistics, the estimates for the boy indicator alone are statistically significant and negative for schooling, studying at home, and household chores. Conversely, they are statistically positive for leisure activities—playing time in both samples and time spent using CGS in the enrolled sample—and for labor time spent helping fathers. These findings suggest that boys' time-allocation patterns are less likely to be "pro-educational" than those of girls. While previous research on pro-educational time use has emphasized studying at home (Nguyen et al. 2022), our results suggest that shorter time allocations for both labor and leisure also contribute to a pro-educational pattern, especially in developing countries like the Philippines. Furthermore, our results contrast with earlier studies showing that girls in developing countries tend to spend less time in school (e.g., Pörtner 2016; Sawada et al. 2006). Interestingly, there is no significant gender difference in the amount of time spent helping mothers with their jobs.

In the enrolled sample ([3] and [4]), the same pattern holds for the boy indicator. This indicates that boys' school enrolment does not reduce the time they spend on leisure activities compared to girls, as the interaction between the boy indicator and school enrolment is statistically insignificant for leisure (playing) time. We interpret these results as further evidence that boys' time-use patterns are less likely to be pro-educational, contributing to their educational disengagement. Regardless of whether they are enrolled in school, boys tend to spend more time playing than girls, even when controlling for other factors.

5.2 *Effect of MLFP on Child Pro-Educational Time-Allocation Patterns*

The estimates of MLFP across all specifications [1]–[4] are statistically negative for leisure time (playing; using CGS). These results suggest that MLFP has a moderate effect on reducing children's leisure time, indicating a pro-educational influence when disregarding child gender heterogeneity. However, the cross-effect of MLFP and the boy indicator is statistically significant and negative for studying at home, with coefficients of −1.71 in specification [2] and −1.97 in specification [4], both at the 5% level. The non-significance of MLFP alone suggests that this negative cross-effect leads to a reduction in boys' study time compared to girls.

Conversely, the interaction between MLFP and the boy indicator is statistically significant and positive for playing time, with coefficients of 2.54 in specification [2] and 1.91 in specification [4], at the 1–5% levels. These values are notable when compared to the negative effect of MLFP alone in the same specifications (−2.96 and −1.90, respectively). This positive cross-effect indicates an increase in boys' playing time relative to girls.

These cross-effects highlight contrasting responses between sons and daughters in their time allocations for studying at home and leisure activities. Specifically, *MLFP* widens the disparity between sons and daughters in terms of the pro-educational time uses, leading to a reduction in sons' pro-educational time uses relative to those of daughters when daughters are used as the reference point. In essence, the inclusion of the boy indicator introduces a gender-specific adjustment, whether positive or negative, relative to a female figure in a binary comparison. These findings underscore a contrasted, discretionary reaction prompted by MLFP in how daughters and sons allocate their time.

5.3 Discussion of Two Mechanisms

To interpret the contrasting responses of sons and daughters to MLFP, where daughters exhibit more pro-educational time use, we incorporate indicators of mothers' employment status. Similar to Shajan and Sumalatha (2022), who compared the effects of mothers in professional versus agricultural sectors on child health, we include dummy variables for "self-employed" and "land-owning farmer" mothers, with "formally employed" as the reference category (as described in Sect. 4).

Locally in Eq. (2), by letting the MLFP indicator and the self-employment and land-owning-farmer indicators be denoted as *MLFP*, *SE*, and *LF*, and their coeffieicents be μ_1, μ_2, and μ_3, , the formal contract-worker effect (base) is expressed as $\mu_1 (= \mu_1 MLFP + \mu_2 SE + \mu_3 LF = \mu_1 * 1 + \mu_2 * 0 + \mu_3 * 0)$. Likewise, the self-employment effect is $\mu_1 + \mu_2 (= \mu_1 MLFP + \mu_2 SE + \mu_3 LF = \mu_1 * 1 + \mu_2 * 1 + \mu_3 * 0)$, and the land-owning farmer effect is $\mu_1 + \mu_3$ $(= \mu_1 MLFP + \mu_2 SE + \mu_3 LF)$ $(= \mu_1 * 1 + \mu_2 * 0 + \mu_3 * 1)$.

In Table 6, the estimates for *mother: self-employed* show statistically significant negative effects on children's study time at home in specifications [3] (–0.98) and [4] (–1.68), while the MLFP indicator alone shows no significant effect. For leisure time, *mother: self-employed* has negative coefficients compared to MLFP, which consistently shows positive effects on playing time (1.31 vs –1.67 for [1], 2.06 vs –2.96 for [2], 0.84 vs –1.13 for [3], and 1.28 vs –1.90 for [4], respectively). However, the cross-effects of *boy indicator* × *mother: self-employed* show opposite directions for both studying (1.23 vs 0 for [2] and 1.59 vs –1.68 for [4], respectively) and playing time (–1.50 vs 2.06 for [2] and –1.02 vs 1.28 for [4], respectively). This suggests that the MLFP effect, which reduces pro-educational time allocation in boys, is attenuated—or even cancelled—if mothers are self-employed rather than formally employed.[17]

The attenuation of the MLFP effect when mothers are self-employed, despite income being controlled, may be attributed to daughters perceiving formally employed mothers as role models. Formal employment generally requires higher

[17] The magnitudes of the *boy indicator* × *mother: self-employed* are smaller than those of the *boy indicator* × *MLFP*, leading us to interpret this as attenuation rather than cancellation.

education (Cameron et al. 2001)[18] and offers more stable and higher wages compared to self-employment, which is common in micro-businesses in the study area (Cabegin and Gaddi 2019). This aligns with interviews conducted during our pilot study, where daughters often viewed formally employed mothers as educational role models, associating their employment with the need to succeed academically.

In this regard, similar comparisons regarding FLFP would also be useful, as one may wonder whether the time-allocation patterns of boys (particularly their labor time helping with their fathers' jobs) can be more affected by the LFPs of the same-gender parents, namely fathers (Estudillo et al. 2001, 2008; Quisumbing 1994). Therefore, although it is not the main variable of concern in this study, we report similar estimates of FLFP and paternal employment status along with their cross effects of *boy indicator* in Table 6, to compare the results regarding MLFP with those concerning FLFP. The results on FLFP in Table 6 are, however, contrary to these expectations. First, the explanatory power of FLFP is much vaguer than MLFP for the children's labor time helping with their fathers' jobs as most of the coefficients of *FLFP* are statistically insignificant.[19] Despite this, the explanatory power and its patterns of MLFP for the children's labor time helping with their fathers' jobs are similar to those for the playing time in the enrolled sample ([3] and [4]).[20] Second, the coefficients of FLFP are negative but their cross effect with *boy indicator* is statistically insignificant for the playing time, unlike the cross effect of MLFP with *boy indicator*. Third, however, the coefficients of *Father: Wage labor* and *Father: Self-employed* alone, respectively, are positive but their cross effects with *boy indicator* are negative in specifications [2] and [4] for the playing time. These are similar to those of MLFP and the cross effects. Likewise, for the studying time at home, the coefficients of *Father: Self-employed* alone are statistically negative in specifications [2] and [4] while its cross effect with *boy indicator* is statistically positive (only in specification [2] and the statistical significance is lower than those for the playing time).

What does this contrast of MLFP with FLFP bring about to our discussions? The most important aspect is to reinforce or reconfirm the aforementioned discussions about the effects of MLFP and the children's role-model type response by their parental employment status. Both for mothers and fathers, the reference category has been the status of formal employment. Therefore, the child responses to pro-education time allocation patterns by the child genders and by the less formal employment status of their parents consistently correspond to the previous interpretations of parents as role models. Concisely, the general effect of MLFP leads more

---

[18] A dramatic increase in female labor force participation is observed among women reaching the college graduate level; this pattern is pronounced in the Philippines (Cameron et al. 2001: 470–472).

[19] This is perhaps because FLFP is virtually a given for the family members in our sample, with the rate exceeding 90% (Table 5).

[20] Another exception is the cross effect of *boy indicator* × *Father: Land-owner farmer* on children's labor time spent helping with their fathers' work, which is –0.70 and significant at the 10% level in specification [2]. In other words, compared to the reference category of fathers with formal employment status, sons of land-owning farmer fathers spend less time assisting with their fathers' work. Yet, since it is not statistically significant in specification [4], the estimate may be less robust.

(less) pro-educational time allocation patterns of daughters (sons) while the effect is attenuated for this path among the working mothers of less formal employment. FLFP also leads to similar results although not as clear as MLFP does, while the paternal less formal employment status attenuates this path as well. In other words, intriguingly, daughters are more responsive pro-educationally if their working parents are more formal workers regardless of whether they are mothers or fathers, than sons are. In this sense, the MLFP–FLFP comparison serves to reconfirm the main discussions so far regarding the MLFP in the current and previous subsections.

In addition to the role-model interpretation, another possibility is the diminished ability of working mothers to monitor playful children (which sons are more likely to be), leading them to spend more time with educationally focused activities. When mothers are working, they are less likely to supervise their children as the children's primary caregivers (Battistella and Conaco 1998; Cawley and Liu 2012; Cortes 2015; Nguyen 2016; Sayer et al. 2004).

A final question arises as to whether the role-model effect of MLFP applies more to daughters and the monitoring effect more to sons. Based on our pilot study, self-employed women often demonstrate flexibility in work hours and locations, which may enable them to better supervise their sons. In contrast, formally employed mothers with longer commutes and stricter work hours might struggle to provide the same level of supervision. This possibility is supported by our findings, considering Bertrand and Pan's (2013) observation that boys require increased maternal involvement during adolescence compared to their female counterparts, as mothers' self-employment attenuates the negative effect of MLFP on boys' time use.

5.4 Tests of the Validity of IV

In this section, we present the statistical tests for the IV. First, Table 7 reports the results of Wooldridge's (1995) robust score test, which assesses the null hypothesis that the MLFP variable is exogenous with respect to the dependent variables of time allocations. Table 7 aligns with the sample classifications and specifications used in Table 6.

For the full sample, the test results show that the robust chi-square statistics for MLFP are statistically significant for time spent on household chores (specification [2] only), as well as for leisure activities—specifically playing time and time spent using CGS (in both specifications). These findings reject the null hypothesis of MLFP exogeneity for these time-use categories. However, for the other time-use variables, the test statistics are not statistically significant, suggesting that MLFP can be treated as exogenous for those time uses.

For the enrolled sample, the null hypothesis is rejected for a broader range of time uses: schooling time (specification [2] only), child labor time helping with fathers' jobs (both specifications), labor time helping mothers (specification [2] only), and playing time (both specifications), all at 5%–10% statistical significance levels. These results suggest that MLFP is endogenous for these time-use categories but can be

Table 7 Robust Chi-square statistics of Wooldridge's robust score test (Null Hypothesis: Exogeneity of MLFP)

Dependent variables (time uses)	Specifications[§]	Full sample		Specifications[§]	Enrolled sample	
Sleeping	[1]	0.06		[3]	0.01	
	[2]	0.35		[4]	2.02	
Studying at home	[1]	1.17		[3]	2.52	
	[2]	1.52		[4]	2.51	
Schooling (in min)	[1]	1.49		[3]	0.13	
	[2]	1.41		[4]	0.17	*
Schooling (in days)	[1]	1.80		[3]	1.82	
	[2]	1.49		[4]	1.83	
Work (fathers' jobs)	[1]	0.73		[3]	2.97	*
	[2]	1.34		[4]	3.78	*
Work (mothers' jobs)	[1]	1.12		[3]	1.98	
	[2]	2.46		[4]	3.10	*
Household chores	[1]	3.15		[3]	2.16	
	[2]	3.16	*	[4]	2.31	
Playing	[1]	8.59	***	[3]	3.90	**
	[2]	8.61	***	[4]	3.38	*
Computer-game shops	[1]	3.20	*	[3]	0.22	
	[2]	3.91	**	[4]	0.03	

***$p < 0.01$; **$p < 0.05$; *$p < 0.10$

§ Specifications [1] do not include and specifications [2] include some interaction terms of the *boy indicator* variable in Table 6

Source Author's calculations

treated as exogenous for the remaining time uses. Based on these findings, and given the focus of this study on pro-educational time uses, MLFP has been treated as endogenous in the empirical analysis.

Second, Table 8 provides the estimates for the IV in the first-stage equation along with the Stock–Yogo F-statistics. For the IV to be considered strong, two conditions must be met: the IV must be statistically significant in predicting MLFP, and the Stock–Yogo F-statistics must meet or exceed the commonly accepted threshold of 10. The results indicate that the first-stage coefficients of the IV are statistically significant and positive at the 1% level across all samples and specifications. Consequently, the IV is confirmed as relevant and explanatory for MLFP. Additionally, the Stock–Yogo F-statistics consistently exceed the threshold value of 10, indicating that the IV is not weak. Therefore, the likelihood of encountering a weak instrument problem is minimal.

To test and validate the exclusion restriction, Table 9 shows the regression of z_{ij}, the IV, on t_{ki}, the dependent variables, in Eq. (2) that ensures that the IV does not have

Table 8 First-Stage estimators and F-statistics (Dependent Variable = MLFP; Instrument = MLFP Wage-Trend Indicator)

Second-stage Specifications		Coef. of Instrument	Robust S.E	p-value	Stock–Yogo F-statistics	Corresponding Specifications	
Full sample:							
	Without interaction terms	0.30***	0.05	0.00	36.65***	Table 6	[1]
	With interaction terms	0.19***	0.05	0.01	15.58***	Table 6	[2]
Enrolled sample:							
	Without interaction terms	0.32***	0.05	0.00	34.92***	Table 6	[3]
	With interaction terms	0.21**	0.07	0.00	14.03***	Table 6	[4]

*** $p < 0.01$; ** $p < 0.05$; * $p < 0.10$
Source Author's calculations

a direct effect on children's time use, independent of MLFP. The results indicate that the IV does not exhibit statistically significant direct effects on most of the time-use categories, supporting the validity of the exclusion restriction in the analysis.

As demonstrated in the results above, the IV (wage trend increase) does not show statistically significant direct effects on children's time use. Hence, these results further support the validity of the exclusion restriction, confirming that the wage trend influences children's time use indirectly via MLFP. An exception is the time

Table 9 Regression results for exclusion restriction

Dependent Variable (child time uses)	Coef. of IV	Robust S.E	p-value	95% CI	R-squared
Sleep	–0.02	0.17	0.91	[–0.36, 0.32]	0.00
Study at home	0.10	0.17	0.59	[–0.25, 0.44]	0.00
Schooling	0.11	0.17	0.52	[–0.23, 0.45]	0.00
Labor: for Fathers' Job	0.03	0.17	0.88	[–0.31, 0.36]	0.00
Labor: for Mothers' Job	0.05	0.18	0.80	[–0.30, 0.39]	0.00
Household Chores	0.17	0.18	0.33	[–0.17, 0.52]	0.00
Playing	–0.14	0.17	0.42	[–0.48, 0.20]	0.00
CGS	–0.30	0.17	0.08	[–0.64, 0.04]	0.01

Notes IV = instrumental variable; S.E. = standard error; CI = confidence interval
Source Author's calculations

for CGS, where the coefficient is negative and weakly significant at the 10% level. However, the time for CGS is not a key time-use element in the study's main analysis.

6 Conclusions

This study sheds light on the impact of MLFP on child time allocation in rural poverty settings, with a particular focus on boys' educational disengagement. Using time-use data from rural Philippines and leveraging institutional changes in the regional labor market, we explore the influence of MLFP on key time inputs of children (Fuwa et al. 2006; Jacobs et al. 2004; Kurosaki et al. 2006; Lloyd et al. 2008; Nguyen et al. 2022).

Our findings reveal that MLFP significantly affects children's time use, with daughters more likely to engage in pro-educational activities than sons. Importantly, the negative effect on boys is unintended. This reflects the rational coping mechanisms of mothers facing poverty-driven livelihood fluctuations, rather than exercising their empowered status (Cabegin 2013; Torres-Yu 2011), which will be further discussed in Chap. 5. Furthermore, this unintended effect exacerbates boys' time-use patterns particularly in cases where mothers are formally employed. The data suggest that daughters, influenced by their mothers' role-modeling, tend to engage in pro-educational activities. This highlights the importance of fostering female role models to encourage girls' educational aspirations. At the same time, this unintended effect may leave scarring in boys' study habits, lowering the likelihood of re-establishing study-oriented routines even after the shock abates, which is consistent with a form of hysteresis whereby the shock's adverse consequences create path dependence (Andrew 2014).

Our further discussion from Sect. 5.3 suggest that working mothers' capacity to monitor their children's activities, particularly those of boys, may be diminished, which has potential consequences for boys' educational engagement. While we find a connection between the reversed gender gap and MLFP in poverty settings, the results also reflect the complexities of achieving true gender equality given women's dual burdens. In the contemporary era of inclusive development, this study's exploration of the relationship between boys' disengagement from education and MLFP highlights complex family dynamics and a persistent challenge to achieving gender parity, calling into question the validity of framing boys' disengagement as merely a "reversed" gender disparity in the end.

Taken together with the findings from Chaps. 2 and 3, this chapter highlights a triangular structure of gendered educational divergence in rural Philippines: while boys are more likely to fall behind (Chap. 2) and girls benefit from intergenerational support (Chap. 3), this chapter reveals how household dynamics—particularly maternal labor—can further shape boys' disengagement from education. These interlinked patterns reinforce the structural asymmetry that underlies the broader phenomenon of gender reversal.

Policies should focus on encouraging men and women's education and MLFP while supporting mothers in balancing caregiving and economic roles. Strengthening social support systems and extending educational resources, such as extracurricular activities and evening schooling, could help mitigate the negative effects of reduced maternal supervision (Halim et al. 2022). Additionally, poverty alleviation programs, including conditional cash transfers, should be enhanced, and addressing the gender wage gap is crucial for ensuring the positive impact of MLFP outweighs any negative consequences (Ermisch and Francesconi 2013; Yamauchi and Tiongco 2013).

Finally, this study acknowledges several limitations, which open avenues for future research. Although we inferred mothers' reduced time availability at home, we could not directly analyze mothers' or fathers' time use. Future research should collect direct data on parental time use to gain a clearer picture. Moreover, our assumptions about parental involvement after employment might be too rigid, as evidence from developed countries shows parents adapt to changing circumstances (Sayer et al. 2004). Further studies should explore this adaptability over time, especially in the Philippine context.

It should also be reminded, as discussed in Sect. 4, that the "pro-educational" time-use patterns observed in this study are highly gendered from the outset, although this is why this study has aimed to go beyond simply being male or female to further explore the factors behind these gender differences. Lastly, while our findings provide important insights into rural villages in the Philippines, caution is necessary in generalizing these results to other developing countries. Further research is needed to build a more comprehensive understanding of the complex interactions between MLFP, child time use, and educational outcomes across different socioeconomic and cultural settings.

While this chapter provides crucial insights into the unintended consequences of MLFP, it also raises further questions regarding the underlying factors driving maternal employment and whether family structures can mitigate the unintended effect. These questions will be explored in Chap. 5, which extends the analysis by examining the socioeconomic determinants of MLFP, particularly the roles of FLFP and household poverty, as well as the potential of extended family settings to offset the gendered impacts of MLFP on boys' educational engagement.

Appendix

For other disaggregated activities, the questionnaire survey collected frequency-level data (e.g., if a child participated in an activity, the frequency was counted as one). Regarding labor engagements, there is a *qualitative* distinction between boys and girls. Boys were observed to assist their fathers at work more frequently than daughters, who rarely did so. In contrast, there was no significant difference between boys and girls in terms of helping their mothers at work. Similarly, the roles and activities children undertake in household chores differ notably between boys and girls. Table A.1 illustrates that field chores occurring outside the home, such as animal care

Table A.1 Decomposed activities within each category

Variables	Means	(1)		(2)	(1) / (2)*
		Of girls		Of boys	
Household chores (= 1 if experienced at least once)					
Young sibling caregiving	0.2	0.2	≈	0.2	1.00
Carry heavy materials	0.3	0.2	<<	0.4	0.50
Animal caregiving	0.1	0.1	<<	0.2	0.50
Cloth wash	0.5	0.6	>	0.4	1.50
Shopping daily consumables	0.1	0.1	≈	0.1	1.00
Cooking	0.6	0.7	>	0.5	1.40
Cleaning	0.7	0.8	>	0.5	1.60
Studying at home (=1 if did at least once)					
Reviewing	0.4	0.5	>	0.3	1.67
Doing the day's homework	0.7	0.8	>	0.6	1.33
Preparing for exam	0.2	0.3	>	0.2	1.50
Doing "project"	0.4	0.3	<	0.5	0.60
Playing (weekly days of engagement)					
With neighbors	1.3	0.6	<<	2.0	0.30
With classmates	0.4	0.3	<	0.5	0.60
Alone	0.2	0.1	<<	0.3	0.33
Computer-Game Shop (weekly minutes)†					
Online game	16.9	1.8	<<	32.4	0.06
Facebook	24.3	19.5	<	29.1	0.67
YouTube	29.9	14.9	<<	45.2	0.33
Chatting	11.7	8.9	<	14.6	0.61
Preparation for classes	35.7	32.6	<	38.9	0.84
Pesos spent (in peso)	35.0	26.0	<	44.3	0.59

Notes * "(1) / (2)" means the index of gender parity

† Minutes of each category for computer-game shop usage may overlap and, therefore, may exceed the mean value reported in Table 2 due to simultaneous multitasking

Source Author's calculations

and carrying heavy items, disproportionately fall on boys. Conversely, contrary to popular belief, girls do not always dominate in household chores. While cooking and cleaning were observed to be performed more often by girls, the gender disparity is less pronounced compared to field chores. Boys also participated in tasks traditionally perceived as feminine, such as cleaning and cooking. According to individual responses, boys reported washing dishes and organizing clean items after meals, tasks they often shared with their female siblings.

In addition to the quantitative questionnaire survey, personal interviews revealed that some boys expressed frustration and resentment toward their parents, particularly their mothers, for stereotyping them as lazy. Their comments suggested an effusion that their female siblings were more likely to remain at home and spend more time with their mothers. Boys often mentioned having "appointments" to go out with their friends or *barkada*.[21] They also admitted that their household contributions were frequently criticized as insufficient. During "behind-the-scenes" interviews, boys revealed their resentment toward their female siblings, as they felt mothers and older siblings consistently assigned them physically demanding chores. They emphasized that the extent of their contribution was not fully captured by the length or frequency of tasks alone. Typically, the chores assigned to boys were performed outside the home, including fetching water, gathering or chopping firewood, farming, and animal husbandry, all of which required considerable physical strength. Girls, on the other hand, were more frequently tasked with laundry and babysitting.

Physically demanding chores often involved carrying heavy items, such as transporting large water bottles from water stations back home, or feeding and caring for animals outside in the hot sun or rain. Boys reported feeling extremely fatigued after completing these tasks, expressing envy toward their female siblings, who could perform some tasks inside the house. Boys noted that their sisters could sit indoors, chat with their mothers, and complete what they described as "*medyo magagaang gawain*" ("somewhat light chores") "*kahit gaano kahaba silang gumagawa*" ("even though the chores take a long time"). The boys added, "*kami po ... paminsan lang po ... gumagawa ng mas mabibigat na gawain*" (#we are the ones ... doing the heavier chores sometimes") and "*parang 'one-shot' [at] nakakapagod lang po [ang] gawa namin ay*" ("it is like we did the one-shot heavy chores").

References

Acosta P (2011) School attendance, child labour, and remittances from international migration in El Salvador. J Dev Stud 47(6):913–936. https://doi.org/10.1080/00220388.2011.563298

Afridi F, Mukhopadhyay A, Sahoo S (2016) Female labor force participation and child education in India: evidence from the national rural employment guarantee scheme. IZA J Labor Dev 5(1):1–27. https://doi.org/10.1186/s40175-016-0053-y

[21] *Barkada* is a peer group or a friend group observed nationwide in the Philippines. Chapter 7 discusses this topic.

Ahn J, Yoo JP (2022) Patterns of time use among 12-year-old children and their life satisfaction: a gender and cross-country comparison. Child Indic Res 15(5):1693–1717. https://doi.org/10.1007/s12187-022-09938-0
Alcaraz C, Chiquiar D, Salcedo A (2012) Remittances, schooling, and child labor in Mexico. J Dev Econ 97(1):156–165. https://doi.org/10.1016/j.jdeveco.2010.11.004
Andrew M (2014) The scarring effects of primary-grade retention? A study of cumulative advantage in the educational career. Social Forces 93(2):653–685. https://doi.org/10.1093/sf/sou074
Antman FM (2011) The intergenerational effects of paternal migration on schooling and work: what can we learn from children's time allocations? J Dev Econ 96(2):200–208. https://doi.org/10.1016/j.jdeveco.2010.11.002
Antman FM (2013) The impact of migration on family left behind. In: Constant AF, Zimmermann KF (eds) International handbook on the economics of migration. Edward Elgar Publishing, Cheltenham, UK, pp 293–308
Asadullah MN, Chaudhury N (2009) Reverse gender gap in schooling in Bangladesh: insights from urban and rural households. J Dev Stud 45(8):1360–1380. https://doi.org/10.1080/00220380902935824
Asian Development Bank (ADB) (2020) Asia's journey to prosperity: policy, market, and technology over 50 years. Asian Development Bank, Manila, Philippines. https://doi.org/10.22617/TCS190290
Attanasio OP, Kaufmann KM (2009) Educational choices, subjective expectations, and credit constraints. No. w15087. National Bureau of Economic Research. https://www.nber.org/system/files/working_papers/w15087/w15087.pdf. Accessed on 1 Aug 2019
Attanasio OP, Kaufmann KM (2014) Education choices and returns to schooling: intra-household decision making, gender and subjective expectations. J Dev Econ 109:203–216. https://doi.org/10.1016/j.jdeveco.2014.04.003
Bai J, Wang Y (2020) Returns to work, child labor and schooling: the income vs. price effects. J Dev Econ 145:102466. https://doi.org/10.1016/j.jdeveco.2020.102466
Basu K, Sanghamitra D, Bhaskar D (2010) Child labor and household wealth: theory and empirical evidence of an inverted-U. J Dev Econ 91(1):8–14. https://doi.org/10.1016/j.jdeveco.2009.01.006
Battistella G, Conaco MCG (1998) The impact of labour migration on the children left behind: a study of elementary school children in the Philippines. J Soc Issues Southeast Asia 13(2):220–241. https://doi.org/10.1355/SJ13-2C
Beegle K, Dehejia R, Gatti R (2009) Why should we care about child labor? The education, labor market, and health consequences of child labor. J Hum Resour 44(4):871–889
Bertrand M, Pan J (2013) The trouble with boys: Social influences and the gender gap in disruptive behavior. Am Econ J Appl Econ 5(1):32–64. https://doi.org/10.1257/app.5.1.32
Bianchi SM, Milkie MA (2010) Work and family research in the first decade of the 21st century. J Marriage Fam 72(3):705–725. https://doi.org/10.1111/j.1741-3737.2010.00726.x
Blau FD, Kahn LM (2007) The gender pay gap: have women gone as far as they can? Acad Manag Perspect 21(1):7–23. https://www.jstor.org/stable/4166284
Blundell R, Pistaferri L, Saporta-Eksten I (2016) Consumption inequality and family labor supply. Am Econ Rev 106(2):387–435. https://doi.org/10.1257/aer.20121549
Borga LG (2019) Children's own time use and its effect on skill formation. J Dev Stud 55(5):876–893. https://doi.org/10.1080/00220388.2018.1499893
Boserup E (1970) Woman's role in economic development. George Allen & Unwin Ltd, London, UK
Bouis HE, Palabrica-Costello M, Solon O, Westbrook D, Limbo AB (1998) Gender equality and investments in adolescents in the rural Philippines. International Food Policy Research Institute. https://doi.org/10.22004/ag.econ.37905
Browning M, Chiappori PA, Weiss Y (2014) Economics of the family. Cambridge University Press, Cambridge, UK. https://doi.org/10.1017/CBO9781139015882

Cabegin ECA (2013) Gendered labor supply response to Filipino spouses' overseas migration and remittances. Asian Pac Migr J 22(2):147–175. https://doi.org/10.1177/011719681302200201
Cabegin ECA, Gaddi RS (2019) Determinants of female labor force participation in the Philippines. National Economic and Development Authority. The Philippines. https://economicsph.org/sites/default/files/Determinants%20of%20Female%20Labor%20Force%20Participation%20%28Edillon%29.pdf
Cameron LA, Dowling JM, Worswick C (2001) Education and labor market participation of women in Asia: evidence from five countries. Econ Dev Cult Change 49(3):459–477. https://doi.org/10.1086/452511
Cawley J, Liu F (2007) Mechanisms for the association between maternal employment and child cognitive development. NBER Working Papers 13609. National Bureau of Economic Research. https://doi.org/10.3386/w13609
Cawley J, Liu F (2012) Maternal employment and childhood obesity: a search for mechanisms in time use data. Econ Hum Biol 10(4):352–364. https://doi.org/10.1016/j.ehb.2012.04.009
Chen M, Vanek J, Lund F, Heintz J, Jhabvala R, Bonner C (2005) Progress of the world's women 2005: women, work and poverty. UNIFEM
Cortes P (2015) The feminization of international migration and its effects on the children left behind: evidence from the Philippines. World Dev 65:62–78. https://doi.org/10.1016/j.worlddev.2013.10.021
Deaton A (1997) The analysis of household surveys: a microeconometric approach to development policy. World Bank
Del Boca D, Monfardini C, Nicoletti C (2017) Parental and child time investments and the cognitive development of adolescents. J Law Econ 35(2):565–608. https://doi.org/10.1086/689479
Desai S, Jain D (1994) Maternal employment and changes in family dynamics: the social context of women's work in rural South India. Popul Dev Rev 20(1):115–136. https://doi.org/10.2307/2137632
Dinkelman T, Ngai LR (2022) Time use and gender in Africa in times of structural transformation. J Econ Perspect 36(1):57–80. https://doi.org/10.1257/jep.36.1.57
DOLE (2012) DOLE provides definition of child labor-related terms. https://www.dole.gov.ph/news/dole-provides-definition-of-child-labor-related-terms/. Accessed 12 Sep 2022
Dong XY, An X (2015) Gender patterns and value of unpaid care work: findings from China's first large-scale time use survey. Rev Income Wealth 61(3):540–560. https://doi.org/10.1111/roiw.12119
Duflo E (2012) Women empowerment and economic development. J Econ Lit 50(4):1051–1079. https://doi.org/10.1257/jel.50.4.1051
Edmonds EV, Shrestha M (2014) You get what you pay for: schooling incentives and child labor. J Dev Econ 111:196–211. https://doi.org/10.1016/j.jdeveco.2014.09.005
Ermisch J, Francesconi M (2013) The effect of parental employment on child schooling. J Appl Economet 28(5):796–822. https://doi.org/10.1002/jae.2260
Estudillo JP, Quisumbing A, Otsuka K (2001) Gender differences in land inheritance, schooling and lifetime income: evidence from the rural Philippines. J Dev Stud 37(4):23–48. https://doi.org/10.1080/00220380412331322031
Estudillo JP, Sawada Y, Otsuka K (2008) Poverty and income dynamics in Philippine Village 1985–2004. Rev Dev Econ 12:877–890. https://doi.org/10.1111/j.1467-9361.2008.00458.x
Esquivel V, Budlender D, Folbre N, Hirway I (2008) Explorations: time-use surveys in the south. Fem Econ 14(3):107–152. https://doi.org/10.1080/13545700802075135
Eswaran M (2014) Why gender matters in economics. Princeton University Press, Princeton, New Jersey
Faria JR, Sachsida A (2012) Demographic dynamics in poor countries: labour market conditions and gender inequalities. J Dev Stud 48(1):99–114. https://doi.org/10.1080/00220388.2010.527957
Fertig A, Glomm G, Tchernis R (2009) The connection between maternal employment and childhood obesity: inspecting the mechanisms. Rev Econ Househ 7(3):227–255. https://doi.org/10.1007/s11150-009-9052-y

Field E, Pande R, Rigol N, Schaner S, Stacy E, Moore CT (2023) Measuring time use in rural India: design and validation of a low-cost survey module. J Dev Econ 103105:35. https://doi.org/10.1016/j.jdeveco.2023.103105

Fuwa N (2014) Pro-girl bias in intra-household allocation in the rural Philippines: revisiting the "adult goods" approach. Rev Dev Econ 18(4):727–740. https://doi.org/10.1111/rode.12115

Fuwa N, Ito S, Kubo K, Kurosaki T, Sawada Y (2006) Intrahousehold resource allocation, child labor, and school enrollment: evidence from rural India. Econ Rev 57(4):328–343. https://doi.org/10.15057/21948

Fuwa N, Ito S, Kubo K, Kurosaki T, Sawada Y (2012) How does credit access affect children's time allocation? Evidence from rural India. J Glob Dev 3(1):4. https://doi.org/10.1515/1948-1837.1095

Glick P (2008) What policies will reduce gender schooling gaps in developing countries: evidence and interpretation. World Dev 36(9):1623–1646. https://doi.org/10.1016/j.worlddev.2007.09.014

Goldin C (1995) The U-shaped female labor force function in economic development and economic history. In: Schultz P (ed) Investment in women's human capital. University of Chicago Press, Chicago, USA, pp 61–90

Grootaert C, Kanbur R (1995) Child labor: an economic perspective. Int Labour Rev 134(2):187–203

Grootaert C, Patrinos HA (eds) (1999) Policy analysis of child labor: a comparative study. St. Martin's Press, New York, USA

Grootaert C, Patrinos HA (Eds.) (2002) A four-country comparative study of child labor. Presented at the international economics of child labor seminar in Oslo, Norway, May 28–29

Haveman R, Wolfe B (1995) The determinants of children's attainments: a review of methods and findings J Econ Lit 33(4):1829–1878. https://www.jstor.org/stable/2729315

Halim D, Perova E, Reynolds S (2022) Childcare and mothers' labor market outcomes in lower- and middle-income countries. World Bank Res Obs 38(1):73–114. https://doi.org/10.1093/wbro/lkac003

Heady C (2003) The effect of child labor on learning achievement. World Dev 31(2):385–398. https://doi.org/10.1016/S0305-750X(02)00186-9

Hirway I (2010) Time-use surveys in developing countries: An assessment. In: Antonopoulos R, Hirway I (eds) Unpaid work and the economy. Palgrave Macmillan, London, UK, pp 252–324

Ilahi N (2010) The intra-household allocation of time and tasks: What have we learnt from the empirical literature. World Bank policy research working paper series, 20785

Jacobs JE, Vernon MK, Eccles JS (2004) Relations between social self-perceptions, time use, and prosocial or problem behaviors during adolescence. J Adolesc Res 19(1):45–62. https://doi.org/10.1177/0743558403258225

Jensen R (2012) Do Labor market opportunities affect young women's work and family decisions? experimental evidence from India. Quart J Econ 127(2):753–792. https://doi.org/10.1093/qje/qjs002

Jha J, Bakshi S, Faria EM (2012) Understanding and challenging boys' disadvantage in secondary education in developing countries. UNESCO, Background paper prepared for the EFA Global Monitoring Report

Kahneman D, Krueger AB, Schkade DA, Schwarz N, Stone AA (2004) A survey method for characterizing daily life experience: The day reconstruction method. Science 306(5702):1776–1780. https://doi.org/10.1126/science.1103572

Kan MY, Pudney S (2008) Measurement error in stylized and diary data on time use. Sociol Methodol 38(1):101–132

Kudo Y, Shonchoy AS, Takahashi K (2019) Can solar lanterns improve youth academic performance? Experimental evidence from Bangladesh. World Bank Econ Rev 33(2):436–460. https://doi.org/10.1093/wber/lhw073

Kurosaki T, Ito S, Fuwa N, Kubo K, Sawada Y (2006) Child labor and school enrollment in rural India: Whose education matters? Dev Econ 44(4):440–464. https://doi.org/10.1111/j.1746-1049.2006.00024.x

Lam CB, McHale SM (2015) Time use as cause and consequence of youth development. Child Dev Perspect 9(1):20–25. https://doi.org/10.1111/cdep.12100

Larson RW, Verma S (1999) How children and adolescents spend time across the world: Work, play, and developmental opportunities. Psychol Bull 125(6):701–736. https://doi.org/10.1037/0033-2909.125.6.701

Le K, Nguyen M (2020) Shedding light on maternal education and child health in developing countries. World Dev 133:105005. https://doi.org/10.1016/j.worlddev.2020.105005

Lloyd CB, Grant M, Ritchie A (2008) Gender differences in time use among adolescents in developing countries: implications of rising school enrollment rates. J Res Adolesc 18(1):99–120. https://doi.org/10.1111/j.1532-7795.2008.00552.x

Mapa DS (2021) Working children and child labor situation. Reference Number 2021–484. Philippine statistics authority. https://psa.gov.ph/content/working-children-and-child-labor-situation

McHale SM, Crouter AC, Tucker CJ (2001) Free-time activities in middle childhood: links with adjustment in early adolescence. Child Dev 72(6):1764–1778. https://doi.org/10.1111/1467-8624.00377

McKenzie D, Rapoport H (2011) Can migration reduce educational attainment? Evidence from Mexico. J Popul Econ 24(4):1331–1358. https://doi.org/10.1007/s00148-010-0316-x

Meyerhoefer CD, Chen CJ (2011) The effect of parental labor migration on children's educational progress in rural China. Rev Econ Household 9(3):379–396. https://doi.org/10.1007/s11150-010-9105-2

Nankinga O, Kwagala B, Walakira EJ (2019) Maternal employment and child nutritional status in Uganda. PLoS ONE 14(12):e0226720. https://doi.org/10.1371/journal.pone.0226720

Nazier H, Ezzat A (2022) Gender differences and time allocation: A comparative analysis of Egypt and Tunisia. Q Rev Econ Financ 85:174–193. https://doi.org/10.1016/j.qref.2021.01.001

Nguyen CV (2016) Does parental migration really benefit left-behind children? Comparative evidence from Ethiopia, India, Peru and Vietnam. Soc Sci Med 153:230–239. https://doi.org/10.1016/j.socscimed.2016.02.021

Nguyen HT, Brinkman S, Le HT, Zubrick SR, Mitrou F (2022) Gender differences in time allocation contribute to differences in developmental outcomes in children and adolescents. Econ Educ Rev 89:102270. https://doi.org/10.1016/j.econedurev.2022.102270

Okabe M (2025) Unintended effect of mothers' labor force participation on child time allocations under family dynamics in rural Philippines. Rev Econ Household. https://doi.org/10.1007/s11150-024-09758-x

Parish WL, Willis RJ (1993) Daughters, education, and family budgets: Taiwan experiences. J Hum Resour 28(4):863–898. https://doi.org/10.2307/146296

Patrinos HA, Psacharopoulos G (1997) Family size, schooling and child labor in Peru–an empirical analysis. J Popul Econ 10(4):387–405. https://doi.org/10.1007/s001480050050

Parreñas RS (2007) The gender ideological clash in globalization: women, migration, and the modernization building project of the Philippines. Soc Thought Res 28:37–56. https://doi.org/10.17161/STR.1808.5223

Philippine Statistics Authority (2017) Functional literacy, education, and mass media survey 2013. Philippine Statistics Authority

Philippine Statistics Authority (2021) Functional literacy, education, and mass media survey 2019. Philippine Statistics Authority

PIA MIMAROPA, 2017. DOLE MIMAROPA issues new minimum wage rates for domestic workers. https://pia4b.wordpress.com/2017/07/24/dole-mimaropa-issues-new-minimum-wage-rates-for-domestic-workers/. Accessed on 1 Aug 2018

Pörtner CC (2016) Effects of parental absence on child labor and school attendance in the Philippines. Rev Econ Household 14:103–130. https://doi.org/10.1007/s11150-014-9266-5

Psacharopoulos G (1997) Child labor versus educational attainment: some evidence from Latin America. J Popul Econ 10(4):377–386. https://doi.org/10.1007/s001480050049

Quisumbing AR (1994) Intergenerational transfers in Philippine rice villages. Gender differences in traditional inheritance customs. J Dev Econ 43(2):167–195. https://doi.org/10.1016/0304-3878(94)90003-5

Ravallion M, Wodon Q (2000) Does child labour displace schooling? Evidence on behavioural responses to an enrollment subsidy. Econ J 110(462):C158–C175. https://doi.org/10.1111/1468-0297.00527

Reggio I (2011) The influence of the mother's power on her child's labor in Mexico. J Dev Econ 96(1):95–105. https://doi.org/10.1016/j.jdeveco.2010.07.002

Rubiano-Matulevich E, Viollaz M (2019) Gender differences in time use allocating time between the market and the household. Policy research working paper 8981. World Bank

Sawada Y, Kubo K, Fuwa N, Ito S, Kurosaki T (2006) On the mother and child labor nexus under credit constraints: findings from rural India. Dev Econ 44(4):465–499. https://doi.org/10.1111/j.1746-1049.2006.00025.x

Sayer LC, Bianchi SM, Robinson JP (2004) Are parents investing less in children? Trends in mothers' and fathers' time with children. Am J Sociol 110(1):1–43. https://doi.org/10.1086/386270

Seymour G, Malapit H, Quisumbing A (2020) Measuring time use in developing country agriculture: evidence from Bangladesh and Uganda. Fem Econ 26(3):169–199. https://doi.org/10.1080/13545701.2020.1749867

Shajan J, Sumalatha BS (2022) Maternal employment and children's health in India: an exploratory analysis. J Public Aff 22(3):e2580. https://doi.org/10.1002/pa.2580

Sharma K, Bisht R (2022) Gender, time-use, and health: a scoping review. Int Health Trends Perspect 2(2):193–216. https://doi.org/10.32920/ihtp.v2i2.1637

Srinivasan S, Bhat CR (2005) Modeling household interactions in daily in-home and out-of-home maintenance activity participation. Transportation 32(5):523–544. https://doi.org/10.1007/s11116-005-5329-z

Stewart J (2013) Tobit or not Tobit? J Econ Soc Meas 38(3):263–290. https://doi.org/10.3233/JEM-130376

Strauss J, Thomas D (1995) Human resources: Empirical modeling of household and family decisions. Handb Dev Econ 3:1883–2023

Torres A (2011) Analysis on why boys do poorly: Philippines case study [Mimeo]. United Nations Girls' Education Initiatives

Torres-Yu R (2011) Childhood and family in contemporary children's fiction: resilience, agency, and emerging gender norms. Kritika Kultura 16:44–64

UNESCO (2022) Leave no child behind: Global report on boys' disengagement from education. United Nations Educational, Scientific and Cultural Organization

UNGEI (2012) Why are boys under-performing in education? Gender analysis of four Asia–Pacific countries. United Nations Girls' Education Initiative

Welmond MJ, Gregory L (2021) Educational underachievement among boys and men. World Bank

Williams JR, Masuda YJ, Tallis H (2016) A measure whose time has come: formalizing time poverty. Soc Indic Res 128(1):265–283. https://doi.org/10.1007/s11205-015-1029-z

Wooldridge JM (1995) Score diagnostics for linear models estimated by two stage least squares. In: Maddala GS, Phillips PCB, Srinivasan TN (ed) Advances in econometrics and quantitative economics: essays in Honor of Professor C. R. Rao. Oxford: Blackwell

Xu S, Shonchoy AS, Fujii T (2022) Assessing gender parity in intrahousehold allocation of educational resources: evidence from Bangladesh. World Dev 151:105730. https://doi.org/10.1016/j.worlddev.2021.105730

Yang D (2008) International migration, remittances and household investment: evidence from Philippine migrants' exchange rate shocks. Econ J 118(528):591–630. https://doi.org/10.1111/j.1468-0297.2008.02134.x

Yamauchi F, Tiongco M (2013) Why women are progressive in education? Gender disparities in human capital, labor markets, and family arrangement in the Philippines. Econ Educ Rev 32:196–206. https://doi.org/10.1016/j.econedurev.2012.09.003

Zimmermann T, Williams JH (2016) Parents' educational expectations, their determinants, and consequences in explaining students' dropout in an area in Cambodia. In: Kitamura Y, Edwards DB, Sitha Jr. C, Williams JH (ed) The political economy of schooling in Cambodia: issues of quality and equity. Palgrave Macmillan, London UK

Chapter 5
Families to Mothers?—Poverty-Driven Maternal Labor, Extended Family's Potential for Support, and Boys' Educational Disengagement: Further Investigation in Marinduque, MIMAROPA, Southern Luzon

Abstract This chapter investigates the unintended effect of maternal labor force participation (MLFP) in rural Philippine households, focusing on its determinants and the potential for extended family support to mitigate this effect. Using data from Marinduque, the study employs empirical analyses to examine the drivers of MLFP and assess whether extended family settings can offset its unintended impact on boys' educational time use. A bivariate probit analysis reveals that MLFP is primarily driven by economic necessity, with household poverty and insufficient fathers' labor force participation (FLFP) compelling mothers to enter the labor market as a compensatory strategy. While MLFP sustains family livelihoods, it reduces boys' time spent on educational activities and increases their leisure time. Extended family settings, though more common in rural areas, provide only limited relief and fail to fully mitigate the unintended effect of MLFP. These findings challenge interpretations of the unintended effect as merely causing a reversed gender disparity in education, instead highlighting how entrenched traditional gender norms continue to burden mothers while indirectly affecting boys. The chapter underscores the need for systemic policies to address household poverty, enhance employment stability, and foster equitable educational opportunities to mitigate these challenges.

Keywords Dual burden · Extended family · Poverty-driven labor · Primary child-care responsibilities · Unintended effect of mothers' labor force participation

1 Introduction

The preceding chapters have illustrated the complex interplay between gender, parental labor force participation, and children's pro-educational time inputs. Chapter 4 demonstrated that maternal labor force participation (MLFP) often had an unintended effect, amplifying gendered gaps in time-use patterns between sons and daughters, potentially contributing to boys' disengagement from pro-educational

This chapter is based on part of Okabe (2025).

M. Okabe, *Economics of the Reversal in Gender Disparities in Education and Development*, Economics, Law, and Institutions in Asia Pacific,
https://doi.org/10.1007/978-981-96-9271-2_5

activities. Specifically, Chapter 4 identified two mechanisms through which MLFP impacts children: (1) reduced maternal capacity for supervising children and (2) a role-model effect, where working mothers more strongly influence daughters compared to sons.

In line with these findings from Chapter 4, it is also important to recall the findings and discussions in Chapter 3, which highlighted the intergenerational transmission of educational disparities in Bukidnon, another rural province of the Philippines. Chapter 3 revealed that maternal education plays a critical role in shaping daughters' educational trajectories, particularly in the long term beyond primary education. These findings reflect broader societal and cultural dynamics, where mothers often serve as role models for their daughters. Together, these dynamics raise an important question: Is it fair to attribute the consequences of MLFP's unintended effect on child time allocations, as examined in Chapter 4, solely to working mothers?

This chapter challenges such a simplistic interpretation by examining the structural and socioeconomic drivers behind MLFP and evaluating whether extended family—a family system commonly observed in rural settings—can mitigate its unintended effect on boys' educational time use. Extended families, including grandparents and other adult relatives, are often seen as potential buffers against socioeconomic hardship and caregiving challenges (Mare 2011; LaFave and Thomas 2017). However, their capacity to counteract these unintended consequences is not guaranteed and may even exacerbate household inequalities when existing gendered labor divisions are reinforced (Liversage and Jakobsen 2010).

This chapter addresses two interrelated questions: (1) What drives MLFP in rural households, and to what extent is it influenced by FLFP and household poverty? (2) Can extended families effectively offset the unintended effect of MLFP on boys' education? Drawing on primary data from Marinduque, this study extends Chapter 4's analysis to explore these questions, emphasizing the need to situate MLFP within the broader structural constraints of poverty and family dynamics.

The remainder of this chapter is structured as follows. Section 2 reviews the conceptual framework and relevant literature. Section 3 outlines the data and methodological approach. Section 4 presents empirical findings, and Sect. 5 discusses the results and implications. Finally, Sect. 6 concludes this chapter, discussing policy implications and future research warranted.

2 Conceptual Framework

The empirical results in Chapter 4 demonstrate that MLFP widens the gap between sons' and daughters' pro-educational time use. This is termed an "unintended" effect of MLFP. In the Philippine context, mothers are expected to shoulder dual responsibilities: childrearing and contributing to household income, often filling the breadwinner role traditionally held by fathers (Torres-Yu 2011). In the societal context of the Philippines, a Filipino phrase "*ilaw ng tahanan*," meaning "light of the family," is a time-worn expression that highlights the traditional maternal role of providing guidance and support to children. In contrast, fathers are referred to as another similar Filipino phrase, "*haligi ng tahanan*," meaning "pillar of the home," often associated with the breadwinner role, responsible for sustaining the household livelihood. This well-referred norm, aside from education, emphasizes mothers' key roles in holistic human development such as child health (Le and Nguyen 2020).

Therefore, MLFP in rural households is assumed to be rarely a purely voluntary decision; instead, it is often induced by household poverty and insufficient income from fathers' labor force participation (FLFP). Previous studies demonstrate that economic necessity frequently compels mothers to enter the labor market, acting as a compensatory mechanism during periods of low male earnings or unemployment (Meyerhoefer & Chen 2011; Razavi 2007). This dual burden—balancing both income generation and child caregiving responsibilities—challenges mothers' ability to supervise children's education effectively, as touched upon in Chapter 4. Household poverty and traditional gender norms exacerbate these dynamics, reinforcing time-use disparities that disproportionately affect boys (Blau et al. 2010; Bianchi and Milkie 2010).

The phenomenon referred to in Chapter 4 as the "unintended" effect of MLFP underscores that reducing boys' pro-educational time is neither the intention nor the choice of working mothers. In the Philippine context, mothers often assume dual responsibilities, filling the breadwinner role traditionally held by fathers (Torres-Yu 2011). These challenges are further magnified in patriarchal and agrarian societies, where traditional gender roles persist, and subsistence living places additional pressures on women and children. FLFP, often treated as a predetermined or pseudo-exogenous factor, influences maternal employment decisions through its impact on household livelihoods (Kabeer 2015; Jayachandran 2021).

Extended family systems are frequently cited as potential buffers against these challenges, particularly in rural and developing regions (Croll 2006; Mare 2011). Grandparents or other adult relatives, such as uncles and aunts, have been shown to provide long-term benefits for child welfare and education through resource sharing, caregiving, or even direct educational interactions (Adermon et al. 2021; Edmonds 2006; LaFave and Thomas 2017; Li and Cao 2023; Quisumbing 1997; Zeng and Xie 2014). However, the effectiveness of such support varies. While extended family members may step in to supervise children, their contributions do not always fully offset the dual burden on mothers or mitigate MLFP's unintended effect (Afridi et al. 2016). In some cases, extended family structures may even reinforce existing gendered responsibility divisions, creating additional inequalities.

This chapter situates MLFP within these broader structural and cultural constraints, examining how FLFP, household poverty, and extended family support interact to influence boys' educational outcomes. By integrating these elements, the analysis highlights the interconnected nature of economic and cultural factors shaping household decisions in rural settings.

3 Data and Methods

This chapter continuously uses the same primary data collected in rural Marinduque as used in Chapter 4 to further explore and analyze the unintended effect of MLFP through the two questions stated in Sects. 1 and 2. The dataset includes detailed information on household composition, parental employment, children's time use, and educational engagement. For descriptions of the data collection process, sampling methods, and summary statistics, readers are referred to Chapter 4. This section highlights the variables and analytical methods specific to the two research questions addressed in this chapter.

3.1 Determinants of MLFP

To examine the factors influencing MLFP, this study focuses on the interaction between MLFP and FLFP. Both MLFP and FLFP are categorized into formal employment, self-employment, and underemployment. Before econometric analyses, our preliminary descriptive findings from self-reported reasons for MLFP—mothers' subjective responses—reveal economic necessity is the primary driver: 86% of working mothers cited issues related to their husbands' earnings, including inadequate income (79.2%) and unemployment (6.9%). In contrast, voluntary MLFP—measured by the response "I like working"—was reported by only 11.1%. These findings suggest that MLFP is closely tied to FLFP and household economic strain, which are further explored through the econometric analysis in Sects. 4 and 5.

3.2 Time Allocation and Extended Family Setting

The second research question investigates whether extended family members mitigate the unintended effect of MLFP on boys' educational engagement. The dataset distinguishes between nuclear and extended households, with extended families defined as those including at least one relative beyond the nuclear unit (e.g., grandparents, aunts, or uncles).

As explained in Chapter 4, time-use data collected from children through a diary-based method capture daily activity patterns, including time spent on education, household labor, and leisure. This chapter examines whether extended family settings influence the unintended effect of MLFP on boys' time allocation differently compared to nuclear families, building on insights from Chapter 4 while extending the analysis to address the impact of household composition.

3.3 Methods

The analysis employs two econometric approaches. For the first research question, a bivariate probit model is employed to jointly estimate the determinants of MLFP and FLFP. This model allows for the analysis of key factors shaping MLFP decisions, such as household poverty, fathers' employment status, and other household characteristics, while accounting for potential interdependence between FLFP and MLFP. By modeling these decisions jointly, the bivariate probit approach provides insights into how MLFP decisions are influenced by economic necessity and gendered household dynamics.

The model also includes a test of whether FLFP can be treated as a predetermined or exogenous variable for the determination of MLFP. Specifically, the Wald test assesses whether the error terms of the MLFP and FLFP equations are uncorrelated, as assumed under the null hypothesis. Rejection of the null hypothesis suggests that FLFP is endogenous or not predetermined, implying that unobserved factors jointly influence both variables. This dual focus ensures that the analysis not only captures the socioeconomic determinants of MLFP but also rigorously evaluates the independence of FLFP in shaping maternal employment decisions.

For the second research question, an instrumental variable (IV) regression model, similar to the approach used in Chapter 4, is applied to examine the relationship between MLFP and children's time allocation patterns, with an additional focus on the interactions between MLFP and extended family settings. This model addresses the potential endogeneity of MLFP in determining children's time use by using regional minimum wage changes as an IV, which satisfies the exclusion restriction. As in Chapter 4, validity tests for this extended analysis confirm the validity of the IV. These results, detailed later in Sect. 5.3, support the reliability of the empirical findings.

3.4 Summary Statistics

Table 1 summarizes the dependent and independent variables used in this chapter's analysis. As the dataset overlaps with that of Chapter 4, the summary statistics remain unchanged. Of particular relevance to this chapter, the extended family indicator—coded as 1 for households with members beyond children and parents—shows that approximately one-third of households in the sample are classified as extended families. Other covariates, including FLFP, household income, and children's individual attributes, are incorporated into the analysis as described in Sects. 4.1 and 4.2.

Table 1 Summary statistics of variables

Variables			Full sample (*n* = 284)		Enrolled sample (*n* = 258)	
			Mean	Std. dev	Mean	Std. dev
Dependent variables:						
	Time allocation, 7 days					
		Sleeping	3610.23	435.94	3598.72	429.73
		Studying at home	279.14	267.17	307.71	271.19
		Schooling (in min)	2097.54	913.50	2307.52	663.46
		Schooling (in days)	4.31	1.61	4.71	0.95
		Helping with fathers' jobs	111.48	253.88	86.53	186.64
		Helping with mothers' jobs	76.72	175.54	83.82	182.75
		Household chores	447.04	367.75	450.72	365.22
		Playing	228.65	308.90	198.99	291.19
		Computer-game shops	54.30	131.46	48.15	103.17
Independent variables and covariates:						
	Individual characteristics					
		Enrolled (=1)	0.91	0.28	n.a.	n.a.
		Male (=1)	0.46	0.50	0.41	0.49
		Age	15.22	2.84	15.14	2.62
		Lowly aspired child	0.10	0.29	0.05	0.22
		Eldest (=1)	0.18	0.38	0.19	0.39
		Youngest (=1)	0.21	0.41	0.20	0.40
		Elder siblings	2.68	2.33	2.69	2.44
		Younger siblings	1.80	1.45	1.77	1.38
	Household characteristics					
		FLFP indicator (=1 father is working)	0.93	0.25	0.94	0.24
		Father: Land-owner farmer (=1)	0.05	0.22	0.05	0.22
		Father: Wage labor (=1)	0.13	0.33	0.13	0.33
		Father: Self-employment (=1)	0.31	0.46	0.31	0.46
		FLFP: Wage-increase indicator (=1 if increasing)	0.19	0.39	0.19	0.39

(continued)

Table 1 (continued)

Variables			Full sample (n = 284)		Enrolled sample (n = 258)	
			Mean	Std. dev	Mean	Std. dev
		MLFP indicator (=1 if mother is working)	0.50	0.50	0.53	0.50
		Mother: Land-owning farmer (=1)	0.01	0.08	0.01	0.09
		Mother: Self-employment (=1)	0.35	0.48	0.38	0.49
		MLFP: Wage-increase indicator (=1 if increasing)[a]	0.14	0.34	0.13	0.34
		ln per capita income	6.97	1.05	7.08	1.02
		per capita income	1871.68	2867.10	1952.46	2959.60
		Income shares to non-parental household members' earnings (%)	0.14	0.24	0.13	0.24
		Father's age	47.17	7.81	46.93	7.56
		Mother's age	44.91	6.89	44.57	6.39
		Father's education (=1 if college graduate)	0.11	0.31	0.12	0.33
		Mother's education (=1 if college graduate)	0.14	0.35	0.14	0.35
		Female headed (=1)	0.04	0.19	0.03	0.16
		Separate father (=1)	0.13	0.34	0.13	0.34
		Separate mother (=1)	0.09	0.29	0.09	0.28
		Extended family (=1)	0.32	0.47	0.32	0.47
	School variables					
		Public school (=1)	n.a.	n.a.	0.90	0.29
		Commuting time (mins., one-way)	n.a.	n.a.	18.72	14.63
		Walking to school (=1)	n.a.	n.a.	0.20	0.40
		Distance (km, one-way)	n.a.	n.a.	3.58	5.07

[a]Instrument variable for MLFP

Note Dependent variables are standardized into z-scores in regression analyses for the comparison. FLFP and MLFP refer to fathers' and mothers' labor force participation, respectively

Source Author's calculations

4 Empirical Analysis

4.1 *Joint Estimation of Determinants of Parental Labor Force Participation*

To better examine the dual burden experienced by working mothers, we investigate whether MLFP is self-determined and voluntary or compelled by economic necessity, particularly household poverty. In addition to the self-reported reasons for maternal employment summarized in Sect. 3.1, this section employs econometric analysis to identify the determinants of MLFP and assess the extent to which it is voluntarily chosen, independent of husbands' characteristics and household living standards (as the null hypothesis).

A bivariate probit model (Cameron and Trivedi 2005) is used to jointly estimate MLFP and FLFP, allowing for nonzero correlation between the two error terms. This approach evaluates whether MLFP is independently determined from FLFP and explores the extent to which MLFP is self-determined by mothers (Sawada et al. 2006). The model assumes that FLFP is predetermined relative to MLFP, based on the traditional breadwinner role attributed to men in rural Philippine households. This assumption follows the framework of Sawada et al. (2006), who analyzed similar dynamics in rural India. The bivariate probit equation for household j with child i is specified as follows:

$$\begin{cases} P_j = \mathbf{z}_j \boldsymbol{\beta}_\mathbf{P} + \epsilon_P, & P_j = \mathrm{I}\left(P_j^* > 0\right); \\ M_j = \mathbf{z}_j \boldsymbol{\beta}_\mathbf{M} + \mathbf{h}_j \boldsymbol{\gamma} + \epsilon_M, & M_j = \mathrm{I}\left(M_j^* > 0\right). \end{cases} \tag{5.1}$$

where $\mathrm{I}(\cdot)$ denotes the indicator function; the vector $\mathbf{z}_j$ contains the common covariates of household characteristics, and the vector $\mathbf{h}_j$ includes additional covariates that are included only in the equation for M_j. P_j^* and M_j^* represent the underlying latent variables for P_j and M_j, which are the indicators for FLFP and MLFP, respectively, taking the value 1 if participating in the labor force and 0 otherwise. The vector $\mathbf{z}_j$ includes the number of children, husband's education, age, monthly income, and a wage-trend indicator for the labor market (=1 if wages have increased in the husband's occupation). The vector $\mathbf{h}_j$ includes the husband's employment status (=1 if employed), wife's age, education, and a wage-trend indicator for the labor market in the wife's occupation[1] (=1 if wages have increased). This analysis focuses on testing the null hypothesis that the two equations are simultaneously determined, while also examining the estimated coefficients of the husband's working and income profiles in determining M_j.

[1] This wage-trend indicator, conceptually the same as the IV in Chapter 4, is also applied in the estimation of Eq. (5.2) in this chapter.

4.2 Analysis on the Potential of Extended Family Offsetting the Unintended Effect of MLFP

To test whether extended family settings can offset the unintended effect of MLFP, we introduce an extended family indicator variable (EX_{ij}), which takes the value of 1 if a household is classified as an extended family and 0 otherwise. This variable, constructed using household demographic data, identifies households including at least one additional adult relative (e.g., grandparents, uncles, or aunts), providing a measure of extended family composition. These members may help monitor children during their working mothers' absence from home.

Accordingly, the extended family indicator variable (EX_{ij}), its interaction term with the MLFP indicator ($MLFP_{ij} * EX_{ij}$), and the three-way interaction term with the MLFP and boy indicators ($G_i * MLFP_{ij} * EX_{ij}$) are incorporated into the model as an extension of Eq. (5.1) from Chapter 4. The updated model is specified as follows:

$$\begin{aligned} t_{ki} = \gamma_k^G G_i + \mu_{1k} MLFP_{ij} + \mu_{2k}\left(G_i * MLFP_{ij}\right) + \mu_{3k} EX_{ij} \\ + \mu_{4k}\left(G_i * EX_{ij}\right) + \mu_{5k}\left(MLFP_{ij} * EX_{ij}\right) \\ + \mu_{6k}\left(G_i * MLFP_{ij} * EX_{ij}\right) + \mathbf{x_i}\boldsymbol{\beta}_1^G + \mathbf{x_j}\boldsymbol{\beta}_2^G + \omega_k^G + u_{ki}^G, \end{aligned} \quad (5.2)$$

where $\mathbf{x_i}$ and $\mathbf{x_j}$ are vectors of the individual characteristics of child i and household$j$, respectively. The term ω_k^G represents region- and school-level fixed effects specific to the barangay where the household resides and the school where the child is enrolled. The stochastic error term is denoted by u_{ki}^G. The additional effectsμ_{3k},μ_{4k},μ_{5k}, and μ_{6k} in Eq. (5.2) are of particular interest, as they allow us to assess whether the extended family structure mitigates the unintended effect of MLFP.

Using the same 2SLS strategy as in Chapter 4, the estimation method and the instrument for MLFP are implemented similarly. Specifically, the fitted value of $\widehat{MLFP}_{ij}$ is derived from the first-stage regression:

$$\widehat{MLFP}_{ij} = \widehat{\zeta^G} z_{ij} + \mathbf{x_i}\widehat{\boldsymbol{\eta}_1^G} + \mathbf{x_j}\widehat{\boldsymbol{\eta}_2^G}, \quad (5.3)$$

where z_{ij} is the IV, and$\widehat{\zeta^G}$,$\widehat{\boldsymbol{\eta}_1^G}$, and $\widehat{\boldsymbol{\eta}_2^G}$ are the estimated coefficients from the first stage. This fitted value, $\widehat{MLFP}_{ij}$, is then used in place of $MLFP_{ij}$ in the second-stage estimation of Eq. (5.2). The validity tests for the IV in estimating Eqs. (5.2) and (5.3) are detailed in Sect. 5.3.

5 Results

5.1 Determinants of Parental Labor Force Participation

In what situations are mothers more likely to participate in the labor force? The bivariate probit results for Eq. (5.1) are displayed in Table 2. According to the estimates, mothers with higher levels of education and those whose husbands have low incomes are more likely to participate in the labor force. This suggests that MLFP is influenced by both the mothers' own human capital and their husbands' economic instability. These results align with the self-reported reasons discussed in Sect. 3.1, confirming that the majority of MLFP occurs as a compensatory response to insufficient earnings by husbands.

While the educational level of mothers is a significant positive predictor of MLFP, the relationship is not linear; there is a sharp, kinking, and dramatic increase in MLFP participation among mothers who are college graduates. This aligns with findings by Cameron et al. (2001: 470–472), who observed that such a sharp increase is more pronounced in the Philippines than in South Korea, Thailand, Indonesia, and Sri Lanka.

However, these results do not imply that fathers deliberately choose to remain unemployed, underemployed, or lower-income earners, relying on their wives' employment. Rather, FLFP appears to be a given or predetermined factor in MLFP decisions. This hypothesis is tested using Wald statistics to assess whether FLFP can be treated as exogenous to MLFP. The Wald test results, shown in the bottom row of Table 2, indicate that the null hypothesis of exogeneity cannot be rejected at conventional significance levels (p-value= 0.46). Consequently, FLFP is identified as exogenous or predetermined with respect to MLFP decisions, reinforcing the traditional social norm in rural Philippine households that fathers (husbands) are expected to be the primary breadwinners (Torres-Yu 2011).

The coefficients for husbands' age indicate that older husbands are less likely to be working, which can be attributed to early retirement or physical limitations. Meanwhile, wives of older husbands are more likely to participate in the labor force, whereas no significant relationship is observed for wives' age. Additionally, as husbands' earnings decline, wives (mothers) are more likely to work, consistent with the self-reported reasons for MLFP. Similarly, the presence of young children significantly reduces mothers' likelihood of labor force participation, consistent with prior studies (Cabegin 2013), inhibited by the parental role.

In summary, MLFP is shown to be a strategic choice to cope with poverty resulting from their husbands' lower earning power or vulnerability in their household's income. For mothers, MLFP is largely determined by their husbands' attributes. As interpreted by the bivariate probit analysis, which is also validated by the mothers' self-reported reasons, MLFP is, on the one hand, a transformation of mothers' own human capital. On the other hand, it also indicates an *insurance* function in the event that their husbands' earnings are insufficient. One motivation for MLFP is the poverty faced by mothers' households; therefore, MLFP is a rational strategy to deal with

Table 2 Bivariate probit analysis of labor force participation determinants, husbands (FLFP), and wives (MLFP)

Variables	FLFP	MLFP
Number of younger children	0.27	−0.31***
	[0.17]	[0.08]
Number of elder children	−0.08	0.00
	[0.06]	[0.05]
Husband's education (years)	0.02	−0.02
	[0.05]	[0.04]
Husband's education (= 1 if college graduate)	5.21***	2.15***
	[0.36]	[0.48]
Husband's age	−0.15***	0.11***
	[0.05]	[0.03]
Husband: Industry wage-trend indicator (= 1 if increased)	5.38***	−0.49*
	[0.20]	[0.25]
Husband's monthly income (thousand pesos)		−0.06***
		[0.00]
FLFP (= 1 if husband working)		1.34
		[1.22]
Wife's age		−0.01
		[0.02]
Wife's education (years)		0.00
		[0.05]
Wife's education (= 1 if college graduate)		1.12***
		[0.43]
Wife: Industry wage-trend indicator (= 1 if increased)		2.46***
		[0.34]
Constant	3.28***	−1.92
	[0.95]	[2.17]
ρ	−0.94[a]	
	[1.27]	
Log likelihood	−204.00	
No. of observations	292	
[a]Wald test of error term correlation parameter ($H_0: \rho = 0$):	$\chi^2(1) =$	0.55
	p-value =	0.46

***$p < 0.01$; **$p < 0.05$; *$p < 0.10$

Notes Numbers in brackets are robust standard errors

Source Author's calculations

poverty or fluctuations in a family's income. This is consistent with the literature stating that female LFP is a rational strategy to cope with the poverty situation or additional demands and fluctuations in a household's livelihood (Blundell et al. 2016; Sawada et al. 2006) and with the findings from the Philippine national-scale Labor Force Survey (Cabegin and Gaddi 2019: 63; David et al. 2018: 16–19).

Notably, rural societies in the Philippines continue to uphold traditional norms that designate men as the primary breadwinners (Cabegin 2013; Torres-Yu 2011). This social climate, which affects the stride of contemporary women in attaining high educational levels, can also promote MLFP, which needs to be understood in terms of the family dynamics under poverty situations not only by women but also by men. Thus, MLFP and its unintended consequences for boys' pro-educational time use, as discussed in Chapter 4, cannot be attributed solely to working mothers. Instead, they must be understood within the broader context of family dynamics, where both maternal and paternal attributes play significant roles.

5.2 *Extended Family Setting*

The results for estimators of γ_k^G, μ_{1k}, μ_{2k}, μ_{3k}, μ_{4k}, μ_{5k}, and μ_{6k} are reported in Table 3 where specifications correspond to the full sample ([1] and [2]) and enrolled sample ([3]) and [4]), respectively, as in Table 6 of Chapter 4. Because the estimates of γ_k^G, μ_{1k}, and μ_{2k} are qualitatively similar to those in Table 6 of Chapter 4, we particularly look into the estimates of μ_{3k}, μ_{4k}, μ_{5k}, and μ_{6k}.

The coefficients μ_{3k}, capturing the effect of EX_{ij} alone, are statistically negative on the school attendance for the specifications [1] (–0.28) and [3] (–0.28), and positive on the child labor time with mothers' jobs for the specification [3] (0.35) and the leisure time (playing time) for the specifications [1] (0.42) and [3] (0.31).

The coefficients μ_{4k}, capturing the interaction effect of $G_i * EX_{ij}$ (boys in extended families), are statistically positive on the child labor time with mothers' jobs for the specifications [2] (0.61) and [4] (0.87), the leisure (playing) time for the specification [2] (0.75), and the time spent on computer-game shops (CGS) for the specification [2] (1.03), respectively. That is, the matched interaction setting of boys in an extended family, regardless of MLFP, predicts that they are more likely to devote more time to labor (helping with mother's jobs) and more time to leisure (playing) than they would otherwise.

The coefficients μ_{5k}, capturing the interaction effect of $MLFP_{ij} * EX_{ij}$ (regardless of child gender), are statistically positive on the child labor time with fathers' jobs for the specification [4] (0.84) and that with mothers' jobs for the specifications [2] (1.12) and [4] (1.49), the leisure (playing) time at the specification [2] (1.72), and the time spent on CGS for the specifications [2] (1.48) and [4] (0.83), respectively.

Finally, the coefficients μ_{6k}, capturing the interaction effect of $G_i * MLFP_{ij} * EX_{ij}$, which is our concern in particular, are statistically negative on the leisure time (playing) for the specifications [2] (–1.99) and [4] (–1.38) and the time spent on CGS for the specifications [2] (–1.36) and [4] (–1.04), respectively. Yet, their magnitudes

Table 3 Marginal effects of mothers' labor force participation and extended family on children time allocations

Variables	Sleep				Education											
					Studying at Home				Schooling				Attendance			
	[1]	[2]	[3]	[4]	[1]	[2]	[3]	[4]	[1]	[2]	[3]	[4]	[1]	[2]	[3]	[4]
Boy indicator (=1)	−0.13	−2.11***	−0.10	1.28*	−0.42***	1.78**	−0.45***	0.44	−0.16*	0.46	−0.16*	−0.26	−0.07	0.34	−0.10	−0.16
	[0.12]	[0.78]	[0.12]	[0.66]	[0.13]	[0.83]	[0.14]	[0.88]	[0.08]	[0.54]	[0.09]	[0.41]	[0.07]	[0.44]	[0.08]	[0.37]
Maternal LFP	−0.79	−1.39	−0.61	−0.97	1.14	2.60*	1.46*	2.85*	0.88*	1.46*	0.63	1.16	0.44	0.69	0.46	0.76
	[0.56]	[0.95]	[0.56]	[0.95]	[0.79]	[1.43]	[0.85]	[1.55]	[0.52]	[0.89]	[0.53]	[0.93]	[0.46]	[0.75]	[0.49]	[0.81]
Boy× Maternal LFP		1.10		0.77		−2.71**		−3.02**		−1.17		−1.08		−0.59		−0.71
		[0.84]		[0.80]		[1.14]		[1.21]		[0.73]		[0.75]		[0.57]		[0.60]
Extended family (=1)	−0.10	−0.14	−0.08	−0.04	0.15	0.30	0.02	0.31	−0.26	−0.13	−0.18	−0.23	−0.28**	−0.12	− 0.28**	−0.15
	[0.18]	[0.35]	[0.19]	[0.37]	[0.21]	[0.44]	[0.23]	[0.48]	[0.16]	[0.31]	[0.16]	[0.31]	[0.13]	[0.21]	[0.14]	[0.23]
Boy × Extended family		−0.33		−0.59		−0.16		−0.41		0.22		0.11		0.02		−0.04
		[0.45]		[0.46]		[0.48]		[0.55]		[0.36]		[0.39]		[0.26]		[0.31]
Mother's LFP× Extended family		0.54		0.32		−0.56		−0.78		−0.57		−0.19		−0.46		−0.40
		[0.59]		[0.61]		[0.86]		[0.93]		[0.56]		[0.57]		[0.45]		[0.48]

(continued)

Table 3 (continued)

Variables		Sleep				Education											
						Studying at Home				Schooling				Attendance			
		[1]	[2]	[3]	[4]	[1]	[2]	[3]	[4]	[1]	[2]	[3]	[4]	[1]	[2]	[3]	[4]
	Boy × Mother's LFP × Extended family		−0.48		−0.07		0.99		1.54		0.42		0.28		0.39		0.50
			[0.72]		[0.74]		[0.91]		[0.97]		[0.62]		[0.63]		[0.46]		[0.49]
Controlling covariates:																	
	Other individual variables	Yes	Yes	Yes	Yes	Yes	Yes	Yes	Yes	Yes	Yes	Yes	Yes	Yes	Yes	Yes	Yes
	Other household variables	Yes	Yes	Yes	Yes	Yes	Yes	Yes	Yes	Yes	Yes	Yes	Yes	Yes	Yes	Yes	Yes
	School variables	No	No	Yes	Yes	No	No	Yes	Yes	No	No	Yes	Yes	No	No	Yes	Yes
	Region dummies	Yes	Yes	Yes	Yes	Yes	Yes	Yes	Yes	Yes	Yes	Yes	Yes	Yes	Yes	Yes	Yes
	Enumerator dummies	Yes	Yes	Yes	Yes	Yes	Yes	Yes	Yes	Yes	Yes	Yes	Yes	Yes	Yes	Yes	Yes
R^2		0.15	0.13	0.16	0.17	0.17	0.07	0.05	0.10	0.58	0.58	0.26	0.28	0.74	0.75	0.23	0.26
No. of observations		284	284	258	258	284	284	258	258	284	284	258	258	284	284	258	258

(continued)

Table 3 (continued)

Variables	Labor and Chores											
	Father's Job				Mother's Job				Household Chores			
	[1]	[2]	[3]	[4]	[1]	[2]	[3]	[4]	[1]	[2]	[3]	[4]
Boy indicator (=1)	0.46***	2.21*	2.21*	2.21*	2.21*	2.21*	2.21*	0.84	0.84	0.84	− 0.38***	− 0.38***
	[0.11]	[0.11]	[0.11]	[0.11]	[0.11]	[0.79]	[0.79]	[0.79]	[0.79]	[0.79]	[0.12]	[0.12]
Maternal LFP	− 0.44	− 0.58	− 0.88*	− 1.26	− 0.68	− 1.58	− 0.89	− 2.14*	− 0.74	− 0.95	− 0.52	− 0.65
	[0.54]	[0.89]	[0.48]	[0.80]	[0.71]	[1.14]	[0.71]	[1.11]	[0.54]	[0.93]	[0.58]	[0.97]
Boy × Maternal LFP		− 0.30		0.03		0.93		1.17		0.39		0.25
		[0.76]		[0.64]		[0.93]		[0.90]		[0.89]		[0.89]
Extended family (=1)	0.07	− 0.17	0.25	− 0.39*	0.28	− 0.63**	0.35*	− 0.88**	0.22	− 0.17	0.27	− 0.17
	[0.17]	[0.24]	[0.16]	[0.22]	[0.22]	[0.31]	[0.21]	[0.36]	[0.18]	[0.30]	[0.19]	[0.29]
Boy × Extended family		− 0.24		0.38		0.61*		0.87**		0.27		0.38 ara>
		[0.38] lePara>		[0.32]		[0.34]		[0.38]		[0.40]		[0.40]
Mother's LFP × Extended family		0.34		0.84*		1.12*		1.49**		0.53		0.40
		[0.52]		[0.45]		[0.64]		[0.66]		[0.57]		[0.58]
Boy × Mother's LFP × Extended family		0.89		0.22		0.06		0.20		− 0.47		− 0.36
		[0.69]		[0.58]		[0.76]		[0.82]		[0.73]		[0.73]

(continued)

Table 3 (continued)

Variables		Labor and Chores											
		Father's Job				Mother's Job				Household Chores			
		[1]	[2]	[3]	[4]	[1]	[2]	[3]	[4]	[1]	[2]	[3]	[4]
Controlling covariates:													
	Other individual variables	Yes	Yes	Yes	Yes	Yes	Yes	Yes	Yes	Yes	Yes	Yes	Yes
	Other household variables	Yes	Yes	Yes	Yes	Yes	Yes	Yes	Yes	Yes	Yes	Yes	Yes
	School variables	No	No	Yes	Yes	No	No	Yes	Yes	No	No	Yes	Yes
	Region dummies	Yes	Yes	Yes	Yes	Yes	Yes	Yes	Yes	Yes	Yes	Yes	Yes
	Enumerator dummies	Yes	Yes	Yes	Yes	Yes	Yes	Yes	Yes	Yes	Yes	Yes	Yes
R^2		0.30	0.38	0.18	0.25	0.23	0.27	0.27	0.31	0.25	0.31	0.26	0.30
No. of observations		284	284	258	258	284	284	258	258	284	284	258	258

Variables	Leisure							
	Playing				CGS			
	[1]	[2]	[3]	[4]	[1]	[2]	[3]	[4]
Boy indicator (=1)	0.67***	− 0.06	− 0.06	− 0.06	0.24**	0.24**	0.24**	0.24**
	[0.12]	[0.83]	[0.83]	[0.83]	[0.83]	[0.83]	[0.10]	[0.10]
Maternal LFP	− 1.59**	− 3.29**	− 1.02	− 2.24*	− 1.57**	− 2.79**	− 0.97**	− 1.30*
	[0.64]	[1.30]	[0.62]	[1.16]	[0.61]	[1.23]	[0.46]	[0.78]

(continued)

Table 3 (continued)

Variables	Leisure							
	Playing				CGS			
	[1]	[2]	[3]	[4]	[1]	[2]	[3]	[4]
Boy × Maternal LFP		3.19***		2.39**		1.89*		0.56
		[1.06]		[0.96]		[1.01]		[0.66]
Extended family (=1)	0.42**	– 0.44	0.31*	– 0.22	0.30	– 0.76**	0.02	– 0.52*
	[0.17]	[0.39]	[0.18]	[0.37]	[0.20]	[0.37]	[0.15]	[0.30]
Boy × Extended family		0.75*		0.65		1.03**		0.53
		[0.44]		[0.43]		[0.46]		[0.40]
Mother's LFP × Extended family		1.72**		1.06		1.48**		0.83*
		[0.78]		[0.68]		[0.72]		[0.50]
Boy × Mother's LFP × Extended family		– 1.99**		– 1.38*		– 1.36*		– 1.04*
		[0.84]		[0.74]		[0.81]		[0.60]
Controlling covariates:								
Other individual variables	Yes	Yes	Yes	Yes	Yes	Yes	Yes	Yes
Other household variables	Yes	Yes	Yes	Yes	Yes	Yes	Yes	Yes
School variables	No	No	Yes	Yes	No	No	Yes	Yes
Region dummies	Yes	Yes	Yes	Yes	Yes	Yes	Yes	Yes
Enumerator dummies	Yes	Yes	Yes	Yes	Yes	Yes	Yes	Yes

(continued)

Table 3 (continued)

Variables	Leisure							
	Playing				CGS			
	[1]	[2]	[3]	[4]	[1]	[2]	[3]	[4]
R^2	0.25	0.12	0.31	0.27	0.14	0.08	0.21	0.22
No. of observations	284	284	258	258	284	284	258	258

***$p < 0.01$; **$p < 0.05$; *$p < 0.10$

Notes Numbers in brackets are the small-sample adjusted standard errors; CGS = computer-game shops

Source Author's calculations

are smaller than those of the "unintended" effect of MLFP captured as μ_2 (3.19 and 2.39 for the specifications [2] and [4], respectively).

In summary, the unintended effect of MLFP on sons' time spent studying at home and playing—represented by negative values of μ_2 (–2.71 and –3.02 for specifications [2] and [4], which resembles the equivalent estimates in Table 6 of Chapter 4)—is not fully offset by the presence of an extended family (μ_6,μ_3,μ_4, and μ_5 coefficients). Similarly, the magnitudes of MLFP's positive impact on playing time (μ_2 coefficients of 3.19 and 2.39 for specifications [2] and [4]) are only partially reduced by the extended family context (3.19–1.99 and 2.39–1.38, respectively).

Thus, extended family settings appear to provide some relief for boys affected by MLFP, as suggested by the interaction terms. However, the magnitude of this effect is small and not consistently statistically significant across specifications. Therefore, the mitigating role of extended families should be interpreted cautiously, highlighting the limited capacity of these settings to counteract the unintended consequences of MLFP under the structural constraints faced by rural households.

5.3 *Test of the Validity of IV*

Similar to Chapter 4, the statistical tests of IV for the estimates for Table 3 are performed. Table 4 presents the result of Wooldridge's (1995) robust score test (its chi-square statistics and statistical significance) on the null hypothesis that the MLFP variable is exogenous to the dependent variables of time allocations. The test result indicates that the chi-square statistics of MLFP are statistically significant for home study time and leisure time (playing) across the two samples, refuting the null hypothesis that MLFP is exogenous. Since the primary focus of this study is on pro-educational time allocations, it is determined that the MLFP should be treated as endogenous, as shown in Table 3.

Then, Table 5 reports the results for the coefficient of IV in the first-stage equation, including robust standard errors and significance levels, and the Stock–Yogo F-statistics. To conclude that the IV is not weak, both the IV must be statistically significant to the MLFP and the F-statistics must have a rule-of-thumb value of 10 or higher. According to the findings, the first-stage coefficients of IV are statistically significant and positive at the 1% level across all samples, specifications, and models, including the extended-family study. Consequently, the IV is deemed pertinent and explanatory for the MLFP. In addition, the first-stage Stock–Yogo F-statistics are consistently greater than the value of ten. We conclude that the IV is statistically valid and relevant across all samples, specifications, and models for the aforementioned reasons. Consequently, we conclude that the weak IV problem is least likely here as well.

To test and validate the exclusion restriction, Table 6 shows the regression of t_{ki}, the dependent variables, on z_{ij}, the IV in Eqs. (5.2) and (5.3), which ensures that the IV does not have a direct effect on children's time use, independent of MLFP. The results indicate that the IV does not exhibit statistically significant direct effects on

Table 4 Chi-square statistics of Wooldridge's robust score test (null hypothesis: Exogeneity of MLFP)

Dependent variables	Specifications[a]	Full sample	Specifications[a]	Enrolled sample
Sleeping	[1]	2.61	[3]	2.46
	[2]	3.09*	[4]	2.13
Studying at home	[1]	2.92*	[3]	4.35**
	[2]	5.13**	[4]	5.87**
Schooling (in min)	[1]	3.06*	[3]	1.24
	[2]	2.75*	[4]	1.36
Schooling (in days)	[1]	1.10	[3]	1.24
	[2]	0.71	[4]	1.01
Work (fathers' jobs)	[1]	0.47	[3]	2.48
	[2]	0.42	[4]	2.52
Work (mothers' jobs)	[1]	0.90	[3]	1.71
	[2]	1.11	[4]	2.31
Household chores	[1]	1.40	[3]	0.61
	[2]	1.10	[4]	0.44
Playing	[1]	7.12***	[3]	3.34*
	[2]	8.47***	[4]	4.03**
Computer-game shops	[1]	4.74**	[3]	1.98
	[2]	5.67**	[4]	1.79

***$p < 0.01$; **$p < 0.05$; *$p < 0.10$

[a]Specifications [1] and [3] do not include and specifications [2] and [4] include, some interaction terms with the boy indicator variable in Table 3

Source Author's calculations

most of the time-use categories, supporting the validity of the exclusion restriction in the analysis.

As demonstrated in the results above, the IV (wage trend increase) does not show statistically significant direct effects on children's time use. Hence, these results further support the validity of the exclusion restriction, confirming that the wage trend influences children's time use indirectly via MLFP. An exception is the time for CGS, where the coefficient is negative and weakly significant at the 10% level. However, the time for CGS is not a key time-use element in the study's main analysis.

5.4 *Further Exploration of Dual Burden*

The results reveal that sons exhibit less pro-educational time use under MLFP scenarios compared to daughters, a disparity that is not effectively mitigated by the extended family setting, with the presence of other adult household members

Table 5 First-stage estimators and F-statistics (dependent variable = MLFP; instrument: MLFP wage-trend indicator)

Second-stage Specifications		Coef. of Instrument	Robust S.E	p-value	Stock–Yogo F-statistics	Corresponding tables and specifications[a]	
Full sample:							
	Without interaction terms	0.28***	0.05	0.00	35.03***	Table 3	[1]
	With interaction terms	0.17**	0.05	0.02	14.07***	Table 3	[2]
Enrolled sample:							
	Without interaction terms	0.30***	0.05	0.00	34.14***	Table 3	[3]
	With interaction terms	0.18**	0.06	0.02	12.04***	Table 3	[4]

***$p < 0.01$; **$p < 0.05$; *$p < 0.10$
[a]Specifications [1] and [3] do not include and specifications [2] and [4] include some interaction terms with the boy indicator variable in Table 3
Source Author's calculations

Table 6 Regression results for exclusion restriction

Dependent variable (child time use)	Coef. of IV	Robust S.E	p-value	95% CI	R-squared
Sleep	–0.02	0.17	0.91	[–0.36, 0.32]	0.00
Study at home	0.10	0.17	0.59	[–0.25, 0.44]	0.00
Schooling	0.11	0.17	0.52	[–0.23, 0.45]	0.00
Labor: assisting fathers' jobs	0.03	0.17	0.88	[–0.31, 0.36]	0.00
Labor: assisting mothers' jobs	0.05	0.18	0.80	[–0.30, 0.39]	0.00
Household chores	0.17	0.18	0.33	[–0.17, 0.52]	0.00
Playing	–0.14	0.17	0.42	[–0.48, 0.20]	0.00
CGS	–0.30	0.17	0.08	[–0.64, 0.04]	0.01

Notes IV = instrumental variable; S.E. = standard error; CI = confidence interval; CGS = computer-game shops
Source Author's calculations

who might otherwise monitor their activities. This underscores the pivotal role mothers play in supervising their sons' educational endeavors. In contrast, daughters appear to be more sensitive to the nature of their mother's employment, whether formal or informal. Furthermore, the findings reinforce the dual burden faced by mothers. On one hand, mothers actively participate in supplementary and "insurance" roles to support the primary breadwinner and cope with poverty. On the other hand, they remain the central figures responsible for their children's education and well-being—roles that are only partially compensated for by other household members.

This interpretation is further substantiated by further data from our questionnaire survey additionally collected. Both children and parents were asked to identify the family member most concerned with child-related issues (Table 7). A significant majority of children (77.7%) identified their mothers as the primary caregiver. Similarly, among parents, 82.7% indicated that mothers are the most involved, a sentiment echoed not only by mothers themselves but also by fathers.

Table 8 further decomposes the evidence of this shared perception in Table 7 into the cross-tabulation by children's and adults' beliefs. It highlights the mutuality of beliefs between mothers and children regarding the mother's central role in addressing child-related concerns. Specifically, among the 234 adult family members who identified the mother as the most concerned family member, 194 cases (82.9% of these adults) also aligned with the child's perception. In contrast, among the 44 adult family members who identified the father, only 17 cases (38.6% of these adults) aligned with the child's view. This stark difference underscores the prominent role mothers play in child-related issues compared to fathers and other adult family members. The relatively low percentages for other adult family members further illustrate that the mother's role in addressing child-related concerns is largely irreplaceable within the household.

While Table 8 primarily emphasizes column-based percentages (vertical interpretation) to directly support the argument of this paper—highlighting the dominant role of mothers as perceived by both children and adult family members—an alternative analysis based on row-based percentages (horizontal interpretation) also provides additional insights. Specifically, among the 220 children who identified their mother

Table 7 Children's and parents' perceptions of the family member most concerned with child-related issues

Relation to children	Child-own perceptions			Adult-own perceptions		
	Freq.	Percent	Cum.	Freq.	Percent	Cum.
Father	39	13.8%	13.8%	44	15.5%	15.5%
Mother	220	77.7%	91.5%	234	82.7%	98.2%
Grandfather	0	0.0%	91.5%	2	0.7%	98.9%
Grandmother	1	0.4%	91.9%	1	0.4%	99.3%
Elder brother	11	3.9%	95.8%	0	0.0%	99.3%
Elder sister	9	3.2%	98.9%	0	0.0%	99.3%
Other	3	1.1%	100%	2	0.7%	100%
Total	283	100%		283	100%	

Note "Freq." = frequency; "cum." = cumulative percentage
Source Author's calculations

Table 8 Cross-tabulation of agreement between children's and parents' perceptions of the family member most concerned with child-related issues

		Adult-own perceptions					
		Father	Mother	Grandfather	Grandmother	Other	Total
Child-own perceptions							
	Father	**17 (38.6%)**	21 (9.0%)	0 (0.0%)	1 (100%)	0 (0.0%)	39 (100%)
	Mother	24 (54.5%)	**194 (82.9%)**	2 (100%)	0 (0.0%)	0 (0.0%)	220 (100%)
	Grandmother	0 (0.0%)	1 (0.4%)	0 (0.0%)	0 (0.0%)	0 (0.0%)	1 (100%)
	Elder brother	1 (2.3%)	8 (3.4%)	0 (0.0%)	0 (0.0%)	2 (100%)	11 (100%)
	Elder sister	1 (2.3%)	8 (3.4%)	0 (0.0%)	0 (0.0%)	0 (0.0%)	9 (100%)
	Other	1 (2.3%)	2 (0.9%)	0 (0.0%)	0 (0.0%)	0 (0.0%)	3 (100%)
Total		44 (100%)	234 (100%)	2 (100%)	1 (100%)	2 (100%)	283 (100%)

Note The upper numbers in each cell represent raw counts, while the lower numbers in parentheses indicate column-based percentages. These percentages highlight the distribution of child perceptions within each adult perception category, emphasizing the importance of understanding the child's perspective. Bolded numbers denote mutual agreements where children and parents identified the same family member as most concerned with child-related issues
Source Author's calculations

as the most concerned family member, 88.2% also aligned with the perception of adult family members. Similarly, for the 39 children who identified their father, 43.6% were in agreement with the view of adult family members. This horizontal perspective underscores the strength of children's recognition of their mother's role in addressing their concerns. Furthermore, it suggests that children are more likely to perceive their mother as a central figure in their upbringing, regardless of whether this perception is explicitly mirrored by other adult members in the household.

As described in Table 1 of Chapter 4, this questionnaire survey collected information through two main approaches: categories where adult household members represented the family and answered questions about household characteristics, and categories where children directly provided information about their own activities and experiences. The majority of adult respondents were mothers (82.7%), followed by fathers (15.5%),[2] with grandparents and others accounting for only a small minority

[2] Notably, during many household visits, fathers initially interacted with the researchers but often deferred to mothers once they learned that the survey concerned household finances and children's education. This pattern underscores the primary role mothers play in managing household and child-related matters. At the same time, a substantial number of fathers did serve as respondents, which suggests that their involvement in household surveys is not entirely absent or rejected.

(1.8%), as shown in Table 8. However, the choice of respondent in each household was not randomly assigned but rather emerged as a result of household-specific decision-making processes. This introduces a potential selection bias, as the decision on who responded may itself reflect underlying household dynamics or traditional roles.[3]

The findings from Sect. 4 highlight the dual burdens faced by mothers, as they navigate the challenges of supporting their families economically while simultaneously bearing primary responsibility for their children's education. These results are further supplemented by the insights from Tables 7 and 8, which reveal patterns of mutual recognition between children and adult family members regarding caregiving roles. Specifically, mothers are overwhelmingly identified as the family members most concerned with child-related matters, reflecting their pivotal role in monitoring children's educational time. Fathers and other adult family members, while involved to varying degrees, are less frequently recognized in this capacity. These descriptive insights complement the main analysis in Sects. 4 and 5 by shedding light on the relational dynamics and trust within families, providing a richer understanding of mothers' central roles.

This broader notion of dual burdens, even in domestic settings, can also be analogous to the context of overseas working mothers, as known as "martyr mothers" in the Philippine studies (Parreñas 2007: 51). These mothers dedicate themselves to their accompanying family members and those left behind in the Philippines, reflecting the "feminization era" of overseas Filipino workers (Cortes 2015).[4] In summary, these findings collectively underscore the significant role of mothers in monitoring their children's educational time and the differing responses of sons and daughters to their working mothers. The challenges and sacrifices experienced by mothers, even among the local labor force, exemplify the complex nature of their roles within family dynamics.

Moreover, this era of reversed gender disparity in education, where women's educational attainment surpasses that of men and their economic participation continues to grow, represents undeniable progress. However, the dual burdens faced by women and the unintended effect of MLFP, as highlighted in this chapter, subtly yet unmistakably suggest the persistence, maintenance, and even reinforcement of traditional gender roles, despite the phenomenon superficially appearing as a positive reflection of women's active participation in the workforce. While the unintended effect of MLFP, quite literally unintended, contributes to the reversed gender disparity by facilitating women's educational and economic advancements, they also call into question the very meaning of "reversed." The findings in the study and from Chapter 4 underscore the need to critically examine how this reversal impacts not only women but also men and broader family dynamics.

---

[3] As such, interpretations of Table 8 should take this potential bias into account, as it reports raw distributions and does not account for potential confounders. Unlike the findings from the multivariate analysis, which represent the main results of this study and control for confounding factors, Table 8 is supplementary and intended to provide additional interpretative context.

[4] Nevertheless, this type of normative distinction between fathers and mothers can be observed as an entrenched social norm in many societies (Rubiano-Matulevich and Viollaz, 2019, p. 20).

6 Conclusions

This chapter has examined two interconnected aspects of MLFP in rural households: its economic drivers and the role of extended family support in mitigating its unintended effect on pro-educational child time inputs. The analysis reveals that MLFP is a rational response to economic constraints, particularly in households where fathers' income is unstable or insufficient. The unintended effect of MLFP is, therefore, understood as the consequence not maternal but of family dynamics.

When extended family settings are focused, they can provide some relief but their ability to offset these gendered disparities is identified to be limited. The findings suggest that relying on extended family as a buffer against the dual burdens faced by mothers has its limits, and does not fully address the broader implications of maternal employment for gender equity in education. The persistence of these disparities, despite increased female participation in the labor force, calls into question the real meaning of "reversed" gender disparity in education.

These findings have important implications for policy. Addressing the root causes of MLFP requires efforts to reduce economic vulnerability, particularly by improving fathers' employment stability and increasing access to flexible employment for mothers. In addition, interventions aimed at improving boys' educational engagement—such as after-school programs or mentorship—could help counteract the negative time allocation patterns observed in this study. Moreover, efforts to redistribute domestic responsibilities through community-based campaigns could promote greater gender equality in educational participation.

This study underscores the need for a broader rethinking of support systems for working mothers. Rather than relying solely on extended family support, comprehensive policies should focus on addressing both the economic and caregiving needs of families. Future research should explore the long-term impacts of MLFP on children's educational outcomes and investigate the role of extended families in different cultural contexts to better understand how household labor dynamics affect intergenerational educational patterns.

Taken together, the four chapters in **Part II** demonstrate a structural asymmetry in how gendered educational outcomes are shaped and sustained. Chapter 2 showed how boys fall behind at key educational transitions; Chapter 3 revealed how girls benefit from intergenerational transmission, especially through educated mothers; Chapter 4 examined the unintended effects of maternal labor on boys' educational involvement; and this chapter has shown that neither extended families nor broader socioeconomic conditions are sufficiently mitigating these effects. What emerges is not a reversal of gender inequalities, but a redistribution of burdens within structurally constrained households.

To conclude this chapter, while the analysis identified boys' disengagement from education through time-use patterns, it also highlighted the deeply entrenched traditional gender norms that mothers are forced to navigate—norms that are neither reversed nor novel. The unintended effect of MLFP reveals how conventional gender inequities, far from being eliminated, resurface in altered forms. Could boys' disengagement from education, in part, reflect the continuation of longstanding gender biases against women, merely expressed in new ways? At the very least, interpreting boys' educational disengagement as a simple reversal of gender disparities warrants critical reevaluation, suggesting that such phenomena may be symptomatic of more pervasive, underlying inequities. The sacrifices of "martyr mothers" serve as a poignant reminder of the resilience and inequities embedded within household decision-making, underscoring the urgent need for policies that support both families and gender equity.

References

Adermon A, Lindahl M, Palme M (2021) Dynastic human capital, inequality, and intergenerational mobility. Am Econ Rev 111(5):1523–1548. https://doi.org/10.1257/aer.20190553

Afridi F, Mukhopadhyay A, Sahoo S (2016) Female labor force participation and child education in India: evidence from the national rural employment guarantee scheme. IZA J Lab Dev 5(1):1–27. https://doi.org/10.1186/s40175-016-0053-y

Bianchi SM, Milkie MA (2010) Work and family research in the first decade of the 21st century. J Marr Fam 72(3):705–725. https://doi.org/10.1111/j.1741-3737.2010.00726.x

Blau FD, Ferber MA, Winkler AE (2010) The economics of women, men, and work, 6th edn. Prentice Hall, Upper Saddle River, NJ

Blundell R, Pistaferri L, Saporta-Eksten I (2016) Consumption inequality and family labor supply. Am Econ Rev 106(2):387–435. https://doi.org/10.1257/aer.20121549

Cabegin ECA (2013) Gendered labor supply response to Filipino spouses' overseas migration and remittances. Asian Pac Migr J 22(2):147–175. https://doi.org/10.1177/011719681302200201

Cabegin ECA, Gaddi RS (2019) Determinants of female labor force participation in the Philippines. National Economic and Development Authority, Manila, Philippines. https://economicsph.org/sites/default/files/Determinants%20of%20Female%20Labor%20Force%20Participation%20%28Edillon%29.pdf

Cameron AC, Trivedi PK (2005) Microeconometrics: methods and applications. Cambridge University Press, Cambridge, UK

Cameron LA, Dowling JM, Worswick C (2001) Education and labor market participation of women in Asia: Evidence from five countries. Econ Dev Cult Change 49(3):459–477. https://doi.org/10.1086/452511

Cortes P (2015) The feminization of international migration and its effects on the children left behind: evidence from the Philippines. World Dev 65:62–78. https://doi.org/10.1016/j.worlddev.2013.10.021

Croll E (2006) The intergenerational contract in the changing asian family. Oxf Dev Stud 34(4):473–491. https://doi.org/10.1080/13600810601045833

David CC, Albert JRG, Vizmanos JFV (2018) Sustainable development Goal 5: How does the Philippines fare on gender equality? Research Paper Series. Philippine Institute for Development Studies, 2018–2004.

Edmonds EV (2006) Child labor and schooling responses to anticipated income in South Africa. J Dev Econ 81(2):386–414. https://doi.org/10.1016/j.jdeveco.2005.05.001

Jayachandran S (2021) Social norms as a barrier to women's employment in developing countries. IMF Econ Rev 69:576–595. https://doi.org/10.1057/s41308-021-00140-w

Kabeer N (2015) Gender, poverty, and inequality: a brief history of feminist contributions in the field of international development. Gend Dev 23(2):189–205. https://doi.org/10.1080/13552074.2015.1062300

LaFave D, Thomas D (2017) Extended families and child well-being. J Dev Econ 126:52–65. https://doi.org/10.1016/j.jdeveco.2016.11.006
Le K, Nguyen M (2020) Shedding light on maternal education and child health in developing countries. World Dev 133:105005. https://doi.org/10.1016/j.worlddev.2020.105005
Li M, Cao J (2023) Multi-generational educational mobility in China in the twentieth century. China Econ Rev 80:101990. https://doi.org/10.1016/j.chieco.2023.101990
Liversage A, Jakobsen V (2010). Sharing space-gendered patterns of extended household living among young Turkish marriage migrants in Denmark. J Comp Fam Stud 41(5):693–715. http://www.jstor.org/stable/41604399
Mare RD (2011) A multigenerational view of inequality. Demography 48:1–23. https://doi.org/10.1007/s13524-011-0014-7
Meyerhoefer CD, Chen CJ (2011) The effect of parental labor migration on children's educational progress in rural China. Rev Econ Household 9(3):379–396. https://doi.org/10.1007/s11150-010-9105-2
Okabe M (2025) Unintended effect of mothers' labor force participation on child time allocations under family dynamics in rural Philippines. Rev Econ Household: 1–53. https://doi.org/10.1007/s11150-024-09758-x
Parreñas RS (2007) The gender ideological clash in globalization: Women, migration, and the modernization building project of the Philippines. Soc Thou Res 28:37–56. https://doi.org/10.17161/STR.1808.5223
Quisumbing AR (1997) Better rich, or better there? Grandparent wealth, coresidence, and intra-household allocation. Food Consumption and Nutrition Division (FCND) Discussion Paper, 23. International Food Policy Research Institute, Washington, DC
Razavi S (2007). The political and social economy of care in a development context: conceptual issues, research questions and policy options. United Nations Research Institute for Social Development (UNRISD) Programme on Gender and Development Paper, no. 3. Geneva: UNRISD
Rubiano-Matulevich E, Viollaz M (2019) Gender differences in time use allocating time between the market and the household. Policy Research Working Paper 8981. World Bank.
Sawada Y, Kubo K, Fuwa N, Ito S, Kurosaki T (2006) On the mother and child labor nexus under credit constraints: Findings from rural India. Dev Econ 44(4):465–499. https://doi.org/10.1111/j.1746-1049.2006.00025.x
Torres-Yu R (2011) Childhood and family in contemporary children's fiction: resilience, agency, and emerging gender norms. Kritika Kultura 16:44–64
Wooldridge JM (1995) Score diagnostics for linear models estimated by two stage least squares. In: Maddala GS, Phillips PCB, Srinivasan TN (eds) Advances in econometrics and quantitative economics: essays in honor of Professor C. R. Rao. Blackwell, Oxford
Zeng Z, Xie Y (2014) The effects of grandparents on children's schooling: evidence from rural China. Demography 51(2):599–617. https://doi.org/10.1007/s13524-013-0275-4

Part III
School Environment and Poverty

Chapter 6
Teachers to Boys?—Scoring Bias, Stereotypes, and the Teacher Market in Rural Philippines: A Natural Experiment in Marinduque, MIMAROPA, Southern Luzon

Abstract This chapter examines teacher evaluation bias as a potential driver of reversed gender disparities in academic performance in rural Philippines. Leveraging a natural experimental design, we analyze a difference-in-differences (DID) estimand between "non-blind" report-card (RC) scores and "blind" standardized test (NAT) scores for the same students. Despite controlling for individual, household, and other school characteristics, boys consistently underperform in teacher-assigned scores—a discrepancy not observed in blind assessments. We identify two mechanisms: (i) implicit stereotypes favoring girls, and (ii) the tendency for teacher evaluations to capture diligence-related behaviors where boys may fall short. This gendered biasing effect on the scores is compounded by a highly gender-skewed teacher labor market, where female teachers dominate due to limited professional alternatives for educated women in underdeveloped local economies. Our findings suggest that evaluation bias is not merely pedagogical but rooted in broader institutional and labor market structures. The chapter concludes with implications for gender equalizing education policy and the importance of integrating educational reforms with economic development strategies aimed at diversifying employment pathways, rather than attributing disparities solely to individual teacher consciousness.

Keywords Boys' underperformance · External assessment · Rating systems · Stereotypes · Teacher gender diversification · Difference in differences (DID)

1 Introduction

Previous chapters explored how poverty, particularly its manifestations through income shocks, domestic responsibilities, and boys' breadwinning expectations, intersects with family dynamics to shape educational disparities. In contrast, starting **Part III: School Environment and Poverty**, this chapter shifts the focus to the school environment, examining whether and how evaluation mechanisms within the

---

This chapter draws on Okabe (2025).

M. Okabe, *Economics of the Reversal in Gender Disparities in Education and Development*, Economics, Law, and Institutions in Asia Pacific,
https://doi.org/10.1007/978-981-96-9271-2_6

Philippine education system contribute to the observed underperformance of boys. Using a natural experimental framework, it compares teacher-assigned scores with blind assessments to identify potential gender bias.

Gender disparities in education manifest not only in access indices such as enrollment rates but also in academic performance, which shapes students' motivations, expectations, and self-beliefs (Attanasio and Kaufmann 2014; Buhl-Wiggers et al. 2021; Doornkamp et al. 2022; Welmond and Gregory 2021; Wright and Arora 2022; Xu et al. 2022; Yamauchi and Liu 2013). In this context, gender bias in academic evaluations may play a critical role (Wright and Arora 2022). Even a single episode of grading bias can scar subsequent learning behavior via official records, track placement, and teacher expectations, generating path dependence or a form of hysteresis in attendance and effort (Andrew 2014; DiPrete and Eirich 2006; Dutt 2023).

Empirically, this chapter adopts the "blind" versus "non-blind" test score comparison framework developed by Goldin and Rouse (2000) and Lavy (2008). The Philippine education system incorporates blind assessments through the National Achievement Tests (NATs), nationwide standardized exams administered by the government and scored independently of teachers. In contrast, report card (RC) grades reflect teacher evaluations and are non-blind. When substantial discrepancies exist between these two scores, the divergence can serve as a natural experiment setting, potentially revealing implicit stereotypes—positive or negative—toward particular social groups (Doornkamp et al. 2022; Hinnerich et al. 2011; Lavy 2008; Lavy and Sand 2018).

This chapter exploits the same data as Chapters 4 and 5. The specific data parts used for this chapter include non-blind scores along with individual and household-level characteristics from 275 students across nine villages in Marinduque Province, the same region studied in the earlier chapters. Sampling was conducted using a stratified random method across municipalities, representing all income classes. Within this sample, we observed persistent underperformance among boys in non-blind teacher evaluations, a pattern absent in blind external assessments. We further matched 135 individual students to confidential NAT score data obtained from the local government. This integration reduced the sample size but allowed us to compare blind and non-blind scores for the same individuals. The matching approach effectively eliminated individual-level fixed effects, such as unobservable ability, enabling the analysis of systematic deviations. Section 6 discusses the implications of the reduced sample size.

Despite these advanced empirical settings, the Philippines remains understudied in the literature, primarily due to restricted access to nonpublic, micro-level data on both score types—a common limitation in developing country contexts. This study overcomes that challenge by combining confidential NAT score data from the Philippine Department of Education (DepEd) with original survey data collected in rural areas. Our data encompass school subjects often overlooked in the literature, including Filipino, English, science, social studies, and two practice-based subjects, thus broadening the scope of analysis.

Our empirical analysis identifies two key mechanisms contributing to the observed score discrepancies for boys: implicit bias against male students and the broader scope of diligence-based teacher assessments, including attendance and behavior. Additionally, student–teacher gender (mis)match intensifies these biases, reflecting labor market imbalances in developing countries,[1] where female teachers often outnumber male counterparts. As such, we consider teacher labor market structures alongside score bias in our interpretation. These findings align with literature identifying teacher behavior as a significant predictor of educational disparities (Dee 2005; Lavy 2008; Torres 2011; UNGEI 2012; Hanushek and Woessmann 2017; Alan et al. 2018; Alesina et al. 2018; Jouini et al. 2018; Burgess et al. 2022; Doornkamp et al. 2022; Ferman and Fontes 2022; Rakshit and Sahoo 2023).

Teachers may deviate from norms of fairness and impartiality when forming expectations and judgments (Glock and Krolak-Schwerdt 2013; Alesina et al. 2018; Hanna and Linden 2012; Legette et al. 2021), thereby influencing educational outcomes. Although interest in gender stereotypes and test score gaps has grown, most empirical evidence remains confined to high-income countries. Even in such contexts,[2] findings regarding consistent gender bias and its origins are mixed. Studies in Denmark, France, Israel, Italy, and the United States have found that stereotypes hamper female students' performance in math and science (Lavy 2008; Cornwell et al. 2013; Lavy and Sand 2018; Carlana 2019; Terrier 2020; Burgess et al. 2022).[3,4] In contrast, a Swedish study found no significant gender bias in score discrepancies, possibly due to the country's high level of gender equality and the narrow focus on Swedish language assessments (Hinnerich et al. 2011: 689–690).

This study contributes to the literature by applying similar frameworks and motivations to the Philippine context—a developing country with uniquely advanced gender parity in education. While facing persistent economic challenges, the Philippines is often considered gender equal, complicating the interpretation of reversed gender gaps in education. The institutionalization of blind assessments through NATs provides a rare opportunity for natural experimental analysis. If substantial gaps exist between blind and non-blind scores, they may reflect evaluators' implicit stereotypes, making this setting particularly useful for testing such hypotheses (Lavy 2008; Hinnerich et al. 2011; Lavy and Sand 2018; Doornkamp et al. 2022).

The remainder of this chapter is organized as follows. Section 2 outlines the research setting and motivations. Section 3 describes the data and research site. Section 4 elaborates on the empirical methodology. Section 5 presents the results,

[1] Such is the case even for math, where existing studies elaborate that boys excel globally (Guiso et al. 2008; Hadjar et al. 2014; Nollenberger et al. 2016).

[2] Here, the "high-income (developed) countries" refers to member countries of the Organisation for Economic Co-operation and Development (OECD).

[3] These studies posit that female students on the science track are likely to be stereotyped because math and science are considered male-dominated (Dusek and Joseph 1983; OECD 2014; Muñoz 2018). Teachers can stereotype female pupils in particular academic disciplines, like math, which is compatible with educational psychology (Dusek and Joseph 1983; Riegle-Crumb and Humphries 2012; Tiedemann 2000, 2002).

[4] Teacher-stereotype topics range from gender to other personal attributes such as race and caste (Alesina et al. 2018; Alston et al. 2022; Botelho et al. 2015; Burgess and Greaves 2013; Gershenson et al. 2016; Glock and Krolak-Schwerdt 2013; Hanna and Linden 2012).

while Sect. 6 explores mediation mechanisms. Section 7 concludes with key findings and policy implications.

2 Setting

Torres (2011) identified multiple concerns regarding boys' crisis in education, including higher dropout rates, earlier entry into economic activities, lower functional literacy, lower scores on NATs and RCs, and greater vulnerability to corporal punishment. UNGEI (2012) emphasized that hidden curricula in classrooms, though unconsciously enacted, are often perceived by students as discriminatory. Torres (2011) further argued that the Philippine school environment is not gender-neutral and that prevailing stereotypes hinder boys' potential and academic achievement. The lack of male role models, particularly male teachers, may reinforce these stereotypes, although Torres noted the lack of robust data on this issue. Testing for bias and stereotypes in educational environments requires disaggregated microdata by gender, region, socioeconomic status, and ethnicity—data that remain scarce. A persistent reliance on aggregated data in Philippine educational research has been noted by David et al. (2017).

While school-related factors are difficult to quantify, rich literature exists on demand-side determinants of educational outcomes. Torres (2011) found that poverty compels boys to contribute to household livelihoods once they reach physical maturity. Estudillo et al. (2008) highlighted men's comparative advantage in agriculture—a sector less profitable than non-agricultural employment. Other studies note egalitarian parental behaviors, such as sons inheriting land and daughters receiving investment in education as compensation (Quisumbing 1994; Estudillo et al. 2001). Mapa (2021) documented boys' dominance in child labor, while Fuwa (2014) reported a pro-girl intrahousehold bias in rural areas. Yamauchi and Tiongco (2013) attributed this to women's need to accumulate greater human capital in response to labor market pressures. Bouis et al. (1998) even referred to boys' disinterest and irresponsibility in schooling. These studies, including this book's earlier chapters, have further indicated that poverty's effects are not limited to financial constraints, but also manifest in children's informal labor duties, expectations of income contribution, and gendered household roles.

In contrast to the growing evidence on demand-side factors, teacher and supply-side perspectives remain underexplored. Teacher gender has emerged as a significant variable, with teachers tending to favor students of the same gender (Dee 2005; Torres 2011; Alan et al. 2018; Carlana 2019; Doornkamp et al. 2022). Consequently, student–teacher gender (mis)match becomes crucial in understanding teacher-perceived stereotypes (Dee 2005; Carrell et al. 2010). In developing countries, the predominance of female teachers amplifies gender imbalances (Crawfurd and Pugatch 2022). This study seeks to connect differences in rating systems with biases linked to teacher gender ratios, both of which are specific to the setting.

While this chapter shifts the analytical lens from household and family domains to the school environment, it must be noted that school-level dynamics do not operate in isolation. In particular, poverty, manifesting as unstable household income, limited resources for schooling, and expectations for boys to contribute economically, continues to shape student performance, even within formal institutions. Teacher perceptions and scoring practices are not immune to such external structural pressures.

3 Data

3.1 Data Outline and Research Site

The data used in this chapter are the same as in Chapters 4 and 5, collected in Marinduque Province (Fig. 1 in Chapter 4). As yielded by the data sampling manner explained in Sect. 3 of Chapter 4, the final dataset for this chapter comprised 275 children. We collected unique information on children (explained in the following subsections), including confidential, nonpublic microdata; unlike nationally representative surveys with large-scale samples, the government does not provide the data provision scheme to external users. This chapter uses three data sources: (1) an original survey of sample household parents and children; (2) administrative, highly confidential NAT score data provided by DepEd exclusively for this study; and (3) administrative data provided by Region IV-B Office of DepEd regarding the female TGRs of sample children enrolled schools.

The information from survey (1) was grouped into three categories as follows: (i) individual characteristics of the sampled children, who were predominantly adolescents/in high school; (ii) the children's education profiles; and (iii) basic information about their families. Category (i) included names, gender, date of birth, birth order, number of siblings and weekly home study time.[5] Category (ii) comprised the student's enrolment status and school information. Category (iii) included the home address, contact information, demographics, educational, employment and income details of parents and other family members.

[5] To ensure inclusive and neutral wording, respondents could indicate gender as male, female, or "other" (no respondent chose "other").

3.2 Descriptive Statistics

3.2.1 Individual Characteristics

Table 1 presents the sample characteristics based on the descriptive statistics of the dependent and independent variables.[6] The male indicator variable indicates that 47% of the children in our sample are males (the remaining 53% are females). The birth-order information (which uses the indicators of the oldest, firstborn and youngest, or lastborn children among siblings) shows that 15% and 22% of children are firstborn and lastborn, respectively. On average, a child has 1.73 younger siblings and 2.72 older siblings, resulting in an average of approximately 5.5 children (= 1.73 + 2.72 plus 1.0 for the individual). Thus, the average birth-order among siblings is between second and third. Of the sample, 46% had one or more role models in their communities whom they admire and aspire to emulate. Using diary-style questionnaires, we standardize students' study and school attendance time into *z*-scores for regression analysis.

3.2.2 Household Characteristics

On average, parents completed the third year of a four-year secondary education and did not complete secondary school.[7] Mothers generally had more years of education than fathers and fathers were older than their wives. Of all households, 62% had at least one mobile phone. On average, mothers contributed 19% of their household income, whereas nonparent members contributed 13%. Beneficiary households of the Philippine conditional cash transfer program—known in Filipino as the *Pantawid Pamilyang Pilipino Program* (4Ps)—accounted for 40%, implying that these households are poorer than the majority. The co-residential status revealed that 10% of households were female-headed due to the death of husbands (fathers) or separation[8]; fathers and mothers live separately in 11% and 9% of households due to working in another location or a foreign country, respectively.

The indicators for parental employment categories were used, with self-employment as the reference category. Of the total fathers, 6%, 5% and 8% were landowner farmers, tenant farmers and agricultural wage laborers, respectively; 15% were fishermen and 1% were in proprietor/ownership positions such as management. Meanwhile, 48% of mothers were employed. Consequently, fathers and mothers were primarily self-employed.

---

[6] This is based on the variables from the final complete model in Table 11.

[7] In their parents' generation, secondary education lasted only four years (see also Chapters 2 and 3).

[8] Civil divorce is generally unavailable under Philippine law. Limited exceptions exist (e.g., under Muslim personal law or through judicial recognition of a valid foreign divorce) but are unlikely to apply to the present study's sample and locale. In this survey, respondents who no longer cohabited or shared income reported their status as "separated."

Table 1 Descriptive statistics

Variables	Obs.	Mean	Std. Dev.	Min.	Max.
Dependent variables:					
Scores on RC (original scores out of 100)					
Filipino	275	83.18	5.32	64.00	98.00
Math	274	81.88	4.84	71.00	96.00
English	274	82.48	5.27	67.00	97.00
Science	270	82.80	4.88	73.00	98.00
Social Studies	259	83.44	4.67	73.00	98.00
MAPEH	269	84.90	5.06	71.00	97.00
TLE	240	84.67	5.12	74.00	99.00
Scores on NATs (original scores out of 100)					
Filipino	135	64.74	21.82	15.00	97.50
Math	135	55.05	31.90	3.70	100.00
English	135	55.65	29.31	5.00	97.50
Science	135	49.87	26.51	7.50	97.50
Social Studies	135	55.63	24.61	11.11	95.00
Independent variables:					
Individual characteristics					
Male indicator (= 1 if yes)	275	0.47	0.50	0.00	1.00
Eldest (= 1 if yes)	275	0.15	0.36	0.00	1.00
Youngest (= 1 if yes)	275	0.22	0.41	0.00	1.00
No. of younger siblings	275	1.73	1.43	0.00	7.00
No. of elder siblings	275	2.72	2.33	0.00	11.00
Having a role-model person (= 1 if yes)	275	0.46	0.50	0.00	1.00
Studying time at home (weekly, *z*-scores)	268	0.00	1.00	−1.06	5.20
Weekly frequency of going to school (weekly, *z*-scores)	268	0.07	0.92	−2.67	1.67
Household characteristics:					
Father's years of education	259	8.84	3.18	1.00	14.00
Mother's years of education	274	8.97	3.15	2.00	14.00
Log per capita income	275	6.87	1.18	0.00	9.72
Father's age	275	46.77	7.65	31.00	74.00
Mother's age	258	44.72	6.58	31.00	73.00

(continued)

Table 1 (continued)

Variables	Obs.	Mean	Std. Dev.	Min.	Max.
Having a mobile phone (= 1 if yes)	275	0.62	0.49	0.00	1.00
Income shares of mother's earnings	273	0.19	0.26	0.00	1.00
Income shares of non-parent members	273	0.13	0.24	0.00	0.89
CCT beneficiary family (= 1 if yes)	275	0.40	0.49	0.00	1.00
Female-headed family (= 1 if yes)	275	0.10	0.30	0.00	1.00
Father not living together (= 1 if yes)	275	0.11	0.32	0.00	1.00
Mother not living together (= 1 if yes)	275	0.09	0.28	0.00	1.00
Father is a land-owning farmer (= 1 if yes)	275	0.06	0.23	0.00	1.00
Father is a contract farmer (= 1 if yes)	275	0.05	0.22	0.00	1.00
Father is an agricultural wage laborer (= 1 if yes)	275	0.08	0.27	0.00	1.00
Father is a fisherman (= 1 if yes)	275	0.15	0.36	0.00	1.00
Father is proprietor (= 1 if yes)	275	0.01	0.12	0.00	1.00
Working mother indicator (= 1 if yes)	258	0.48	0.50	0.00	1.00
Mother is a land-owning farmer (= 1 if yes)	275	0.01	0.09	0.00	1.00
Mother is proprietor (= 1 if yes)	275	0.00	0.00	0.00	0.00
School variables:					
Public school indicator (= 1 if yes)	255	0.93	0.26	0.00	1.00
Going to school on foot (= 1 if yes)	254	0.25	0.44	0.00	1.00
Minutes of commuting to school	254	18.58	14.38	2.00	120.00
Home–school distance (km)	254	3.26	4.75	0.03	39.00
Female Teacher Gender Ratio (TGR):					
Filipino	275	0.81	0.16	0.50	1.00
Math	275	0.68	0.16	0.00	1.00

(continued)

Table 1 (continued)

Variables	Obs.	Mean	Std. Dev.	Min.	Max.
English	275	0.91	0.11	0.50	1.00
Science	275	0.88	0.12	0.00	1.00
Social Studies	275	0.84	0.08	0.50	1.00
MAPEH	275	0.65	0.19	0.00	1.00
TLE	275	0.72	0.23	0.00	1.00

Note MAPEH = Music, arts, physical education and health. TLE = Technology and livelihood education
Source Author's calculations using the primary data

Importantly, these household-level indicators, such as income poverty, parental education, employment, and participation in the 4Ps, are used in empirical models for control variables. As such, the results isolate the effects of school-side mechanisms—particularly non-blind teacher evaluations—from confounding effects of income poverty. The analysis, therefore, captures the marginal effects of teacher-based evaluation structures, conditional on the controlled factors being held constant.

3.2.3 School Variables

Table 1 shows the public-school indicator (1 if the school is public and 0 if it is private), commuting mode indicator (1 if walking), commuting time (in minutes), home–school distance (in kilometers) and school female TGRs for each subject. In the sample, 93% of children were enrolled in public schools and 7% were enrolled in private schools. In rural areas, 24% of students walked to school daily, while the remaining children commuted via pedicabs, tricycles or jeepneys. The average commute takes about 18 min and the average distance between home and school is about 3.3 km. Female TGRs are discussed later in Sects. 4.3 and 5.3.

3.3 Two Scores on Report Cards and National Achievement Test

Table 2 summarizes the two-score types used in this chapter. Comparing the RC and NAT, the visibility of examinees' attributes, such as gender for score markers, differs. In the Philippines, all students are expected to have RC scores for every school semester and NAT scores for grades 6 and 10. RC and NAT scores are also used in entrance exams in higher-level education, meaning that teachers and students have the same incentive to perform well on both assessments; however, visibility is not a choice variable; examinees cannot choose whether scores are blind or non-blind.

The data collection focuses on teenagers in high school; thus, students' NAT scores are recorded once they reach seventh grade (first year of high school) or higher.

In the household survey, we interviewed parents/guardians, asking about their children's latest semester RC scores in Filipino (national language), math, English, science, social studies, MAPEH (music, arts, physical education and health) and TLE (technology and livelihood education). The Bureau of Education Assessment of the DepEd (BEA-DepEd) provided individual level NAT score information for children in or above grade 7; the BEA-DepEd allowed us to track NAT data for exclusive use. The office tracks individual NAT scores by running all eligible students' names, birth dates and years, home addresses and enrolled school names against a huge BEA-DepEd database containing nationwide data. RC scores range from 0 to 100; a score below 70 indicates failure. Unlike RC scores, NAT scores range from 0 to 100 with no threshold. Mean values and standard deviations have different meanings; therefore, we standardized RC and NAT scores into z-scores by each school subject for regression analyses.

The NAT is a standardized, multiple-choice, objective test administered nationwide, and its scores are evaluated blindly. In contrast, schoolteachers evaluate RC scores non-blind, so they know who they are evaluating. According to RC evaluation policies, students' nonacademic, attitude-based 'observed values' are scored separately from each school subject in four components: *maka-diyos* (piety), *makatao* (humane personality), *maka-kalikasan* (respect for the environment and nature) and *makabansa* (nationalism and citizenship). In this sense, attitude-based evaluations, like accounting for students' proactive learning personalities, are independent of the RC and NAT scores. This advantage trait is derived from the institutional setting for empirical analysis (Sect. 6).

DepEd circulates the RC grading policy to all schoolteachers and asks them to base their RC scores on (1) performance tasks, (2) written works and (3) quarterly assessments (Philippine Department of Education 2015). Policies (1) and (3) require quarterly assessments based on semester exam results. Conversely, policy (2) may add routine student factors, such as homework completion, to the RC score rating compared to the externally administered NAT score rating. Section 6.1 discusses this potentiality.

3.4 RC–NAT Score Differences with Multiple Hypothesis Tests

Table 3 compares the gender distribution of collected score averages by school subject, where the scores that are summarized in Table 1 are standardized into z scores. Figure 1 illustrates radar charts for visualization purposes. The average of male students is lower across all subjects for the non-blind rating but not for the blind rating. This contrasting pattern is robust, referring to Romano–Wolf step-down

Table 2 Score type classification by source

Score type	School subject coverage							Source	Blindness	Score marker
	Filipino	Math	English	Science	Social Studies	MAPEH	TLE			
RC (report card)	○	○	○	○	○	○	○	RC collected via household survey	Non-blind	Teachers
NAT (National Achievement Test)	○	○	○	○	○	n.a.	n.a.	BEA-DepEd	Blind	Mechanical scoring (externally administered)

Note MAPEH = music, arts, physical education and health; TLE = technology and livelihood education; BEA-DepEd = Bureau of Education Assessment, Department of Education. Scores are at the individual student level

Source Author's classification

adjusted *p*-values in Table 3 (Romano and Wolf 2005), which considers multiple hypothesis testing for all the school subjects.

The Romano–Wolf step-down adjustment is applied in this analysis to address the issue of multiple hypothesis testing across the school subjects. Without adjustment, testing for gender differences in each subject independently increases the risk of false positives (erroneously detecting significant differences due to chance alone). By sequentially adjusting the *p*-values across all subjects, the Romano–Wolf method ensures that the reported results reflect robust gender differences, even after accounting for the multiple comparisons. In Table 3, adjusted *p*-values (in brackets) represent results accounting for these multiple comparisons, while unadjusted *p*-values (in parentheses) show results from single hypothesis tests conducted for each subject independently.

The gaps between male and female averages range from 0.56 SD for math to 0.87 SD for English in the non-blind scores. Female students outperform their male counterparts in math despite the generally stylized trend that male students excel in math (Guiso et al. 2008: 1164; Hadjar et al. 2014: 118; Nollenberger et al. 2016: 259–261). Overall, male students consistently underperform compared to their female counterparts in all the subjects, including MAPEH and TLE; in contrast, no such gender differences are detected in NAT scores.

4 Empirical Analysis

4.1 Benchmark Model

Our empirical analysis first examines whether teachers stereotype students' academic performance. As a benchmark, two estimations with gender as an independent variable are performed separately on RC and NAT scores, allowing us to focus on the coefficient stability of the student male dummy variable when other controls are added to regression equations and transitive changes in R^2 (Altonji et al. 2005; Bellows and Miguel 2009; Oster 2019). This approach treats students' gender variable as if it has an omitted variable bias (Oster 2019). Suppose the effect of students' gender variable is not generated by the teachers' stereotype but is caused by variables omitted until one specification is included. In that case, its coefficient should be less significant or insignificant because the included covariates now capture the effect of students' gender variable along with transitive changes in R^2 and vice versa. The sequence of added covariates is based on Bronfenbrenner's (1989, 1995) ecological systems theory for standard educational production function models, starting with microsystems, i.e. the individual (self), the family, community and school levels.

Following the benchmark model, the same steps are repeated to estimate the two-score differences calculated at the same student level for the other dependent variable. This approach aligns with the extant literature. Additionally, we examined the interactions between the students' gender variable and the female TGRs. Based

Table 3 *Z*-score comparisons between NAT and RC scores, and multiple hypothesis tests of gender differences in score gaps by child gender and subject

Scores and Subjects	Obs	All	Female (F)	Male (M)	Δ(F-M)
Non-blind score (RC)					
Filipino	275	0.00	0.34	−0.38	0.72 (0.00)*** [0.00]***
Math	274	0.00	0.26	−0.30	0.56 (0.00)*** [0.00]***
English	274	0.00	0.40	−0.47	0.87 (0.00)*** [0.00]***
Science	270	0.00	0.33	−0.39	0.72 (0.00)*** [0.00]***
Social Studies	259	0.00	0.34	−0.38	0.72 (0.00)*** [0.00]***
MAPEH	269	0.00	0.32	−0.38	0.71 (0.00)*** [0.00]***
TLE	240	0.00	0.28	−0.35	0.63 (0.00)*** [0.00]***
Blind score (NAT)					
Filipino	135	0.00	0.00	0.00	0.00 (0.98) [0.98]
Math	135	0.00	−0.01	0.02	−0.03 (0.88) [0.98]
English	135	0.00	0.04	−0.06	0.10 (0.57) [0.81]
Science	135	0.00	0.04	−0.07	0.11 (0.52) [0.79]
Social Studies	135	0.00	0.06	−0.10	0.16 (0.36) [0.63]
Difference (Δ Score (RC–NAT))					
Filipino	125	0.18	0.35	−0.10	0.46 (0.04)** [0.08]*

(continued)

Table 3 (continued)

Scores and Subjects	Obs	All	Female (F)	Male (M)	Δ(F-M)
Math	123	0.14	0.30	−0.09	0.39 (0.10)* [0.15]
English	125	0.17	0.34	−0.12	0.46 (0.02)** [0.07]*
Science	121	0.32	0.47	0.05	0.42 (0.03)** [0.08]*
Social Studies	114	0.23	0.31	0.10	0.21 (0.33) [0.33]

* $= p < 0.10$; ** $= p < 0.05$; *** $= p < 0.01$

Notes

1. Numbers in parentheses are the model *p*-values following single hypothesis tests regarding H_0: $\Delta(F - M) = 0$ at each school subject
2. Numbers in brackets are the Romano–Wolf step-down adjusted *p*-values considering the multiple hypothesis tests regarding H_0: $\Delta(F - M) = 0$ over all the school subjects
3. Music, arts, physical education and health (MAPEH) and technology and livelihood education (TLE) are not examined at the National Achievement Tests (NATs). RC = report card

Source Author's calculations using his primary and administrative data provided by DepEd

on the reviewed literature, the interactions must be statistically significant if the students' RC–NAT score gaps capture the teachers' stereotypes towards one gender of students.

The benchmark model is written as:

$$S_{ijs} = \delta_{js} M_i + \mathbf{X_i} \boldsymbol{\beta}_{\mathbf{js}} + \mathbf{X_h} \boldsymbol{\gamma}_{\mathbf{js}} + \mathbf{X_k} \boldsymbol{\theta}_{\mathbf{js}} + \omega_{1js} + \varphi_{1js} + u_{ijs}. \tag{1}$$

Here, the dependent variable (S_{ijs}) is student *i*'s *z*-scores on the test type $j =$ {NAT, RC} of the school subject $s =$ {Filipino, math, English, science, social studies, MAPEH, TLE}; MAPEH and TLE are available only in the RC case. M_i is the student's gender indicator (male dummy variable), taking 1 if the individual *i* is male and 0 otherwise. The vectors $\mathbf{X_i}$, $\mathbf{X_h}$ and $\mathbf{X_k}$ contain the student *i*'s characteristics, the family background at the household-level of *i*'s household (h) and the school-level characteristics at *i*'s enrolled school (k), respectively. Using Bronfenbrenner's (1989, 1995) ecological systems theory framework, this study controls for different-level unobservables using fixed effects at different levels. ω represents the village-level fixed effect to control for unobservable heterogeneity across the barangays of each student's residential area. φ represents the school-level fixed effect to control for unobservable teacher and school factors not captured by $\mathbf{X_k}$. We include fixed effects for grade (and educational stage) to net out curricular and cohort differences across RC and NAT implementations. The scalar δ and vectors $\boldsymbol{\beta}$, $\boldsymbol{\gamma}$ and $\boldsymbol{\theta}$ are the

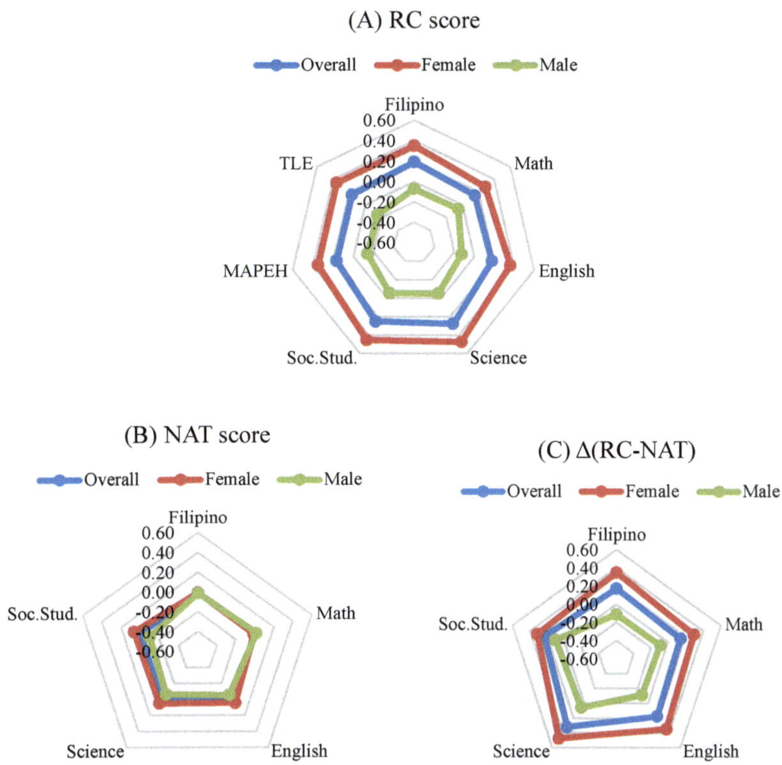

Fig. 1 Radar charts of mean score comparisons among children with both scores, Arranged by score type. *Note* Soc. Stud. = Social Studies. MAPEH = music, arts, physical education, and health. TLE = technology and livelihood education.
Source Author's calculations based on primary and administrative data supplied by DepEd

estimated parameters. We interpret the RC–NAT difference as teacher-side discretion in non-blind RC assessments. This requires that NAT is externally administered and blind and RC is non-blind; that there are no gender-differential shocks or time trends between the two tests; that both tests capture the same latent subject proficiency up to a monotone transformation; and that stakes and incentives are comparable across tests (Sects. 3.2–3.3 for test administration and Sect. 4.2 for identification).

4.2 Identification Strategy with Two-Score Difference Estimations

We used data containing the two-score profiles regarding the same individual students to directly regress the differences between the two scores for the same individuals. We exploited the identification strategy that views the switch in 'blindness' setting as an exogenous quasi-experimental variation. All eligible-grade students (in both public and private schools) in the Philippines must take NATs; thus, test takers and markers have no choice whether the scores are blind or non-blind (Goldin and Rouse 2000; Lavy 2008; Hinnerich et al. 2011; Doornkamp et al. 2022). Furthermore, the researchers, students and teachers cannot change the NAT and RC rating manners based on their preferences and characteristics.

Moreover, NAT and RC scores serve as base materials for individual performance considered for entering further education (from primary to junior secondary and from junior to senior secondary); thus, NATs and RC scores have similar significance. Therefore, our Philippine setting plausibly satisfies the required assumptions. Accordingly, the model is augmented by replacing S_{ijs} with the two-score difference. Now the model can be written as:

$$\Delta S_{is} = \delta_{\mathrm{D},js} M_i + \mathbf{X_i \beta_{D,js}} + \mathbf{X_h} \boldsymbol{\gamma}_{Djs} + \mathbf{X_k} \boldsymbol{\theta}_{Djs} + \omega_{2js} + \varphi_{2js} + \epsilon_{ijs}, \quad (2)$$

where the dependent variables are defined as $\Delta S_{is} \equiv S_{i,RC,s} - S_{i,NAT,s}$ for every school subject (s) as in Eq. (1). The coefficient of interest, $\delta_{D,s}$, means $\delta_{RC,s} - \delta_{NAT,s}$; if $\delta_{D,s} \lesseqgtr 0$, then $\delta_{RC,s} \lesseqgtr \delta_{NAT,s}$. After adding $\mathbf{X_k}$ and φ, we use the female TGRs by school subject and their interaction terms with M_i as control variables. Regressing ΔS_{is} on M_i yields a difference-in-differences (DID) estimand: the male–female gap under non-blind RC minus the corresponding gap under blind NAT. In a stacked specification with the test-type index $j \in \{\text{NAT, RC}\}$ and allowing all controls to have test-specific coefficients; then this DID estimand equals the coefficient on $M_i \times 1\{j = RC\}$ (where $1\{\cdot\}$ denotes an indicator, i.e., $\delta_{D,s}$).

4.3 *Female Teacher Gender Ratios at the School Level*

In the data, individual students' school names are linked to their enrolment (24 school names); however, the data do not include teachers' genders. Thus, we used data provided by the Region IV-B Office of DepEd regarding the female teacher gender ratios (TGRs) of each enrolled school as the proxy variable. TGRs are assumed to be associated with RC scores, of which students are known to be scored by teachers in the non-blind assessment. Female TGRs take the value between 0 and 1 (i.e. 1 – 'female TGR' = 'male TGR'). Our interviews with DepEd and school principals show that teacher gender assignments are made randomly. Higher female TGRs for a certain subject at each student's school imply that the student is more likely to be taught by a female teacher.

Gender disparity is common in the teacher labor market in developing (vs developed) countries, where private sectors are still underdeveloped; thus, teaching as a profession is dominated by women (Crawfurd and Pugatch 2022). Given Dee's (2005) discussion, student–teacher gender mismatches are viewed as a default setting for Filipino boys due to a severe lack of male teachers; the opposite applies to female students. This compatibility between same-sex and opposite-sex teachers for a student is a comparative mechanism of the discussed source of teacher-perceived stereotypes (Dee 2005; Carrell et al. 2010).

Table 4 presents the summary statistics of female TGRs by subject. Female TGRs are 91% for English and science and 68% for math. These figures are higher than expected but capture the typical commonality of teacher labor market situations in developing countries (Crawfurd and Pugatch 2022). Figure 2 depicts female TGR averages by school level. Overall, 81.7% of schoolteachers were female: 87.1% in elementary and 72.0% in secondary. According to World Development Indicators, these figures are consistent with the Philippines' national average rates: 87%–88% (2015–2020) in primary education vis-à-vis 64% as the world average and 71%–73% (2014–2020) in secondary education vs 53%–54% as the world average. Figure 3 shows female TGR averages in secondary education by subject sets. More women teach NAT subjects (Filipino, math, English, science and social studies) than non-NAT subjects (MAPEH and TLE) (79.3% vs. 57.4%). These numbers confirm that the research site and country are consistent with Crawfurd and Pugatch's (2022) review of the gender-unbalanced teacher labor market in developing countries.

Table 4 Female teacher gender ratio in schools enrolled by sample students by NAT subject

Subject	Mean	S.D.	Min.	Max.
Filipino	0.81	0.16	0.50	1.00
Math	0.68	0.16	0.00	1.00
English	0.91	0.11	0.50	1.00
Science	0.88	0.12	0.00	1.00
Social Studies	0.84	0.08	0.50	1.00

Note NAT = National Achievement Test
Source Administrative data were provided by the Region IV-B Office, DepEd

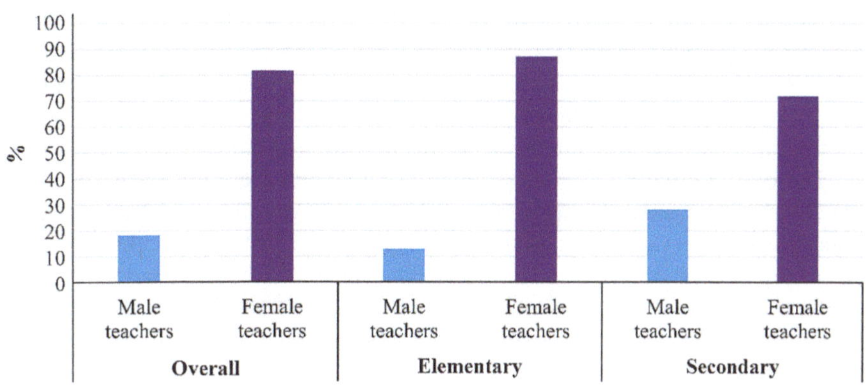

Fig. 2 Female teacher gender ratio (TGR) in schools enrolled by sample students: Arranged by educational level. *Source* Author's calculations using administrative data supplied by the DepEd's Region IV-B Office

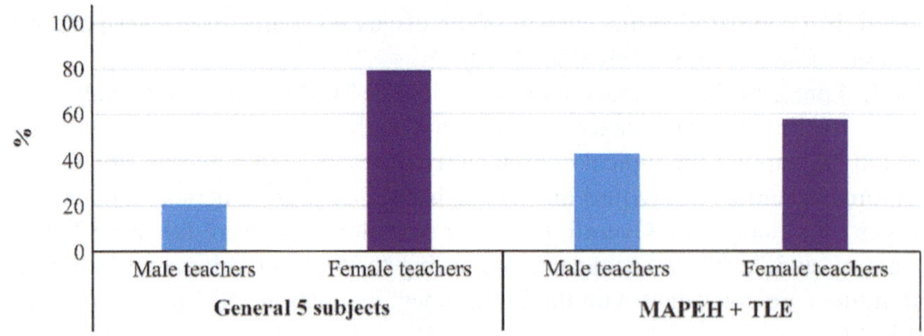

Fig. 3 Female teacher gender ratio (TGR) in secondary schools enrolled by sample students: Arranged by subject set. *Note* Five general subjects, Filipino, math, English, science and social studies, are examined in NATs. *Source* Author's calculations using administrative data supplied by the DepEd's Region IV-B Office

5 Results

5.1 Male Effect on the Benchmark Model

Table 5 presents the estimated male effects in model Eq. (1). Panels (a)–(g) correspond to school subjects, while columns (1)–(4) show successive additions of covariates. Table 5 indicates that across all subjects, the male students' scores are lower for the non-blind rating but not for the blind rating (see also Table 3 for discussions about the gender difference in the two scores and the multiple hypothesis tests). This pattern remains consistent in the RC ratings when comparing the entire sample (central four rows) with the subsample of children whose NAT scores are matched (right four rows), enabling a robust comparison with the NAT score sample. Nonetheless, male students' NAT performance suggests they are not underperforming.

Regarding transitive changes of adjusted R^2, columns (1)–(2) show a drastic increase for dependent variables, particularly non-blind rating scores. Individual- and household-level characteristics, such as demographic profiles and socioeconomic status, have considerable explanatory power of the dependent variable distributions; however, the male effect remains robustly negative even after including these covariates. The blind rating NAT score estimations show that the adjusted R^2 increases from column (2) backwards; therefore, including village- and school-level characteristics and unobservable can explain dependent variable distributions. Despite these controls, the source of the negative male effect remains. The included variables at these levels have some explanatory power for the distributions; however, they are not the 'omitted variable' for the negative male effect.

Table 5 Male effect on NAT and RC scores: Benchmark estimations by academic subject

	NAT				RC							
					Full Sample				Subsample with NAT scores			
	(1)	(2)	(3)	(4)	(1)	(2)	(3)	(4)	(1)	(2)	(3)	(4)
(a) Filipino												
Male (= 1)	0.03 [0.16]	−0.1 [0.17]	−0.16 [0.28]	−0.23 [0.24]	−0.72*** [0.11]	−0.72*** [0.11]	−0.71*** [0.06]	−0.65*** [0.08]	−0.42** [0.18]	−0.49*** [0.17]	−0.46*** [0.13]	−0.56*** [0.11]
Adj. R^2	0.08	0.20	0.20	0.26	0.13	0.24	0.26	0.29	0.03	0.28	0.26	0.24
No. of Obs.	135	128	128	127	275	256	256	228	125	118	118	118
(b) Mathematics												
Male (= 1)	0.13 [0.13]	0.10 [0.14]	0.11 [0.22]	0.03 [0.23]	−0.56*** [0.12]	−0.59*** [0.11]	−0.56*** [0.06]	−0.63*** [0.10]	−0.34* [0.18]	−0.53*** [0.17]	−0.50*** [0.07]	−0.63*** [0.10]
Adj. R^2	0.41	0.46	0.48	0.55	0.08	0.30	0.34	0.28	0.02	0.27	0.27	0.28
No. of Obs.	135	128	128	127	274	255	255	227	123	116	116	115
(c) English												
Male (= 1)	0.00 [0.14]	−0.07 [0.15]	−0.08 [0.22]	−0.15 [0.21]	−0.87*** [0.11]	−0.92*** [0.10]	−0.90*** [0.06]	−0.85*** [0.07]	−0.49*** [0.18]	−0.66*** [0.16]	−0.63*** [0.14]	−0.69*** [0.11]
Adj. R^2	0.35	0.44	0.46	0.51	0.18	0.35	0.37	0.38	0.05	0.31	0.30	0.31
No. of Obs.	135	128	128	127	274	255	255	229	125	118	118	118
(d) Science												
Male (= 1)	−0.02 [0.13]	−0.11 [0.15]	−0.11 [0.26]	−0.13 [0.24]	−0.72*** [0.11]	−0.81*** [0.11]	−0.82*** [0.11]	−0.85*** [0.13]	−0.52*** [0.19]	−0.69*** [0.19]	−0.66** [0.23]	−0.89*** [0.09]
Adj. R^2	0.74	0.73	0.75	0.74	0.18	0.35	0.37	0.38	0.05	0.34	0.33	0.32
No. of Obs.	134	127	127	126	274	255	255	229	121	114	114	114
(e) Social Studies												

(continued)

Table 5 (continued)

	NAT				RC							
					Full Sample				Subsample with NAT scores			
	(1)	(2)	(3)	(4)	(1)	(2)	(3)	(4)	(1)	(2)	(3)	(4)
Male (= 1)	−0.06	−0.1 [0.14]	−0.11 [0.19]	−0.12 [0.11]	−0.72*** [0.12]	−0.70*** [0.12]	−0.67*** [0.09]	−0.66*** [0.11]	−0.51** [0.20]	−0.64*** [0.18]	−0.58*** [0.14]	−0.58*** [0.11]
Adj. R^2	0.37	0.43	0.43	0.49	0.12	0.30	0.34	0.26	0.05	0.30	0.28	0.21
No. of Obs.	135	128	128	127	259	241	241	214	114	107	106	106
(f) Music, Arts, Physical Education and Health (MAPEH)												
Male (= 1)	n.a. n.a.	n.a. n.a.	n.a. n.a.	n.a. n.a.	−0.71*** [0.12]	−0.78*** [0.11]	−0.78*** [0.14]	−0.65*** [0.12]	−0.49*** [0.19]	−0.64*** [0.19]	−0.64*** [0.15]	−0.58*** [0.14]
Adj. R^2	n.a.	n.a.	n.a.	n.a.	0.12	0.32	0.31	0.31	0.05	0.27	0.26	0.26
No. of Obs.	n.a.	n.a.	n.a.	n.a.	269	250	250	224	125	118	118	117
(g) Technology and Livelihood Education (TLE)												
Male (= 1)	n.a. n.a.	n.a. n.a.	n.a. n.a.	n.a. n.a.	−0.63*** [0.12]	−0.62*** [0.12]	−0.63*** [0.10]	−0.67*** [0.09]	−0.50*** [0.19]	−0.49** [0.19]	−0.49** [0.19]	−0.57** [0.20]
Adj. R^2	n.a.	n.a.	n.a.	n.a.	0.10	0.32	0.30	0.29	0.05	0.25	0.24	0.21
No. of Obs.	n.a.	n.a.	n.a.	n.a.	240	221	221	198	114	107	106	106
Controls:												
Male dummy (= 1)	Yes	Yes	Yes	Yes	Yes	Yes	Yes	Yes	Yes	Yes	Yes	Yes
Child and household characteristics	No	Yes	Yes	Yes	No	Yes	Yes	Yes	No	Yes	Yes	Yes

(continued)

Table 5 (continued)

	NAT				RC							
					Full Sample				Subsample with NAT scores			
	(1)	(2)	(3)	(4)	(1)	(2)	(3)	(4)	(1)	(2)	(3)	(4)
ω (Region-level FE)	No	No	Yes	Yes	No	No	Yes	Yes	No	No	Yes	Yes
School-related characteristics	No	No	No	Yes	No	No	No	Yes	No	No	No	Yes
φ (School-level FE)	No	No	No	Yes	No	No	No	Yes	No	No	No	Yes

$^{*} = p < 0.10$; $^{**} = p < 0.05$; $^{***} = p < 0.01$

Notes 'n.a.' = not tested at NATs. Numbers in brackets are robust standard errors. NAT = National Achievement Test; RC = report card

Source Author's calculations using his primary and administrative data provided by DepEd

5.2 *Male Effect on Two-Score Difference Estimations*

Table 6 shows the regression results of estimating Eq. (2) by school subject. The first four columns correspond to those in Table 5 and the estimates are qualitatively similar to those in Table 5. When only individual- and household-level characteristics are added as covariates, the male effect estimate is significantly negative, which contrasts with the global trend (Guiso et al. 2008: 1164; Hadjar et al. 2014: 118; Nollenberger et al. 2016: 259–261). The male effect explains a 0.39 standard deviation (SD) (social studies) to 0.64 SD (English) downward bias for non-blind rating compared to the female counterparts. Column (3) controls for village-level unobservables, showing that the male effect estimate remains negative for English and social studies; it is insignificant but negative for other subjects. In column (4), where school-level fixed effects are controlled for, the male effect coefficients turn significantly negative again. The Eq. (2) estimation shows that the male effect is detected across all subjects (including Filipino, math and science).

Even with the addition of the school-level fixed effect and the other covariates and fixed effects, the downward bias from the male effect alone is still present. This result contrasts with other research, such as Hinnerich et al. (2011: 689–690), who found no gender effect in the blind–non-blind score differences in Sweden. Furthermore, Lavy and Sand (2018) and Carlana (2019) showed that the stereotype bias was downwards for female students in Italy and Israel. Consequently, the score rating difference from students' exposure to non-blind teacher evaluations increases the likelihood of male students underperforming. This effect occurs even when considering the heterogeneity students experience across schools, communities, household characteristics and personal profiles.

5.3 *The Female Teacher Gender Ratios and Likelihood of Teacher–Student Gender (Mis)match*

Table 7 presents the estimation results, incorporating the TGRs of each school subject in the enrolled institution as additional covariates within the comprehensive model. The TGR variables operate at the school level and the number of clusters (i.e. schools) is not extensive; thus, we omitted the school-level fixed effect. Instead, we reported the wild-bootstrapped clustered standard errors outlined by Cameron et al. (2008) and referred to in Tables 7, 8, 10, and 11.

Table 7 indicates that the male effect on the results remains consistent with Table 6. Notably, the TGR variable in science shows sensitivity to the distinction between blind and non-blind rating scores. This outcome indicates that a student's likelihood of having a female teacher is a statistically significant predictor for the score difference between blind and non-blind ratings in the science subject. However, this predictor is insignificant for the other subjects in Table 7.

Table 6 Male effect on two-score differences between NAT and RC scores by academic subject

	(1)	(2)	(3)	(4)
(a) Filipino				
Male (= 1)	−0.47** [0.20]	−0.43* [0.22]	−0.37 [0.20]	−0.36* [0.16]
Adj. R^2	0.04	0.18	0.17	0.23
No. of Obs.	125	118	118	118
(b) Mathematics				
Male (= 1)	−0.40* [0.22]	−0.50** [0.24]	−0.42 [0.26]	−0.41* [0.20]
Adj. R^2	0.03	0.19	0.13	0.17
No. of Obs.	123	116	116	115
(c) English				
Male (= 1)	−0.51*** [0.19]	−0.64*** [0.19]	−0.64** [0.22]	−0.61*** [0.13]
Adj. R^2	0.11	0.2	0.17	0.21
No. of Obs.	125	118	118	118
(d) Science				
Male (= 1)	−0.45** [0.19]	−0.55*** [0.20]	−0.54 [0.30]	−0.78*** [0.16]
Adj. R^2	0.04	0.19	0.18	0.27
No. of Obs.	121	114	114	114
(e) Social Studies				
Male (= 1)	−0.28 [0.20]	−0.39* [0.21]	−0.34* [0.18]	−0.31* [0.15]
Adj. R^2	0.14	0.24	0.24	0.19
No. of Obs.	114	107	106	106
Controls:				
Male dummy (= 1)	Yes	Yes	Yes	Yes
Child and household characteristics	No	Yes	Yes	Yes
ω (Region-level FE)	No	No	Yes	Yes
School-related characteristics	No	No	No	Yes
φ (School-level FE)	No	No	No	Yes

$^{*} = p < 0.10$; $^{**} = p < 0.05$; $^{***} = p < 0.01$

Notes Numbers in brackets are robust standard errors. NAT = National Achievement Test; RC = report card

Source Author's calculations using his primary and administrative data provided by DepEd

Table 7 Male effect on differences between RC and NAT Scores by academic subject (with TGRs added)

	Filipino	Math	English	Science	Soc. Stu.
Male (= 1)	−0.40*** [0.11]	−0.48** [0.14]	−0.62*** [0.12]	−0.63*** [0.15]	−0.43** [0.18]
Female TGR (own subject)	1.63 [0.96]	0.21 [0.76]	−0.61 [0.81]	−1.89* [0.85]	1.30 [2.37]
Adj. R^2	0.19	0.17	0.19	0.21	0.23
No. of Obs.	116	114	116	112	105

* $= p < 0.10$; ** $= p < 0.05$; *** $= p < 0.01$

Notes

1. TGRs = teacher gender ratios; Soc. Stu. = Social Studies; NAT = National Achievement Test; RC = report card
2. Numbers in brackets are the wild-bootstrapped cluster standard errors at the school level

Source Author's calculations using his primary and administrative data provided by DepEd

Table 8 Male effect on differences between RC and NAT scores by subject (with the Interaction term of TGRs with male dummy variable added)

	Filipino	Math	English	Science	Soc. Stu.
Male (= 1)	−0.39** [0.11]	−0.64*** [0.18]	−0.63*** [0.11]	−0.67*** [0.15]	−0.58** [0.18]
Female TGR (own subject)	1.51 [1.23]	1.90* [0.87]	−0.07 [0.91]	−2.74** [0.84]	4.43 [2.84]
Male × Female TGR (own subject)	0.33 [1.15]	−2.99** [0.99]	−1.47* [0.67]	2.68* [1.31]	−5.77** [2.38]
Adj. R^2	0.19	0.18	0.18	0.21	0.24
No. of Obs.	116	114	116	112	105
Joint Hypothesis Test (*p*-values) H_0: Male + Male × Female TGR = 0	0.27	0.01***	0.00***	0.04**	0.02**

* $= p < 0.10$; ** $= p < 0.05$; *** $= p < 0.01$

Notes

1. TGRs = teacher gender ratios; Soc. Stu. = Social Studies; NAT = National Achievement Test; RC = report card
2. Numbers in brackets are the wild-bootstrapped cluster standard errors at the school level

Source Author's calculations using his primary and administrative data provided by DepEd

The estimation in Table 8 adds the TGRs' interaction with the male dummy variable, allowing us to examine student–teacher gender (mis)match (Dee 2005; Carrell et al. 2010). The results show that the interaction term *Male* × *FemaleTGR* is estimated to be responsive in math, English, science and social studies. The interaction term coefficients are statistically negative for math, English and social studies and positive for science. This outcome suggests that male students taught by female teachers (math, English and social studies) are likelier to receive lower non-blind ratings than their male counterparts taught by male teachers and their female counterparts; the opposite holds for science. This same-sex compatibility is consistent with previous studies (Dee 2005; Carrell et al. 2010). Without the teachers' stereotype, attributes like TGRs cannot explain the difference between non-blind and blind scores in either direction (Lavy and Sand 2018). Nevertheless, the results in Table 8 reaffirm and strengthen the conclusion that teacher stereotypes contribute to bias in student scores.

The contrast between science and math is puzzling; thus, we conducted additional remote interviews with selected teachers. They suggested that learning science entails more fieldwork, such as collecting botanical, animal and mineral samples outdoors, compared to learning math, which primarily involves desk studies. Teachers may perceive a greater comparative advantage for boys than girls in such outdoor activities; however, at the same time, any chance variation may have influenced the result. Therefore, further studies are warranted to explore the observed contrast. This need also applies to the subsequent arguments in the next section.

6 Mediation Discussion

6.1 On Tracking of the National Achievement Test Scores

Table 5 shows a decline in NAT vs RC observations. The BEA-DepEd did not intentionally omit some students' NAT scores. Tracking success or failure is out of our control and not an individual choice variable; therefore, this study assumes random tracking rates. Nevertheless, some students might have recently migrated to our research site without having their NAT scores tracked. BEA-DepEd tracked all sample children's names and addresses; however, suppose some students skipped the NAT. This subsection discusses whether this situation could misconstrue our results.

Based on population, the first 'migration' option is least likely. As explained in Sect. 3.1, the sampling framework used the CBMS master list as the population. Only four households not listed in the CBMS participated in the questionnaire survey because their families had moved. BEA-DepEd did not track the NAT scores of only two children from one of the four households. Thus, migration is the least associated with tracking rates.

In the Philippines, every eligible student must take the NAT regardless of public or private school enrolment. Section 3.3 outlined that students need both NAT and RC scores for higher education entrance. Local teachers said a few cases might arise where students did not take a test because they had no penalty mechanism. Given this possibility, how likely are better-performing students to miss the NAT? For our empirical analysis, it matters if the direction underestimates or overestimates the male effect. If underestimating possibility is the case, result interpretations are unaffected. They are interpreted as the least existing effect, which would be no less significant than if more tracking was successful because the male effect estimates in Eq. (2)

were underestimated. However, if overestimating occurred, the male effect estimates in Eq. (2) might be overestimated enough that they led to a false interpretation of the estimated bias.

Therefore, we used probit estimations to check whether NAT scores were tracked. The dependent variable is a binary dummy variable, taking 1 if the student's NAT scores were tracked and 0 otherwise. The regressors include the male dummy variable and the RC scores of the same school subjects to check for associations with lower academic performance. Table 9 presents probit estimates; in column (1), the direction is neutral for Filipino, math, English and social studies, and of the former type (underestimation). In contrast, the statistical significance is at the 10% level for science, where the NAT scores of better-performing students in RC scores are more likely to be tracked. Column (2) shows that the male effect occurs among better-performing male students only in English; it does not affect the other four subjects. Moreover, both columns show that gender alone is irrelevant for tracking probability. Overall, the estimates indicate a neutral case for almost all subjects, with a former underestimating case for a few subjects. Thus, tracking the NAT scores does not affect the results and interpretations because the estimated male effects are theoretically equivalent to what could have been estimated in the counterfactual.

6.2 *On the Possibility of Alternative Mechanisms*

Given the setting and two assessment systems described in Sects. 2 and 3, this subsection discusses the possibility that NAT–RC score differences may only capture attitudes proactively evaluated in students' RC scores but not in external assessments such as NAT scores. The RC scoring policy by DepEd and the assessment of NATs described in Sect. 3.3 can counter-argue that students' attitudes and personalities are isolated from the respective RC scores of each subject. In this sense, the institutional settings would ensure the concern is irrelevant.

Nonetheless, we conducted a further analysis to address the concern within the empirical framework. Our current data include school attendance (one-week records) and diary-based time for home study (one-week records). The regression uses these two variables as the proxy for the student's diligence.[9] We assume that students who attend school more often or study at home for longer (or both) are likelier to have personality traits that teachers evaluate as actively participating in and preparing for class (Ferman and Fontes 2022).

Table 10 presents the result. First, school attendance positively correlates with two-score differences in math and science. This outcome suggests that upwards RC scores are likely in these subjects because children who attend school regularly miss fewer classes and appear more engaged to their teachers. Second, studying time at home does not affect the two-score differences in any subjects, contrasting with

[9] The school attendance and study-time variables here were not collected by school subject; they are measured at the student level and therefore do not vary across school subjects.

Table 9 Probit estimation of probability of tracking NAT scores

Independent variables	(1)	(2)
Male (= 1)	0.03 [0.20]	−1.81 [1.22]
Age	0.16*** [0.04]	−0.05 [0.13]
Male × Age		0.26* [0.14]
Enrolled Grade	−0.02** [0.01]	0.19 [0.14]
Male × Enrolled Grade		−0.22 [0.14]
z score on RC, Filipino	0.01 [0.14]	0.00 [0.19]
Male × *z* score on RC, Filipino		−0.18 [0.29]
z score on RC, math	−0.22 [0.14]	−0.2 [0.17]
Male × *z* score on RC, math		−0.05 [0.29]
z score on RC, English	−0.11 [0.16]	−0.42* [0.24]
Male × *z* score on RC, English		0.83** [0.34]
z score on RC, science	0.30* [0.15]	0.43* [0.23]
Male × *z* score on RC, science		−0.26 [0.31]
z score on RC, social studies	0.20 [0.13]	0.16 [0.19]
Male × *z* score on RC, social studies		0.09 [0.26]
Regional-level dummy	Yes	Yes
Intercept	−2.34*** [0.69]	−0.95 [1.02]
Pseudo R^2	0.14	0.18
No. of Obs.	231	231

* $= p < 0.10$; ** $= p < 0.05$; *** $= p < 0.01$

Note Numbers in brackets are robust standard errors. NAT = National Achievement Test

Source Author's calculations using his primary and administrative data provided by DepEd.

Table 10 Male effect on differences between RC and NAT scores by subject (with studying time at home and school attendance times added)

	Filipino	Math	English	Science	Soc. Stu.
Male (= 1)	−0.35** [0.14]	−0.67*** [0.12]	−0.61*** [0.16]	−0.57** [0.19]	−0.52** [0.19]
Female TGR (own subject)	1.48 [1.22]	2.84** [0.88]	−0.01 [0.84]	−3.95*** [1.03]	4.99 [3.02]
Male × Female TGR (own subject)	0.49 [1.26]	−3.70*** [0.82]	−1.52* [0.75]	2.09 [1.44]	−5.61* [2.81]
Studying time at home	0.03 [0.11]	−0.03 [0.17]	−0.04 [0.12]	−0.04 [0.09]	0.02 [0.11]
School attendance times	0.05 [0.28]	0.86*** [0.18]	0.05 [0.14]	0.67*** [0.14]	0.57 [0.30]
Adj. R^2	0.17	0.22	0.17	0.25	0.24
No. of Obs.	115	113	115	111	104
Joint Hypothesis Test (*p*-values) H_0: Male + Male × Female TGR = 0	0.92	0.00***	0.03***	0.28	0.08*

* $= p < 0.10$; ** $= p < 0.05$; *** $= p < 0.01$

Notes

1. TGRs = teacher gender ratios; Soc. Stu. = Social Studies; NAT = National Achievement Test; RC = report card
2. Numbers in brackets are the wild-bootstrapped cluster standard errors at the school level

Source Author's calculations using his primary and administrative data provided by DepEd

Ferman and Fontes (2022). Students studying at home longer are likelier to appear diligent; thus, the result implies that the bias is more of a *pure* stereotype against boys than one conditional on the student attitudinal proxy measured as studying time. Importantly, including these diligence factors does not eliminate the male effect, remaining robustly negative over all the subjects.

Compared to Table 8, the coefficients of *Female TGR* and *Male × Female TGR* are similar. Specifically, the signs of the coefficients of *Male × Female TGR* and the joint tests remain consistent in math, English and social studies. Therefore, while RC scores may capture additional aspects like students' diligence, the previous understanding in Table 8 still holds.

Finally, Table 11 includes the interaction terms of the male indicator with the diligence factors to investigate their mechanism. As shown, the increase in female TGR remains unfavorable for boys in math and social studies and for all students in science; it has no significance for English. Notably, the interaction term with school attendance is statistically significantly negative in four subjects (Filipino, math, English and science), and study time at home is likewise significant in English and science. Surprisingly, these estimates suggest that more diligent boys score lower than their less diligent male counterparts compared to their female counterparts. However, our interpretations are always relative, with the male dummy capturing the

Table 11 Male effect on differences between RC and NAT scores by subject (with the interaction terms of studying time at home and school attendance times with male dummy and female TGRs added)

	Filipino	Math	English	Science	Soc. Stu.
Male (= 1)	0.04 [0.15]	−0.40** [0.14]	−0.39* [0.18]	−0.31 [0.20]	−0.54* [0.24]
Female TGR (own subject)	1.24 [1.22]	2.91*** [0.75]	0.11 [0.87]	−3.94*** [1.01]	5.07 [3.25]
Male × Female TGR (own subject)	0.03 [1.31]	−4.13*** [0.65]	−0.93 [0.83]	1.86 [1.92]	−5.73* [2.95]
Studying time at home	0.11 [0.13]	0.02 [0.19]	0.02 [0.13]	0.00 [0.10]	0.01 [0.12]
Male × Studying time at home	−0.36 [0.20]	−0.25 [0.14]	−0.25** [0.10]	−0.25** [0.10]	0.05 [0.17]
School attendance times	0.73* [0.32]	1.08*** [0.25]	0.37** [0.15]	0.87*** [0.14]	0.56 [0.33]
Male × School attendance times	−1.33** [0.44]	−0.86* [0.45]	−0.78*** [0.17]	−0.90** [0.27]	0.03 [0.19]
Adj. R^2	0.23	0.22	0.19	0.26	0.22
No. of Obs.	115	113	115	111	104
Joint Hypothesis Test (*p*-values) H_0: Male + Male × Female TGR = 0	0.96	0.00***	0.20	0.41	0.09*

$^* = p < 0.10$; $^{**} = p < 0.05$; $^{***} = p < 0.01$

Notes

1. TGRs = teacher gender ratios; Soc. Stu. = Social Studies; NAT = National Achievement Test; RC = report card

2. Numbers in brackets are the wild-bootstrapped cluster standard errors at the school level

Source Author's calculations using his primary and administrative data provided by DepEd.

difference between female and male students; therefore, we can also interpret that diligent girls are more likely to score higher overall than boys.

Differences between blind and non-blind rating scores can be attributed to student diligence aspects measured as attendance; however, the outcome of student–teacher gender (mis)match indicates a teacher bias in scoring, particularly disadvantaging male students in math, English and social studies. We maintain the approach discussed in Sect. 5.3 regarding the opposite sign of science. Notably, diligence favors girls much more in the non-blind rating than their male counterparts. Even if RCs capture student diligence more than NATs, they should be gender neutral as long as students are equally diligent.

While these score discrepancies are institutionally embedded, they may be compounded by the fact that boys from lower-income households are more frequently absent or less prepared, not necessarily out of disinterest but because of their broader economic responsibilities at home.

Our findings indicate that the non-blind rating favors girls more than boys, even within the group of likewise diligent girls and boys. Tables 8 and 10 allow us to compare how adding the diligence factors affected the regressions, showing that (1) the negative male effect persists across all school subjects afterwards. Even after controlling for other variables, including the diligence factors, male students still scored lower in the non-blind rating. (2) Including diligence factors does not eliminate the cross effect of *Male* × *Female TGR* that was statistically significant in Table 8. When student diligence factors are controlled, the cross effect remains responsive.

Additionally, the interaction term of the diligence factors with the male indicator (Table 11) is negative, implying that the more diligent male (female) students are, the less (more) favorably they are evaluated in the non-blind rating compared to their female (male) counterparts. In other words, the stereotype regarding diligent students is amplified compared to the blind rating, potentially leading male students to feel unrewarded even when they exhibit diligence similar to their female counterparts. Moreover, the joint tests in Tables 8 and 10 support the robustness of the findings; however, our results cannot definitively determine which of the two narratives is the sole explanation, necessitating further exploration.

7 Conclusions

This chapter explored gender disparities in basic education subjects, expanding the analysis beyond math and science. Using a natural experimental framework based on students' exposure to visibility in score rating systems, we applied the blind–non-blind score comparison approach of Goldin and Rouse (2000) and Lavy (2008) to the Philippine context. Our findings reveal a consistent underperformance by boys in teacher-assigned scores, a pattern not observed in standardized blind assessments.

Our findings highlight two potential sources of gender disparity. The first is the possibility of differential teacher scoring bias, favoring girls over boys. Second, while students' diligence is reflected in their non-blind rating scores, the blind rating scores show that male students who are equally diligent as their female counterparts are disproportionately unrewarded. We approached the first possibility by observing the increased likelihood for students, especially boys, to be taught by female teachers. The results suggested this possibility in some school subjects, including math. Nonetheless, we should exercise caution against overgeneralizing all the subjects, as contradictory findings occurred between math and science (Sect. 5.3). Nonetheless, this finding aligns with some previous studies on student–teacher gender mismatch, reflecting a female-teacher-dominated market in developing countries, even in math; however, other studies suggest that boys excel globally (Guiso et al. 2008; Hadjar et al. 2014; Nollenberger et al. 2016).

We approached the second possibility by considering diligence factors such as students' school attendance and study time at home. In our recognized quasi-experimental setting, the results implied that the non-blind rating may capture diligence more than the blind rating. However, if teachers merely capture diligence when rating RC scores and reflect the difference between boys and girls, comparing the likewise diligent male and female students should reveal equal treatment. Conversely, our results imply that female students are rated even more favorably than their male counterparts, even for similarly diligent students. This suggests that male students may perceive an absence of reward for their efforts, potentially weakening their academic motivation.

Importantly, the estimation models in this chapter already controlled for individual and household-level economic factors, including income and poverty status. Therefore, the teacher scoring biases we observe can be interpreted as marginal effects net of household poverty—capturing institutional variations across schools and teachers. The evidence holds policy implications for gender-equalizing public policies in the Philippines and similar emerging economies (Sects. 1 and 2).

First, in gender-balancing policymaking in human development fields, it is crucial to identify which evaluation system the policymakers primarily reference. Unlike the Swedish case of Hinnerich, Höglin and Johannesson (2011), we found that boys underperform on teacher-scored evaluations despite equal performance on standardized tests. Given the study's findings, improving the student evaluation system is one option in the global trends post-COVID, given a decline in the proactive introduction of external assessments into regular student evaluations (Burgess et al. 2022). Empirical evidence from Burgess et al. (2022) suggests that exposing students to semi-blind or 'semi-external assessment' in math can alleviate the gender gap, offering policy relevance for governments in developing countries that face severe financial constraints.

Gender diversification of the teacher labor market can be another fundamental option. In developing countries, teacher labor markets are closely tied to the country's economic development stage and tend to be disproportionately represented by female teachers. Teaching is a significant source of formal, professional employment in developing countries with a growing demand for education; it offers a substantial share of employment opportunities for women and individuals with diplomas as economies progress (Goldin 1995; Crawfurd and Pugatch 2022). Therefore, further studies on the unbalanced teacher market are warranted to determine whether the high female teacher domination is an outcome of labor-market discrimination against women, especially in gender-segregated occupations and rural employment settings. This situation contrasts with that of educated males, who have broader and more diverse occupational choices (Takayama et al. 2010; Yamauchi and Tiongco 2013; Estudillo and Otsuka 2015).

Therefore, regional-level poverty and underdevelopment may still exert structural influence on the institutional dynamics examined in this chapter. For instance, in rural areas such as Marinduque, the underdevelopment of the private sector constrains employment opportunities for educated women, reinforcing the occupational clustering of female workers in teaching and public administration. This occupational pattern results in a highly gender-imbalanced teacher labor market, which in turn manifests in the student–teacher gender mismatch observed in our study. In this light, the gendered configuration of the teacher labor market is not merely an educational phenomenon but one deeply embedded in broader economic structures.

Although these macroeconomic constraints lie beyond the empirical scope of this chapter, their relevance is clear. Policies aimed at industrial upgrading and the creation of gender-neutral employment opportunities are essential for long-term educational equity. Development and education policy, therefore, must be treated as interdependent, not separate domains.

Lastly, we acknowledge limitations and outline directions for future research. First, as this chapter primarily covers secondary education, its direct applicability to higher education—where gender disparities may reverse—is limited (Goldin et al. 2006). Nonetheless, the findings remain relevant, as secondary education forms a direct pathway to higher levels (Carrell et al. 2010). Second, the relatively small sample size, while limiting generalizability, enabled access to rare microdata on NAT scores through close collaboration with BEA–DepEd and local governments. While broader studies would aid generalizability, the rarity of such data justifies prioritizing depth over breadth. Third, while this study used female teacher ratios (TGRs) as proxies, richer data on individual teacher characteristics are needed. That said, even aggregate indicators proved statistically meaningful in explaining blind–non-blind score gaps (Alesina et al. 2018), underscoring the importance of expanding this line of research.

Beyond these methodological constraints, this chapter signals a shift in analytical focus, from household-level dynamics explored in **Part II** to institutional mechanisms that reinforce gender disparities. As the opening to **Part III**, it reframes schools not as neutral platforms but as sites where bias can be reproduced. Mechanisms such as teacher gender ratios (TGRs) and subjective internal assessments emerge as key channels through which gendered inequalities are shaped, particularly in settings where external evaluations are limited. In this institutional frame, even single episodes of bias, regardless of intent, may leave, to some extent, scarring persistent traces in records and placements that are carried forward through expectations (Andrew 2014; DiPrete and Eirich 2006).

These perspectives prepare the ground for Chapter 7, which explores how disengaged boys from education may still find pathways to educational re-engagement. In contrast to the exclusionary forces outlined here, the next chapter foregrounds resilience and student agency. Taken together, the two chapters reveal how gendered outcomes are not only shaped by systems but are also challenged—and at times, subverted—through individual effort and adaptation.

References

Alan S, Ertac S, Mumcu I (2018) Gender stereotypes in the classroom and effects on achievement. Rev Econ Stat 100(5):876–890. https://doi.org/10.1162/rest_a_00756

Alesina A, Carlana M, La Ferrara E, Pinotti P (2018) Revealing stereotypes: evidence from immigrants in schools. NBER working paper no. 25333. https://doi.org/10.3386/w25333

Alston M, Darity WA, Eckel CC, McNeil L, Sharpe R (2022) The effect of stereotypes on black college test scores at A historically black university. J Econ Behav Organ 194:408–424. https://doi.org/10.1016/j.jebo.2021.12.005

Altonji JG, Elder TE, Taber CR (2005) An evaluation of instrumental variable strategies for estimating the effects of catholic schooling. Journal of Human Resources, 40(4):791–821. https://doi.org/10.3368/jhr.40.4.791
Andrew M (2014) The scarring effects of primary-grade retention? A study of cumulative advantage in the educational career. Social Forces 93(2):653–685. https://doi.org/10.1093/sf/sou074
Attanasio OP, Kaufmann KM (2014) Education choices and returns to schooling: intra-household decision making, gender and subjective expectations. J Dev Econ 109:203–216. https://doi.org/10.1016/j.jdeveco.2014.04.003
Bellows J, Miguel E (2009) War and local collective action in Sierra Leone. J Public Econ 93(11–12):1144–1157. https://doi.org/10.1016/j.jpubeco.2009.07.012
Botelho F, Madeira RA, Rangel MA (2015) Racial discrimination in grading: evidence from brazil. Am Econ J Appl Econ 7(4):37–52. https://doi.org/10.1257/app.20140352
Bouis H, Palabrica-Costello M, Solon O, Westbrook D, Limno A (1998) Gender equality and investments in adolescents in the rural Philippines. International Food Policy Research Institute, Washington, DC
Bronfenbrenner U (1989) Ecological systems theory. In: Vasta R (ed) Six theories of child development: revised formulations and current issues. Jessica Kingsley Publishers Ltd., London, pp 187–249
Bronfenbrenner U (1995) Developmental ecology through space and time: A future perspective. In: Moen P, Elder GH, Luscher K et al (eds) Examining lives in context: perspectives on the ecology of human development. American Psychological Association, Washington, DC, pp 619–647. https://doi.org/10.1037/10176-018
Buhl-Wiggers J, Jones S, Thornton R (2021) Boys lagging behind: unpacking gender differences in academic achievement across East Africa. Int J Educ Dev 83:102382. https://doi.org/10.1016/j.ijedudev.2021.102382
Burgess S, Greaves E (2013) Test scores, subjective assessment, and stereotyping of ethnic minorities. J Labor Econ 31(3):535–576. https://doi.org/10.1086/669340
Burgess S, Hauberg DS, Rangvid BS, Sievertsen HH (2022) The importance of external assessments: high school math and gender gaps in STEM degrees. Econ Educ Rev 88:102267. https://doi.org/10.1016/j.econedurev.2022.102267
Cameron AC, Gelbach JB, Miller DL (2008) Bootstrap-based improvements for inference with clustered errors. Rev Econ Stat 90(3):414–427. https://doi.org/10.1162/rest.90.3.414
Carlana M (2019) Implicit stereotypes: evidence from teachers' gender bias. Quart J Econ 134(3):1163–1224. https://doi.org/10.1093/qje/qjz008
Carrell SE, Page ME, West JE (2010) Sex and science: how professor gender perpetuates the gender gap. Quart J Econ 125(3):1101–1144. https://doi.org/10.1162/qjec.2010.125.3.1101
Cornwell C, Mustard DB, Van Parys J (2013) Noncognitive skills and the gender disparities in test scores and teacher assessments: evidence from primary school. J Human Resources 48:236–264. https://doi.org/10.3368/jhr.48.1.236
Crawfurd L, Pugatch T (2022) Teacher labor markets in developing countries. In: McCall BP (ed) The Routledge handbook of the economics of education. Routledge, New York, NY, pp 193–217
David CC, Albert JRG, Vizmanos JFV (2017) Sustainable development goal 5: how does the Philippines fare on gender equality? Research paper series. Philippine Institute for Development Studies, Quezon City
Dee TS (2005) A teacher like me: does race, ethnicity, or gender matter? American Econ Rev 95(2):158–165. https://doi.org/10.1257/000282805774670446
Department of Education, Philippine Government (DepEd) (2014) Philippine education for all 2015 review report. Philippines Department of Education, Manila
Department of Education, Philippine Government (DepEd) (2017) Gender-responsive basic education policy. Philippines Department of Education, Manila
Department of Education, Philippine Government (DepEd), Order, D.E. (2015). Policy guidelines on classroom assessment for the K to 12 basic education program-no. 8. Philippine Department of Education

DiPrete TA, Eirich GM (2006) Cumulative advantage as a mechanism for inequality: A review of theoretical and empirical developments. Annual Rev Sociology 32(1):271–297. https://doi.org/10.1146/annurev.soc.32.061604.123127

Doornkamp L, Van der Pol LD, Groeneveld SM, Mesman J, Endendijk JJ, Groeneveld MG (2022) Understanding gender bias in teachers' grading: the role of gender stereotypical beliefs. Teaching and Teacher Educ 118:103826. https://doi.org/10.1016/j.tate.2022.103826

Dusek JB, Joseph G (1983) The bases of teacher expectancies: a meta-analysis. J Educ Psychol 75(3):327–346. https://doi.org/10.1037/0022-0663.75.3.327

Dutt AK (2023) Hysteresis and path dependence in economic analysis: formalizations causes and implications. Rev Keynesian Econ 11(4):435–459. https://doi.org/10.4337/roke.2023.04.01

Estudillo JP, Otsuka K (2015) Moving out of poverty: an inquiry into the inclusive growth in Asia. Routledge, New York

Estudillo JP, Quisumbing AR, Otsuka K (2001) Gender differences in land inheritance, schooling and lifetime income: evidence from the rural Philippines. J Dev Stud 37(4):23–48. https://doi.org/10.1080/00220380412331322031

Estudillo JP, Sawada Y, Otsuka K (2008) Poverty and income dynamics in Philippine Villages, 1985–2004. Rev Dev Econ 12(4):877–890. https://doi.org/10.1111/j.1467-9361.2008.00458.x

Ferman B, Fontes LF (2022) Assessing knowledge or classroom behavior? Evidence of teachers' grading bias. J Public Econ 216:104773. https://doi.org/10.1016/j.jpubeco.2022.104773

Fortin NM, Oreopoulos P, Phipps S (2015) Leaving boys behind: gender disparities in high academic achievement. J Human Resources 50(3):549–579. https://doi.org/10.3368/jhr.50.3.549

Fuwa N (2014) Pro-girl bias in intra-household allocation in the rural Philippines: Revisiting the "adult goods" approach. Rev Dev Econ 18(4):727-740. https://doi.org/10.1111/rode.12115

Gershenson S, Holt SB, Papageorge NW (2016) Who believes in me? The effect of student–teacher demographic match on teacher expectations. Econ Educ Rev 52:209–224. https://doi.org/10.1016/j.econedurev.2016.03.002

Glock S, Krolak-Schwerdt S (2013) Does nationality matter? The impact of stereotypical expectations on student teachers' judgments. Soc Psychol Educ 16(1):111–127. https://doi.org/10.1007/s11218-012-9197-z

Goldin C (1995) The U-shaped female labor force function in economic development and economic history. In Schultz P (ed) Investment in women's human capital and economic history. University of Chicago Press, Chicago

Goldin C, Katz LF, Kuziemko I (2006) The homecoming of American College women: the reversal of the college gender gap. J Econ Perspect 20(4):133–156. https://doi.org/10.1257/jep.20.4.133

Goldin C, Rouse C (2000) Orchestrating impartiality: the impact of 'blind' auditions on female musicians. Am Econ Rev 90(4):715–741. https://doi.org/10.1257/aer.90.4.715

Guiso L, Monte F, Sapienza P, Zingales L (2008) Diversity. Culture, gender, and math. Science 320(5880):1164–1165. https://doi.org/10.1126/science.1154094

Hadjar A, Krolak-Schwerdt S, Priem K, Glock S (2014) Gender and educational achievement. Educ Res 56(2):117–125. https://doi.org/10.1080/00131881.2014.898908

Hanna RN, Linden LL (2012) Discrimination in grading. Am Econ J Econ Pol 4(4):146–168. https://doi.org/10.1257/pol.4.4.146

Hanushek EA, Woessmann L (2017) School resources and student achievement: a review of cross-country economic research. In: Rosén M, Hansen KY, Wolff U (eds) Cognitive abilities and educational outcomes: A festschrift in honor of Jan-Eric Gustafsson. Springer International Publishing, Cham, pp 149–171

Hinnerich BT, Höglin E, Johannesson M (2011) Are boys discriminated in Swedish high schools? Econ Educ Rev 30(4):682–690. https://doi.org/10.1016/j.econedurev.2011.02.007

Jouini E, Karehnke P, Napp C (2018) Stereotypes, underconfidence and decision-making with an application to gender and math. J Econ Behav Organ 148:34–45. https://doi.org/10.1016/j.jebo.2018.02.002

Lavy V (2008) Do gender stereotypes reduce girls' or boys' human capital outcomes? Evidence from a natural experiment. J Public Econ 92(10–11):2083–2105. https://doi.org/10.1016/j.jpubeco.2008.02.009

Lavy V, Sand E (2018) On the origins of gender gaps in human capital: short- and long-term consequences of teachers' biases. J Public Econ 167:263–279. https://doi.org/10.1016/j.jpubeco.2018.09.007

Legette KB, Halberstadt AG, Majors AT (2021) Teachers' understanding of racial inequity predicts their perceptions of students' behaviors. Contemp Educ Psychol 67:102014. https://doi.org/10.1016/j.cedpsych.2021.102014

Mapa DS (2021) Working children and child labor situation. Reference Number 2021–484. Philippine Statistics Authority. Retrieved from https://psa.gov.ph/content/working-children-and-child-labor-situation

Muñoz JS (2018) The economics behind the math gender gap: Colombian evidence on the role of sample selection. J Dev Econ 135:368–391. https://doi.org/10.1016/j.jdeveco.2018.08.007

Nollenberger N, Rodríguez-Planas N, Sevilla A (2016) The math gender gap: the role of culture. American Econ Rev 106(5):257–261. https://doi.org/10.1257/aer.p20161121

Okabe M (2025) Boys' underperformance, teacher scoring bias and unbalanced teacher market in rural Philippines. J Dev Stud 61(1):40–62. https://doi.org/10.1080/00220388.2024.2398449

Organisation for Economic Co-operation and Development (OECD) (2014) Are boys and girls equally prepared for life? OECD, Paris

Oster E (2019) Unobservable selection and coefficient stability: theory and evidence. J Bus Econ Stat 37(2):187–204. https://doi.org/10.1080/07350015.2016.1227711

Quisumbing AR (1994) Intergenerational transfers in Philippine rice villages. Gender differences in traditional inheritance customs. J Dev Econ 43(2):167–195. https://doi.org/10.1016/0304-3878(94)90003-5

Rakshit S, Sahoo S (2023) Biased teachers and gender gap in learning outcomes: evidence from India. J Dev Econ 161:103041. https://doi.org/10.1016/j.jdeveco.2022.103041

Riegle-Crumb C, Humphries M (2012) Exploring bias in math teachers' perceptions of students' ability by gender and race/ethnicity. Gend Soc 26(2):290–322. https://doi.org/10.1177/0891243211434614

Romano JP, Wolf M (2005) Stepwise multiple testing as formalized data snooping. Econometrica 73(4):1237–1282. https://doi.org/10.1111/j.1468-0262.2005.00615.x

Takayama N, Fuwa N, Yurugi T (2010) The role of non-agricultural sectors in rural poverty reduction: A case study in Mindanao, Philippines. Japanese J Southeast Asian Stud 48:46–73 [Japanese]

Terrier C (2020) Boys lag behind: how teachers' gender biases affect student achievement. Econ Educ Rev 77:101981. https://doi.org/10.1016/j.econedurev.2020.101981

Tiedemann J (2000) Parents' gender stereotypes and teachers' beliefs as predictors of children's concept of their mathematical ability in elementary school. J Educ Psychol 92(1):144–151. https://doi.org/10.1037/0022-0663.92.1.144

Tiedemann J (2002) Teachers' gender stereotypes as determinants of teacher perceptions in elementary school mathematics. Educ Stud Math 50(1):49–62. https://doi.org/10.1023/A:1020518104346

Torres A (2011) Analysis on why boys do poorly: Philippines case study [Mimeo]. UNGEI, Bangkok

United Nations Girls' Education Initiative (UNGEI) (2012) Why Are Boys Under-Performing in Education? Gender Analysis of Four Asia-Pacific Countries. UNGEI, Bangkok, p 2012

Welmond MJ, Gregory L (2021) Educational underachievement among boys and men. World Bank, Washington, DC

Wright NA, Arora P (2022) A for effort: incomplete information and college students' academic performance. Econ Educ Rev 88:102238. https://doi.org/10.1016/j.econedurev.2022.102238

Xu S, Shonchoy AS, Fujii T (2022) Assessing gender parity in intrahousehold allocation of educational resources: evidence from Bangladesh. World Dev 151:105730. https://doi.org/10.1016/j.worlddev.2021.105730

Yamauchi F, Liu Y (2013) Impacts of an early stage education intervention on students' learning achievement: evidence from the Philippines. J Dev Stud 49(2):208–222. https://doi.org/10.1080/00220388.2012.700395

Yamauchi F, Tiongco M (2013) Why women are progressive in education? Gender disparities in human capital, labor markets, and family arrangement in the Philippines. Econ Educ Rev 32:196–206. https://doi.org/10.1016/j.econedurev.2012.09.003

Chapter 7
Peers to Boys?—Fed-Up na sa Barkada—Resilience Amid Schooling Disengagement: A Qualitative Inquiry into a Case in Antique, Western Visayas

Abstract This chapter qualitatively explores the resilience of Filipino boys who re-engaged with formal education after dropping out, focusing on peer influence and educational trajectories in Antique Province, Philippines. While existing research emphasizes causes of boys' disengagement, it often overlooks pathways to re-engagement. Using qualitative methods, including focus group discussions and household interviews with students aged 13–19, the study examines how socioeconomic pressures, family dynamics, and *barkadahan* (peer groups) shape boys' educational outcomes. Findings show that economic hardship, the need to work, and diminished motivation contribute to disengagement, while *barkadahan* often acts as a barrier by fostering behaviors that divert boys from school. However, the study highlights *barkadahan*'s dual role, showing how peer bonds can also foster resilience when boys reassess their priorities. Moments of awakening prompt boys to return to school, challenging the notion of formal education as a linear, irreversible process. This research situates boys' experiences within a social capital framework, emphasizing the transition from bonding to bridging social capital as a key re-engagement mechanism. The study advocates for flexible educational policies and second-chance programs that accommodate re-entering students, emphasizing recovery and growth after setbacks, with implications for both local contexts and global educational discourse.

Keywords Awakening · *Barkadahan* · High school dropouts · Educational resilience · Schooling re-engagement · Nonlinear educational trajectories

This chapter draws on Okabe (2018).

M. Okabe, *Economics of the Reversal in Gender Disparities in Education and Development*, Economics, Law, and Institutions in Asia Pacific,
https://doi.org/10.1007/978-981-96-9271-2_7

1 Introduction

Chapters 2–6 examined the factors behind the reversed gender disparity through the lenses of household poverty, family dynamics, and school environments. Ultimately, a shared conclusion across these chapters is that boys' educational disadvantages cannot be fully understood without considering the interplay between family dynamics, poverty, and school environments. The rigorous econometric evidence presented in these chapters demonstrates that boys face educational disadvantages from the start of compulsory elementary education (Chapter 2), with these disadvantages persisting and even intensifying at secondary and tertiary levels (Chapter 3). Assuming the linear and irreversible nature of formal education, schooling delays and discontinuity reflect the internal inefficiencies in educational investment, which boys are consistently more likely to experience than girls.

Microeconomic analyses in Chapters 4–5 show that boys exhibit less pro-educational behavior compared to girls, including lower enrollment rates and poorer academic performance. However, these behaviors should be understood within the context of poverty-driven family dynamics, where gendered roles and interactions play a critical role in shaping children's welfare. Chapter 6 further highlights implicit grading bias influenced by teacher stereotypes toward students of different genders. However, this bias amplified in the school environment is also rooted in teacher labor market conditions and regional industrial development, both of which remain gender biased.

While this chapter, as in Chapter 6, continues to focus on the school environment, it shifts to another aspect of educationally disengaging boys' personalities: their resilience. Although earlier chapters highlighted boys' tendencies to underperform and frequently drop out, it is in this chapter that the lens of resilience is introduced and explored. To achieve this, the chapter combines an exploratory approach to unique schooling experiences with household interviews within the same geographic area. In this chapter, educational *resilience* refers not to recovery from trauma, but to the capacity of students to reconnect with formal education after disengagement, that is, academic rebound or nonlinear perseverance (Henderson and Milstein 2003). While previous chapters largely engaged with educational continuity as a linear function of household or institutional conditions, this chapter challenges that assumption by examining cases of nonlinear educational trajectories among rural boys. In light of the mechanisms discussed earlier in this book, such resilience may counteract prospective scarring at the individual (micro) level and soften path-dependent dynamics (a form of hysteresis) at the meso level by reopening schooling trajectories after periods of disengagement. Here, "hysteresis" is used in the economic sense (Dutt 2023; Palley 2023), not in Bourdieu's sense of a habitus–field mismatch (Bourdieu 1990).

In contrast to the previous chapters, this chapter adopts a more qualitative and exploratory approach. It begins by presenting the stories of informants before organizing the findings. Fieldwork conducted in Antique Province, Western Visayas

Region (Region VI), reveals intriguing aspects of resilience. Focus group discussions (FGDs) and household interviews with students aged 13–19 shared their unique schooling histories, detailing various reasons for dropping out, including economic, family-related, physical, and social challenges. Some students cited their involvement in *barkada*—Philippine peer groups characterized by social activities such as drinking and games—as a factor in their disengagement from school (Alinsug and Dechavez 2019; Bouis et al. 1998; Collantes 2016; Dumont 1993).

These peer groups can have both positive and negative effects on members' progress and behaviors (Dumont 1993). Generally, membership in a *barkada* during adolescence, which can be prone to misconduct, is regarded as a negative predictor of educational attainment (Ellis et al. 2018). Despite these challenges, some students chose to return to school even after being overaged and expressed moments of frustration and self-doubt related to their time spent with their *barkada*. While *barkada* is often statically associated with negative educational outcomes, this study highlights the dynamic relationships members have with their *barkada*. The experiences they shared, particularly how those who disengaged re-entered formal education later, reveal their resilience and agency. Drawing on Woolcock and Narayan's (2000) framework of bonding and bridging social capital, the chapter examines how peer networks, often associated with dropout, can, under certain conditions, become vehicles of re-engagement.

These findings challenge the conventional view that formal education—and, by extension, disengagement from it—follows a linear and irreversible trajectory, underscoring their significant yet underexplored potential. They offer new insights into our understanding of underperforming and disengaging boys by suggesting that underperformance or disengagement from education is not necessarily permanent. Rather, it reflects a capacity for resilience and change, highlighting the potential for students to alter their educational trajectories when given opportunities or encouragement. The significant role of resilience cannot be overemphasized, as children and youth often exhibit resilient responses even when facing negative experiences such as bullying (Shemesh and Heiman 2021). Although the official discourse on education promotes linear advancement, local youth practices reveal alternative logics of engagement that do not easily align with institutional trajectories.

This chapter is structured as follows: Sect. 2 reviews the literature. Section 3 introduces the research aims, the study site, and outlines of the field study. Section 4 discusses the survey and case school outlines. Section 5 discusses the results based on the field observations of focal male students who initially dropped out and then returned to school. This section identifies the socioeconomic and familial factors that hindered their education and the factors that encouraged their return. Section 6 elaborates the discussions from two perspectives, awakening and *barkadahan*. Finally, Sect. 7 concludes this chapter and discusses future research.

2 Literature Review

Various factors contribute to boys' disengagement from education, including socioeconomic pressures, peer influence, and school-related challenges (see the previous chapters). They often encounter socioeconomic and emotional difficulties as well as behavioral challenges within traditional schooling environments, which can result in disengagement, while not unique to boys (Epstein et al. 1998). As discussed in the chapters of **Part II**, poverty frequently compels boys to prioritize labor over education, particularly in rural settings where family labor is prevalent (Acosta 2011; Bai and Wang 2020; Beegle et al. 2009; Estudillo et al. 2001, 2008; Gorman-Smith et al. 2012; Patrinos and Psacharopoulos 1997). However, the discussions on poverty primarily focus on the causes of disengagement but overlook how boys re-engage with education after dropping out. This study seeks to address the gap by exploring how boys overcome barriers and return to formal schooling.

Peer groups also play a critical role in boys' disengagement. Boys associating with peers who devalue academic achievement are more likely to disengage from school (Crosnoe et al. 2003; Wentzel and Caldwell 1997). In the Philippines, *barkada* peer groups significantly shape members' behaviors, often contributing to negative educational outcomes (Alinsug and Dechavez 2019; Bouis et al. 1998). However, their focus primarily frames peer influence as a static barrier, offering limited insights into how the members distance themselves from such groups to re-enter education. By situating the *barkada*-ship (*barkadahan* hereafter) in a changing life course, this study highlights the dynamic distancing between members and their *barkadahan*, resulting in an "awakening."

The resilient potential of boys in re-engaging with education has been underexplored. Research suggests that social support networks and flexible programs facilitate boys' return to schooling (Ungar 2013; Shemesh and Heiman 2021). However, much of this literature emphasizes institutional interventions, with less attention to personal and community-level dynamics. This study explores how resilience, shaped by peer dynamics, contributes to their educational re-engagement.

Finally, this study further aims to challenge the notion of formal education as linear and irreversible. Modernization theory assumes a linear trajectory of progress (Endresen 2021), and the modern formal education systems, shaped by these principles and originating in modern Western societies, likely inherit this perspective (Kurlaender and Hibel 2018; Benner et al. 2021). In this context, once disengaged, re-engaging with public formal education is often challenging and widely regarded as irreversible, except through nonformal education programs—provided in the Philippines as the Alternative Learning System (ALS) (Alvarez 2024; Endresen 2021; Igarashi 2018; Pascual et al. 2022; Kurlaender and Hibel 2018; Benner et al. 2021). However, the nonformal education formed as the ALS is also known to be facing various challenges in developing learners' academic performance and problems of facilities, logistics, and provisions (Wayas and Dinoro 2023).[1] While acknowledging

[1] Note that this chapter does not deny that the nonformal education—the ALS in the Philippines—provides significant and invaluable learning opportunities—providing alternative pathways for

the significant social potential of ALS, this chapter is motivated by the idea that relying solely on ALS to address school dropouts, without considering the flexible accommodation capacity of formal education, can limit students' opportunities.

Interestingly, some degree of flexibility has been documented even within the trajectories of formal education, allowing for dropout and re-engagement later in life (e.g., during or after working, marriage, or parenthood) (Pallas 2003: 170). Nonetheless, Pallas (2003: 170) explains that learners in later life pathways, who are "outside of the 18–24 age range," are considered "nontraditional" students and are identified as "potential markets for their educational wares" by many postsecondary institutions. In other words, for traditional educational systems, learners who follow the standard educational trajectories are considered traditional and standard.

Moreover, the aforementioned flexibility, despite the traditional view of educational trajectories, is primarily observed in cases of late learning during or after stages of work, marriage, or parenthood. This type of re-engagement is typical and more akin to postsecondary-level lifelong learning, which is now widely promoted in industrialized societies, particularly in the context of civil service. However, little attention has been given to the possibility of re-engagement in basic formal education during the juvenile schooling period, particularly in poverty-stricken rural contexts. Drawing on a case study from the Philippines, this study examines an often-overlooked aspect of boys' disengagement: their capacity for resilience. By presenting observations from Antique Province, this chapter highlights that disengagement is not necessarily irreversible, demonstrating the adaptability of formal educational trajectories even during the juvenile schooling period.

---

vulnerable students who have deviated from the "standard" tracks in formal education for various reasons (Alvarez 2024; Igarashi 2018; Pascual et al. 2022). That said, by visiting some ALS schools in different regions, including rural areas of Antique and Marinduque as well as urban centers like Metro Manila and Metro Cebu, I observed local voices indicating that the nonformal education offered through ALS also faces challenges, such as issues related to schooling facilities and perceptions of program completers. For example, ALS programs often share the facilities of existing formal schools. Therefore, ALS classes are typically held before or after regular school hours (e.g., early morning or late evening), unless the formal schools allow overlapping use of their facilities during the same hours. Regarding teacher duties, while some teachers work exclusively for ALS, not a few are responsible for both formal schooling and ALS, leading to fatigue. To enhance time flexibility for working learners, ALS classes are sometimes offered as mobile schooling, where teachers travel to on-demand, convenient locations for learners. However, this practice results in personal financial costs for teachers, as some reported that they are not always reimbursed by local governments. On the student perception side, although ALS completers receive an official certificate of completion, I was told that completing ALS is sometimes perceived as stigmatizing, as it implicitly suggests a past failure to continue within the formal education system.

3 Outlines of Research Site and Survey

This chapter discusses fieldwork conducted in Antique Province, Visayas. Examining a Visayan case provides several advantages for this book. First, Visayas is one of the three major regions of the Philippine archipelago, alongside Luzon (where Marinduque is studied in Chapters 4–5) and Mindanao (where Bukidnon is covered in Chapters 1–2). Located between Luzon and Mindanao, Visayas shares similar characteristics with Mindanao, such as a predominance of poverty and agriculture. Second, these traits place Visayas behind Luzon in terms of educational development. By including this case, the book expands its geographical and socioeconomic coverage, enhancing its diversity.

Gender disparities in educational outcomes, favoring girls, are evident nationwide across all regions, though their severity varies depending on them. For example, Fig. 1 shows region-level net enrollment rates (NER) for secondary education, highlighting two key trends: (1) NERs are generally lower in Visayas and Mindanao compared to Luzon; but (2) females outnumber males in enrollment across regions, with the female rate 14.72% higher than the male rate on the national average. These underscore the more pronounced gender disparities in provincial areas. Also in Region VI, the female NER is 18.31% higher than the male rate, exceeding the national average gap of 14.72%.

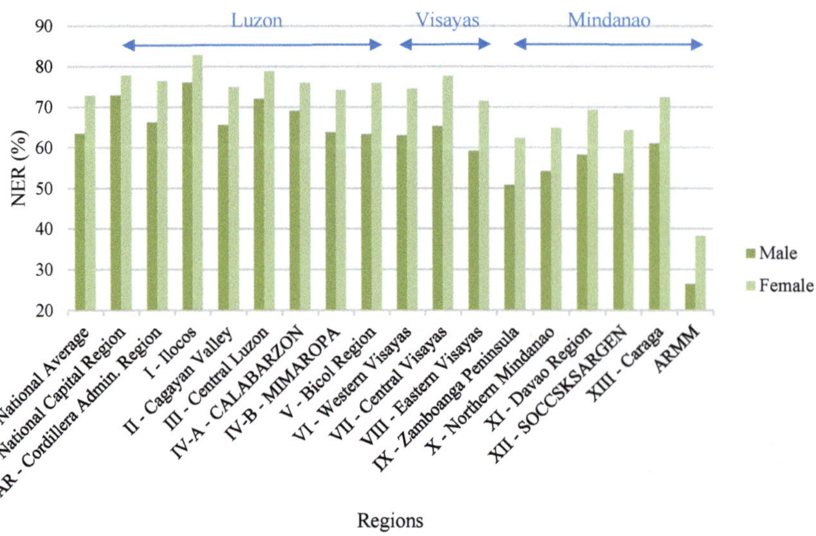

Fig. 1 Net enrollment rate in public and private secondary level schools. *Notes* CALABARZON = Cavite–Laguna–Batangas–Rizal–Quezon; MIMAROPA = Mindoro–Marinduque–Romblon–Palawan; SOCCSKSARGEN = South Cotabato–Cotabato City–North Cotabato–Sultan Kudarat–Sarangani–General Santos City; ARMM = Autonomous Region in Muslim Mindanao (as of 2017).
Source 2017 *Philippine Statistical Yearbook*, Philippine Statistics Authority

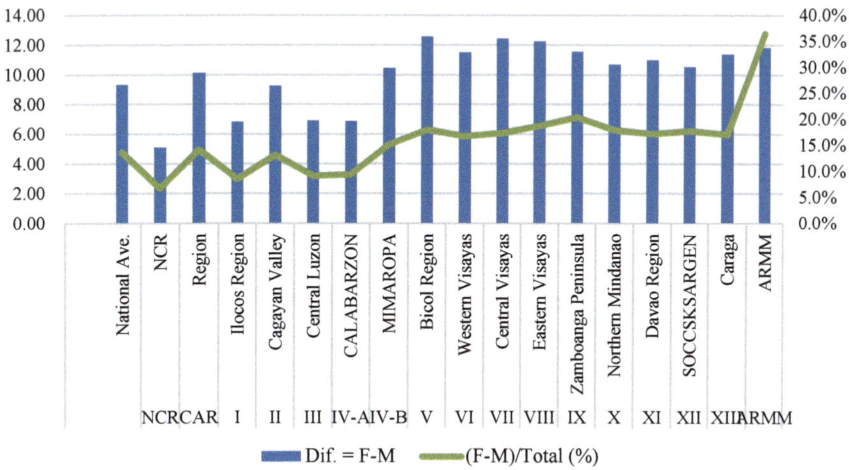

Fig. 2 Gender gap disaggregation of net enrollment rates in public and private secondary level schools. *Notes* CALABARZON = Cavite–Laguna–Batangas–Rizal–Quezon; MIMAROPA = Mindoro–Marinduque–Romblon–Palawan; SOCCSKSARGEN = South Cotabato–Cotabato City–North Cotabato–Sultan Kudarat–Sarangani–General Santos City; ARMM = Autonomous Region in Muslim Mindanao (as of 2017).
Source 2017 Philippine Statistical Yearbook, Philippine Statistics Authority

Similar related trends are also found in Fig. 2. It exhibits the differences between male and female NERs and the relative proportions in percentages that account for the differences in total NER across regions. The visual information in Fig. 2 is clearer in the male–female gaps in NER across the regions. Likewise, the regions outside of Luzon, such as MIMAROPA, Visayas, and Mindanao show higher gaps unfavorable to male students.

Region VI comprises the islands of Panay and Guimaras, where various Visayan languages are spoken. In Antique, the primary languages include Hiligaynon (the region's lingua franca) and Karay-a (a provincial language). Filipino is also widely used in education and media.

The study area for this chapter, Antique Province, is part of Region VI, the Western Visayas Region (Fig. 3). Region VI encompasses Panay Island and Guimaras Island, with the provinces of Aklan, Antique, Capiz, and Iloilo on Panay Island, and Guimaras on Guimaras Island. In Region VI, various local languages from the Visayan language family are spoken, not Tagalog, which serves as the basis for the national language, Filipino. In Antique Province, the primary languages spoken include Kinaray-a (Karay-a), the provincial language, and Hiligaynon (Ilonggo), the region's lingua franca, both of which are part of the Visayan language family. However, Filipino (Tagalog) is also spoken due to its status as the national language, which is taught through education and widely used in mass media, including TV programs, music, and news reports. Antique stretches along the western coast of Panay Island, facing the Sulu Sea. Its economy is primarily based on fishing and

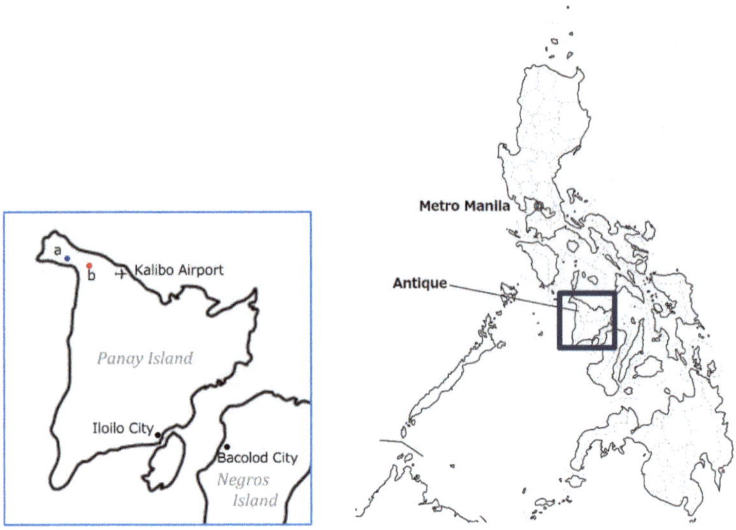

Fig. 3 Map of Antique Province and research sites.
Note Point "a" corresponds to Barangay Mag-Aba in Pandan, Antique. Point "b" corresponds to Barangay Sta. Ana in Pandan, Antique.
Source Author's creation

agriculture, contrasting with the tourism-driven economy of nearby Boracay Island to the north.[2]

We stayed from July 23–30, 2017, in several local residential areas within the Municipality of Pandan. During this period, I conducted household and school visitations and interviews in English and Filipino (Tagalog). Responses in local Visayan languages by students and adults were translated into Filipino or English by schoolteachers and a local research assistant to facilitate understanding.

Pandan is located in northern Antique, a two-hour drive from Kalibo Airport, a gateway to Panay Island. We visited three elementary schools, two high schools, and one vocational school. Most schools were in Barangay Mag-Aba (point a in Fig. 3), near the *poblacion*—municipality's central areas—while one high school in Barangay Sta. Ana (point b in Fig. 3) was situated on a steep mountainous site. This study focuses on observations from School A in Barangay Mag-Aba, because it offers both primary and secondary education, providing a unique opportunity to examine students' transitions between these levels, though we also incorporate experiences from the other schools visited during the study.

[2] At a farmers' meeting in Pandan, it was noted that while some rice paddies are irrigated, others are less well-equipped. Rice seeds are still sown directly in the paddies, a practice that, although less labor-intensive, results in lower yields compared to the more labor-intensive equal-distance (row) sowing method.

4 Survey and Case School Outlines

At School A, we conducted a focus group discussion (FGD) on the afternoon of July 24, 2017, with eight male students aged 13–19 to explore their schooling histories. All participants had previously dropped out of high school but later returned. Preliminary household interviews were also conducted in selected villages, locally referred to as barangays. Before presenting our findings, we first provide an overview of the school's data profile.

Table 1 shows enrollment data for secondary-level students over the five school years (SY) preceding our field study, spanning SY 2011–12 to SY 2015–16. Unlike the earlier cross-regional data, these enrollment figures do not indicate significant gender disparities. During SY 2011–12 and SY 2012–13, more boys than girls were enrolled (244 vs. 218 and 277 vs. 247, respectively). However, these figures exclude "out-of-school" youth—students who were not enrolled but resided in the community, as noted by schoolteachers.

In contrast, Table 2 highlights dropout statistics from SY 2012–13 to SY 2015–16, revealing significantly higher dropout rates among male students. In the Philippine educational system, students who fail exams must repeat the grade, which exacerbates the ongoing issue of boys' disengagement from education (Miralao 2008; UNICEF EAPRO 2009). Although Table 1 indicates no significant gender differences in enrollment numbers over the same period, dropout rates were consistently higher among male students (as shown in Table 2). Promotion rates—calculated as 100% minus failure rates—reflect a similar trend, with more male students failing to advance (Table 3). The requirement to repeat a grade after failing exams further contributes to the problem of male students falling behind academically.

In sum, the issues of boys' underperformance (UNGEI 2012), boys' crisis (Miralao 2008), and the observations by UNICEF EAPRO (2009) are evident at School A. This chapter focuses on male students who have dropped out and later returned to school. Our study design sought to investigate their schooling histories and family circumstances through interactive discussions. A schoolteacher and a local assistant facilitated and translated the discussions from Kinaray-a or Hiligaynon to Filipino (Tagalog) or English, although the informant students spoke Filipino as well. During the FGD, follow-up questions were posed to gain deeper insights into their experiences.

Table 1 School A's enrollment data (head count by sex)

	SY 2011–12	SY 2012–13	SY 2013–14	SY 2014–15	SY 2015–16
Males	244	277	271	270	285
Females	218	247	280	297	287
Total	452	524	551	567	572

Source Provided by School A on request

Table 2 Number of dropouts for the last four school years, School A (by sex)

	SY 2012–13			SY 2013–14			SY 2014–15			SY 2015–16		
	M	F	Both	M	F	Both	M	F	Both	M	F	Both
Grade 7	4	1	5	1	3	4	5	0	5	1	0	1
Grade 8	6	1	7	4	0	4	7	0	7	0	0	0
Grade 9	2	1	3	2	0	2	3	0	3	0	0	0
Grade 10	4	1	5	1	0	1	0	0	0	1	0	1
Total in number	16	4	20	8	3	11	15	0	15	2	0	2
(in %)	(80)	(20)	(100)	(73)	(27)	(100)	(100)	(0)	(100)	(100)	(0)	(100)

Notes 1. "M" refers to "Male" and "F" to "Female."
2. Grade 7 refers to the first grade in high school.
Source Provided by School A on request

Table 3 Promotion rates and failure rates, School A (by sex)

	SY 2014–15						SY 2015–16					
	Promotion rate			Failure rate			Promotion rate			Failure rate		
	M	F	Both	M	F	Both	M	F	Both	M	F	Both
Grade 7	92	100	97	8	0	3.4	87	98	93	12.6	0	7.2
Grade 8	92	100	96	8	0	4	91	99	95	9	1	5
Grade 9	95	100	98	5	0	2.4	95	97	94	5	3	4
Grade 10	100	100	100	0	0	0	98	98	98	1	1	2

Notes 1. "M" refers to "Male" and "F" to "Female."
2. Grade 7 refers to the first grade in high school.
Source Provided by School A on request

5 Results and Observations on the Backgrounds of Dropouts

All the informant male students, aged 13–19, were enrolled in the school at the time of FGD. They exhibited a range of appearances: some were notably tanned and seemed mature, while others appeared more passive. We discussed their reasons for leaving school. The facilitator initiated the conversation, prompting the students to share and discuss their personal backgrounds and reasons for dropping out. During the FGD, follow-up questions were conducted to gain deeper insights into their experiences.

5.1 *Economic Hindrances: Even Traveling Across the Sea to Negros Island*

The students discussed the economic challenges they faced in attending school. Consistent with the literature, many cited labor-related reasons for absenteeism. One student mentioned working seasonal jobs to fund his education, such as selling merchandise to cover tuition fees and earning ₱15 per hour (approximately US$0.30 at the time). High school students in rural areas often face financial pressures due to poverty and limited family support. Teachers and students noted that many villagers rely on fishing and agriculture, which are unstable income sources, particularly during rainy seasons lasting half the year. This instability often compels children to contribute to their family's livelihood.

Another student shared his experience of engaging in seasonal labor outside the province and even beyond Panay Island. During school vacations, he traveled through Iloilo City, the urban center of Panay Island, to Bacolod City, the provincial capital of Negros Occidental on Negros Island (see Fig. 3). There, he worked in manufacturing and took up seasonal labor in sugarcane fields, driven by the high demand for short-term workers in the island's sugarcane industry. Although his initial intention was to work only during school breaks, financial necessity often extended his work periods, negatively impacting his schooling and potentially contributing to his dropout.

A local elementary school teacher highlighted the cultural expectation for boys to contribute to the family income, especially through agricultural and fishing activities. She noted that this norm often frames child labor as acceptable if it stems from necessity. To support struggling students, the teacher occasionally provided financial assistance from her own resources, expressing her belief that reducing the need for child labor could improve educational outcomes.

5.2 *Personal Dispositions or Noncognitive Skills in Learning*

Some students attributed their dropout to personal factors, such as a lack of interest in learning or feelings of *tamad* (laziness). One student described himself at the time as *walang interes* (no interest) in attending school. Citing "no interest" is not uncommon, as national reports using representative data have also highlighted this factor (PSA 2021). These cases often reflect a recursive interaction between personality traits or dispositions and the schooling environment. As their interest diminishes, intrinsic motivation declines, prompting students to seek alternative, more engaging activities.

Thus, one respondent who mentioned "laziness" elaborated that he frequently spent time with his *barkada*. When asked about its activities, he hesitantly explained that *barkada* often engaged in activities such as *maagang pag-inom ng alak* (underage drinking, e.g., gin and beer), *paninigarilyo* (smoking), *pagpasyal-pasyal* (roaming around), and *paglalaro ng basketbol* (playing basketball), among others. Other boys added, *"Sa totoo lang, wala kaming plano mula pa nung simula*" ("Actually, we had no specific plans from the start about what to do"). These activities, described as spontaneous or ad hoc, underscore the informal and aimless nature of their peer group interactions.

Additionally, two students repeatedly described themselves as "addicted" to online computer games. According to them, their villages have "computer-game shops" equipped with up to a dozen computers. For a relatively affordable fee (e.g., ₱15 for 30 min), those without personal computers at home can use computers at these shops and enjoy online games. The youth are particularly sensitive to "bandwagon" trends, including fashion, gaming, and celebrity culture. Social media such as Facebook, Messenger, and Instagram also play a significant role in their daily lives. A lack of interest in school or feelings of laziness often translate into frequent visits to these game shops. Some mothers we interviewed expressed concern over their sons' frequent visits to these establishments, noting that this behavior interferes with their schooling. As adolescents grow older, mothers often find it increasingly difficult to regulate their children's engagement in such activities (Alampay et al. 2011).

5.3 Negative Experiences: Physical and Mental

Another set of issues involved both physical and mental challenges. One student mentioned asthma, highlighting how illness or physical disabilities can hinder concentration and disrupt academic progress. Similarly, bullying and teasing were significant barriers to education (Alinsug and Dechavez 2019). One student privately shared that he had considered dropping out after being repeatedly called "biggums," a derogatory term referencing his body size. While such negative experiences are not unique to the Philippines, they underscore the universal nature of these challenges. Notably, *barkadahan*, typically associated with friendship and camaraderie, can occasionally become a source of conflict or emotional harm among its members (Alinsug and Dechavez 2019).

5.4 Parents' Reactions to Their Sons' Dropping Out

Parents' reactions to their sons dropping out varied significantly. Some students reported that their parents expressed anger or disappointment, with remarks such as "*Nagalit ang nanay ko* (My mother got angry)", "*Pinagalitan ako* (I was scolded)", or "*Nasermonan ako* (I was reprimanded)". In other cases, parents apologized or expressed regret, using phrases like "*patawad* (deep apologies)" to convey their sorrow, often because they could no longer afford to support their children's education.

Notably, some students mentioned that their parents reacted indifferently, saying nothing special when they dropped out. While the students themselves were unsure how to interpret this lack of response, a schoolteacher suggested it might reflect parental detachment—not only from their children's education but also from their overall behavior. This detachment, in turn, can further exacerbate boys' educational challenges in a cyclical manner. Such an indifferent attitude raises concerns, as it reflects a limited capacity to guide and support their children. Without this support, children may struggle to make important decisions, compounding the difficulties they already face.

6 Discussion: Back to School—Exploring the Pathways and Motivations

6.1 Awakening

The informant students reflected on their motivations for returning to school. One student described a pivotal moment with his *barkada* when he realized that their activities were "*sayang lang ang oras*" (a waste of time). He repeatedly expressed feelings of being "*fed-up na* (already fed up)" against *barkada* relations and activities and "*nagsawa na ako* (tired of them)". Other students echoed this sentiment, noting the financial burdens of *barkada* activities (e.g., buying alcohol and cigarettes). As their reflections deepened, some students expressed growing concerns about their futures, asking pessimistically, "*Paano na lang kaya ako kung magpapatuloy sa ganitong barkadahan at hindi na mag-aaral?* (What if I continued staying out of school because of such *barkadahan*?)." Over time, they began to recognize the negative impacts of dropping out on their long-term prospects. While much of the literature focuses on the reasons for students not attending school, an intriguing aspect of our observations was the inclusion of students who had returned to school. These informants spanned various age groups, from older students (aged 17–19) to younger ones aged 13. Their narratives illustrate the boys' capacity to discern what is beneficial or detrimental to their futures.

These narratives highlight moments of awakening—turning points where students reassessed their situations and made deliberate decisions to return to school. This suggests that while *barkadahan* is often seen as a long-term process across the life cycle, levels of commitment and disengagement can change, influenced by personal growth and life circumstances. Indeed, similar patterns have been noted in other studies. For example, Dumont (1993) describes how men in Central Visayas who achieved higher social status later reevaluated their ties to their *barkada*. This underscores how life trajectories and social positions shape individuals' relationships with *barkada* culture, which remains widespread but highly context-dependent across the Philippines. Although *barkada* culture is prevalent across the Philippines, individuals' engagement with it varies depending on their life stage and circumstances. In this context, our findings from School A align with broader patterns documented elsewhere in the Philippines, illustrating the adaptability of *barkada* relationships and the potential for individuals to distance themselves from such affiliations as their priorities and perspectives shift.

6.2 *Barkadahan*: Social Bonds and Educational Challenges

Both the informant students and local residents observed that boys often spend significant time with their *barkada*, to the extent that *barkadahan* can divert their focus from education. Activities associated with *barkadahan*, such as early-age drinking, smoking, roaming, and basketball are seen as undermining academics, a pattern also noted elsewhere in the Philippines. For instance, Bouis et al. (1998), in their ethnographic survey of Bukidnon, Northern Mindanao, highlighted parental concerns regarding the strong bond between boys and their *barkada*. Furthermore, the connection between *barkadahan* and masculinity in the Philippines has been extensively studied (e.g., Collantes 2016; Dumont 1993; Eviota 1992), illustrating its pervasive influence on male peer identity formation.

Recognizing *barkada* as both a barrier and support offers nuanced insights into addressing boys' educational disengagement. The concept of *barkada* parallels homosocial peer groups observed in other cultural contexts, such as youth gangs and peer groups in urban settings globally. These groups exhibit similar dynamics of identity formation, peer influence, and educational disengagement (Crosnoe et al. 2003; Ellis et al. 2018). *Barkada* is deeply rooted in the Filipino value system, making it a unique yet globally comparable cross-cultural phenomenon. Likewise, *barkada* transcends specific boundaries of gender, age, class, residence, religion, or politics, forming trans-social groups ubiquitous across the Philippines (Dumont 1993). While both men and women form *barkada*, these groups are predominantly associated with male peer dynamics in contemporary settings (Collantes 2016; Dumont 1993). For instance, Collantes (2016) observed in Cavite and Laguna that *barkada* often operates as distinct male spaces, where men and women coexist yet remain socially and spatially separated.

Takahashi (1972: 197) described *barkada* as a "primary group" in Philippine society, emphasizing the Filipino value of *tayo-tayo*-ism. The term *tayo* translates to "we" in English but specifically includes the second person(s), unlike *kami*, which excludes them. This linguistic distinction reflects the Filipino sensitivity to insider–outsider boundaries. Strong *barkada* relationships often embody this value, fostering solidarity and a sense of belonging. Takahashi (1972) further noted that *barkada* embodies this solidarity, essential for maintaining group norms. In this context, it parallels *kapitbahay* (neighborhood) relationships in fostering social cohesion, illustrating its local community dynamics.

In our observations, some students who were initially deeply involved in their *barkada* eventually recognized its negative impact on their educational prospects. However, as Takahashi (1972) observed, *barkada* is not inherently linked to vice. Within the Filipino value system, *barkadahan* serves as a mechanism for harmonizing human relations and forms a fundamental basis for social networks. While *barkadahan* is often seen as a distraction from education, it also plays a constructive role in strengthening local social ties and fostering mutual support. Collantes

(2016), Dumont (1993), and Eviota (1992) further highlight the generational aspects of *barkadahan* and the nuanced balance between its positive and negative effects. These findings underscore the importance of situating *barkadahan* within the broader social dynamics of the Philippines, rather than framing it solely as an educational barrier. Future research could further explore how the social strengths of *barkadahan* might be leveraged to mitigate its drawbacks and support educational attainment.

7 Conclusion

This chapter investigated male students in a Western Visayan province who had dropped out of high school, synthesizing insights from schoolteachers, family members, and the students themselves. Using a qualitative approach, this chapter prioritized depth of exploration and insight over the breadth of sample emphasized in more quantitative chapters, such as Chapters 2–6. The focus here is on the unique trajectories and socio-cultural factors influencing the decisions of boys who re-engaged with education.

On the one hand, the findings align with previous chapters and existing literature, indicating that Filipino boys lag behind their female counterparts in education due to factors such as economic deprivation and societal expectations to contribute to family livelihoods (King and Hill 1998; Miralao 2008; UNGEI 2012). These pressures create an ambivalent relationship between labor and education, as boys often leave school to work.

On the other hand, noncognitive skills such as perseverance also play significant roles in educational outcomes. A lack of these skills often leads boys to disengage from school, gravitating toward peer groups like *barkadahan*, which reinforce societal attitudes that hinder academic success (Bouis et al. 1998; Collantes 2016). However, a notable finding of this study is the resilience demonstrated by boys who returned to school, challenging the notion that dropping out is irreversible. Read in light of earlier chapters, this resilience may operate as resilience to scarring by attenuating the persistence of earlier setbacks and, at the margin, by disrupting path dependence (a form of hysteresis) in schooling pathways. This resilience is evident in their reevaluation of the importance of education for their futures. For example, some students expressed regret over time wasted with their *barkada*, and this realization rekindled their commitment to schooling. These findings align with those of Dumont (1993) and Collantes (2016), who observed that changes in personal and social circumstances—shaped by life stages and trajectories—can significantly influence not only educational outcomes but also the extent to which individuals distance themselves from their peer groups and associated activities.

From a social network perspective, *barkadahan* offers a valuable opportunity for further research into its role in human development (Woolcock and Narayan 2000). Defined by geographic proximity, generational cohorts, and shared contemporaneity (e.g., Portes and Sensenbrenner 1993; Lin 2001), *barkadahan* exemplifies bonding social capital (Putnam 2000; Coleman 1988). While fostering solidarity, its dual nature—both supportive and restrictive—reflects broader dynamics of bonding social capital (Bourdieu 1986; Putnam 2000). The "awakening" observed among students highlights the potential to transition from bonding to bridging social capital. Bridging social capital, which connects individuals to broader networks and role models, encourages forward-looking attitudes and alternative life trajectories (Granovetter 1973; Woolcock and Narayan 2000).

In terms of the implicit progressivist assumption about the linearity and irreversibility of public formal education, our findings also challenge this notion by demonstrating the nonlinear and reversible educational trajectories experienced by the informant students. When discussing out-of-school students and youth, or so-called dropouts, there is a tendency to expect that nonformal education programs—such as the ALS in the context of the Philippines—should accommodate them or are capable of providing alternatives to or remedying the perceived failure of formal schooling. Undoubtedly, today's nonformal education programs offer significant potential as alternative opportunities for these students and youth to re-engage in educational experiences. Nonetheless, alongside the "awakenings" experienced by the returning students, our findings highlight that the accommodating environment and inherent flexibility of the public formal schooling system itself at the research site, without immediately resorting to the ALS, played a critical role in fostering their resilience and re-engagement.[3] This presents an eye-opening insight that challenges conventional perspectives on the contemporary school system, whose foundations are largely rooted in modern Western societies.

In sum, this chapter extends the book's core concept of "reversal" beyond structural inversion, suggesting instead that reversal may emerge through nonlinear pathways of rupture and reconnection. Rather than portraying boys as passive casualties of institutional bias, the chapter foregrounds their capacity to reposition themselves through informal peer networks and reflective agency. In doing so, it invites a rethinking of educational outcomes not merely as endpoints in a trend, but as dynamically negotiated trajectories shaped by both cultural logic and situated practices—often beyond the purview of formal systems.

Lastly, several areas not fully addressed in this chapter warrant future research. First, empirically identifying the conditions that facilitate the "awakening" and educational re-engagement remains a critical area of exploration. This requires more longitudinal and participatory analyses to investigate the interactions among individual resilience, peer dynamics, and systemic factors—such as national policies and global trends. Given the universality of *barkada* dynamics, with equivalents in other societies, parallels can be drawn worldwide with similar youth groups, including not only male but also gender-diverse and community-based collectives. Second, adopting a more inclusive approach to gender dynamics by incorporating girls and nonbinary individuals would contribute to a more comprehensive understanding of educational challenges. Finally, the capacity of schools and public formal education

[3] While this may not have applied to the student informants in our study, this does not preclude the possibility that nonformal education can function as a preparatory stage for reintegration into formal schooling.

systems to accommodate re-engaging students is a vital topic. These research directions hold the potential to connect local insights with broader comparative societal perspectives, paving the way for meaningful advancements in the field.

While the empirical basis of this chapter is grounded in a particular rural setting, the social dynamics surrounding *barkada* are not unique to this locality. As a widespread mode of youth association across the Philippines, *barkada* culture may offer a common yet underexplored mechanism through which disengaged boys renegotiate their relationship with formal education. Recognizing this potential allows for future comparative inquiry across regions, as well as deeper theorization of informal peer support as a form of educational resilience.

References

Acosta P (2011) School attendance, child labour, and remittances from international migration in El Salvador. J Dev Stud 47(6):913–936. https://doi.org/10.1080/00220388.2011.563298

Alampay LP, Jocson MRM (2011) Attributions and attitudes of mothers and fathers in the Philippines. Parenting 11(2–3):163–176. https://doi.org/10.1080/15295192.2011.585564

Alinsug E, Dechavez J (2019) *Barkada*–not always a friend: peer aggression in the Philippines. In: Skrzypiec G, Wyra M, Didaskalou E (eds) A global perspective of young adolescents' peer aggression and well-being. Routledge, New York, pp 126–146. https://doi.org/10.4324/9780429426797-7

Alvarez AJ (2024) Second chances: exploring the philippine alternative learning system. Intern J Schol Educ 7(1):1–16. https://doi.org/10.52134/ueader.1445226

Bai J, Wang Y (2020) Returns to work, child labor and schooling: the income Vs. price effects. J Dev Econ 145:102466. https://doi.org/10.1016/j.jdeveco.2020.102466

Beegle K, Dehejia R, Gatti R (2009) Why should we care about child labor? The education, labor market, and health consequences of child labor. J Human Resour 44(4):871–889. https://doi.org/10.3368/jhr.44.4.871

Benner AD, Chen S, Mistry RS, Shen Y (2021) Life course transitions and educational trajectories: Examining adolescents who fall off track Academically. J Youth Adolesc 50:1068–1080. https://doi.org/10.1007/s10964-020-01376-x

Bouis HE, Palabrica-Costello M, Solon O, Westbrook D, Limbo AB (1998) Gender equality and investments in adolescents in the rural Philippines, research report, (108). International Food Policy Research Institute, Washington DC. https://doi.org/10.2499/0896291111rr108

Bourdieu P (1986) The forms of capital. In: Richardson JG (ed) Handbook of theory and research for the sociology of education. Greenwood, New York, pp 241–258

Bourdieu P (1990) The logic of practice. Stanford University Press, Standord

Coleman JS (1988) Social capital in the creation of human capital. Am J Sociol 94(Suppl.): S95–S120. https://doi.org/10.1086/228943

Collantes CF (2016) Reproductive Dilemmas, labour and remittances: gender and intimacies in Cavite, Philippines. South East Asia Res 24(1):77–97. https://doi.org/10.5367/sear.2016.0293

Crosnoe R, Cavanagh S, Elder GH (2003) Adolescent friendships as academic resources: the intersection of friendship, race, and disadvantage. Sociol Perspect 46(3):331–352. https://doi.org/10.1525/sop.2003.46.3.331

Dumont J-P (1993) Visayan male *Barkada*: Manly behaviour and male identity on a Philippine Island. Philipp Stud 41(4):401–436. https://doi.org/10.13185/2244-1638.4881

Dutt AK (2023) Hysteresis and path dependence in economic analysis: formalizations causes and implications. Rev Keynesian Econ 11(4):435–459. https://doi.org/10.4337/roke.2023.04.01

Ellis Wendy, Lynne Zarbatany, Xinyin Chen, Megan Kinal, Lisa Boyko (2018) Peer groups as a context for school misconduct: the moderating role of group interactional style. Child Devel 89(1):248–263. https://doi.org/10.1111/cdev.12722
Endresen SB (2021) Technological retrogression: A Schumpeterian interpretation of modernization in reverse. Anthem Press, London. https://doi.org/10.2307/j.ctv1ns7nhc
Epstein D, Elwood J, Hey V, Maw J (1998) Failing boys? Issues in gender and achievement. Open University Press, Buckingham
Estudillo JP, Quisumbing A, Otsuka K (2001) Gender differences in land inheritance, schooling and lifetime income: Evidence from the rural Philippines. J Dev Stud 37(4):23–48. https://doi.org/10.1080/00220380412331322031
Estudillo JP, Sawada Y, Otsuka K (2008) Poverty and income dynamics in Philippine village 1985–2004. Rev Dev Econ 12:877–890. https://doi.org/10.1111/j.1467-9361.2008.00458.x
Eviota EU (1992) The political economy of gender: women and the sexual division of labour in the Philippines. Zed Books, London
Gorman-Smith Deborah, Elizabeth Grisa Hunt, Dylan Robertson (2012) Fatherhood and fathering among low-income and minority men. In *Oxford Handbook of Poverty and Child Development*, edited by Rosalind King and Valerie Maholmes. Oxford: Oxford University Press
Granovetter M (1973) The strength of weak ties. Am J Sociol 78(6):1360–1380. https://doi.org/10.1086/225469
Heckman JJ (2013) Giving kids a fair chance. Massachusetts Institute of Technology Press, Massachusetts
Henderson N, Milstein MM (2003) Resiliency in schools: making it happen for students and educators, 2nd edn. Corwin Press, Thousand Oaks, CA
Igarashi T (2018) A second chance to develop the human capital of out-of-school youth and adults: the Philippines alternative learning system. World Bank Policy Note 127978:1–24
King EM, Hill A (1998) Women's education in developing countries: barriers, benefits, and policies. World Bank, Washington, D.C.
Kurlaender M, Hibel J (2018) Students' educational pathways: aspirations, decisions, and constrained choices along the education lifecourse. In *Handbook of the Sociology of Education in the 21st Century*, edited by Schneider, B. Cham: Springer. https://doi.org/10.1007/978-3-319-76694-2_16
Lin N (2001) Social capital: a theory of social structure and action. Cambridge University Press, Cambridge. https://doi.org/10.1017/CBO9780511815447
Miralao VA (2008) Towards post-feminism in Philippine education. In *The Paradox of Philippine Education and Education Reform: Social Scientific Perspectives*, edited by Bernado, A. Quezon City: Philippine Social Science Council, pp 113–132
Okabe M (2018) "'Under-performing' or resilient Filipino boys in education? Listening to students' and adults' perspectives and backgrounds: a western Visayas case. IDE Discussion Paper (unpublished working paper).
Pallas AM (2003) Educational transitions, trajectories, and pathways. In *Handbook of the Life Course*, edited by Mortimer, J.T. & Shanahan, M.J. Boston, MA: Springer. https://doi.org/10.1007/978-0-306-48247-2_8
Palley T (2023) Broadening the application of hysteresis in economics: institutions policy lock-in psychology identity and ideas. Rev Keynesian Econ 11(4):460–488. https://doi.org/10.4337/roke.2023.04.02
Pascual EA, Stella Marie A Virtudez, Karla Carryl B Cambia (2022) Lived-experience of former ALS (Alternative Learning System) Students of Nagcarlan, Laguna, Philippines. Intern J Res Public 110(1):555–569. https://doi.org/10.47119/IJRP1001101110202223980
Patrinos HA, Psacharopoulos G (1997) Family size, schooling and child labor in Peru: an empirical analysis. J Popul Econ 10(4):387–405. https://doi.org/10.1007/s001480050050
Philippine Statistics Authority (PSA) (2021) *2019 FLEMMS Final Report*. Quezon City: PSA
Portes A, Sensenbrenner P (1993) Embeddedness and immigration: notes on the social determinants of economic action. Am J Sociol 98(6):1320–1350. https://doi.org/10.1086/230191

Putnam RD (2000) Bowling alone: the collapse and revival of American community. Simon & Schuster, New York

Sachs JD (2015) The age of sustainable development. Columbia University Press, New York. https://doi.org/10.7312/sach17314

Shemesh DO, Heiman T (2021) Resilience and self-concept as mediating factors in the relationship between bullying victimization and sense of well-being among adolescents. Int J Adolesc Youth 26(1):158–171. https://doi.org/10.1080/02673843.2021.1899946

Takahashi A (1972) The value system of the Philippines [Firipin no kachi taikei]. In *The Value Systems of the Southeast Asia* [*Tonan azia no kachi taikei*] Vol. 4, edited by Yoshiyuki Hagiwara and Akira Takahashi. Tokyo: Gendai Azia Shuppankai (in Japanese)

Wayas S, Dinoro A (2023) An assessment of alternative learning system (ALS) in the Philippine rural areas. Asia Res Netw J Educ 3(2):74–97

Wentzel KR, Caldwell K (1997) Friendships, peer acceptance, and group membership: relations to academic achievement in middle school. Child Dev 68(6):1198–1209. https://doi.org/10.1111/j.1467-8624.1997.tb01994.x

Woolcock M, Narayan D (2000) Social capital: implications for development theory, research, and policy. World Bank Res Observ 15(2):225–249. https://doi.org/10.1093/wbro/15.2.225

Ungar M (2013) The social ecology of resilience: A handbook of theory and practice. Springer, NY. https://doi.org/10.1007/978-1-4614-0586-3

United Nations Children's Fund East Asia and Pacific Regional Office (UNICEF EAPRO) (2009) Education for all mid-decade assessment: gender equality in education: East Asia and Pacific progress note. UNICEF EAPRO, Bangkok

United Nations Girls' Education Initiative (UNGEI) (2012) Why are boys under-performing in education? Gender analysis of Four Asia-Pacific countries. https://www.unicef.org/eapro/report_why_are_boys_underperforming_FINAL.pdf

Yamauchi F, Tiongco M (2013) Why women are progressive in education? Gender disparities in human capital, labor markets, and family arrangement in the Philippines. Econ Educ Rev 32:196–206. https://doi.org/10.1016/j.econedurev.2012.09.003

Part IV
Conclusions

Chapter 8
Reconsidering the Economics of "Reversal": Toward Human Development for All

Abstract This final chapter reexamines the central question of whether the observed gender disparity in education in the Philippines—where boys now appear more disadvantaged than girls—truly constitutes a reversal. Drawing on empirical findings from preceding chapters, the discussion is organized into three interrelated themes: poverty, family dynamics, and school environments. These perspectives reveal that boys' educational disengagement cannot be understood independently of broader social, economic, and institutional structures embedded in local contexts. While girls may outperform boys on certain educational indicators, the underlying labor market and family systems often continue to disadvantage women, suggesting that gendered inequalities are not simply reversed but transformed in complex ways, unfolding intertemporally and across post-school domains. The chapter also reflects on the interdisciplinary approach adopted in this book, combining development economics, educational studies, and area studies. This integrative stance aims to bridge gaps between empirical rigor and contextual sensitivity, offering a model for how localized inquiry can inform broader theoretical and policy debates. The term "reversal" is thus used not to denote a complete inversion of inequality, but to interrogate surface-level shifts that may obscure deeper, enduring asymmetries. In doing so, the book encourages readers to reconsider gender inequality as a dynamic phenomenon shaped by intersecting cultural, institutional, and economic forces.

Keywords Education and inequality · Family dynamics · Informal institutions and local contexts · Resilience · Hysteresis · Gender reversal debate

1 Introduction

This book has highlighted an emerging issue in human development in low- and middle-income countries: boys' disengagement from education. The discussions began by focusing on this as a *reversed* trend compared to the conventional concern of

M. Okabe, *Economics of the Reversal in Gender Disparities in Education and Development*, Economics, Law, and Institutions in Asia Pacific,
https://doi.org/10.1007/978-981-96-9271-2_8

female underrepresentation in education, while acknowledging the continued importance of female empowerment.[1] This book selected the Philippines as the focal case country, after reviewing global trends of the issue across developing countries and then the intranational patterns within the Philippines. Its aim has been to explore the underlying factors and frameworks contributing to this issue, utilizing in-depth case studies from the Philippines. In line with global concerns, this book refers to this phenomenon as a "boys' crisis," a term used by local academics and policymakers in the Philippines to underscore its urgency and raise awareness.

Despite traditionally high levels of basic education throughout the last century, the Philippines began experiencing setbacks in educational attainment at the start of this millennium. Scholars have identified the boys' crisis as a contributing factor to these setbacks. This issue is as crucial to human development in the Philippines as it is becoming in global contexts. In Chap. 1, rural areas with more severe poverty, rather than urban centers with growing economic activities, are identified as the primary source of boys' disengagement from education. Accordingly, this book has presented in-depth studies from three rural provinces, each geographically selected one of the entire three main island groups of the Philippine archipelago: Luzon (as Chaps. 4–6), Visayas (as Chap. 7), and Mindanao (as Chaps. 2 and 3).

Each chapter has explored the rural socioeconomic environment and schooling, introducing both shared and unique perspectives within a framework where poverty is understood not as a parallel factor, but as a structural force that shapes and refracts family dynamics and school environments, and through these domains, ultimately produces the gendered patterns of educational disengagement that constitute the reversal. The empirical research focused on three interconnected areas to elucidate this phenomenon: (i) the same-sex-assorted parent–child nexus in educational attainment, particularly the positive mother–daughter relationship (Chaps. 2 and 3); (ii) boys' playful behavioral patterns in relation to poverty-shaped family dynamics (Chaps. 4 and 5); and (iii) school-rooted gendered bias on students and the resilience exercised in school environment dynamics (Chaps. 6 and 7).

In this final chapter, I organize the findings from each chapter into these three central themes: how poverty, as a structural condition, shapes boys' disengagement from education through family dynamics (Sect. 3) and school environments (Sect. 4), with Sect. 2 first examining poverty itself as a foundational constraint. Section 5 then revisits the notion of a "reversal" in the studied disparity and offers directions for future research. Finally, Sect. 6 concludes the book.

[1] It is repeatedly emphasized throughout this book that addressing the boys' crisis should not be viewed as a zero-sum game. This concluding chapter reiterates this in its later sections.

2 Structuring Role of Poverty in Educational Disengagement

2.1 *Pathways from Poverty to Disengagement: Institutional and Economic Mechanisms*

This book highlights the significant impact of poverty on boys' disengagement from education in the Philippines. While cross-country analyses suggest that male disengagement is more common in middle-income stages, the Philippine case shows that poverty-stricken rural areas are key sources of educational dropout (mainly discussed in Chap. 1). Notably, credit constraints, immediate financial needs, and household resource competition exacerbate this trend (Chaps. 2 and 3). Boys' earlier physical maturity often compels them to seek work during adolescence, further distancing them from formal education (Hulme and Shepherd 2003; Wood 2003; Fuwa 2014).

Rather than reiterating previously covered content, this section emphasizes the overarching role of poverty as a systemic and structuring force that indirectly produces gendered educational outcomes. Chaps. 2 and 3 detailed the micro-level factors linking poverty to educational discontinuation among students from impoverished households. Additionally, socioeconomic and cultural norms surrounding child labor and family dynamics, as discussed in Chaps. 4, 5, and 7, which prioritize short-term economic contribution over long-term educational investment, compound the issue (Balisacan 2003; Clarete et al. 2018). These short-run adjustments can leave persistent adverse (scarring) effects on grade progression and re-entry costs, raising the likelihood of withdrawal at transition grades (Andrew 2014).

2.2 *Econocultural Norms: A Preliminary Note on a Bargain About Long-Term Loss for Short-Term Gain*[2]

Building on the previous chapters, this final chapter explores underlying factors contributing to poverty and boys' educational disengagement in local contexts. It presents additional observations from one of the research sites, which were not explicitly discussed earlier, to complement the preceding findings. In this sense, the chapter serves as a preliminary investigation into the underlying dynamics behind the withdrawal of boys from formal education.

Since the time of my fieldwork and continuing to the present, I have frequently observed seemingly miscellaneous, small-scale jobs, especially in rural areas but also in urban settings. These observations may reflect the influence of econocultural norms prevalent in the rural Philippines—such as *pakikibahagi* (the virtue of sharing),

[2] This section builds on Okabe (2025). I also thank Professor Toru Nakanishi for additional constructive suggestions.

pakikisalo (participation and camaraderie), and *utang na loob* (debt of gratitude).[3] In communities where risks persist, these longstanding norms and informal orders have functioned as mechanisms for maintaining social cohesion and redistributing opportunities among members.[4,5]

Extensions of this logic are evident in everyday practices. For instance, some individuals prepare snacks (*merienda*) at home and go door to door "selling" them. Even if the residents are not hungry, they are often implicitly expected to purchase some, especially if the sellers are perceived as being in need.[6] Local youths—particularly boys—would visit households and, without being asked, climb backyard trees to harvest coconuts. In return, they would receive a portion of the yield or some form of compensation. Those who managed to save some of their earnings often purchased used motorbikes or bicycles to begin offering *tricycle* or *pedicab* services. When they saw neighbors walking, even over short distances, they would call out and offer rides. These types of informal, small-scale jobs appeared to be predominantly undertaken by males.

In rural areas heavily reliant on primary industries such as agriculture, the line between the "haves" and the "have-nots" is often ambiguous and reversible (Barrett 2005). Through pseudo-donations embedded within *pakikibahagi*-like norms, wealth and risks may be redistributed in ways that sustain labor supply systems resembling informal labor markets. These jobs are unstable and nonstandard, yet they require only time, physical strength, and perseverance—not formal educational credentials—thus making them accessible to out-of-school youth or those at risk of dropping out. Their very existence may serve as a psychological buffer—the belief that "even if I drop out, I'll manage somehow."

This situation may be interpreted as a Faustian bargain, in which short-term needs are fulfilled at the cost of long-term stability (Hulme and Shepherd 2003; Nakanishi 2008; Wood 2003). Those authors highlight the role of patron-client power structures in mediating such bargains.[7] In this book's context, however, I argue that communal

---

[3] In urban centers, these normative virtues are becoming less influential than in the past and than in rural areas, due to urbanization and the increasing anonymity of urban society.

[4] These services persist as implicit expectations between the haves and have-nots, even in Manila, such as the role of jeepney barkers (dispatchers).

[5] One such example is the agricultural practice known as *hunusan*, an open-access, low-barrier-to-entry, cooperative crop harvesting (Hayami and Kikuchi 2000). In this practice, neighbors without farmland or resources contribute labor during harvesting and receive a share of the yield. This can be interpreted as a form of wisdom and informal institution for mutual risk sharing deeply rooted in traditional rural life (Hayami and Godo 2005).

[6] I frequently asked local informants why they purchased or accepted the offers. They did not provide specific reasons but often responded with a simple phrase "*Ganun talaga kasi*..." ("That's just how it is... "). This sense of implicit expectation strongly implies the underlying social expectation in these contexts.

[7] While the Faustian bargain view shares similarities with concepts in behavioral economics such as hyperbolic discounting, our usage foregrounds structurally embedded power asymmetries and informal institutional orders rather than attributing outcomes solely to individual-level cognitive mechanisms such as present bias, intertemporal inconsistency, or time preferences (Laibson 1997; O'Donoghue and Rabin 1999; Wood 2003; Wood 2015).

norms and practices long embedded in local life and intended to mitigate poverty can, ironically, stabilize informal employment and reinforce patterns of social immobility by providing this very buffer. Conceptually, I frame the mechanism as a three-level framework: micro—an individual Faustian bargain that prioritizes immediate earnings, belonging, or relief from risk over future human-capital returns; meso—adverse incorporation, i.e., inclusion on subordinate, low-return terms in markets, state programs, and patronage that restricts voice and exit (Hickey and du Toit 2007; Wood 2015); and macro—shared poverty, in Geertz's sense of the involutionary spreading of work and income that equalizes downward and dampens incentives for prolonged schooling (Geertz 1963; Wood 2015).

A related argument emerges from theories of comparative advantage in labor. Physical work, such as farming, demands strength but not necessarily formal education, whereas many non-agricultural jobs require higher educational attainment. Empirical research across several Asian countries shows that women's labor force participation tends to increase sharply only after they attain a college degree, with the Philippines being a notable case (Cameron et al. 2001, Deolalikar 1993). If this is so, men—having access to jobs across a broader educational spectrum—may feel they have a fallback by accepting a Faustian bargain, while women experience greater pressure to stay in school due to a lack of viable alternatives without higher education. In light of this, does women's higher educational attainment truly represent a "reversal" of the gender gap?

If these preliminary observations are substantiated by empirical data, they may provide a further compelling answer to the question of why poverty matters in understanding the reversal of gendered educational outcomes. They also suggest the possibility that reversed gender disparities may become further entrenched in poor and rural areas. Moreover, this framework could be extended to other Southeast Asian contexts characterized by stark intra-country urban–rural divides. Moving forward, sustained cross-country analysis of the interplay among poverty, traditional norms, and children's life trajectories will be essential.

Finally, it remains an open question whether the apparent demand for male youth labor in rural areas is inherently stronger than that for females, or whether such demand is generated by the availability of these informal jobs (Heintz 2010). This chapter suggests that youths who drop out of school may enter these small-scale occupations, implying that labor supply itself could generate demand in the short term. Further inquiry into these hypothetically Faustian bargains is warranted. In aggregate, such bargains can generate a form of hysteresis—familiar from macroeconomics (Dutt 2023) but applied here to cohort-level persistence in schooling gaps even after the immediate shock recedes.

3 Family Dynamics and Boys' Disengagement from Education

3.1 Intergenerational Dynamics: Parent–Child Nexus in Education

In this book, family dynamics is presented as another equally important underlying theme associated with gender disparity in education, alongside poverty. This book intentionally places high value on this perspective not only due to economic literature that focuses on intrahousehold resource allocations but also because the family is the most important and most cherished institution in the Philippines (Jocano 1998; Medina 2015).

Chapters 2 and 3 examined the continuity of demands for education and focused on the same-sex-assorted parent–child nexus (i.e., father–son and mother–daughter nexus) in their levels of educational attainment. It was found that the mother–daughter nexus was stronger than the father–son nexus, particularly at higher levels of education. Furthermore, the discussions in Chaps. 2 and 3 revolved around the concern that these detected intergenerational gendered associations might perpetuate current gender gaps, especially considering the persisting trend of men's lower average educational attainment compared to women's.

The findings of the same-sex parent–child educational assortative nexus in Chap. 2 and the further specifically identified mother–daughter nexus in Chap. 3 have been particularly significant to the subsequent chapters, as they suggest a dynamic within the family where children and parents interact in ways that influence children's educational outcomes. Indeed, the literature widely reports a bias favoring investment in daughters in the Philippine context (Estudillo et al., 2001a, b, 2008, 2009; Fuwa 2014). This parental preference for daughters' education over sons' one is consistent with the literature, indicating that parents are more inclined to invest in their daughters' human capital.[8]

While these findings provide intriguing insights into the identified patterns of how family dynamics influence boys' and girls' educational attainment, Chaps. 2 and 3 did not delve deeply enough into specific aspects of the interactions beyond the very pattern between mothers (and fathers) and their children concerning schooling. This limitation partly stemmed from the nature of the data used, which was collected by IFPRI, a third-party institute, with the relevant yet different research focus—investigating the impact of agricultural commercialization, which was the IFPRI's primary motivation to perform the survey (recall Chap. 2 and Bouis and Haddad 1990). This limitation eventually motivated me to collect tailor-made primary survey data that directly aligns with the current research topic. Consequently, we proceeded to explore these dynamics further by examining the specific challenges boys and

[8] This behavior contrasts with that observed in South Asia, where sons are typically favored over daughters (Asadullah and Chaudhury 2009; Kurosaki et al. 2006; Sawada et al. 2006).

girls face within the family and in school, as presented in Chaps. 4 and 5 as well as Chap. 6.

3.2 Mothers' Labor Force Participation and Its Impact on Family Dynamics

Therefore, Chaps. 4 and 5 highlighted the need to situate boys' underperformance within the context of family dynamics, affecting *both* men and women. After Chaps. 2 and 3 explored family dynamics through the intergenerational parent-to-child nexus of educational attainment, Chaps. 4 and 5 revealed another crucial family dynamic where mothers and children play significant roles for each other through mothers' labor force participation (MLFP), which is an outcome of women's human capital investment. It was initially expected that MLFP would increase children's time spent on household chores, thereby reducing their time for education. However, this was not observed. Instead, the analysis found that daughters and sons responded differently regarding the time spent on their educational activities, which Chaps. 4 and 5 termed an "unintended" effect of MLFP.

3.3 Maternal Dual Burden in Family Dynamics: Rural and Cultural Contexts

In considering these family dynamics, it is important to reconfirm that some initial conditions of the Philippines, known from rural studies, indicate a lower resistance to female labor activities compared to countries in South Asia or the Middle East for example. Since the 1960s–70s, Filipino women have been recognized as being able to participate in the labor force with less cultural and social resistance from their surroundings (Takahashi 1972). Bilateral descent has broadly taken hold in the Philippines (and in Southeast Asia as well). Even matrilineal systems and matrilateral descent were found in some regions, such as Bukidnon Province in Chap. 3 (Sudo 1989). These findings suggest that, historically, women in the Philippines were not substantially unfavored compared to men.

According to the observations in Chaps. 4 and 5, mothers are flexibly responsive to collectively maintaining their household livelihoods alongside fathers. While fathers (men) may appear to exercise authority and power within families, mothers (women) are indeed no weaker than fathers, e.g., controlling the purse strings (Takahashi, 1973: 159). However, there is an equivocal aspect when it comes to female labor. Recent studies report that Filipino female workers are still not treated or compensated as favorably as men in the labor market, even if they possess similar attributes and qualifications (Asuncion 2018; Serrano and Certeza 2014; Yamauchi and Tiongco 2013).[9]

Even under these less favorable conditions, mothers in rural areas still have to work. It is important to note that these mothers are qualitatively different from middle-class working mothers in urban centers, who can afford to hire *yaya* (babysitters) to compensate, even partially, for childcare responsibilities. In rural areas, MLFP is significantly driven by poverty or low levels of livelihood. The rural poor's situations are at subsistence levels, rather than responding to what Ivan Illich referred to as the "radical monopoly" that dominates contemporary technological urban centers (Illich 2001=1973). While relying on government provisions, the rural poor also face high demands to maintain their subsistence levels of livelihood.

Although working mothers might recognize the potential impact of their MLFP on child behavior, as measured in Chaps. 4 and 5, they often face immediate demands to earn a living. This situation compels mothers to meet these demands, particularly when fathers' earnings are insufficient (in Sect. 2.2). Similar to the previous section, this scenario can be viewed as a form that forces the rural poor into adverse incorporation (Hickey and du Toit 2007; Hulme and Shepherd 2003; Wood 2003; Nakanishi 2008): Here, MLFP exerts gendered influences on children's educational behaviors, generally having a negative impact on sons. However, this impact is driven by the pressing need to support the household livelihood and supplement the role of the breadwinner.

It is crucial to emphasize that while MLFP might be socially and culturally accepted or face less resistance, this does not necessarily translate into gender equality in terms of compensation (Asuncion 2018; Serrano and Certeza 2014; Yamauchi and Tiongco 2013). Similarly, the gender inequality that boys are underachieving and facing more difficulties in education does not necessarily signify a reversal of the conventionally universal gender disparity against women seen in most of the world. Alternatively, the highly traditional aspects of gender inequality in the Philippines may persist, despite global discourse recognizing the country as one of the top achievers in gender equality in society.

At least, according to the discussions in Chaps. 4 and 5, it is important to reiterate that women's *voluntary* decisions or preferences to work must always be respected by their family members, as well as by firms, communities, and governments. However, MLFP that is somewhat forced, *involuntarily* decided by mothers themselves, or triggered by their husbands' lesser economic capacity, should be addressed as a policy variable. The U-shaped hypothesis of MLFP rates as per welfare levels states that higher MLFP rates do not necessarily correspond to higher wealth levels for women and vice versa (Goldin 1995; Sawada et al. 2006). Even when a woman

[9] In advanced economies, studies in labor economics have shifted their focus from the level of education to the type or academic specialty, as women increasingly attain higher education and gender equality in the quantitative sense is being achieved. Therefore, at least in developed countries, if differences in these educational aspects persist between men and women, understanding the wage gaps between them becomes more complex than before (O'Reilly et al.2015; Rubery and Grimshaw 2011; ILO 2016).

works, the wealth level of her family or her own wealth level can remain low, despite the fact that she appears empowered because she is employed.

4 School Environment and Boys' Disengagement from Education

4.1 School Environment Matters

Previous chapters and much of the literature have primarily addressed gender bias in education from the perspectives of poverty, family dynamics, and other socioeconomic (demand-side) factors. Chapter 6, while still considering students' socioeconomic circumstances, integrates primary data with confidential, student-level administrative data from the Philippines' national achievement tests (NATs). This approach intentionally shifts the focus to the supply side, particularly the school environment. This is the other underlying research agenda set in this book alongside poverty and family dynamics.

Chapter 6 specifically examines gendered stereotypes held by those scoring the tests. Using a natural experimental identification strategy, the empirical analysis compares the sources of the persistent negative male effect on test scores. By analyzing the variations in "blindness" between the NAT rating system and teacher-rated report cards (RCs), the study finds that male students are systematically more likely to receive lower scores when evaluated in a non-blind system where teachers know the identity of the examinees. These findings suggest that gender stereotypes held by teachers may contribute to the underperformance of Filipino schoolboys.

However, Chap. 6 does not aim to blame teachers, as the study does not prove that they consciously or intentionally applied these stereotypes. Nevertheless, the findings are significant. The literature has provided empirically sound perspectives on the demand-side factors that contribute to boys' poor academic performance or their decision to drop out of school. Chapter 6 introduces additional channels for intervention on the supply side, such as addressing teacher-related factors, including the high proportion of female teachers in the Philippines. These interventions could complement demand-side measures like employment and stipend programs.

Importantly, Chap. 6 also finds that this augmentation of underperformance is attributable to pure stereotyping based on the students' gender, rather than any observable factors like tidiness that might influence their scores on RCs. Given the erratic directions of gendered stereotypes found in the literature, it is crucial to note that stereotyping can be exercised in a purely social and context-dependent manner, rather than in an essentialistic or deterministic way, as discussed in Chap. 1.

4.2 Exposure to Augmentation

Paradoxically, even essentialism-based interpretations can appear reasonable in the context of the discussions so far. The data supported certain tendencies: boys tend to study less diligently than girls, spend less time in school, are more likely to leave class, and play longer than girls (Chaps. 4 and 5). Additionally, boys are more likely to prefer or be required to start working while still of school age (Sect. 2 in this chapter). One might argue that the educational outcomes that arise from these behavioral differences between boys and girls—labeled as "*tamad/katamaran*" (laziness) or "*sipag/kasipagan*" (diligence) in local terms—could ultimately be attributed to them, respectively. Girls, who tend to put more effort into learning and pro-educational activities, might be seen as deserving of better outcomes. In this sense, the resulting gender disparity might be viewed as the natural consequence of meritocracy or equity, where those who work harder are rewarded.

Nevertheless, this book does not endorse these interpretations, even if they seem reasonable in some respects. A key example is the study in Chap. 6. The primary academic contribution of this chapter was not merely to reconfirm the negative male effect, which had already been established in previous chapters. Instead, the significant insight was the concept of augmentation through the stereotype bias. While male students may generally perform worse than their female counterparts, this underperformance can be amplified when they are evaluated in school, compounding scarring by increasing the subjective cost of schooling. Without this augmentation, their academic performance might appear closer to that of female students. Chapter 6 explored teacher-side characteristics unique to the Philippines, such as gender ratios among teachers and the teaching labor market.

This raises further questions about boys' underperformance as a form of reversed gender disparity in education. Two interpretations seem plausible. First, due to augmentation, boys are evaluated more harshly than they might be in the absence of gender-based stereotypes. This suggests that boys are not "rewarded" as fairly as girls for the same level of effort, potentially decreasing their motivation (even if they are not consciously aware of the augmented effect). Consequently, boys' less diligent or more playful behaviors in school environment as well as in out-of-school one might be linked to this experience of unfair evaluation. In this regard, Appendix B illustrates another lens of these perspective in the research site. Their exposure to augmentation is thus a significant factor contributing to boys' underperformance in education, making it appear as though there is a reversal of the typical gender disparity.

Second, the augmentation effect implies that boys might not perform significantly worse than girls if the augmentation did not exist. Conceptually removing the augmentation effect allows us to consider that boys' performance could be more equal to that of girls in a setting free from such biases. Therefore, this book presents an alternative narrative: boys are not inherently underperforming. With proper guidance and support, boys could catch up with girls in education, suggesting that boys'

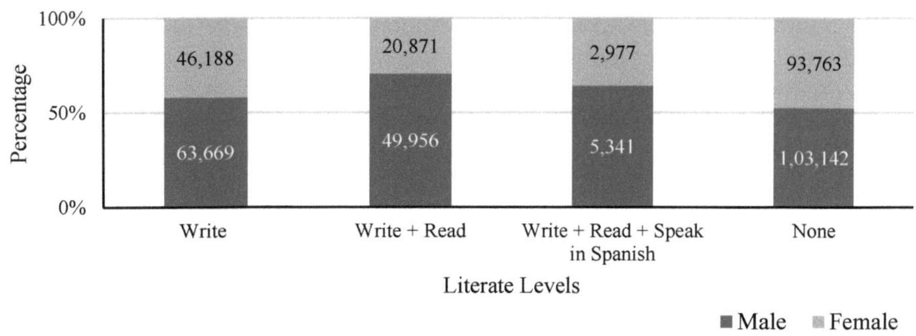

Fig. 1 Literacy-level comparisons by Genders (1876). *Source* Author's illustration based on Abella (1965: 29)

underperformance is not predestined by essentialistic factors.[10] This book does not argue that only boys should receive intervention and support. Instead, true gender equality must eliminate disparity for any gender, whether male or female.

4.3 Resilience, Social Network, and Role Models

Chapter 7 introduces findings that diverge from those discussed in previous chapters, focusing on the resilience demonstrated by boys who initially left school but later returned. This chapter sheds light on a different aspect of educational disengagement: the resilience they showed during their absence. As highlighted earlier, economic hardship was a key factor driving these boys to leave school. Confronted with poverty, they were often required to contribute to their families' income through child labor. Some moved from Panay Island to Negros Island to engage in informal, seasonal work in sugarcane fields and manufacturing, which disrupted their school attendance and contributed to their perceived lack of diligence, making their reintegration into the classroom challenging.

Additionally, Chap. 7 examines the role of social networks, particularly the local concept of *barkadahan*, which refers to a group of friends. Literature often associates *barkadahan* with educational disengagement and underperformance. This social network is sometimes linked to behaviors considered detrimental to academic commitment, as seen by parents, teachers, and local adults. Although some ethnographies and rural studies recognize *barkadahan* as a form of social capital with positive aspects, the negative connotations tend to dominate.

[10] The reversal of gender differences in education, confirmed in Chap. 1 and increasingly pronounced in recent generations, does not appear to be a permanent long-term trend. For instance, as shown by Abella (1965), around 1876 during the Spanish colonial period, boys had higher literacy levels than girls (Fig. 1).

Our findings, however, reveal a pivotal moment when some individuals experienced a sense of being "fed up" with *barkadahan*. This turning point prompted them to reevaluate their life choices and return to school, despite being overage. Similar patterns have been observed in ethnographic studies, where individuals who moved up the social ladder from rural to urban environments transitioned from lower socioeconomic status to middle-class status. While our informants' experiences do not mirror such dramatic social mobility, their return to school represents a significant instance of resilience and personal development.

As discussed in Chaps. 4 and 5 as well as will be introduced in Appendix A, children navigate a complex environment that includes family, school, and various out-of-school activities such as playing, socializing, sports, arts, ceremonies, religious practices, shopping, and labor. The school environment remains central to children's everyday life, especially during enrollment and even during their out-of-school period—even if it is just in the back of their mind—and children must maintain a connection to it unless they complete their education. The sense of awakening experienced by the returned students, despite their engagement in non-school activities, indicates ongoing reflection on their association with schooling.

As previously mentioned, social groups can function both positively and negatively depending on timing and members. One positive aspect is the potential for these groups to foster or bridge role models for students. A possible factor behind the return of students to school could be the influence of role-model figures. While affiliating with a *barkada*, a child also interacts with other friends outside the group. In my local observations in Antique and Marinduque Provinces, children reported having their own *huwaran* (role-model persons) within their small living world, such as within the same barangay and schools. Interestingly, the age of the *huwaran* did not seem to matter much—some were older, while others were around the same age. This perspective is closely related to peer effects, a research topic actively studied in the economics of education (Sacerdote 2011: 268–269).

For a deeper understanding of these dynamics, the interplay between social network group membership and educational outcomes remains underexplored. Chapter 7 highlights the need for further research into the specific experiences that led these students to feel "fed up," reassess their lives, and ultimately return to school. Future studies should employ participatory observation and fieldwork methods to enhance our understanding of resilience within the context of *barkadahan*, particularly given the allegedly closer associations of *barkadahan* with boyhood and thereafter with manliness.

5 Questioning the "Reversed" Gender Disparity

5.1 Reconsidering the "Reversal": Empirical Nuances

In this section, we reconsider the notion of "reversal" by revisiting the findings from the previous chapters, highlighting how poverty-driven processes produce gendered consequences that cannot be fully understood within a simple binary framework.

First, the main finding in Chap. 4, the "unintended" effect of MLFP contributed to boys' undiligent behaviors, offered a nuanced implication. While the effect of MLFP has been identified in the chapter as a source of the boys' underperformance through affecting the child gendered pro-educational time allocations, this effect emerged from MLFP functioning as a rational, poverty-induced household insurance strategy, where mothers took on supplementary breadwinner roles to stabilize family livelihoods. Indeed, this issue has been documented as a growing hardship among vulnerable groups and within informal-economy settings (ILO and ADB 2011).

Chapter 5 conceptualizes the "dual burden" of responsibilities assumed by mothers, who must balance childrearing duties while also taking on part of the breadwinner role. This dual burden, structurally shaped by persistent rural poverty, echoes the sacrifices of female Overseas Filipino Workers (OFWs), often described through terms such as *sakripisyo/pagsasakripisyo* and *pagmamalasakit* (Pinzon 2021; Piocos 2019; Sobritchea 2007).[11,12] These maternal roles, both local and transnational, suggest that gendered household strategies under poverty have far-reaching intergenerational effects.

Second, Chap. 6 also aligns with this interpretation. While it identified scoring bias against boys linked to the predominance of female teachers, it also interrogated the socioeconomic background that leads to female domination in the teaching profession. In the Philippines, the proportion of female teachers typically falls within the 70 to 80% range, regardless of subject (Sect. 4.3 of Chap. 6). That section states that this reflects, in part, the structural lack of private-sector alternatives for educated rural women, which makes public teaching one of the few socially respected and formally

---

[11] In the OFW context, *dobleng sakripisyo* (double sacrifices) (Pinzon 2021: 299) may correspond to what is expressed here as the dual burden in the domestic context.

[12] Notwithstanding, Chaps. 4 and 5 have not explored female Overseas Filipino Workers (OFWs) as extensively as locally working mothers in their resident locations, due to the limited number of reported OFWs in our data; the majority are working locally. For further details, see Appendix Chapter A. This appendix explains that, contrary to the global discourse which often depicts the Philippines as an immediate labor-sending country, not many local people can transition directly to overseas jobs in the rural setting studied in Chaps. 4 and 5. Instead, labor migration occurs in a stepwise, concentric manner: from home vicinities to *poblacions* within villages and municipalities, from *poblacions* to provincial capitals, from provincial capitals to urban centers, from urban centers to the national capital, Metro Manila, and finally, from Metro Manila to overseas destinations. This labor migration process heavily relies on the amount of and access to financial capital (cash and savings), social capital (friends, social networks, and access to accurate and timely information), and public capital (governmental assistance). This heterogeneous, gradual process continues through and within the destinations abroad as well.

recognized career paths, especially for those not migrating abroad for work. In this context, the "bias" in schools may be less an educational failure than a labor market adaptation to structural gendered inequalities.

Third, that being said, another finding from Chap. 4 regarding the role-model dynamic between mothers and daughters, with its emphasis on economic independence and responsibility, further underscores the unintended effect of MLFP. The female dominance in school teaching environments likely favors female students in both family dynamics and the learning environment compared to male students. These mechanisms align with, and may even reinforce and be reinforced by, the intergenerational same-sex parent–child assortative education nexus discussed in Chaps. 2 and 3.

Boys' disengagement from education affects not only the boys themselves—some of whom will become fathers—but also the girls—some of whom will become mothers—resulting in long-term intergenerational effects when they assume these roles. Since poverty-induced MLFP is an economic response where mothers supplement the breadwinner roles typically filled by fathers, the identified "unintended effect" of MLFP suggests the need to view boys' disengagement from education or boys' crisis as part of a broader crisis impacting individuals regardless of gender.

Therefore, overemphasizing the "reversal" of the educational disparity pattern would no longer be appropriate. It is time to question whether the reversed gender disparity is genuinely occurring or if it represents a transformation of a broader gender crisis that should be addressed by society as a whole. This book suggests that our observations and empirical findings support the idea of gender disparities *ingeniously transforming one after another*—against men at one stage and against women at another—and between schooling and post-schooling systems—all strongly linked to local conditions.

In other words, now, this book does not stand at the view that these disparities align with the so-called zero-sum game perspective, which interprets experiences in other girl-outperforming countries as leading to unintended negative consequences for boys due to nationally large-scale affirmative actions aimed at addressing the problem of female education (Asadullah and Chaudhury 2009: 1374). Both types of disparities—both educational and post-educational, and those affecting both men and women—should be considered and addressed collectively.

5.2 Consolidating What We Have Learned: A Conceptual Framework of This Book's Perspective

To synthesize the structural, institutional, and intergenerational processes discussed throughout the book, the following conceptual framework (Fig. 2) offers a visual consolidation of how gendered educational disengagement—particularly among boys—is shaped, mediated, and reinforced within broader socioeconomic contexts.

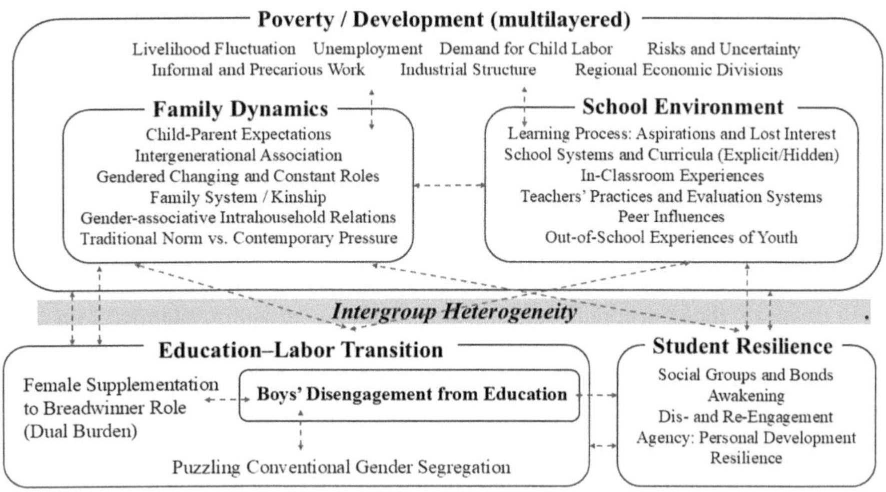

Fig. 2 Conceptual framework of this book's perspective. *Source* Author's conceptualization

This framework is organized around three interrelated domains—poverty and (under)development, family dynamics, and school environment—that collectively shape boys' disengagement from education. These domains are not independent; rather, they interact dynamically. For example, poverty-induced maternal labor force participation (MLFP) transforms traditional household roles, leading to the unintended educational consequences shown in Chaps. 4 and 5. School environments, in turn, are shaped by curricular structures, evaluation practices, teacher labor markets, and peer group cultures. Chapter 6 shows how implicit biases in scoring and classroom interactions can amplify gendered perceptions of ability, while Chap. 7 highlights how peer affiliations and students' out-of-school experiences affect their resilience and learning trajectories. These dynamics often interact with household role modeling, reinforcing or mediating gendered outcomes in education.

At the center of the framework is intergroup heterogeneity, which represents the differentiated ways in which social groups—typically gender groups in this book—respond to these structural conditions. While this book primarily focuses on gender, such heterogeneity could also emerge along lines of religion, ethnicity, socioeconomic class, or political orientation. It is crucial to note that this concept does not imply the absence of intragroup variation. For example, while this book highlights the disengagement of boys as a group-level trend, it fully acknowledges that many boys are academically successful—and conversely, that not all girls perform well. Intergroup heterogeneity reflects average tendencies across groups, not essentialist divisions, and can coexist with substantial individual-level diversity.

Surrounding the central pathways are mediating behavioral responses, including bonding, awakening, disengagement and re-engagement, personal development, and resilience. These elements reflect the agency of children as they navigate educational constraints—some reinforcing, others resisting structural disadvantages.

Importantly, the framework also draws attention to the broader systemic implications: namely, how educational disengagement translates into puzzling labor market outcomes, such as the persistence of conventional gender segregation in employment despite reversed trends in schooling. This mismatch between the education and labor systems calls for a rethinking of how we conceptualize gender inequality—not as a linear progression, but as a recursive and layered transformation. Initial disparities can set in motion cumulative (dis)advantage processes, progressively amplifying inequality within and across groups and domains (DiPrete and Eirich 2006), exhibiting a form of hysteresis (Dutt 2023).

In this way, the conceptual framework presented here is not intended as a fixed model, but as a synthesized map of the empirical and theoretical insights developed throughout the book. It allows us to step back and view the multiple, interacting layers—structural, institutional, and individual—that together shape the educational trajectories of young people in rural Philippines.

6 Epilogue: In Lieu of a Conventional Conclusion

6.1 Structural Disparities and Policy Imperatives

As discussed in the previous section, what appears to be a reversal in gender disparity may be misleading if viewed solely through educational indicators. This section extends that argument by examining its structural and policy implications under conditions of persistent poverty. One major socioeconomic challenge lies in ensuring that women's educational gains are translated into equitable outcomes in the economic sphere, alongside those of men (Asuncion 2018; Serrano and Certeza 2014; Yamauchi and Tiongco 2013).

In this context, the book cautions against reductive narratives that position the Philippines as a frontrunner in gender equality solely on the basis of educational indicators. While the country ranks highest in Asia in the World Economic Forum's *Global Gender Gap Reports*, with education cited as a key driver of gender parity (WEF 2021: 24), this assessment overlooks the paradox that apparent improvements in one domain of gender equality—namely, girls' educational attainment—may be driven by persisting inequalities in another, such as the labor market's unfavorable treatment of women. While boys may underperform in education, they may still fare better in labor market outcomes and economic opportunities.

Given the findings of this book, which reveal stark educational disadvantages among boys, particularly among certain subgroups, there is an urgent need for educational policy to selectively address these issues. Globally, few low- and middle-income countries have adopted targeted policies to confront boys' disengagement from education (Jha et al. 2012; UNESCO 2022: 98). In the Philippine context, this recognition has emerged gradually. The government's *Education for All 2015* review acknowledged that most gender equity initiatives in education had primarily focused on girls (Philippine Department of Education 2014). Yet it also emphasized the need to tackle boys' higher dropout rates and lower engagement. Only in recent years has the government begun to explicitly recognize boys' underperformance, especially during and after secondary school (Philippine Department of Education 2017).

Improving boys' educational outcomes may ultimately benefit both genders, as educational decisions are often made collectively within households. In this sense, it is vital to move beyond zero-sum framings of gender. Designing male-specific programs should not be seen as exclusionary or as marginalizing the needs of girls. Rather, gender-specific efforts must be embedded within a structural understanding of poverty and opportunity. That said, there remains considerable scope to clarify target populations, practical approaches, and the deeper structural causes behind boys' educational challenges. One certainty, as repeatedly underscored in development economics, is that anti-poverty strategies must remain central—not just as background measures, but as forces that actively shape family strategies and school systems. This book has demonstrated that such strategies influence educational outcomes through multiple, interrelated pathways.

In addition to these interpersonal and household-level effects, addressing boys' disengagement from education also carries significant macro-level implications unless addressed. Widening gender disparities in education can lead to long-term imbalances in labor market participation, earnings potential, and social mobility across generations. In contexts like the Philippines, where certain sectors of the economy remain male-dominated while others increasingly rely on the educational advancement of women, such asymmetries may undermine inclusive growth and exacerbate structural inequality. Furthermore, if boys continue to disengage from formal education, the country risks a growing underclass of men with limited access to stable, skilled employment, potentially fueling social disaffection and political instability. Thus, investing in equitable educational outcomes is not only a matter of gender justice but also a matter of economic resilience and inclusive national development.

6.2 *Methodological Reflections and Future Directions*

Throughout, this book has adopted an interdisciplinary approach. Some sections highlighted local norms and socioeconomic or econocultural conditions through fieldwork that prioritized local languages, while others relied heavily on empirical econometric methods. This combination was intentional: to integrate hypothesis formation with hypothesis testing even within a single book.

This interdisciplinary stance, in addressing such a nuanced issue as the one this book has taken up, aims to contribute to bridging a gap in today's highly specialized social sciences, where integrative approaches remain relatively underutilized. For instance, development economists, for their part, have long played a leading role in modeling poverty dynamics and evaluating policy interventions using rigorous empirical methods. Yet, relative to cross-country work, in-depth, country-specific research conducted in local languages is less routine, often reflecting training, incentives, and data access. Likewise, many scholars in qualitative area studies and educational development studies have made rich and important contributions through exploratory and interpretive methods, while economics-grounded empirical approaches—such as optimization and equilibrium models, econometrics, and causal inference—are not particularly mainstream in these two fields. Of course, there are notable exceptions in each of the three fields. Recognizing these complementary strengths, this book advocates collaboration that integrates contextual knowledge with analytical tools.

In fact, this stance has at times made me feel this in-between position quite acutely, in different ways. Yet over time, I have come to appreciate—and even enjoy—the vantage point afforded by being at the boundaries: a position that allows one to move between domains, to translate between vocabularies, and to see structural connections that might otherwise be overlooked. It is in this spirit that I have drawn on my academic training across economics, educational development, and area studies to approach the issues discussed in this book from a more integrative perspective. The goal has never been to privilege one disciplinary approach over another, but rather to explore how combining diverse perspectives can enhance our understanding of complex social realities.

Naturally, this approach entails trade-offs. It may be criticized for limitations in national representativeness, as the research focuses on just three provinces—albeit selected from each of the Philippines' three major island groups. The findings should not be overgeneralized. At the same time, there is substantial opportunity to enhance generalizability by combining micro-level field data with nationally representative datasets. Achieving both local depth and broad validity remains an enduring challenge in social research.

To mitigate these limitations, the book has provided extensive interpretation, caveats against overgeneralization, and supplementary data and context throughout the main chapters and appendices. These efforts are intended to help navigate the inherent trade-offs of the interdisciplinary and case-based approach taken. Future research collaborations with scholars from other regional or disciplinary fields are highly encouraged. Some might argue that interdisciplinary work can only truly succeed through team-based research, and the extent to which this single-authored book has managed to do so is ultimately left to the judgment of the readers. As a researcher, I recognize the value of division of labor and collaborative inquiry. Working across disciplinary and regional boundaries will be essential for extending the relevance of the findings presented here.

Ultimately, the perspectives and conclusions offered in this book are made possible by its commitment to examining not only education, but also the broader systems that shape it, most notably poverty as a structuring force, and family and school as domains through which its effects manifest, through the combined lenses of development economics, educational development, and area studies. If this book encourages readers to view the reversal of gender disparity not merely as a statistical anomaly, but as a phenomenon embedded in complex and evolving economic, social, and cultural structures, then it will have achieved its aim. In short, I use "reversal" to interrogate surface shifts that can mask deeper gendered dynamics.

This is why I use the phrase *economics of the reversal* in the title of this book. It highlights how individual choices—often rational in the short term—meet locally embedded structural constraints that are themselves entangled with micro-, meso-, and macro-level dynamics within state, market, and institutional orders from the local to the regional and global levels. The phrase is deliberately multivalent: most immediately, it points to the apparent *gender reversal* in education; also to the *intertemporal reversal* in which short-term payoffs dominate long-term returns (e.g., Faustian-bargain dynamics nested within adverse incorporation); and to the *domain reversal* whereby boys' underachievement in education coexists with women's disadvantage in post-school economic outcomes. Taken together, these layered reversals and a form of hysteresis dynamic that they can induce at both the individual and collective levels point toward the necessity of non-zero-sum, structural responses that advance human development for all.

References

Abella D (1965) State of higher education in the Philippines to 1863: a historical reappraisal. Philipp Hist Rev 1(1):1–46

Andrew M (2014) The scarring effects of primary-grade retention? A study of cumulative advantage in the educational career. Social Forces 93(2):653–685. https://doi.org/10.1093/sf/sou074

Asadullah MN, Chaudhury N (2009) Reverse gender gap in schooling in Bangladesh: insights from urban and rural households. J Dev Stud 45(8):1360–1380. https://doi.org/10.1080/00220380902935824

Asuncion RA (2018) Aging societies and gender mainstreaming in the Philippines. In: *Why Asia must up female workforce participation: women hold the key to growing productivity in a sustainable way, as aging shrinks workforces*, by Asian Productivity Organization (APO). Tokyo: APO. https://doi.org/10.61145/DOGT5393

Balisacan AM (2003) The Philippine economy: development, policies, and challenges. Ateneo de Manila University Press, Quezon City

Barrett CB (2005) The Social Economics of Poverty. London: Routledge. https://doi.org/10.4324/9780203799659

Bouis HE, Haddad LJ (1990) *Agricultural commercialization, nutrition, and the rural poor: A study of Philippine farm households*. Boulder and London: Lynne Rienner

Cameron LA, Dowling M, Worswick C (2001) Education and labor market participation of women in Asia: Evidence from five countries. Econ Dev Cult Chang 49(3):459–477. https://doi.org/10.1086/452511

Clarete RL, Esguerra EF, Hill H (eds) (2018) *The Philippine economy: no longer the East Asian exception?* Singapore: ISEAS Publishing. https://doi.org/10.1355/9789814786621

Deolalikar AB (1993) Gender differences in the returns to schooling and in school enrollment rates in Indonesia. J Human Resources 28(4):899–932. https://doi.org/10.2307/146297

Department of Education, Philippine Government (DepEd) (2014) Philippine education for all 2015 review report. Manila: Philippines Department of Education

Department of Education, Philippine Government (DepEd) (2017) Gender-responsive basic education policy. Manila: Philippines Department of Education

DiPrete TA, Eirich GM (2006) Cumulative advantage as a mechanism for inequality: A review of theoretical and empirical developments. Annual Rev Sociology 32(1):271–297. https://doi.org/10.1146/annurev.soc.32.061604.123127

Dutt AK (2023) Hysteresis and path dependence in economic analysis: formalizations causes and implications. Rev Keynesian Econ 11(4):435–459. https://doi.org/10.4337/roke.2023.04.01

Estudillo JP, Quisumbing A, Otsuka K (2001a) Gender differences in land inheritance and schooling investment in the rural Philippines. Land Econ 77(1):130–143. https://doi.org/10.2307/3146985

Estudillo JP, Quisumbing A, Otsuka K (2001b) Gender differences in land inheritance, schooling and lifetime income: evidence from the rural Philippines. J Dev Stud 37(4):23–48. https://doi.org/10.1080/00220380412331322031

Estudillo JP, Sawada Y, Otsuka K (2008) Poverty and income dynamics in Philippine village 1985–2004. Rev Dev Econ 12(4):877–890. https://doi.org/10.1111/j.1467-9361.2008.00458.x

Estudillo JP, Sawada Y., Otsuka K (2009) Income dynamics, schooling investment, and poverty reduction in Philippine villages, 1985–2004. In: K Otsuka, JP Estudillo, Y Sawada (eds) Rural poverty and income dynamics in Asia and Africa. New York: Routledge

Fuwa N (2014) Pro-girl bias in intra-household allocation in the rural Philippines. Rev Dev Econ 18(4):727–740. https://doi.org/10.1111/rode.12115

Geertz C (1963) Agricultural involution: The processes of ecological change in Indonesia. University of California Press, London. https://doi.org/10.1525/9780520341821

Goldin C (1995) The u-shaped female labor force function in economic development and economic history. In: P Schultz (ed) Investment in women's human capital. Chicago: University of Chicago Press

Hayami Y, Godo M (2005) Development economics: From the poverty to the wealth of nations. Oxford University Press, Oxford. https://doi.org/10.1093/0199272700.001.0001

Hayami Y, Kikuchi M (2000) A rice village saga: three decades of green revolution in the Philippines. McMillan Press, London. https://doi.org/10.1057/9780230599185

Heintz J (2010) Defining and measuring informal employment and the informal sector in the Philippines, Mongolia and Sri Lanka. United Nations Development Account Project: Interregional Cooperation on the Measurement of the Informal Sector and Informal Employment 2006–2009 Working Paper 3. UN Economic and Social Commission for Asia and the Pacific (ESCAP)

Hickey S, du Toit A (2007) Adverse incorporation, social exclusion and chronic poverty. Chronic Poverty Research Centre Working Paper 81. https://doi.org/10.2139/ssrn.1752967

Hulme D, Shepherd A (2003) Conceptualizing chronic poverty. World Dev 31(3):403–423. https://doi.org/10.1016/S0305-750X(02)00222-X

Illich I (2001) Tools for conviviality. New York: Marion Boyars (first edition in 1973)

International Labour Organization (ILO) (2016) Global wage report 2016/17: wage inequality in the workplace. Geneva: ILO

International Labour Organization (ILO) and Asian Development Bank (ADB) (2011) Women and labour markets in Asia: rebalancing for gender equality. Bangkok: ILO. http://hdl.handle.net/11540/977

Jha J, Bakshi S, Faria EM (2012) Understanding and challenging boys' disadvantage in secondary education in developing countries. Background paper prepared for the Education for All Global Monitoring Report 2012. Paris: UNESCO

Jocano FL (1998) Filipino social organization: traditional kinship and family organization. PUNLAD Research House, Manila

Kurosaki T, Ito S, Fuwa, N, Kubo K, Sawada Y (2006) Child labor and school enrollment in Rural India: whose education matters? Dev Econ 44(4):440–464. https://doi.org/10.1111/j.1746-1049.2006.00024.x

Laibson D (1997) Golden eggs and hyperbolic discounting. Quart J Econ 112(2):443–477. https://doi.org/10.1162/003355397555253

Medina B-G (2015) The Filipino family, 3rd edn. University of the Philippines Press, Manila

Nakanishi T (2008) Deepening communities. In: T Takahashi, S Yamakage (eds) Human security. Tokyo: University of Tokyo Press

Okabe M (2025) HRD implications of Filipino boys' underperformance in school in the context of rural poverty, family dynamics, and the school environment. Presented at the 11th Research Dissemination Forum, School of Labor and Industrial Relations, University of the Philippines Diliman, March 22.

O'Donoghue T, Rabin M (1999) Doing it now or later. Am Econ Rev 89(1):103–124. https://doi.org/10.1257/aer.89.1.103

O'Reilly J, Smith M, Deakin S, Burchell B (2015) Equal pay as a moving target: international perspectives on forty years of addressing the gender pay gap. Camb J Econ 39(2):299–317. https://doi.org/10.1093/cje/bev010

Pinzon MJL (2021) Defamiliarized family: the '*Anak ng OFWs*' emergent narratives on mediated communication and parent-child relationships. Plaridel 18(2):281–307. https://doi.org/10.52518/2021.18.2-04pnzon

Piocos CM, III (2019) Suffering that counts: the politics of sacrifice in Philippine labor migration. Humanities Diliman 16(2):26–48. https://journals.upd.edu.ph/index.php/humanitiesdiliman/article/view/7107

Rubery J, Grimshaw D (2011) Gender and the minimum wage. In: S Lee, D McCann (eds) Regulating for decent work. Advances in Labour Studies. London: Palgrave Macmillan. https://doi.org/10.1057/9780230307834_9

Sacerdote B (2011) Peer effects in education: how might they work, how big are they, and how much do we know thus far? In: EA Hanushek, S Machin, L Woessmann (eds) Handbook of the economics of education 3. Amsterdam: Elsevier, pp 249–277. https://doi.org/10.1016/B978-0-444-53429-3.00004-1

Sawada Y, Kubo K, Fuwa N, Ito S, Kurosaki T (2006) On the mother and child labor Nexus under credit constraints: findings from Rural India. Dev Eco 44(4):465–499. https://doi.org/10.1111/j.1746-1049.2006.00025.x

Serrano MR, Certeza RA (2014) Gender, unions and collective bargaining in the Philippines: issues and critical factors. In: C Scherrer (ed) Labor and globalization, vol 4. Munich: Rainer Hampp Verlag

Sobritchea CI (2007) Constructions of mothering: the experience of female Filipino overseas workers. In: TW Davasahayam, B Yeo (eds) Gendering Asia. Singapore: NUS Press, pp 173–194

Sudo K (1989) The structure in matrilineal societies (Bokei shakai no kozō). Tokyo: Kinokuniya Shoten Press (in Japanese)

Takahashi A (1972) The value system of the Philippines [Firipin no kachi taikei]. In: Y Hagiwara, A Takahashi (eds) *The value systems of the Southeast Asia* [*Tonan azia no kachi taikei*] Vol 4. Tokyo: Gendai Azia Shuppankai Press (in Japanese)

Torres A (2011) Analysis on why boys do poorly: Philippines case study. *mimeo*, UNGEI

United Nations Educational, Scientific and Cultural Organization (UNESCO) (2022) Leave no child behind: global report on boys' disengagement from education. Paris: UNESCO. https://doi.org/10.54675/BDLL3314

Wood G (2003) Staying secure, staying poor: the 'Faustian Bargain.' World Dev 31(3):455–471. https://doi.org/10.1016/S0305-750X(02)00213-9

Wood G (2015) Situating informal welfare within imperfect well-being regimes. J Int Comp Soc Pol 31(2):132–150. https://doi.org/10.1080/21699763.2015.1047786

World Economic Forum (WEF) (2021) Global gender gap report 2021. Genova: World Economic Forum

Yamauchi F, Tiongco M (2013) Why women are progressive in education? Gender disparities in human capital, labor markets, and family arrangement in the Philippines. Econ Educ Rev 32:196–206. https://doi.org/10.1016/j.econedurev.2012.09.003

Appendices

Appendix A: Socioeconomic Context and Household Livelihoods in Marinduque

A glimpse into a rural Filipino *tiangge*—an informal weekend marketplace where everyday life and local tradition meet

M. Okabe, *Economics of the Reversal in Gender Disparities in Education and Development*, Economics, Law, and Institutions in Asia Pacific,
https://doi.org/10.1007/978-981-96-9271-2

Women at work in a local handicraft workshop, surrounded by their wood-based creations. (Both scenes captured in Gasan.)

Appendix A and B provide supplementary information on Marinduque Province, from which the primary data for Chapters 4–6 were sourced. They provide essential insights into the region's geography, socioeconomic conditions, household livelihoods, and educational status. Compared to other regions in the Philippines, such as Central and Southern Luzon, Western Visayas (see Chapter 7), and parts of Mindanao (see Chapters 2, 3), Marinduque Province has been considerably less studied in development and area studies.[1] Accordingly, these appendices serve as a comprehensive report on Marinduque, a region that has been insufficiently examined in socioeconomic development studies. Appendix B will specifically focus on the educational conditions and out-of-school experiences of the sample children examined in Chapters 4–6.

The structure of this appendix is as follows. Section A.1 provides foundational information about Marinduque Province, explains the rationale behind its selection, and describes the preliminary fieldwork conducted in its villages. Section A.2 details the research methodology, including sampling strategies for municipalities, barangays, and households, and presents an overview of the questionnaire survey. Section A.3 analyzes household livelihoods based on descriptive statistics of the

[1] Noteworthy exceptions include the ecological and geographical research conducted by environmental scientist Arnold Salvacion (e.g., Salvacion 2017; Salvacion 2018; Salvacion and Magcale-Macandog 2015). With regard to the other provinces, among others, refer to existing studies such as Hayami and Kikuchi (2000) for a comprehensive overview of the rural economies in Southern Luzon; Fornier (1998), Fornier (1999), and Menz (1989) for insights into Western Visayas; and Bouis and Haddad (1990), Bouis et al. (1998), and Takayama et al. (2010) for information on Northern Mindanao.

sample data, covering occupations, employment status, educational attainment, co-residential arrangements, and income profiles. Section A.4 examines the role of parental education through quantile regression analysis, highlighting heterogeneous returns to education between the heads (lower returns at the middle–upper quantiles with a rebound at the top) and spouses (increasing returns toward higher quantiles). This finding may contribute to the reversed gender disparity in education discussed in this book; further formal studies are warranted. Finally, Sect. A.5 summarizes this appendix.

A.1 Marinduque Province and Sampled Villages

A.1.1 Marinduque Province in MIMAROPA Region

Marinduque Province is located in the MIMAROPA Region of the Philippines. The MIMAROPA Region was part of the Southern Tagalog Region until 2002, when it was divided into Regions IV-A (CALABARZON) and IV-B (MIMAROPA).[2] Due to this historical association, these regions are still sometimes referred to as Southern Tagalog or Southern Luzon today. The acronym MIMAROPA stands for Mindoro (comprising two provinces, Occidental Mindoro and Oriental Mindoro), Marinduque, Romblon, and Palawan. Although MIMAROPA and CALABARZON (Cavite, Laguna, Batangas, Rizal, and Quezon) were once a single region, MIMAROPA now lags behind CALABARZON economically. CALABARZON, situated near Metro Manila, has evolved into a suburban region that absorbs people and industrial complexes from the capital.[3] In contrast, MIMAROPA has not achieved similar levels of development.

In MIMAROPA, Palawan Province and Occidental Mindoro Province are classified in the 1st income class, with Palawan serving as a regional center. Marinduque Province ranks 4th in income class, following Romblon (3rd) and Oriental Mindoro (2nd). While Palawan is rich in natural resources, agriculture (particularly plantations), and the resort industry, and Mindoro is also abundant in agriculture (especially coconut and rice), Marinduque is less resource-rich.

Marinduque, an island province, includes Marinduque (Boac) Island and several small surrounding islands. It is the smallest province in the region, with a land area of approximately 96,000 hectares, compared to Romblon (around 136,000 hectares), Oriental Mindoro (around 436,000 hectares), Occidental Mindoro (around 588,000 hectares), and Palawan (around 1.49 million hectares). The geographic center of

[2] More precisely, the Southern Tagalog Region once comprised 11 provinces: five on the mainland of Luzon (now Region IV-A or CALABARZON), five island provinces (now Region IV-B or MIMAROPA), and Aurora Province (now part of Region III or Central Luzon Region).

[3] For instance, CALABARZON stands out for hosting industrial parks and attracting international firms through economic zones such as the Cavite Economic Zone. IT parks/zones and manufacturing economic zones are concentrated in this region (Dumayas 2018).

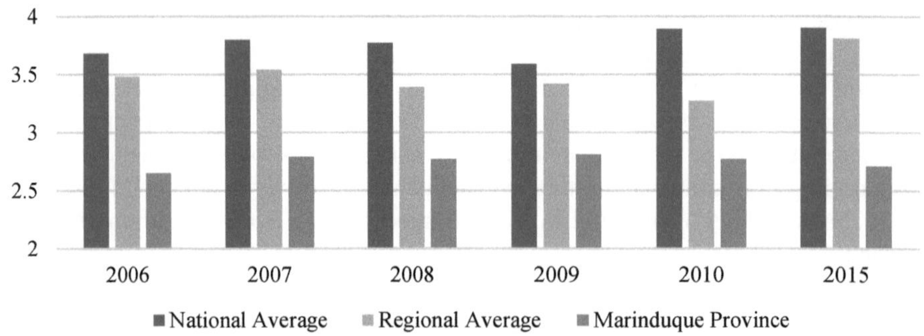

Fig. A.1 The *Palay* Yield-per-Hectare Productivity (t/ha). *Note* National average bar in 2010 is actually from 2013. *Source* 2006–2009 = Bureau of Agriculture Statistics and Regional Development Plan 2011–2016 National Economic and Development Authority; 2010–2015 = Selected Statistics on Agriculture 2018 Philippine Statistics Authority and Regional Development Plan 2017–2022 National Economic and Development Authority

Marinduque Island is Mount Malindig, the highest point in the province, which rises to an elevation of 1,157 m. The province's mountainous zones, which descend towards the island's edges, are covered by forests. Residential and agricultural areas are limited to lowlands near the coast. Due to its small land area, coastal agricultural land is susceptible to chloride damage from the sea, resulting in poor soil quality.

This is reflected in the province's low agricultural productivity. For example, Fig. A.1 shows that Marinduque's *palay* land productivity is below both the national and regional averages. Despite the province's economy being heavily reliant on primary sectors like agriculture and fishery, it struggles to improve agricultural productivity.[4] This contrasts sharply with Bukidnon Province, which is discussed in Chapters 2–3 and for which data from IFPRI were used.

Figure A.2 compares land productivity (t/ha) by crop between Marinduque and Bukidnon. Although both provinces are rural and poor, their agricultural productivity varies significantly. Bukidnon demonstrates much higher land productivity for rice, corn, coconut, and mangoes, whereas Marinduque lags significantly behind. Thus, Marinduque, as a case study, is viewed as having less agricultural prominence and contribution to the regional economy compared to Bukidnon, despite both representing rural poverty.[5]

---

[4] In my direct observations during repeated preliminary fieldwork with talks with local farmers, it appears that since the latter half of the previous century, the Green Revolution—originating from Luzon Island and subsequently spreading—has also reached Marinduque Province. Indeed, the introduction of improved rice varieties, following the pioneering IR8 variety from the Green Revolution, has progressed in the province as well. However, dramatic improvements in production levels akin to those observed in rice-growing villages in Central Luzon have not yet been evident.

[5] Note that Marinduque Province's geographical smallness does not affect the comparison with other provinces, as the analysis is based on per hectare productivity.

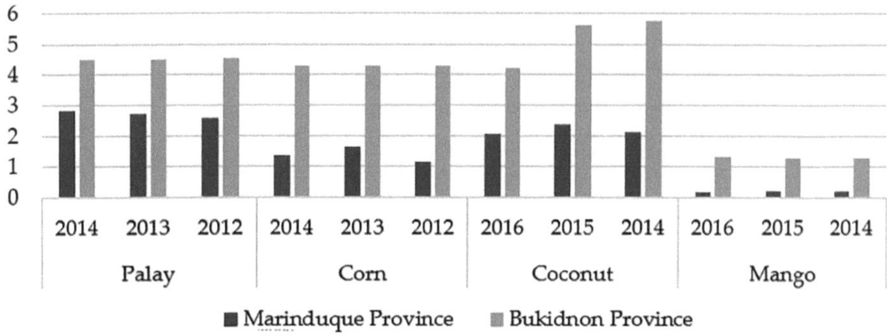

Fig. A.2 Two-province comparison: Land Productivity (MTN/ha), by Crop. *Source* Province Profiles, Philippine Statistics Authority

A.1.2 Choice of Marinduque as Research Site in Chapters 4–6

Marinduque was chosen as the research site for several reasons. It is a rural region where issues related to male schooling are prevalent. Nationally representative statistical indices and a preliminary survey have confirmed that the male-to-female enrollment ratio gap in education typically widens in poorer populations, both during and after secondary education (see Chapter 1). While this chapter does not aim merely to test whether males are underperforming, a key criterion for selecting the research site was the presence of a male-to-female enrollment gap. As illustrated in Chapter 1, it shows the relationship between wealth index deciles and the gender gaps in net enrollment ratios for secondary education in the Philippines. The data indicates that poorer households tend to have a larger gender gap, with fewer males attending school. This suggests that poverty is a significant factor affecting educational access between male and female children.

In a related finding, the most recent version of the national educational survey available at the time of our study preparation, the Functional Literacy, Education, and Mass Media Survey (FLEMMS) conducted by PSA (2016), reports that the gender gap in net enrollment is larger in remote rural regions outside Luzon Island compared to urban centers (including Metro Manila) and rural regions closer to Metro Manila (e.g., Central Luzon Region and CALABARZON). Chapter 1 illustrates this: According to the aforementioned PSA (2016), the MIMAROPA Region is one of the regions with the largest gaps in net enrollment ratios. For children aged 6–18 years (school ages for elementary to upper-secondary education),

Figure A.3 shows the relative numbers of non-attending male and female children by region. The MIMAROPA Region is notably highlighted in this figure. However, high or low relative male counts do not always correspond directly with regional enrollment situations. For example, while the relative male counts in the ARMM (now BARMM) in Fig. A.3 are similar to those in CALABARZON, the ARMM has the highest non-attendance rate in the country (16%), compared to about 12% in

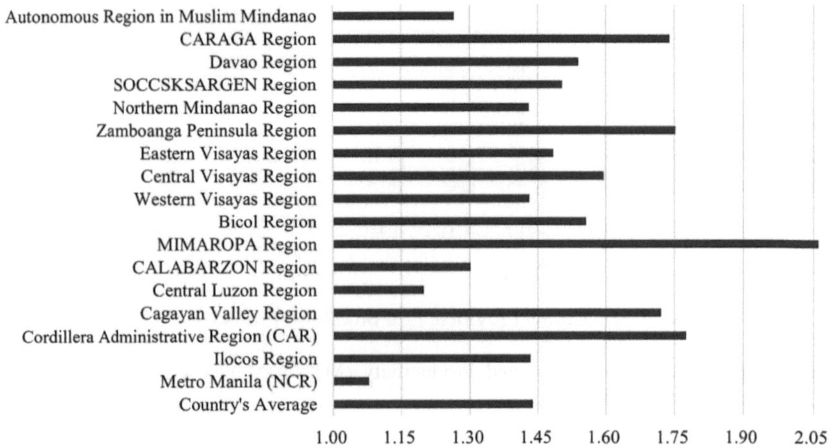

Fig. A.3 Relative numbers of non-attending males to one non-attending female, ages 6–18, by region. *Note* 1.00 means the same frequency of non-attending over males and females. If more (fewer) than 1.00, then it means the higher frequency of non-attending for males (females) than female (male) counterparts in the region. *Source* Author's calculations using PSA (2017)

other regions (see Fig. A.4). Other notable regions include the Zamboanga Peninsula (Region IX) and the Cordillera Administrative Region (CAR). In contrast, gender-equal access to education is relatively better achieved in Metro Manila, followed by the Central Luzon Region (Region III).

I explored the possibility of receiving local assistance by collaborating with members from the Philippine Rural Reconstruction Movement, an NGO based in Quezon City, Metro Manila. Subsequently, a local assistant was identified who worked as a *barangay kagawad* (village council member) in Marinduque and joined the study.

A.1.3 Preparatory Fieldwork to Determine the Research Site

In August 2017, I began preliminary fieldwork in the province, starting with a visit to the barangay of Masiga in the municipality of Gasan (circle D in Fig. A.5). This pilot phase aimed to explore possibilities for research collaboration with local stakeholders. During this phase, no structured questionnaires were used. Instead, I focused on learning about and observing local livelihoods, school environments, and the local economy through unstructured open interviews with selected children and their parents. I also enjoyed simply engaging in everyday conversations, such as *kwentuhan* (storytelling, chatting, and talking) and *tsismis* (rumors and gossips), with local people, which provided a more informal and nuanced understanding of the community compared to formal observation methods.

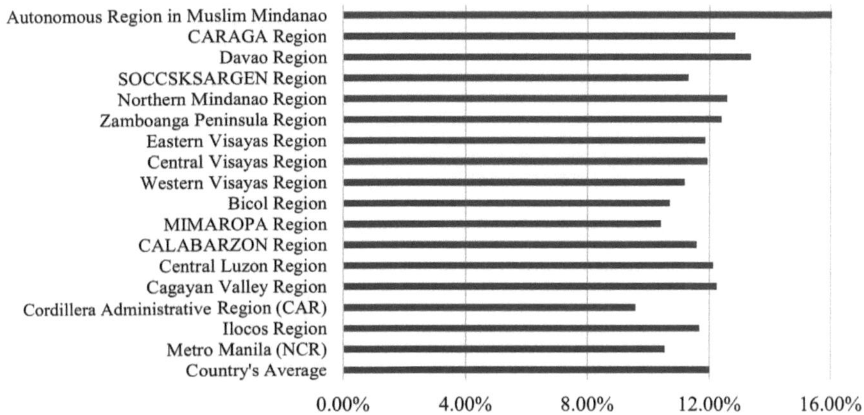

Fig. A.4 Non-attending rates of children at school, ages 6–18, by region. *Note* Non-attending rates = 100% – (Attending Children/Total Children) %. *Source* Author's calculations using PSA (2017)

Simultaneously, I paid courtesy calls to various local government units (LGUs), including *barangay* and mayoral offices, as well as provincial and regional offices of national government departments, and local colleges. These activities continued intermittently until December 2017, alongside other related tasks.

Preliminary interviews and observations revealed that some local people within the LGUs were keenly aware of the issue of "boys' underperformance in education." At times, I inadvertently highlighted this issue to them. Ultimately, my goal was to gauge how the issue of boys' educational underperformance was perceived or problematized by the local population to determine whether the province would be suitable for the research study.

A.2 Household Survey Design

Our household survey was meticulously designed to support the research presented in Chapters 4–6, differing from other datasets whose methodologies, descriptions, and regional overviews are documented in existing literature. Consequently, this section commences with a detailed account of the data collection process, including methodological considerations and preliminary observations.

A.2.1 Sampling Strategy: Stratified Random Sampling

The survey employed a stratified random sampling approach. The entire Province of Marinduque was treated as the target population for statistical analysis. The aim of utilizing stratified random sampling was to ensure a representative sample within

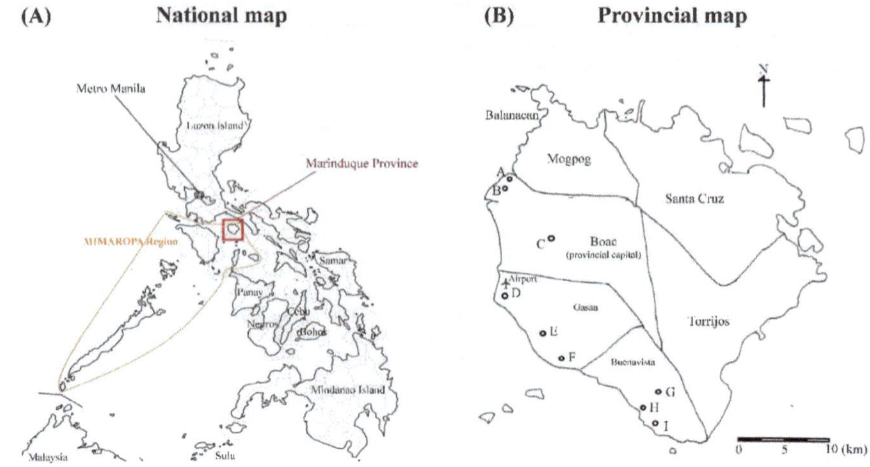

Fig. A.5 Location of Marinduque Province on the National Map. *Notes* Circles A–I in (b) represent the nine sampled *barangays*. *Source* Author's creation

the constraints of budgetary and human resource limitations. The sampling process involved three sequential stages: (1) selection of municipalities, (2) sampling of barangays within the selected municipalities, and (3) sampling of households within the sampled barangays.

In alignment with our resource and budget constraints, as well as econometric feasibility, we initially determined a sample size of 300 children. Two children (siblings) per household were selected from 150 households. The selection criteria aimed to encompass children primarily aged 12 to 18 years, thereby focusing on those at the secondary education level. In instances where fewer than two eligible children were available in some households, the age range was adjusted to include siblings at elementary or tertiary levels. Consequently, the sample predominantly consists of children aged 12 to 18 years, with some younger and older children included.[6]

A.2.2 Choice of Municipalities

During preliminary fieldwork, several notable characteristics of the province were observed:

- The province's economy is predominantly based on primary industries, specifically agriculture and fisheries.

[6] As it transpired, this relaxation resulted in better coverage as we could have the sample with the variation of transitions from elementary to secondary and secondary to tertiary levels.

- The manufacturing sector is relatively small, consisting mainly of handcraft industries and retail services, with varying prevalence across different areas.
- There is considerable heterogeneity in commercial activities and accessibility to educational institutions (particularly secondary schools), influenced by proximity to *poblacion*, that is, municipal centers.[7]
- Local residents inhabit not only the low-lying areas adjacent to the island's contours but also more remote and somewhat isolated mountainous regions. Unlike neighboring islands, few indigenous populations have been reported in Marinduque Province.
- The level of infrastructure development varies significantly across the province.
- There is a lack of awareness among residents of the lowlands regarding the livelihoods of those living in remote mountainous areas.

These observations were gathered during visits to farms, hog-raising operations, fishing areas, women's NGOs, local government offices, and provincial offices of national government agencies, such as the Department of Education (DepEd), the Department of Agrarian Reform, and the Department of Social Welfare and Development (DSWD), among others. Barangay Masiga, Municipality Gasan, appeared to be a representative and average area encompassing these variations.

We also visited Marinduque State College (MSC), a local state institution, and consulted with a faculty member from the School of Liberal Arts regarding the geographic scope necessary for our household survey. Their recommendations indicated that a sample population should reflect diversity beyond a single barangay survey. They suggested focusing on the municipality of Gasan, which includes Barangay Masiga. Municipality Gasan is classified as a third-class municipality but also encompasses areas of both higher and lower economic status. This recommendation informed the decision to conduct a sample survey.

Geographically and administratively, the province is divided into six municipalities: two higher-income municipalities (Boac and Santa Cruz) and two lower-income municipalities (Buenavista and Torrijos), with two intermediate municipalities (Gasan and Mogpog) (see Fig. A.5). According to LGU classifications, these municipalities can be categorized into three income classes. The MSC faculty advised that it would be advantageous to ensure representation across these income classes. Consequently, Boac, Gasan, and Buenavista were selected as sample municipalities to reflect the provincial variations.

A.2.3 Sampling Barangays

Subsequently, the selection of sample barangays was undertaken. Similar to the process for municipalities, it was essential to account for variations within each municipality. We obtained barangay lists from municipal offices, accompanied by

[7] The term *poblacion*, derived from Spanish, refers to the town center.

guidance from local administrators. These lists were categorized into high-, medium-, and low-income groups for each municipality. Each barangay was assigned a unique identifier, and three barangays were randomly selected from each income group per municipality. This approach resulted in a sample of nine barangays (three barangays from each of the three municipalities).

The locations of the nine sampled barangays are depicted in Fig. A.5 (points A–I).[8] Initially, barangays in the municipality of Boac were randomly selected (points A–C). As the provincial capital, Boac has barangays A and B situated near the town center. Barangay A is more affluent than Barangay B, whereas Barangay C is less affluent and situated in the hilly to mountainous highlands, rendering it geographically remote. Access to Barangay C is limited to jeepneys and tricycles, and once there, households are dispersed with no public transportation available. Residents have reported that traveling uphill and downhill is physically and mentally taxing, particularly for children commuting to school.

Next, in the municipality of Gasan, barangays D–F were randomly selected. Barangay D is Masiga, which also served as the base of our operations. Located near Marinduque Airport[9] and the coast, Masiga predominantly features families engaged in micro to small-scale businesses, agriculture, or fisheries. Commercial establishments such as grocery stores, convenience stores, and restaurants are scarce, necessitating trips to the municipality's *poblacion* for such services, typically a 10–20-min tricycle ride. Despite its intermediate income classification, Masiga is relatively underserved in terms of commercial infrastructure. Barangay E, situated within the *poblacion*, is in proximity to the municipal hall, commercial areas with ATM facilities, restaurants, and grocery stores, indicating a higher income level. Conversely, Barangay F, classified as lower income, lies nearby the boundary between the municipalities Gasan and Buenavista. Residents of Barangay F have expressed concerns regarding inadequate infrastructure development, including poor internet access compared to neighboring barangays.

Finally, barangays G–I were randomly sampled from Buenavista. Barangay G, classified as a lower-income area, is situated in a mountainous zone. The geographic challenges encountered by its residents were reported to be similar to those previously

[8] For ethical reasons, the precise names and locations of barangays have been anonymized and are represented by alphabetic codes to ensure confidentiality. While the anonymity of barangays, schools, and households is preserved, efforts have been made to provide the most detailed descriptions possible. It is important to note that while maintaining anonymity is a key consideration, it does not detract from the core discussions of the studies.

[9] At the time of the fieldwork, Air Juan Aviation operated regular commercial seaplane flights connecting the island with Manila Bay; however, the service was suspended during the COVID-19 pandemic and has not resumed since. Beginning in April 2019, Cebgo, a subsidiary of Cebu Pacific, also began operating regular flights between the island and Ninoy Aquino International Airport (Terminal 4), but this service has likewise been discontinued. As of 2025, at the time of writing, there are no scheduled flights to Marinduque Airport. Access is typically by ferry between Lucena (Quezon Province) and Mogpog (Marinduque), often with through buses (e.g., Jac Liner) that roll onto the RoRo ferries. The total travel time between Marinduque and Metro Manila, for example, is roughly 7–10 hours one way, depending on traffic, ferry queues, and weather (in bad weather, I have even experienced a 12-hour trip from Gasan, Marinduque, to Quezon City, Metro Manila).

described by residents of barangay C in Boac. Barangay H is located within the *poblacion* of *Buenavista*, placing it in the municipality's central area, which presents similar issues to those observed in barangay E in *Gasan*. Barangay I, classified as an intermediate-income area within *Buenavista*, is characterized by abundant rivers and groves.

Overall, the livelihoods of the *Marinduqueño* people[10] predominantly rely on primary industries such as agriculture (particularly paddy rice and coconut cultivation), horticulture (vegetable farming), and fisheries. Additionally, craftworks and micro/small enterprises, such as *sari-sari* stores and the sale of homemade foods, play a significant role. The province's economy stands out regionally and nationally for its high rate of self-employment. As shown in Table A.1, the self-employment rate in Marinduque Province is 45.80%, compared to 37.42% in the MIMAROPA Region and 32.94% nationally for rural areas.

However, this high self-employment rate comes at the expense of a lower rate of private establishments, which stands at 26.72% in Marinduque compared to 34.24% regionally and 38.11% nationally for rural areas. This suggests that the private sector

Table A.1 Employment types of Marinduque province in regional and national contexts (%, 2015)

Employment types	National		Region	Province
	Urban	Rural		
Private household	6.66	4.38	4.43	4.58
Private establishment	53.30	38.11	34.24	26.72
Governmental corporation	9.38	8.62	9.62	12.21
Self-employed	23.08	32.94	37.42	45.80
Employer	2.64	4.73	4.31	1.53
Family-owned Business (with pay)	0.43	0.29	0.46	0.00
Family-owned Business (without pay)	4.51	10.94	9.53	9.16
Number of observations (persons)	28,814	49,734	2,392	262

Note Region = MIMAROPA region (Region IV-B); Province = Marinduque
Source PSA (2017)[11]

[10] The adjective for Marinduque is "*Marinduqueño*" in Filipino (an inflected form originally derived from Spanish).

[11] While PSA (2017), the nationally representative Labor Force Survey (LFS), covers all municipalities in Marinduque Province, its sampling framework differs from that of our study. Specifically, within the same three municipalities, the only barangay shared between our sample and the LFS is Buliasnin. The LFS coverage includes: in Boac—Agumaymayan, Balimbingo, Balogo, Buliasnin, Mataas na Bayan (*poblacion*), and Tampus (*poblacion*); in Buenavista—Daykitin; and in Gasan—Bangbang and Tapuyan. In contrast, our sample covers: in Boac—Poras, Buliasnin, and Mogpog; in Buenavista—Barangay III (*poblacion*), Libas, and Mogpog; and in Gasan—Barangay I (*poblacion*), Masiga, and Bacongbacong.

in the province remains underdeveloped. Consequently, the public sector absorbs a larger share of employment compared to regional and national rural averages.[12]

A.2.4 Household Sampling

Following the sampling of barangays, the next step was to sample households. The process began with the creation of a master list based on residential household information from the Community-Based Monitoring System (CBMS) 2014, obtained from each barangay. For a predetermined sample size of 150 households, we computed weights to determine the relative sizes of each barangay according to the population data provided by the CBMS. These weights were then used to allocate the appropriate number of households for sampling in each barangay. Due to the imprecision in aliquot allocations, the final total household sample size was 154. For confidentiality reasons concerning both barangays and households, specific population figures are not disclosed. Instead, at the municipal level, the 154 households were distributed as follows: 39 households across three barangays in Boac; 58 households across three barangays in Gasan; and 57 households across three barangays in Buenavista.

Unique identifiers were assigned to all households on the master list. Using statistical software, random numbers corresponding to the calculated sample sizes for each barangay were generated, resulting in the selection of 154 households. To account for potential absences or refusals, a secondary set of random numbers was generated, excluding those from the initial sampling list. This process provided a list of substitute households to address any issues with non-response. The visitation protocols were established in consultation with local counterparts. Ultimately, fewer cases of absence or refusal were encountered than anticipated, allowing the sample of 154 households to be predominantly drawn from the initial random sampling list.

A.2.5 Questionnaire Survey Process

The design of the questionnaire was informed by insights gained from the preparatory fieldwork I conducted. The questionnaire was structured into three sections: (a) household information, (b) basic information of the sampled children, and (c) a time-use allocation survey for the sampled children over a period of seven days. All questions and response options were prepared in Tagalog (Filipino), the local language,

[12] In this context, Marinduque Province exhibits similarities to Bukidnon Province (as discussed in Chapters 2 and 3) and potentially to Antique Province (as detailed in Chapter 7) regarding the underdevelopment of the private sector within the provincial economy and the compensatory role of the public sector.

given that a significant portion of the sample comprised young children and out-of-school youths who are less comfortable communicating in English. Interviewees were thus permitted to respond in *Tagalog*.

The entire questionnaire underwent validation by a faculty member of MSC. After incorporating minor revisions based on feedback, pilot testing was conducted with a subset of children from Barangay Masiga between December 2017 and early January 2018, spanning the end-of-year holidays. Insights from this pilot phase were utilized to refine both content and language in the final version.

The main body of fieldwork, including home visitations and interviews using the finalized questionnaire, was conducted from January to March 2018. All households across the nine sampled barangays in the three municipalities were visited. I directly instructed local assistants on the research objectives, methodology, potential challenges, and possible solutions. During the fieldwork, daily communication was maintained via Facebook Messenger to facilitate real-time discussions and collaboratively address both minor and major issues. The questionnaire included both self-administered and interviewer-administered components. Detailed descriptions of each section are provided in the respective main chapters of this book. The preparatory work and established relationships resulted in zero refusals. Since the main phase of the research, I continued to visit the research sites to gather supplementary information and to verify any inconsistencies with the initial data, during my periodic stays in the Philippines up to January 2020.

A.3 Households' Livelihood Outlines

A.3.1 Occupations and Working Status

Among the 154 households surveyed, 143 household heads (92.86%) reported being employed within the past six months, while 11 heads (7.14%) were not engaged in work. The spouses of 71 households (48.97%) reported employment within the same period, whereas 74 spouses (51.03%) were not employed. The distribution of workers across various sectors is detailed and visualized in Tables A.2, A.3, Figs. A.6, and A.7. The largest proportion of workers is employed in the service sector (tertiary sector) (29.86%), followed by the agricultural (22.2%), fishery (15.28%), industrial manufacturing (14.58%), retail (9.03%), and public (9.03%) sectors.

Common occupations within the service sector include tricycle drivers, waste collectors, massage therapists, caretakers, cleaners, security personnel, and truck drivers. Retail employment generally involves operating *sari-sari* stores (small-scale shops rooted in local communities), as well as businesses involving small pushcarts or *tindahan* (a Filipino term derived from the Spanish word *tienda*). The free-form responses from the semi-structured sections of the questionnaire reveal a range of retail activities. These range from individual or family-run enterprises selling daily snacks (*merienda*), such as *mani* (roasted peanuts) and *balut/balot* (a traditional

Table A.2 Cross-tabulation of employment status and sector classifications for household heads

Working status, head	Agriculture	Fishery	Manufacturing	Service	Retails	Public	Total
Land-owning farmer	8						8
Contract farmers	7						7
Agricultural worker	13						13
Self-employee	1	21	1	25	9	1	58
Short-term contract worker			11	12	1	3	27
Permanent contract worker	3	1	8	5	2	8	27
Proprietor, business					1	1	2
Managerial position			1	2		1	4
Total	32	22	21	43	13	13	144

Source Author's calculations using the primary data

Table A.3 Cross-tabulation of employment status and sector classifications for household spouses

Working status, spouses	Agriculture	Fishery	Manufacturing	Service	Retails	Public	Total
Land-owning farmer	1						1
Contract farmers							0
Agricultural worker							0
Self-employee	1	2		19	28		50
Short-term contract worker				4			4
Permanent contract worker		1	1	4		10	16
Proprietor, business							0
Managerial position						1	1
Total	2	3	1	27	28	11	72

Source Author's calculations using the primary data

Filipino delicacy consisting of a boiled developing bird embryo, usually a duck), to establishments with shop spaces or permissions to trade in public venues such as schools and markets. Male heads of households are more likely to be employed by shop owners, while their spouses are typically engaged in self-employment activities, including the sale of cooked snacks and street foods, fermented products (*bagoong*), local confectioneries, and textiles (pillows, sheets, bed linens, and handkerchiefs).

Agricultural and fishery work (primary sector) are also predominant industries where many household heads are employed. Among agricultural households,

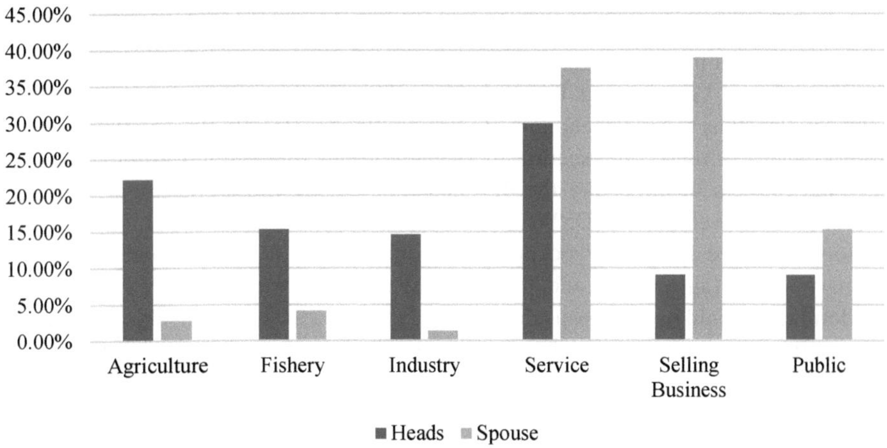

Fig. A.6 Percentages of occupational distribution by industry category for household heads and spouses. *Source* Author's calculations using the primary data

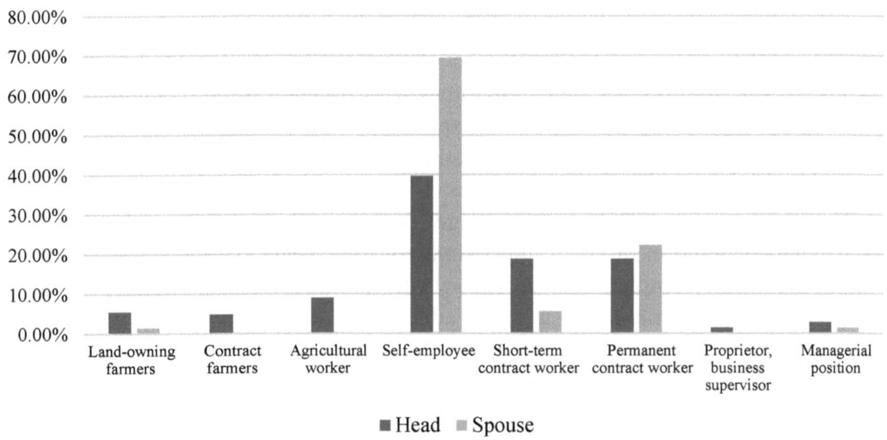

Fig. A.7 Percentages of employment status by household head and spouse. *Source* Author's calculations using the primary data

excluding those primarily engaged in staple crop cultivation (e.g., *palay* or paddy rice farmers), six household heads are involved in horticulture, including the cultivation of vegetables, fruits, and flowers (three households as land-owning farmers and three as agricultural wage laborers). Additionally, three household heads are engaged in animal husbandry, specifically hog raising (one head is self-employed, and three are permanent contract workers). Fishermen are also commonly found in this island province. In contrast, fewer individuals are involved in the manufacturing or industrial (secondary) sector, reflecting the historical trajectory of industrial development in the Philippine economy, particularly in its rural areas.

Lastly, some individuals work in the public sector, with typical occupations including schoolteachers (a profession predominantly occupied by females) and utility workers employed by educational institutions, barangay halls, and other public facilities. Local Government Units (LGUs) also offer employment opportunities, with roles such as barangay captains, *kagawad* (council members), secretaries, treasurers, health workers, civil security personnel (police officers and firefighters), and regional officers in units like the 4Ps headquarters by the Department of Social Welfare and Development (DSWD). Notably, jobs in the service, public, and retail sectors are more frequently occupied by female spouses, while positions in the primary sector (agriculture and fishery) and manufacturing/industrial sectors are predominantly held by male household heads. This indicates a discernible "gendered" pattern in sectoral occupations between men and women.

A.3.2 Educational Attainment by Heads and Spouses

As depicted in Fig. A.8, the majority of both household heads (29.5%) and their spouses (32.1%) completed secondary education (referred to as high school at the time). This is followed by those with elementary education (heads, 16.1%; spouses, 17.6%), individuals who attended some secondary education without graduating (heads, 16.1%; spouses, 15.3%), individuals who attended some elementary education without graduating (heads, 11.4%; spouses, 11.5%), individuals who attended some tertiary education without graduating (heads, 15.4%; spouses, 8.4%), and college graduates (heads, 10.1%; spouses, 14.5%).

These patterns reveal that, on average, both household heads and spouses of the studied generation attained approximately nine years of education, which is slightly below the completion of secondary education. However, a higher proportion of spouses reached graduation at every educational level—elementary, secondary, and tertiary—compared to household heads, who more commonly attained some education without completing graduation at these levels.

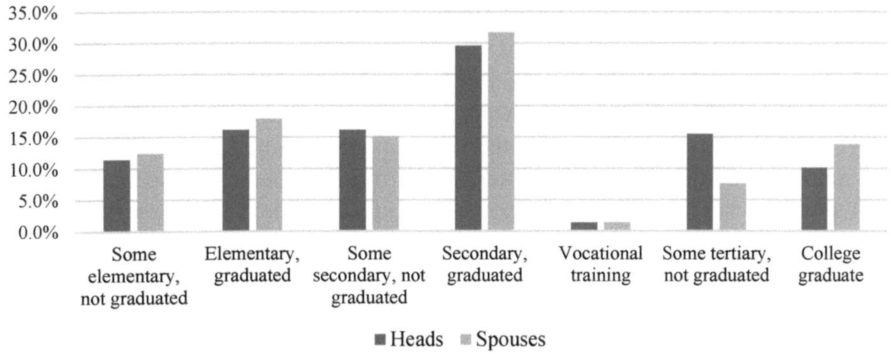

Fig. A.8 Educational attainment by household head and spouse. *Source* Author's calculations using the primary data

A.3.3 Co-residential Status

Table A.4 illustrates the co-residential status of household heads and spouses with other family members. The majority of household heads (85.71%) and spouses (91.03%) reside with their families. Thirteen household heads live elsewhere (8.44%) or abroad as Overseas Filipino Workers (OFWs) (3.90%), while nine spouses live in another location (6.21%) and four spouses reside abroad as OFWs (2.76%). Additionally, three household heads have passed away (1.95%), complicating the relationship status of their surviving spouses (widows or widowers).[13]

Table A.4 Co-residential status of household heads and spouses

Status	Heads		Spouses	
	No	%	No	%
Lives together with family	132	85.71%	132	91.03%
Lives in another place : (Jailed)	13 (2)	8.44%	9 (1)	6.21%
OFWs in a foreign country	6	3.90%	4	2.76%
S/he died	3	1.95%	0	0.00%
Total	154	100.00%	145	100.00%

Source Author's calculations using the primary data

[13] In instances where widows have assumed the role of household head, we classify them as female heads. However, in three cases, the widows did not consider themselves as the new household heads. There are two approaches to coding these cases: (i) automatically designate the widow as new head upon the death of the original head, or (ii) respect the widow's self-identification regarding her role. Because these widows did not identify themselves as the current head, even when asked directly, we adopt approach (ii).

Among the six OFW heads, two are reported to be in Abu Dhabi, one in Riyadh, one in the United States, and two are identified as commercial seafarers. The exact locations of the two seafarers could not be specified as their ships are in transit. Domestically, the remaining three heads are located in Laguna Province, Quezon Province, and Metro Manila, while the locations of the others remain unknown or unidentified. Additionally, two heads are absent from their homes due to incarceration related to drug offenses, with one spouse also jailed for the same reason. The four OFW spouses are reported to be residing in Hong Kong, Australia, and Saudi Arabia (Riyadh).

Table A.5 presents the numbers and percentages of total household members who reside in other locations or are OFWs. In over 62% of households, no members were reported to be living elsewhere, and in over 92% of households, no OFWs were identified. Conversely, in over 37% of households, at least one member lives in another location, and in approximately 7% of households, at least one member is an OFW.

Typically, the family members residing in other cities or working abroad are children who have become independent, pursuing new livelihoods after completing their education and/or getting married. Some of these members are reported to remit funds to family members remaining in Marinduque. Overall, the engagement with OFWs on this sample is less prevalent compared to the national average of 10%.

A.4 Indirect Analysis of Changes in Educational Attainment Over the Past Four Decades

Although our sample data is cross-sectional, it provides an indirect perspective on changes in educational attainment over the past four decades for adults (parents). Table A.6 breaks down the average years of education for fathers and mothers by age cohorts (30s, 40s, 50s, and 60s plus). While this method is not perfectly precise, it

Table A.5 Number of households with members residing in other cities or Overseas Filipino Workers (OFWs)

Numbers	Living in Other Cities		OFW	
	No. of HHs	%	No. of HHs	%
None	96	62.34%	142	92.21%
1 person	40	37.66%	12	7.79%
2 persons	13		0	
3 persons	1		0	
4 persons	4		0	
Total	154	100%	154	100%

Source Author's calculations using the primary data

Table A.6 Average years of educational attainment of sample adults over the past four decades

Age	Males	Females	Average	Dif (Mother–Father)
30s	9.11	9.50	9.31	0.39
40s	8.84	9.22	9.03	0.38
50s	8.36	8.76	8.56	0.40
60s	8.56	9.10	8.83	0.54

Source Author's calculations using the primary data

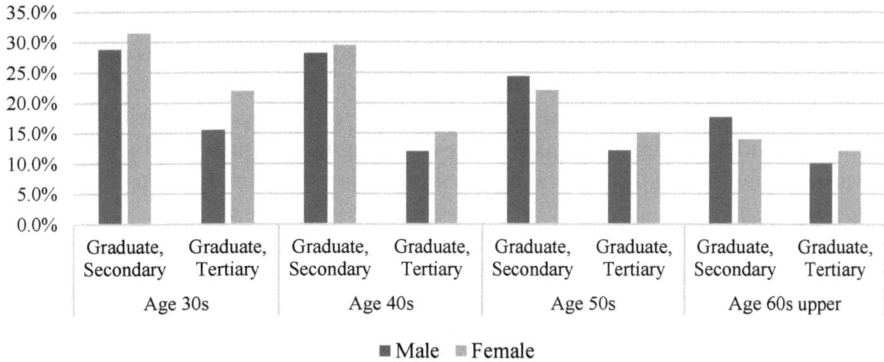

Fig. A.9 Educational attainment of adults over the past four decades in national data (secondary and tertiary graduates). *Source* Author's calculations using PSA (2017)

offers insights into educational trends since fathers and mothers were once students themselves.

The analysis of these age groups into four decade-long categories reveals that women have consistently achieved higher educational attainment compared to men over these decades. Notably, the disparity between women and men has narrowed over time, coinciding with an overall increase in average years of schooling. These trends are also reflected in nationally representative data. Figure A.9, based on PSA (2017), illustrates the percentages of male and female secondary and tertiary-level graduates across the population. Since "years of education" are not available in PSA (2017), we compare the final educational attainments at the secondary and tertiary levels.

A.4.1 Income and Education in the Parental Generation: A Quantile Regression Approach

As current children's incomes or wages are not yet available, we examine the returns to schooling in their parental generation. To understand the relationship between education and income, Mincerian equations are estimated for household heads and spouses.[14] Prior to conducting the regressions, we first perform a visual assessment. Figure A.10 illustrates the distributions of logarithmic mean incomes (in ₱, monthly) for household male heads (husbands) and spouses (wives) across different educational attainment levels.

To analyze the relationship between education and income more comprehensively, we employ quantile regression. Unlike OLS regression, which focuses on the mean of the dependent variable, quantile regression allows us to examine how the effect of education on income varies across different points in the income distribution. This method provides a more nuanced view by assessing how returns to education differ at various quantiles of the income distribution, rather than just focusing on average outcomes.

In Fig. A.10, average log incomes are plotted by educational attainment for household heads and their spouses. While the figure does not distinguish spouses by labor force participation, it suggests that income increases with higher levels of education, particularly for those who completed college. In general, household male heads earn more than their spouses on average. These patterns highlight that completing tertiary education is associated with greater income potential among sample adults in Marinduque Province.

A.4.2 Quantile Regression: Models and Results

Subsequently, we construct a quantile regression model to confirm it further statistically[15]:

$$\ln W_{j,\tau}^{R} = \beta_{0\tau}^{R} + \beta_{1\tau}^{R} S_{j}^{R} + \beta_{2\tau}^{R} A_{j}^{R} + \beta_{3\tau}^{R} \left(A_{j}^{R}\right)^{2} + \beta_{4\tau}^{R} F_{j}^{R} + e_{j,\tau}^{R}.$$

In this equation, at each τ% income quantile, the dependent variable is the logarithm of income W earned by the household head or spouse (denoted as $R =$ {Head, Spouse} in household j). The independent variables include educational

[14] This study employs a simplified variation of the Mincerian (log-wage) equation, which may not guarantee causality because of potential endogeneity (e.g., omitted variable bias). Accordingly, the coefficient(s) on schooling should be interpreted as associations rather than causal effects.

[15] The econometric efficiency of wage equation estimates would be enhanced by using nationally representative microdata, such as the LFS and the Annual Poverty Indicators Survey (APIS). However, since 2003, public-use microdata with person-level detail have not been released, limiting feasibility (Cabgegin 2013: 154).

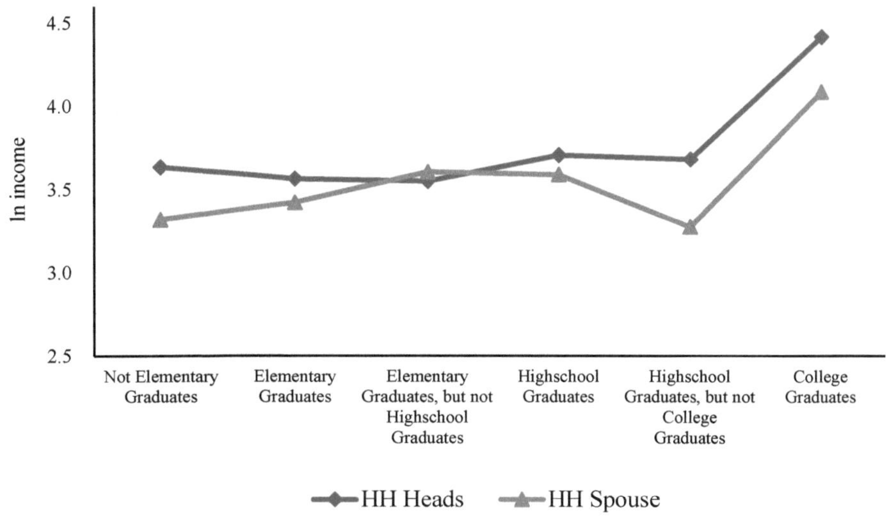

Fig. A.10 Mean values of logarithm income by household head and spouse, by their educational levels attained. *Source* Author's calculations using the primary data

attainment (S), measured by years of completed education, age (A), age squared (A^2) as proxies for experience, and a female dummy variable (F).

First, OLS estimators are reported in the right-hand columns of Table A.7 for household heads and Table A.8 for spouses. Table A.7 indicates that an additional year of schooling results in approximately a 14% increase in the income of household heads (OLS). Table A.8 shows a similar effect for spouses, with an estimated 13% increase in income per additional year of schooling (OLS).

Next, we analyze the results of the quantile regressions, which reveal differences between heads and spouses. The quantile regression estimates indicate that the return on education for household heads is diminishing toward higher quantiles of (conditional) income distribution; it is broadly similar across quantiles (≈0.11–0.12) after the decrease from its highest estimate at $\tau = 90\%$ (≈0.14). A cross-quantile equality test indicates a statistically significant difference (F-statistic 6.56).

In contrast, a qualitatively different pattern emerges in the quantile regression estimators for the spouses of household heads. Table A.8 demonstrates that the return on education for spouses starts lower at lower income levels (beginning from $\tau = 10\%$). As the income of spouses increases (i.e., at higher τ), the return on education rises from 7 to 16%. This pattern is statistically significant at the 10% level, with an F-statistic of 2.90. These results suggest larger estimated returns to schooling for the spouses at higher quantiles of the income distribution. When the spouses are at lower quantiles, their educational attainment is less strongly associated with earnings; however, toward higher quantiles, the association becomes more pronounced. In other words, education is an important correlate of higher earnings among spouses, particularly toward the upper quantiles.

Table A.7 Mincer equation estimation, quantile regression for household heads ($N = 154$)

Variables	Log income					OLS
	$\tau = 10\%$	$\tau = 30\%$	$\tau = 50\%$	$\tau = 70\%$	$\tau = 90\%$	
Female (=1)	−0.01	−0.04	−0.03	0.00	0.01*	−0.04
	[0.16]	[0.03]	[0.03]	[0.01]	[0.00]	[0.04]
Age	−0.02**	−0.02**	−0.01**	0.00	0.00	−0.02**
	[0.01]	[0.01]	[0.00]	[0.00]	[0.00]	[0.01]
Age square	0.01**	0.01**	0.01**	0.000	0.000	0.01**
	[0.00]	[0.00]	[0.00]	[0.00]	[0.00]	[0.00]
Education Attainment	0.14***	0.11***	0.12***	0.12***	0.11***	0.14***
	[0.01]	[0.00]	[0.00]	[0.01]	[0.00]	[0.00]
Constant	1.20***	1.59***	1.36***	1.11***	1.19***	1.46***
	[0.29]	[0.22]	[0.15]	[0.06]	[0.00]	[0.27]
Pseudo R squared	0.69	0.74	0.77	0.81	0.84	0.89¶

***$p < 0.01$; **$p < 0.05$; *$p < 0.10$
¶Adjusted R squared
Note Numbers in brackets are the bootstrapped standard errors with 50 iterations
Source Author's calculations using the primary data

Table A.8 Mincer equation estimation, quantile regression for household spouses ($N = 148$)

Variables	Log income					OLS
	$\tau = 10\%$	$\tau = 30\%$	$\tau = 50\%$	$\tau = 70\%$	$\tau = 90\%$	
Age	−0.13	0.07	−0.04	0.05	0.17	0.05
	[0.18]	[0.13]	[0.10]	[0.11]	[0.11]	[0.08]
Age square	0.00	0.00	0.00	−0.01	−0.01*	−0.01
	[0.00]	[0.00]	[0.00]	[0.00]	[0.00]	[0.00]
Education Attainment	0.07	0.10**	0.12***	0.15***	0.16***	0.13***
	[0.05]	[0.04]	[0.03]	[0.02]	[0.03]	[0.02]
Constant	8.92**	4.16	7.85***	5.94**	3.50	5.35***
	[4.41]	[3.52]	[2.45]	[2.94]	[2.91]	[2.03]
Pseudo R squared	0.05	0.02	0.08	0.16	0.26	0.14¶

***$p < 0.01$; **$p < 0.05$; *$p < 0.10$
¶ Adjusted R squared
Notes Female dummy is omitted because all the spouses in this estimation are female. Numbers in brackets are the bootstrapped standard errors with 50 iterations
Source Author's calculations using the primary data

Conversely, the returns to education for male household heads are lower at the middle–upper quantiles of the conditional wage distribution, with a rebound at the top quantile; the pattern is therefore not strictly monotonic. For the household heads, education is more strongly associated with earnings at the lower quantiles of income distribution. This contrasting difference reflects heterogeneity in the marginal returns to schooling between them.

The increasing returns for female spouses may be influenced by their labor force participation. Higher-educated female spouses might benefit from their education while also managing motherhood. In contrast, those with lower educational attainment may struggle to find similar opportunities, leading to income disparities between working and non-working spouses. Consequently, the pattern of increasing returns to education for female spouses may encourage their daughters to pursue higher educational attainment more than their male counterparts.

A.5 Summary

Appendix A has outlined the regional characteristics that influenced the selection of the research site, provided information on sample households from socioeconomic and educational perspectives, and presented descriptive and econometric analyses related to these issues. Marinduque Province, situated in the MIMAROPA Region, is a typically rural area of the Philippines and demonstrates a recognizable pattern in which males face greater educational disadvantages compared to females. Economically, the province relies heavily on agriculture and fisheries. However, compared to Bukidnon Province, as discussed in Chapters 2 and 3, Marinduque is considerably less productive agriculturally. Furthermore, as an island province, its geographic isolation presents additional challenges that contribute to its economic disadvantages relative to other regions.

Household-level data further highlight the constraints faced by families in Marinduque. A gendered division of labor is evident: male household heads are more likely to work in agriculture and fishing, while female spouses are more commonly employed in the service, retail, and public sectors. The province is characterized by a high rate of self-employment and a relatively underdeveloped private sector. Educational attainment across generations reveals a consistent advantage among women over men, particularly in terms of completing formal education at all levels. Approximately 4 in 10 households (or roughly 38%) have at least one family member living in another city or province, while only about 8% of households report having an Overseas Filipino Worker (OFW)—a figure slightly below the national rural average.

The quantile regression analysis of income and education suggests divergent patterns by gender. For the household heads, returns to education are lower toward the middle–upper quantiles of the income distribution (with a rebound at the top quantile), whereas for the spouses, returns increase toward higher quantiles. This contrast implies that education may play a more strategic and enabling role for women, particularly those aiming to improve household livelihoods through formal employment. These findings offer important insights into the reversed gender disparities in education observed in the broader study. They also underscore the need for policy interventions that recognize both structural and gender-specific barriers to educational and economic opportunities in rural and geographically isolated settings like Marinduque.

Taken together, the descriptive patterns and the quantile regression results presented in this appendix provide preliminary yet important insights into the gendered economic returns to education. Notably, the analysis suggests that for the spouses of household heads, the marginal returns to schooling increase toward higher quantiles of income distribution—a pattern that may be interpreted as evidence of increasing returns. If such a tendency holds more broadly, it could help explain why girls and young women increasingly pursue higher levels of education, even in disadvantaged rural settings. At the same time, these findings remain preliminary due to the limited range of explanatory variables and the exploratory nature of the model specification. Importantly, the patterns reported here concern marginal returns to schooling across the conditional wage distribution; they neither quantify nor imply absolute gender gaps in wages or incomes, and they should not be read as evidence that women's earnings exceed men's in level terms. Further empirical research is essential to assess the robustness of this convexity in women's educational returns and to explore how it interacts with broader institutional and labor market conditions.

References

Bouis HE, Haddad LJ (1990) Agricultural commercialization, nutrition, and the rural poor: a study of Philippine farm households. Boulder and London: Lynne Rienner. https://doi.org/10.1515/9781685858629

Bouis HE, Palabrica-Costello M, Solon O, Westbrook D, Limbo AB (1998) Gender equality and investments in adolescents in the rural Philippines. Washington, DC: International Food Policy Research Institute. https://doi.org/10.2499/0896291111rr108

Cabegin ECA (2013) Gendered labor supply response to filipino spouses' overseas migration and remittances. Asian Pac Migr J 22(2):147–175. https://doi.org/10.1177/011719681302200201

Dumayas ADR (2018) The evolution of economic zones in the Philippines. In: Ishikawa T (ed) Locational analysis of firms' activities from a strategic perspective. Singapore: Springer Singapore, pp 151–174. https://doi.org/10.1007/978-981-13-1684-5_9

Fornier JN (1998) Economic developments in antique province: 1800–1850. Philipp Stud 46(4):407–428. https://doi.org/10.13185/2244-1638.4689

Fornier JN (1999) Economic developments in antique province: 1850–1900. Philipp Stud 47(2):147–180. https://www.jstor.org/stable/42634312

Hayami Y, Kikuchi M (2000) A rice village saga: three decades of green revolution in the Philippines. Basingstoke: Macmillan Press/Barnes & Noble: Lanham. https://doi.org/10.1057/9780230599185

Menz KM (ed) 1989 Rainfed rice production in the Philippines: a combined agronomic/economic study in Antique province. Canberra: Australian Centre for International Agricultural Research

Philippine Statistics Authority (PSA) (2016) Functional literacy, education, and mass media survey 2013. Quezon City: PSA

Philippine Statistics Authority (PSA) (2017) Labor force survey 2015. Quezon City: PSA
Salvacion AR (2017) Exploring determinants of child malnutrition in Marinduque Island, Philippines. Human Ecol 45(6):853–863. https://doi.org/10.1007/s10745-017-9951-0
Salvacion AR (2018) Spatial pattern and determinants of village level poverty in Marinduque Island, Philippines. GeoJ 85:257–267. https://doi.org/10.1007/s10708-018-9944-6
Salvacion AR, Magcale-Macandog DB (2015) Spatial analysis of human population distribution and growth in Marinduque Island, Philippines. J Mar Isl Cult 4:27–33. https://doi.org/10.1016/j.imic.2015.06.003
Takayama N, Fuwa N, Yurugi T (2010) The role of non-agricultural sectors in rural poverty reduction: a case study in Mindanao, Philippines. Jpn J Southeast Asian Stud 48(1):46–73 [Japanese]. https://doi.org/10.20495/tak.48.1_46

Appendix B: Schooling Status and Education of Children in Marinduque

A high-school-aged boy diligently tending to farm work under the midday sun

Highland high school students hauling desks and chairs overhead as they move between classrooms along a steep slope during a break

Appendix B provides essential information on the schooling status of the sample children discussed in Chapters 4–6, situated within their broader livelihood contexts. It serves as supplementary material for both the econometric analyses in the main chapters and the understanding of children's educational conditions, particularly in relation to the reversed gender disparity. These data offer illustrative insights that support the interpretation of the discussions developed in the main chapters.

B.1 Age Cohorts

Table B.1 shows the distribution of the sample by age cohort, separated by sex. The sample includes children aged 8 to 25 (see also Fig. B.1). Females make up slightly more than males, accounting for 52.3% and 47.7%, respectively. The majority of the sample falls within the age range typical for secondary education (ages 12–17), comprising 70.6% of the sample (44.5% in junior high school and 26.1% in senior high school). This is followed by the college/post-secondary level (21.9%) and the elementary level (8.7%). At the junior high school level, the numbers of males and females are relatively equal, but there are slightly more males at the elementary level and fewer in the senior high school and college/post-secondary levels.

Table B.1 Male and female distributions in the sample by Cohort

Age	Female (F)	Male (M)	Both Sexes (B)	M/B per cohort	M/B per school level	B/T per school level	Expected Right Grades*	
8	1	2	3	66.7%	55.6%	8.7%	Elementary	Grade 3
9	2	3	5	60.0%				Grade 4
10	3	6	9	66.7%				Grade 5
11	6	4	10	40.0%				Grade 6
12	10	15	25	60.0%	50.0%	44.5%	JHS	Grade 7
13	19	17	36	47.2%				Grade 8
14	20	23	43	53.5%				Grade 9
15	20	14	34	41.2%				Grade 10
16	19	14	33	42.4%	39.5%	26.1%	SHS	Grade 11
17	30	18	48	37.5%				Grade 12
18	25	12	37	32.4%	41.2%	21.9%	College/PS	College 1/PS 1
19	3	9	12	75.0%				College 2/PS 2
20	10	5	15	33.3%				College 3
21	2	2	4	50.0%				College 4
22	0	2	2	100.0%	80.0%	1.6%		
23	0	1	1	100.0%				
24	0	1	1	100.0%				
25	1	0	1	0.0%				
Total (T)	162	148	310	47.7%	47.7%	100.0%		

* "Expected Right Grades" refer to the grade levels typically associated with a given age. However, they do not necessarily reflect each child's actual grade level, as factors such as grade repetition, delayed school entry, or school dropout may cause discrepancies

Source Author's calculations using the primary data

B.2 School Enrollment Status of the Sample Children

Tables B.2 and B.3 present the school enrollment status of the children in the sample. Table B.2 includes data from 531 children based on responses from the household questionnaire survey, while Table B.3 focuses on 310 children who participated in the time-allocation survey. Table B.2 reveals that 84% of the children are currently enrolled in school, while 16% are not. Of the 16% not enrolled, which corresponds to 85 children, 21% are male and 11.03% are female. This indicates that males are nearly twice as likely as females to be out of school.

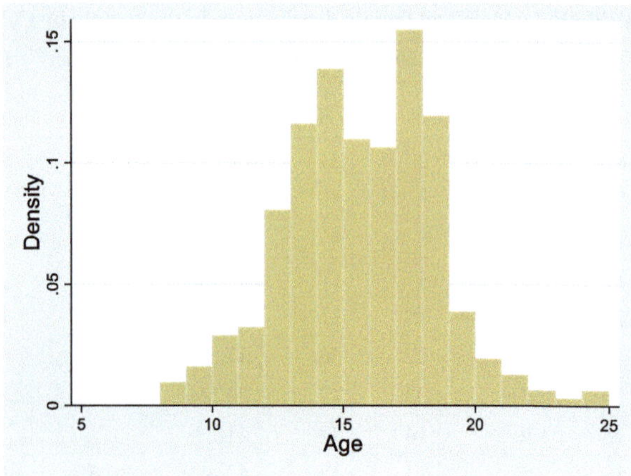

Fig. B.1 Age distribution of sample children. *Source* Author's calculations using the primary data

Table B.3 shows a similar trend among children aged 10–18 who participated in the time-allocation survey. This table provides additional details on whether non-enrollment is due to temporary school absences or permanent dropout. Among the children not attending school, 9.35% have either temporarily stopped attending (4.19%) or have permanently dropped out (5.16%). Notably, there is a significant gender disparity: 2.48% of female children fall into these categories, compared to 16.78% of male children.

The higher proportion of males not attending school in the time-allocation survey compared to the overall sample may be due to the focus on children within the secondary education age range. This age-specific sample is more likely to reflect school-aged children compared to the broader age range in the overall sample.

Regarding school levels of enrollees, Table B.4 shows that among the 446 enrolled children, the majority are at the junior high school level (200 children), followed by elementary school (120 children), senior high school (82 children), college (23 children), nursery/kindergarten (17 children), and post-secondary vocational school or unspecified levels (2 children). At the senior high school level, enrollment is higher among females compared to males, although the reverse is true at the college level, where more males are enrolled. This trend suggests a positive aspect in male enrollment at the college level, but it is important to consider recent changes in the Philippine education system that may affect these figures.

Under the K–12 program, junior high school graduates are now expected to enroll in senior high school before progressing to college. This means that the current college students were high school students prior to the extension of the K–12 program to include senior high school (Okabe, 2018).

Despite the weighted sample-size differences between males and females shown in Table B.4, if the enrollment probability for males at the newly established senior high school level decreases more drastically compared to females, it may indicate a worsening trend for male enrollment in the future. This situation is qualitatively

Table B.2 School enrollment status by sex: all co-resident children

Full sample	Numbers			Percentage		
	Female	Male	Total	Female	Male	Total
Currently enrolled	234	212	446	88.97	79.10	83.99
No longer enrolled/finished school	29	56	85	11.03	20.90	16.01
Total	263	268	531	100	100	100

Source Author's calculations using the primary data

Table B.3 School enrollment status, by sex: children in the time-allocation survey

Diary sample	Numbers			Percentage		
	Female	Male	Total	Female	Male	Total
Currently enrolled	157	124	281	97.52	83.22	90.65
Enrolled but temporarily stopped	2	11	13	1.24	7.38	4.19
No longer enrolled/finished school	2	14	16	1.24	9.40	5.16
Total	161	149	310	100	100	100

Source Author's calculations using the primary data

Table B.4 School levels where enrolled, by sex (whole sample)

Educational level	Numbers			Percentage		
	Female	Male	Total	Female	Male	Total
Nursery/kindergarten	10	7	17	4.3%	3.3%	3.8%
Elementary School	53	67	120	22.6%	31.6%	26.9%
Junior High School	105	95	200	44.9%	44.8%	44.8%
Senior High School	55	27	82	23.5%	12.7%	18.4%
Post-secondary vocational	2	0	2	0.9%	0.0%	0.4%
College	9	14	23	3.8%	6.6%	5.2%
Not specified	0	2	2	0.0%	0.9%	0.4%
Total	234	212	446	100%	100%	100%

Source Author's calculations using the primary data

similar to what is observed in the time-allocation survey participants, as illustrated in Table B.5 for the other sample.

Table B.5 School levels where enrolled, by sex (time-allocation survey sample)

Educational levels	Numbers			Percentage		
	Female	Male	Total	Female	Male	Total
Elementary school	20	33	53	12.74%	26.61%	18.86%
Junior high school	85	66	151	54.14%	53.23%	53.74%
Senior high school	47	17	64	29.94%	13.71%	22.78%
Post-secondary vocational	2	0	2	1.27%	0.00%	0.71%
College	3	8	11	1.91%	6.45%	3.91%
Total	157	124	281	100%	100%	100%

Source Author's calculations using the primary data

B.3 Dropouts and Stopping Schooling

One of the key insights from our survey concerns the issue of dropouts and stopping schooling (*tumigil sa pag-aaral* or *sa paaralan*). The school levels at which individuals decided to stop attending school are listed in Table B.6. It is notable that some boys left school even at the elementary level, while two female students ceased their education just before graduating from high school. In the Philippines, elementary education is compulsory and free in public schools, as is high school education.

Interviews with the children revealed that most decisions to stop attending school were made superficially by the individuals themselves. Out of the 12 children who stopped going to school, nine (one girl and eight boys) reported that the decision was their own. Only one girl and one boy stated that they wanted to continue their education but were compelled to stop. These two children left school in Grade 7 (first year of junior high school) and had hoped to complete high school. The reasons for stopping schooling were not provided for the remaining boy.

Among the 29 children who are no longer attending school, either temporarily or permanently, 26 responded to questions about their future schooling plans (Table B.7). Eleven children (two girls and nine boys) expressed that they do not wish to return to school, while 15 (two girls and thirteen boys) indicated a desire to return. Of those who wish to return, 12 boys stated they want to re-enroll within the next six months, while one girl and one boy expressed a desire to return within the next year.

B.4 Time-Use of Out-of-School Youths (OOSY)

When school-aged children drop out or stop going to school, what activities do they engage in instead? Fig. B.2 uses a cumulative bar chart to illustrate the relative ratios of time use between OOSY and in-school youths. The 50% line indicates the point where the time spent by the two groups is relatively similar.

Table B.6 School levels at which decisions to discontinue schooling were made

School and grade levels	Temporarily			Permanent		
	Female	Male	Total	Female	Male	Total
Halfway through elementary 3	0	1	1	0	1	1
Halfway through elementary 4	0	1	1	0	2	2
Halfway through elementary 5	0	0	0	1	2	3
Elementary, graduate	0	0	0	0	2	2
Halfway through high school 1	0	3	3	0	1	1
Halfway through high school 2	0	1	1	0	1	1
Halfway through high school 3	1	0	1	1	3	4
High school, graduate	1	1	2	0	2	2
Halfway through college 1	0	2	2	0	0	0
Unknown	0	2	2	0	0	0
Total	2	11	13	2	14	16

Source Author's calculations using the primary data

Table B.7 The willingness to go back to school

Willingness	No, do not want to go Back			Yes, do want to go back		
	Female	Male	Total	Female	Male	Total
Current status						
No longer going to school	1	8	9	1	4	5
Yes, but stopped temporarily	1	1	2	1	9	10
Total	2	9	11	2	13	15

Source Author's calculations using the primary data

Figure B.2 classifies time use into sleeping, education, working, and leisure activities. These categories were assessed through both structured and unstructured parts of the time-use survey. The education category includes time allocated to schooling, studying at home, and the frequency (in times per week) of attending school. The working category covers time spent helping with parents' jobs and household chores. Regarding household chores, the survey further disaggregated the frequencies of engagement, capturing differences between girls and boys in the chores performed. The leisure time category includes time spent playing outside or with friends, the frequency (days per week) of playing, the number of playmates (where zero means playing alone), and the nature of these interactions (neighborhood friends, classmates, siblings/relatives, or alone), as well as time spent at computer game shops. The non-structured part of the survey allowed respondents to freely report additional activities, with time spent watching TV, playing with cellphones, using Facebook, and engaging in other activities included in the results

OOSY do not spend any time on schooling or studying at home, and if they play outside, it is not typically with classmates. They are more likely to allocate time to helping with their fathers' jobs and playing outside with more non-classmate friends. Given that more males tend to be OOSY, this suggests that they are often involved in laboring on paternal jobs. In contrast, OOSY do not spend significantly more time on their mothers' jobs and household chores, indicating that these maternal tasks are not substantially replaced even by children who are not attending school. However, while the time spent on household chores is similar between the two groups, OOSY are more likely to engage in field-based chores such as animal husbandry and carrying heavy items.

OOSY also allocate considerable time to leisure activities, including watching TV, playing with cellphones, using Facebook, and engaging in other activities. After leaving school, it is noteworthy that significant portions of their time previously devoted to education are not heavily substituted by work; instead, OOSY seem to choose leisurely activities more frequently than their in-school peers. This contrasts with the education-labor relationship observed in South Asia (Ravallion and Wooden, 2000; Kurosaki et al., 2006). It is important to note that these findings are preliminary and require further analysis with multivariate methods to control for other factors.

B.5 Students Enrolling in Right Grades

To what extent can students remain in the grade level appropriate for their age? In this context, the "right" grade is determined based on the student's age (see Chapter 2). For example, a six-year-old child is expected to enter Grade 1 at the elementary level. Assuming they are promoted to the next grade each year without delay, they should reach Grade 6 by the age of 12.

Figure B.3 and Table B.8 illustrate the proportions of students in the right grade levels and those in delayed grades, categorized by sex. The school-age cohort is adjusted according to the Philippine school calendar, which starts in June and ends in May. The right-hand row of the table shows the average numbers for each category

On average, only one-quarter of enrolled students are in the correct grade level for their age (12.1% + 12.8% = 24.9%), while three-quarters are enrolled with delays (42.5% + 32.6% = 75.1%). Although there is no significant difference between male and female students in terms of being in the right grade, a higher proportion of male students are enrolled with delays compared to female students (42.5% vs. 32.6%). In other words, within the entire school-age cohort, students enrolled with delays are predominantly male, followed by female students with delays, male students in the right grade, and female students in the right grade.

Preliminary fieldwork revealed that being overaged and placed in a lower grade itself can discourage students from continuing their education. For instance, older students in younger grades often feel embarrassed. One case reported to us illustrates this issue: a student felt uncomfortable in his classroom environment due to his age relative to his classmates.

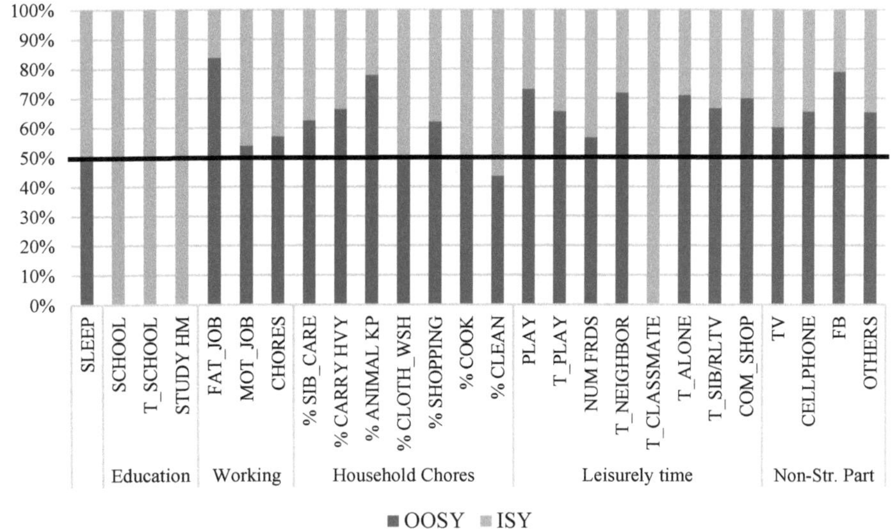

Fig. B.2 Cumulative bar chart of time-use, by OOSY and ISY *Notes*(1) ISY means in-school youth. (2) Education—"SCHOOL" is in minutes spent attending school per week; "T_SCHOOL" is in times (frequencies) of attending schools per week; "STUDY_HM" is in minutes of studying at home per week. (3) Working—"FAT_JOB" is in minutes of helping for father's jobs per week; "MOT_JOB" is in minutes of helping for mother's jobs per week; "CHORES" is in minutes of helping with household chores per week. (4) "Household chores"—Out of all the respondents who did household chores, "%_SIB_CARE" is the percentage of those who did sibling care; "%_CARRY_HVY" is the percentage of those who carried heavy items from/to the houses; "%_ANIMAL_KP" is the percentage of those engaged in animal husbandry; "%_CLOTH_WSH" is the percentage of those who washed or helped wash the clothes; "%_SHOPPING" is the percentage of those who went to buy some items needed by the family; "%_COOK" is the percentage of those who cooked or helped cook; and "%_CLEAN" is the percentage of those who cleaned or helped clean the premises and facilities inside and outside the house. (5) "Leisurely activities"—"PLAY" is in minutes of playing outside and/or with friends per week; "T_PLAY" is the frequency (times) of playing outside and/or with friends per week; "NUM FRDS" is the number of those with whom the respondent played per week; "T_NEIGHBOR" is the frequency of playing with neighborhood friends per week; "T_CLASSMATE" is the frequency of playing with school classmates per week; "T_ALONE" is the frequency of playing alone per week; "T_SIB/RLTV" is the frequency of playing with siblings/relatives per week; and "COM_SHOP" is minutes of using computer game shops. (6) "Non-Str. Part" = non-structured part. "TV," "CELLPHONE," and "FB" are in minutes of enjoying watching TV, cellphones, and Facebook, respectively. *Source*: Author's calculations using the primary data

[The case of a 14-year-old boy, Niko]

Niko, a 14-year-old[16] boy born on December 28, 2003, was enrolled in Grade 7 (first year of junior high school) at the time the author interviewed him and his family. Typically, students at this age are expected to be in Grade 9 (third year of junior high school), but Niko was two years behind his age cohort. He was attending a public high school located in his municipality, the same school where most other high school-aged students in the area are

[16] Age is as of the time of interview.

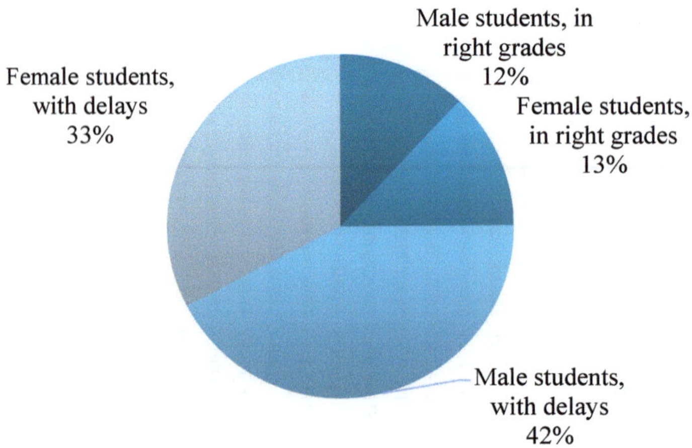

Fig. B.3 Decomposition of Students in Right vs. Delayed Grades by School Age Cohort and Sex (Pie Chart) *Source* Author's calculations using the primary data

enrolled. In his classroom, the majority of his classmates were two years younger than him. Niko already showed visible signs of adolescence and developing masculinity.

One day, some nearby adults observed Niko watering flowers and plants in the school's flowerbed outside the classroom, under the hot sun—and during class time. The neighbors called out to him from outside the school fence, asking why he was doing such a task when he was supposed to be in class. Niko replied that his teacher had instructed him to do it. The neighbors pressed further: why was he, a student, expected to be doing that kind of work during class hours? Hesitantly, Niko explained that his teacher had said he looked older and more mature than his classmates, and had therefore been chosen as the most "suitable" student to take on such duties.

The neighbors later remarked that it was understandable, in a way, that Niko might stand out due to his age. They also noted that he likely felt awkward on a regular basis in the classroom, being older than his peers. Yet, they also described feeling heartbroken watching him being made to work outside while the others were in class. Deep down, they began to feel a sense of resentment toward the teacher.

Niko is the ninth of eleven children. His mother, Melia, is a 51-year-old widow. Her husband (Niko's father) left the family years ago, abandoning his responsibility to support the children. Since then, Melia has singlehandedly raised all eleven children by working as a self-employed producer of pillows, bed covers, and bed sheets. She herself completed only up to Grade 5, having dropped out of elementary school. Nevertheless, she has managed to send some of her children through senior high school, and even to college. Her monthly income from her small business is barely ₱ 1,500, compared to ₱ 3,000 two years ago—business has slowed.

Niko's 17-year-old elder brother dropped out of high school and now works as a restaurant waiter in Metro Manila, sending ₱ 500 home each month. The family leads a modest but difficult life. Life in Manila is also tough, which limits how much of his income the brother can remit. The family was not selected as a beneficiary of the government's 4Ps program, and Niko temporarily stopped going to school. Despite being older than his classmates, Niko was still willing to attend school—perhaps because he had already seen some of his older brothers give up. However, the way he was treated by his teacher was reported to have discouraged him from maintaining a positive attitude toward learning.

Table B.8 Breakdown of students in right vs. delayed grades by school age cohort and gender (%)

Age	8	9	10	11	12	13	14	15	16	17	18	19	20	21	24	**Ave**
(1) **Percentage of Students in the Right Grades:**																
Male	50.0	20.0	0.0	0.0	13.6	3.2	15.4	3.0	0.0	4.8	0.0	22.2	0.0	50.0	0.0	**12.1**
Female	50.0	20.0	12.5	36.4	22.7	12.9	10.3	0.0	22.2	4.8	0.0	0.0	0.0	0.0	0.0	**12.8**
(2) **Percentage of Students in the Delayed Grades:**																
Male	0.0	40.0	62.5	36.4	45.5	48.4	33.3	36.4	37.9	28.6	23.3	55.6	66.7	25.0	100	**42.5**
Female	0.0	20.0	25.0	27.3	18.2	35.5	41.0	60.6	48.3	61.9	76.7	22.2	33.3	25.0	0.0	**32.6**

Note Ave. = average
Source Author's calculations using the primary data

At the same time, as shown in Table B.8, a greater proportion of female students experience enrollment delays between the ages of 14 and 18. This indicates that the issue of delayed enrollment affects female students similarly to male students. Therefore, schooling delays should be recognized as a problem affecting not only male but also female youth.

B.6 Self-Reported Reasons Why They Stopped Schooling

Figure B.4 illustrates the self-reported reasons why students stopped schooling, with up to three reasons given per student. Table B.9 provides a more detailed breakdown for each reason. According to Fig. B.4, the most common reasons for stopping are related to in-classroom experiences and economic/financial issues, followed by work-school trade-offs, lack of interest, and physical aspects. Notably, five children out of 58 provided a tautological response, stating they do not like school simply because they do not like it (expressed in local language as, e.g., "*Wala lang/Ayoko lang, kasi wala nga lang/ayoko nga*" which translates to "Just nothing/Just don't like it because I just don't like it").

While these patterns exhibit variation in frequency, it is important to note that the reasons are interconnected. For instance, as shown in Table B.9, difficulties in the classroom, such as challenges in keeping up with the curriculum, are often related to the students' ability to attend regularly and review material both in and out of class. If students struggle academically, they may fall behind their peers in understanding the material. Moreover, economic or financial difficulties can exacerbate these challenges, leading students to feel pressured to contribute to their household's livelihood, either directly or indirectly.

Thus, it is noteworthy that the intrahousehold contributions, such as helping with parental jobs or performing household chores—more generally classified as "unpaid work"—represent a "silent" burden on children. These contributions are not typically perceived as violating any legislative or ethical mandates concerning child labor. If students experience primarily negative interactions in the classroom, they may begin to view their situation as overwhelmingly adverse, leading to misunderstandings with teachers. Additionally, if students find other activities more enjoyable than schooling, they may be particularly attracted to spending time with friends or engaging in sports. The use of "just because I don't like it" as a reason for dropping out can also reflect this resignation or a regressive attitude towards addressing their educational challenges.

B.7 Summary

Male and female youths and children often face significant challenges even before accessing education. Nevertheless, school dropout is more prevalent among males than their female counterparts. While poverty, specifically economic and financial

Table B.9 Self-reported reasons they stopped schooling (up to three reasons)

Reasons	Male	Female	Total
Economic/Financial aspects:			
No job, parents	1	0	1
School project fee	5	1	6
Transportation fee	1	1	2
Tuition fee	3	0	3
For my other sibling	0	1	1
I don't have/have few stationary goods/school items	1	0	1
Work–school trade-off:			
Need to work for my family needs	4	2	6
Need to work for my own needs	3	0	3
In-classroom aspects:			
Teacher is not understanding me	4	0	4
Bullied by other students	2	1	3
Difficulty in catching up with classes	9	0	9
Physical aspects:			
I am tired always	3	0	3
I have sickness/I am ill	1	0	1
Interest Aspects:			
Love to play/drink/smoking	0	1	1
Lack of interest in schooling	8	1	9
I don't like schools because I just don't like it	4	1	5
Total	49	9	58

Source Author's calculations using the primary data

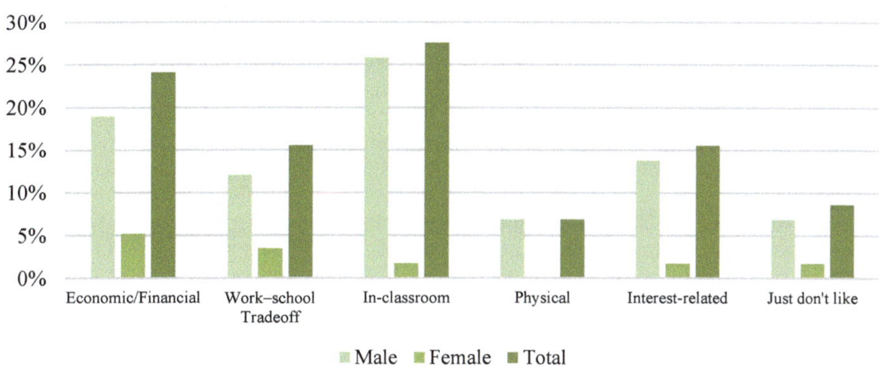

Fig. B.4 Primary reasons for stopping schooling. *Source* Author's calculations using the primary data

barriers, is undoubtedly one of the most common causes, students also encounter non-economic obstacles that lead to school discontinuation. These patterns vary considerably by gender. The data presented here serve as supplementary information to the analyses in Chapters 4–6.

In particular, the data reveal that while both boys and girls face economic and non-economic obstacles, the risk of school dropout and delayed grade progression is significantly higher among male children and youths. Many boys leave school at earlier stages, including the elementary level, while girls are more likely to continue through senior high school. However, a notable share of girls also experience delayed enrollment during the upper secondary years, highlighting that schooling delays are not solely a male issue. The data further indicate that non-enrolled boys are more likely to engage in field-based chores and casual labor, while girls continue to shoulder domestic responsibilities. These findings suggest gendered pathways of school discontinuation and time use after dropout.

Moreover, the subjective reasons students give for leaving school—ranging from financial hardship and academic struggles to emotional detachment from the classroom—point to a complex interplay of individual, household, and institutional factors. The case studies and time-use data demonstrate that school discontinuation does not always lead to increased productive labor; rather, it often results in more unstructured leisure time. These patterns raise concerns about the long-term consequences of dropout, particularly for boys, and underscore the need for policy responses that address both the material and psychological barriers to school participation. Overall, the findings in this appendix reinforce the importance of examining educational outcomes through a gender-sensitive and context-aware lens.

References

Kurosaki T, Ito S, Fuwa N, Kubo K, Sawada Y (2006) Child labor and school enrollment in rural India: Whose education matters? Dev Econ 44(4):440–464. https://doi.org/10.1111/j.1746-1049.2006.00024.x

Okabe M (2018) 'K to 12' program as a national HRD program to develop the workforce. Philipp J Labor Ind Relat 35(1–2):113–129. https://www.journals.upd.edu.ph/index.php/pjlir/article/view/7449

Ravallion M, Wodon Q (2000) Does child labour displace schooling? Evidence on behavioural responses to an enrollment subsidy. Econ J 110(462):158–175. https://doi.org/10.1111/1468-0297.00527

Index

A
Agricultural sector, 148
Aklan (province), 235
Alcohol, 241
Alternative Learning System (ALS), 232, 233, 244
Anthropology, 105
Antique (province), 24, 106, 230, 233–236
Autonomous Region in Muslim Mindanao (ARMM), 15, 104, 235
Awakening, 231, 232, 241, 243, 244, 262, 265

B
Bacolod (city), 14, 239
Bangladesh, 5, 9, 117
Bangsamoro Autonomous Region in Muslim Mindanao (BARMM), 104
Barangay, 40, 119, 120
Barkada/barkadahan, 26, 231, 232, 240–243, 261, 262
Basic Education Sector Reform Agenda, 44
Batangas (province), 14
Bilateral descent, 257
Bilateral kinship, 106
Bivariate provit (biprobit), 167, 170, 172
Boac (municipality), 119, 131
Body mass index (BMI), 53, 58
Boys' crisis, 8, 13, 196, 237, 252, 264
Boys' disengagement, 4, 5, 8, 153, 163, 187, 188, 232, 233, 237, 251–253, 264–267
Boys' underachievement, 8
Boys' underperformance, 5, 8, 13, 14, 17–19, 24, 26, 107, 257, 260, 261, 263, 267
Breadwinner, 81, 82, 116, 136, 164, 165, 170, 172, 174, 184, 258, 263, 264
Bronfenbrenner's ecosystem theory, 204, 206
Buena Vista (municipality), 119, 131
Buffer, 164, 165, 187, 254, 255
Bukidnon Panel Data Survey (BPDS), 42, 43, 53, 90, 91, 95, 105
Bukidnon (province), 24, 27, 39, 41, 42, 45, 89–91, 102–107, 257
Bullying, 231, 240

C
CALABARZON (region), 14, 15
Cambodia, 5, 11, 12, 40
Capiz (province), 235
Cavite (province), 14, 242
Cebuano (language), 47, 52, 54, 91
Central Luzon (region), 14, 15, 41, 105, 107
Child labor, 53, 54, 116, 117, 123, 150, 174, 196, 239, 253, 261
Cohort survival rate, 8, 47, 49
College, 69, 102, 135, 149, 169, 172, 173, 255
Community-based monitoring system (CBMS), 119, 217
Compulsory education, 88
Computer game shop, 240
Conditional cash transfer, 55, 90, 108, 154, 198
Conditional probability, 95–97, 109

M. Okabe, *Economics of the Reversal in Gender Disparities in Education and Development*, Economics, Law, and Institutions in Asia Pacific,
https://doi.org/10.1007/978-981-96-9271-2

Cordillera Administrative Region (CAR), 15, 118
Corn, 41, 42, 105, 107
Cotabato City, 234
Count data, 56, 57, 70, 77

D
Dakar Framework for Action, 4
Delays in schooling, 38, 40, 58
Denmark, 195
Department of Education (DepEd), 28, 44, 51, 194, 197, 202, 203, 206–210, 213, 215–221, 267
Department of Labor and Employment (DOLE), 123, 131
Developed country, 195, 258
Developing country, 4, 5, 7–11
Diminishing return, 98
Discrete dynamic choice model, 96
Dobleng sakripisyo (double sacrifice), 263
Domestic Workers Act, 131
Dropout, 8, 40, 41, 47, 48, 88–90, 98, 110, 196, 231, 233, 237, 239, 253, 267
Dual burden (of mothers), 165, 170, 186, 187
Dummy variable, 51–53, 56, 58, 69, 71, 91, 93, 94, 102, 104, 130, 204, 206, 216, 218

E
Earlier entrance age policy, 39, 70, 81
East Asia, 9, 11, 13
East Asian Miracle, 4
Ecological systems theory, 204
Educational demand, 24, 25, 39, 88, 89, 94, 97, 98, 103, 107, 108
Educational trajectories, 89, 90, 108, 118, 164, 230, 231, 233, 244, 266
Education for all (EFA), 8, 44
EFA Philippine Plan of Action, 44
Elementary school, 44, 45, 51, 53, 54, 70, 81, 82, 236, 239
Empowerment, 104, 114, 117, 252
English (subject), 123–128, 131, 194, 199, 201–206, 209, 210, 214, 216, 218, 220, 221, 236, 237, 242
Equality, 9, 82, 258
Equidispersion, 56
Equity, 18, 28, 89, 107, 108, 187, 188, 224, 260, 266
Essentialism, 19, 260
Exclusion restriction, 132, 151, 152, 167, 181, 182
Extended family, 39, 136, 154, 164–167, 171, 174, 181, 182, 187

F
Family dynamics, 23, 26, 29, 39, 41, 88, 108, 114, 117, 153, 164, 174, 186, 187, 193, 230, 252, 253, 256, 257, 259, 264, 265
Family economics, 21, 94
Farmer, 40, 42, 134–138, 140–143, 145, 146, 148, 149, 168, 169, 198, 200, 236
Farming, 21
Fathers' labor force participation (FLFP), 115, 134–136, 138, 140, 142, 143, 145, 149, 150, 154, 164–170, 172, 173
Faustian bargain, 254, 255
Filipino (subject), 8, 17, 26, 40, 54, 91, 123–128, 131, 164, 165, 186, 194, 198–200, 202, 203, 205, 206, 208–210, 214, 218, 220, 235–237, 242, 243, 257, 259
Formal education, 26, 40, 89, 105, 107, 230–233, 244, 245, 253, 255, 267
Formal worker, 150
France, 195
Free Public Secondary Act (of 1988), 44
Full information maximum likelihood (FIML), 96
F-statistics, 151, 152, 181, 183

G
Gasan (municipality), 119, 131
Gender disparity, 4, 10, 11, 13–17, 26, 28, 88, 153, 156, 187, 222, 256, 258, 260, 266, 268
Gender equality, 4, 19, 29, 153, 187, 195, 258, 261, 266
Gender norm, 27, 114, 115, 117, 165, 187
Gender parity index (GPI), 8–13, 15–17, 118
Genealogy, 106
General Santos City, 234, 235
Global Gender Gap Report, 266
Green Revolution, 41, 105
Guimaras (island, province), 235

H
Haligi ng tahanan, 165
High school, 26, 135, 197, 202, 236–238, 243
  junior, 208
  senior, 208
High-value crop (HVC), 105
Hiligaynon (language), 54, 235
Household chores, 21, 114, 116, 118, 124, 130, 133, 147, 150, 154, 257
Human capital, 4, 6, 19–22, 26, 38, 41, 88–90, 107, 116, 172, 196, 256, 257
Human development, 18, 50, 165, 223, 243, 251, 252
Huwaran, 262
Hysteresis, 20, 23, 25, 38, 108, 153, 194, 230, 243, 255, 266, 269

I
Ilaw ng tahanan, 164
Iloilo (city), 14, 54, 91, 239
Ilokano (language), 54, 71
Ilonggo (language), 54, 91, 235
Income shock, 193
India, 117, 170
Indonesia, 11, 13, 172
Inequality, 5, 27, 29, 38, 48, 89, 90, 104, 258, 266, 267
Informality, 244, 245, 254, 263
Informal worker, 196, 254, 255, 261
Instrumental variable (IV), 24, 131, 132, 150–152, 167, 170, 171, 181–183, 197, 208–210
Intergenerational dynamics, 83, 88, 107, 256
Intergroup heterogeneity, 4, 23, 24, 265
Internal efficiency, 8, 24, 38, 40
International Food Policy Research Institute (IFPRI), 26–28, 42, 43, 47, 51, 52, 63, 68, 76, 80, 90–92, 101, 103, 108, 115, 256
International Labour Organization (ILO), 123
Intragroup heterogeneity, 24
Intrahousehold resource allocation, 24, 106, 256
Islam, 104
Israel, 195, 214
Italia, 195, 214
Ivatan (language), 91

J
Jeepney, 136, 201
Joint estimation, 170
Joint probability, 96

K
K–12 Program, 51
Kinaray-a (Karay-a), 235, 237
Kindergarten/nursery, 45
Kinship, 106
Korea, 172

L
Labor force participation, 132, 163, 255
Labor Force Survey (LFS), 16, 27, 174
Labor market, 6, 7, 19, 21–24, 83, 131, 132, 153, 165, 170, 195, 196, 254, 257, 260, 264, 266, 267
Lack of interest, 239, 240
Laguna (province), 242
Lao People's Democratic Republic (Laos), 5, 11–13
Latent variable, 55, 170
Latin America, 7, 9–11, 13
Leisure, 114–118, 121–123, 133, 147, 148, 150, 166, 174, 181
Lingua franca, 52, 91, 235
Logistic function, 96, 97, 109
Logit, 77
Luzon (island), 14, 15, 28, 41, 54

M
Madrasah, 104
Maguindanao (province), 47
Makabansa (nationalism and citizenship), 202
Maka-diyos (piety), 202
Maka-kalikasan (respect for the environment and nature), 202
Makatao (humane personality), 202
Malaysia, 5, 11, 13
Marinduque (province), 24, 26–28, 115, 119, 120, 194, 197, 262
Martyr mothers, 186, 188
Maternal labor force participation (MLFP), 26, 39, 114–119, 121, 130–137, 140, 142, 145, 147–154, 163–167, 169–174, 181–183, 186, 187, 257, 258, 263–265

Math (subject), 123–128, 195, 199, 200, 202–204, 206, 209, 210, 214, 216–218, 220–223
Matrilineality, 106
Maximum likelihood (ML), 55, 57, 97, 109
Measurement error, 122
Meritocracy, 260
Metro Manila, 14, 15, 118, 233, 263
Mexico, 116
Millennium Development Goals (MDGs), 4, 5, 51
MIMAROPA (region), 15, 24, 115, 118–120, 131
Mindanao, 14, 24, 38, 39, 41, 49, 50, 53, 54, 91, 104, 105, 234, 235, 242, 252
Mindanao Development Authority (MinDA), 28, 49, 50
Minimum wage, 131, 132, 167
Modernization theory, 232
Mothers' labor force participation (MLFP), 114, 135, 169, 175, 257
Multiple hypothesis testing, 204
Music, arts, physical education and health (MAPEH) (subject), 201–203, 206
Muslim, 91, 104, 198
Myanmar, 11, 13

N

National Achievement Test (NAT), 194, 197, 201–206, 208–211, 213, 215–221, 224, 259
National Statistical Coordination Board (NSCB), 47
National Statistics Office (NSO), 45, 48, 49
Natural experiment, 194, 195, 222, 259
Negros (island), 239, 261
Negros Occidental (province), 239
Nested logit, 96
Net enrollment rate (NERs), 9, 10, 15, 16
Net enrollment rates (NER), 9–11, 14–16, 234, 235
Non-agricultural sector, 21, 22, 94, 105, 107
Nonformal education, 232, 244
Nontraditional student, 233
Norm, 6, 7, 21, 29, 51, 122, 135, 136, 165, 172, 186, 239
North Cotabato (province), 235
Northern Mindanao Region (Region X), 24, 42

O

Odds ratio, 101
Opportunity cost, 89
Ordinary least squares (OLS), 55, 130
Organisation for Economic Co-operation and Development (OECD), 6, 195
Out-of-school children (OOSC), 11, 88, 89, 133
Out-of-school youth (OOSY), 11, 88, 89, 254
Overseas Filipino Worker (OFW), 263

P

Pacific, 7, 9, 11, 13, 117
Pagmamalasakit, 263
Pakikibahagi, 253, 254
Pakikisalo, 254
Palawan (province), 234, 235
Panay (island), 54, 235, 236, 239, 261
Pandan (municipality), 236
Pantawid Pamilyang Pilipino Program (4Ps), 198, 201
Patrilineality, 106
Pedicab, 201, 254
Peer influence, 232, 242
Philippine Statistics Authority (PSA), 15–17, 28, 45, 118, 234, 235, 239
Poblacion, 236
Poisson distribution, 56, 57, 70
Poisson model, 56, 57, 70, 77, 78
Poverty dynamics, 41, 267
Poverty reduction, 4, 105
Primary education, 18, 38, 39, 88, 89, 91, 92, 98, 102, 103, 106, 107, 164, 209
Private sector, 105, 208, 223
Public sector, 105, 107

Q

Qualitative approach, 243
Quasi experiment, 208
Quezon (province), 234, 235

R

Rating system, 196, 222, 259
Regimes in family economics, 21
Remittances, 54, 71, 77
Report card (RC), 121, 123, 124, 194, 199, 201–206, 208, 210, 211, 213, 215–218, 220–222, 259
Research Institute for Mindanao Culture (RIMCU), 26–28, 42

Resilience, 26, 89, 188, 224, 230–233, 243–245, 252, 261, 262, 265, 267
Return to schooling, 232
Reversed gender disparity, 5–7, 23, 26, 29, 135, 186, 230, 260, 264
Rice, 41, 105, 236
Risk sharing, 254
Rizal (province), 234, 235
Role model, 115
Romano–Wolf step-down adjustment, 204, 206
Romblon (province), 234, 235
Rural area, 14, 15, 17, 21, 23, 24, 89, 119, 136, 194, 196, 201, 223, 233, 239, 252–255, 258
Rural economy, 94
Rural society, 174

S
Sakripisyo/pagsasakripisyo, 263
Same-sex parent-child nexus, 256, 264
Sarangani (Province), 47, 235
Scarring (persistent adverse effects), 20, 23, 38, 88, 153, 194, 224, 230, 243, 253, 260
Scholarship, 55, 90, 108
School environment, 7, 23, 24, 26, 29, 193, 196, 197, 230, 252, 259, 260, 262, 265
Schools First Initiative, 44
Science (subject), 8, 123, 194, 195, 202, 206, 209, 210, 214, 216–218, 220–222
Scoring bias, 26, 222, 223, 263
Seasonal labor, 239
Secondary education, 4, 8–12, 17, 18, 45, 51, 54, 91, 92, 95, 97, 98, 106, 107, 118, 135, 198, 209, 224, 234, 236
Self-employment, 119, 135, 148–150, 166, 198
Sequential choice, 25, 106, 107
Sequential logit, 96, 97, 109, 110
Service sector, 105, 107
SOCCSKSARGEN (region), 234, 235
Social capital (SC), 71, 77, 94, 231, 243, 244, 261, 263
Social desirability bias, 122
Social media, 240
Social network, 53, 54, 69, 93, 94, 101, 243, 261, 262
Social studies (subject), 123–128, 194, 199, 201–203, 205–207, 209, 210, 214, 216, 218, 220, 221
Sociology, 41, 116
South Cotabato, 234, 235
Sri Lanka, 172
Stereotype, 26, 118, 194–196, 204, 206, 209, 214, 217, 220, 222, 230, 259, 260
Sub-Saharan Africa, 5
Suburban, 14
Sugar, 42, 105
Sugarcane, 105, 107, 239, 261
Sultan Kudarat (province), 235
Sulu (Province), 47, 50
Supervision, 114, 115, 118, 131, 150, 154
Sustainable Development Goals (SDGs), 5, 51
Sweden, 214
System of national accounts (SNA), 116

T
Tagalog (language), 47, 52, 235
Tamad (lazy), 239, 260
Teacher gender ratio (TGR), 196, 197, 201, 204, 208, 209, 214, 216, 217, 220, 221, 224
Teacher labor market, 195, 208, 209, 223, 230, 265
Technology and livelihood education (TLE) (subject), 123–128, 199, 201–203, 205–207, 209
Tertiary education, 18, 82, 83, 89, 92, 95, 97, 98, 102, 114, 136
Test score, 116, 194, 195, 259
Thailand, 5, 11, 13, 172
Time allocation, 26, 115–118, 122, 130, 134, 147–150, 153, 164, 166, 167, 181, 187, 263
Time use, 114, 115, 122, 124, 129–131, 147, 148, 150–154, 164, 166, 167, 174, 181, 182
Tobit, 55–59, 70, 71, 130
Tree diagram, 93, 94
Tricycle, 136, 201, 254
Two-step least squares (2SLS), 132, 133, 171

U
Unemployment, 165, 166
Unintended effect, 115, 153, 154, 163–166, 171, 181, 186, 187, 264
United Nations Educational, Scientific and Cultural Organization (UNESCO), 4, 5, 7–9, 27, 266

United Nations Girls' Education Initiatives (UNGEI), 5–8, 115, 118, 195, 196, 237, 243
Urban center, 14, 15, 98, 118, 233, 239, 254, 258, 263
Urban economy, 252
U-shaped pattern, 6
Utang na loob, 254

V
Validity test, 167, 171
Vietnam, 11
Visayas, 14, 24, 54, 234, 235, 241, 252

W
Wage Order, 131
Wald statistics, 172
Waray (language), 54
Western Mindanao (region), 104
Western Visayas (region), 24, 26, 91, 230, 235
Wild bootstrap, 214, 216, 220, 221
Wooldridge's Robust Score Test, 151, 182
World Bank, 4–6
World Economic Forum (WEF), 18, 266

X
Xavier University, 26, 28

Y
Yaya, 258
Youth, 29, 231, 237, 240, 242, 244, 245, 255

Z
Zamboanga (peninsula, region), 14, 15, 118
Zero-sum game, 7, 28, 252, 264
Z-score, 123, 124, 128, 133, 135, 169, 198, 199, 202, 206

MIX
Papier aus verantwortungsvollen Quellen
Paper from responsible sources
FSC® C105338

If you have any concerns about our products,
you can contact us on
ProductSafety@springernature.com

In case Publisher is established outside the EU,
the EU authorized representative is:
Springer Nature Customer Service Center GmbH
Europaplatz 3, 69115 Heidelberg, Germany

Printed by Libri Plureos GmbH
in Hamburg, Germany